The social dimension of human sexuality

The social dimension of human sexuality

Edited by

Robert R. Bell, Temple University

and

Michael Gordon, University of Connecticut

LITTLE, BROWN AND COMPANY
Boston

Contents

The social
dimension of
human sexuality

part one

Introduction: the study of sexual behavior

There is an honesty in science which refuses to accept the idea that there are aspects of the material universe that are better not known, or the knowledge of which should not be made available to the common man.[1]

There is probably no area of biologically determined behavior that has so intrigued, puzzled, frustrated, and satisfied as many people as sexual behavior. Some of the earliest cave paintings depict sexuality in a manner readily accessible to us today. This is so because all ways in which human beings can achieve sexual satisfaction were probably first discovered early in our history. Over the years we have not developed new forms of sexual expression, but rather the underlying biological possibilities have remained constant, and cultural factors have created variations in the psychological and social responses to sexuality. Some cultures have encouraged the exploration of all facets of human sexuality; others have only begrudgingly permitted the narrowest forms of expression.

Western societies, such as our own, have had a long history of sexual repressiveness. A great deal of lip service has been paid to a code of conduct which limited sexual intercourse to the marital bed, and even there not without certain restrictions. To be sure, much actual behavior has flown in the face of this code as is revealed historically. For example, a large number of couples have entered marriage with their fertility already established. Despite such contradictions the cloud of illicitness has hung over sexual behavior, and still, to some extent, continues to do so. One cannot begin to develop an understanding of the sociology of sexual behavior without an appreciation of this.

A further theme running through the history of sexual behavior in the West is that of patriarchal dominance. This means that most societies have taken similar views toward sexual expression. Just about all that has been written about sex in the past, as well as the present, has been the work of men, and most of it from their point of view. This has been true irrespective of the form of expression: artistic, literary, or scientific. Basically, this view has seen sexual behavior as a pleasurable end in itself for the male and a nonpleasurable means to reproduction for the female.[2] It is useful to look further at some of the assumptions made about sexual expression within a patriarchal framework.

One assumption is that man is sexually superior to woman. It has been believed that man, by the very nature of being a man, has strong sex drives — in other words, this is a basic ingredient of his sense of masculinity. By contrast, it was generally believed that women do not have a strong need for sexual expression. And man, in his defining of woman, linked her assumed low sexual interest with his view of her being

3

passive and dependent. Man was seen as sexually active and expressive and woman as sexually passive and repressive. Any possible reversal of these definitions in a patriarchal society was often cause for alarm. A man with little sexual interest or a woman who passionately responded to sex both might be viewed with suspicion.

Another assumption made in the patriarchal society about sexual expression was that there should be a double standard of sexual rights. The woman was, as suggested, assumed to have no strong interest in sex even in marriage and so would certainly not have any sexual interest outside of marriage. By contrast, man saw himself as possessed of powerful sexual drives that had to be satisfied. In some societies, such as during the Victorian period, the patriarchal man turned to prostitutes and other "loose" women to have his "uncontrollable" sexual needs met. He sometimes even felt sanctimonious about his behavior because he was protecting his passive, repressive wife from his manly, "animalistic" sexual needs. In societies dominated by males it was not difficult to develop rationalizations to fit what they wanted them to fit. It should be remembered that the view of women as sexually inferior was a part of the broader definition of women being inferior in general. The very core of a patriarchal society assumed male superiority.

In this century there have been some dramatic shifts in sexual attitudes and behavior. This is manifested not only in such things as the increasing incidence of premarital intercourse, but also in the related erosion of patriarchal dominance in the overall sexual realm of behavior. Increasingly, women are being seen as the equals of men in their sexual needs and desires. What is developing, then, is a reorientation toward sex in general and female sexuality in particular. These are, of course, related phenomena since an acceptance of nonprocreative or recreational sex hinges on the granting of at least certain sexual rights to women. In general, the articles in this book have been chosen to illustrate the nature of these changes.

The Study of Sexual Behavior

There is often a strong resistance to the idea that one may study sex scientifically since so many moral and ethical questions are associated with it. To some this appears to deprive sex of its mysteriousness and they find this upsetting and unacceptable. However, the interest here is to look at some of the moral assumptions involved in the scientific approach and in what ways those assumptions may be related to studying sexual values and behavior. A commitment to the scientific approach means that there are certain moral values related to being a scientist. The most significant belief is that knowledge is never fixed but always changing. This conviction means resisting as scientifically immoral "any attempt to fix truth once and for all by tradition or by political authority."[3] The fact that the scientist has refused to accept truths as fixed has often brought him into conflict with those who believe in final truths.

Basically, science is a method for objectively attaining reliable knowledge about whatever it is that one studies. This assumption leads to certain judgments by the scientist of the world in which he works. He comes to believe in the purity of science that must not allow itself "to become the handmaiden of theology or economy or state."[4] So while modern science does involve values and ethical judgments, they are only those that are an intrinsic part of the scientific approach. Reiss has described science as being like a monastic order, in that "it demands your allegiance to a way of life with a set of values and it commands you not to 'contaminate' this way of life or these values by introducing any 'alien' values. You may of course profess other values in your role as private citizen but not in your role as scientist."[5]

There is sometimes confusion about the treatment of social values as data for study in the social sciences. The confusion may exist because social research is frequently seen as a threat to existing social values or the social scientist as trying to change social values. In illustration, the sociologist who does a study of some aspect of sexual behavior is not concerned with whether or not people should keep their values, but rather his interest is in the values as social data. His value assumption is that the study of sex will contribute to the scientific body of knowledge about sex. Scientific knowledge presents facts and explanations as to the tentative nature of things, but it does not establish or define standards of moral belief or behavior. "Science cannot give us morality, not even a rational morality. Moral values cannot be scientifically proven; they must be chosen."[6]

Another value assumption of science is that knowledge belongs to no individual or group but rather is the property of the general public. Theoretically, all scientific knowledge is available to all human beings, but in reality only a small part of the general body of scientific knowledge is used by society. Sometimes a scientist is held "responsible" by society for his knowledge, although he does not and cannot control the way in which his findings are used in society. Nevertheless, the scientist may become "the subject of reproach and more violent reactions insofar as these applications are disapproved by the agents of authority or by pressure groups."[7]

It is assumed that the scientific approach can be applied to all aspects of social behavior, although there may be variations in the results due to the special complexities of the area studied. As suggested, human sexual behavior has been of interest since the beginning of time. However, the emergence of a scientific approach to the study of sexual behavior is a relatively recent phenomenon.

The origins of modern sex study are to be found in the writings of Sigmund Freud and Havelock Ellis, both of whom attempted to explain the fundamental and essential character of sexual impulses and how they influence virtually all aspects of human life.[8] They wrote at the end of the 19th and the beginning of the 20th centuries on what they felt to be the developmental sources of unconventional as well as conventional forms of sexual expression, but neither was really concerned with establishing the prevalence of various forms of sexual behavior. Neither by training nor by disposition could Freud and Ellis have been expected to use the social survey techniques that were being developed at the end of the 19th century. Both approached their subject clinically, and as physicians were most sympathetic to the case study approach. However, by taking human sexuality out of the dark recesses of the Victorian attic they paved the way for other researchers to undertake survey studies. They did this not only by changing the prevailing view toward the place of sex in life, but also by creating an atmosphere in which people would be willing to see the possibility of openly and freely discussing their sexual behavior.

One commonly encounters the view that the first significant study of sexual behavior in the United States was that started by Alfred Kinsey, a biologist, at Indiana University in 1938. While it is true that the Kinsey studies have never been equaled in scope or scale they were preceded by a number of important, though unfortunately neglected, studies. In the introduction to their first research report, *Sexual Behavior in the Human Male* (1948), Kinsey and his associates list nineteen previous studies which met their standards of being, "(1) scientific, (2) based on more or less complete case histories, (3) based on a series of at least some size, (4) involving a systematic coverage of approximately the same items on each subject, and (5) statistical in treatment."[9] While they go on generally to dismiss these studies several of them were pioneer efforts which produced important data and thus warrant some individual discussion.

The 1920s was a period of great social change in this coun-

6

try. World War I had erased most remaining Victorian anachronisms, and people began to experience a new freedom. In the sexual sphere these changes were manifested, among other ways, in a marked increase in the rates of premarital coitus. Kinsey found that less than half as many of the women in his sample born before 1900 had had premarital intercourse than women born after that time.

This increase in the incidence of premarital coitus, and the similar increase in the incidence of premarital petting, constitute the greatest changes which we have found between the patterns of sexual behavior in the older and younger generations of American females.[10]

While the extent of these changes was not known at the time the general atmosphere was such as to make at least some people feel that there was a need for some sort of sex education program. Those involved in the newly emerged field of "social hygiene" were particularly concerned with helping people to understand the nature of their sexuality and through this achieve some degree of sexual fulfillment. In order to gather the information they felt necessary to undertake such an educational program, they asked the Bureau of Social Hygiene to do a study of the sexual life of normal women. The product of this study was Katherine Davis's *Factors in the Sex Life of Twenty Two Hundred Women,* begun in 1921 and published in 1929.[11]

Katherine Davis, a sociologist, sent preliminary letters of inquiry to 20,000 women (10,000 married and 10,000 unmarried) whose names were almost all taken from the membership lists of the General Federation of Women's Clubs and alumnae registers of various colleges. The data reported in the book cover a wide variety of behavior including masturbation, contraceptive use, premarital and marital rates of coitus, and homosexual behavior. The data were presented in simple tables and suffered the usual shortcomings associated with studies based on volunteer samples which may not even be representative of the limited group from which they are drawn — in this case urban, highly educated, upper-middle-class women. Such problems have continued to plague sex researchers. Nevertheless, Davis's study marked the beginning of large scale survey studies of human sexuality.

Katherine Davis was not the only researcher active at this time. Gilbert Hamilton, a psychiatrist, published *A Research in Marriage* in the same year (1929) the Davis book appeared.[12] The research reported in that book was sponsored by the National Academy of Science and was based on Hamilton's extensive interviews, some lasting as long as thirty hours, with 200 people, 55 of whom were husband and

7

wife. Most of those interviewed were either his patients or their friends, adding a psychological bias to the already special character of the group he studied. The value of Hamilton's work resides in the breadth of the information he gathered. From that study it is possible to get a sense of the kind of sexual adjustments various couples make and how their sexual histories can shed light, for example, on the relationship between virginity at marriage and their state of marital satisfaction. Hamilton provided a wealth of detailed information and many of the questions he raised were pursued further by Kinsey and his associates.

A study which is often grouped with the work of Davis and Hamilton is Robert Dickinson's *A Thousand Marriages,* though it differed from theirs in a number of ways.[13] Dickinson was an obstetrician-gynecologist who began his practice in the 1880s. In the 1920s, with Lura Bean, he prepared a monograph on marital sexuality based on a thousand cases drawn from his files of five thousand cases. The monograph was published in 1932 under the auspices of the National Committee of Maternal Health.

During most of his practice, Dr. Dickinson insisted that each patient fill out a detailed four-page questionnaire on her family, personal, and physical history before he would see her. He also collected sex histories from many of his patients. It is that group that form the basis of the thousand marriages referred to in the book title. Basically in the work of Dickinson the concern is with the physical aspects of sexuality. As Havelock Ellis noted in the introduction to this book:

Neither Dr. Hamilton's study nor Dr. Davis' involved any physical investigation. But sex is first of all a physical fact, and this relationship of sex is primarily and fundamentally a physical relationship. The report of a gynecologist, even though he is necessarily limited to women who come to him in the first place as patients, becomes, therefore, essential if we are to have an all-around picture of the sexual situation today.[14]

Dickinson was not trained in Freudian thought but he still attempted to explore physical ailments in terms of sexual problems and pursued such avenues of inquiry as the dream lives of his patients. His scrupulously detailed case histories, with their anatomic drawings, complemented the two earlier studies by Davis and Hamilton.

By contemporary standards the data collection of all three of these early sex studies would be strongly criticized. Yet, to do so would not only be unfair but also shortsighted. Those were extremely audacious pieces of research because — although that was a period of social upheaval — sex was not

8

a common topic, and many persons were not willing to answer questions, even on an anonymous basis, concerning their sex lives. The fact that those researchers persevered in the face of such difficulties to collect the data is testimony of their commitment to the importance of scientifically approaching the study of sexual behavior.

Kinsey Studies

Kinsey's contribution was twofold: one, the scientific knowledge that he contributed, and two, his great influence on many in society to accept and to use scientific sexual knowledge. The initial reaction to the Kinsey studies was highly negative. It seems safe to say that no other study of human behavior has had as great an impact on the American population as did the Kinsey studies. The first study of the male was published in 1948 and the second on the female in 1953. In the decade following the publication of the first volume, the name Kinsey became a household word, and the two volumes were sold in large numbers. The great public response was due in part to the books' appearance at a time when the American society was highly receptive both to that which was scientific and to that which was sexual. The prestige of science was high following World War II, and during the war there had developed a public concern about and great interest in sex. During wartime many of the barriers of sexual behavior had been let down; a more open interest had developed, and it continued into the post-war period.[15]

Even with some favorable forces in society there was, among large numbers of Americans, a reaction of indignation, disbelief, and disgust toward the Kinsey studies. The negative reactions may have been due in part to the exposure of the contradictions between what people say one *should* do and what they *actually* do in sexual activity. The public reactions to the Kinsey findings may be summarized under two general reactions on what to do about the disagreement between sexual values and behavior. One reaction was that the values must stand and the deviant sexual behavior be brought into line. In other words, people must be made to behave the way the values said they should. An opposite and much less frequent response was that there should be greater acceptance of common sexual practices and alterations of sex codes to fit the practices.

Generally, it was those who felt that the Kinsey studies posed a threat to their moral beliefs who were most vehement in their attacks on Kinsey and his research. There seemed to exist the belief that one's moral beliefs could only remain strong if one could discredit Kinsey in some way. It seemed to be especially upsetting to many moralists that Kinsey found that many men and women had engaged with some frequency in nonmarital sexual outlets. The moralists were convinced that such frequency must have had undesirable implications. Lerner pointed out that "it became a stereotype in the Kinsey criticism to say that the frequency of sexual outlets no more makes them moral than the frequency of the common cold makes it healthy — an equating of sex with disease which in turn sheds considerable light on the heritage of Puritan repression."[16]

But what is most important about the reactions to the Kinsey studies, the Masters and Johnson research, or any other studies of human sexuality, is the assumption that the findings argue for sexual behavior. For example, nowhere in the Kinsey studies was there a statement that the findings *should* lead people to different behavior, but many of his critics insisted on reading into the studies a variety of moral imperatives. Implied in many of the criticisms of the Kinsey studies was the belief that scientific knowledge should be ignored in many areas of human sexual behavior. For example, one critic wrote that "having been a victim for some thousands of years of a great hoax, which tried to limit his orgasm experience to masturbation and spousal heterosexual relations, he is finally freed by science. This will be an inevitable reaction."[17] Twenty-five years after the appearance of the Kinsey study on the male, there is no evidence that the sexual behavior of males was greatly influenced by the study.

After the Kinsey studies there were many small studies on sexual behavior but none of them had any great impact on society until the first Masters and Johnson book appeared in 1966.[18] Four weeks after that study was published, it made *The New York Times* general best seller list, (as did their second book published in 1970).[19] One news magazine observed after the 1966 publication that even more remarkable than the book's high sales was the minimal public hostility to it. In a short period after the book's publication, its authors had received about 1,000 letters, "10 percent favorable, 20 percent hostile and 70 percent pleas for help with sexual problems."[20] This public reaction was certainly very different from that which greeted the first Kinsey volume. However, it would be a mistake to assume that the battles for the legitimacy of sex research are over. One example is the great controversy that some right-wing groups have been able to create over sex education in the public schools. In fact, it may be possible that we in the United States are moving into an era of greater sexual repression, at least politically. This would be a reaction to what many believe has been too rapid and liberal a development in public sexual expression. There is a great potential for conflict here, especially between generations that represent divergent views about sexual expression.

For a better understanding of some of the findings and interpretations that are presented in the selections that make up this book it is useful to look at some of the problems encountered in doing studies of sexual attitudes and behavior These are problems that may be encountered in studying other aspects of human behavior but which are often intensified in the study of sexual behavior because of its great sensitivity for many people.

Who Gets Studied?

No other aspect of the Kinsey studies was subjected to greater professional criticism than the nature of the sample that was studied. The Kinsey study was not based on a probability sample, in which each individual in the universe to be studied has an equal chance of being selected. Because of the great problem of acquiring a random sample, Kinsey and his associates attempted to substitute 100 per cent participation of persons in various groups. Their assumption was that, in groups, the members could exert internal pressure and get fellow group members to be interviewed who normally would not volunteer on their own. This approach did bring in some respondents they would not normally have gotten. However, the persons interviewed did not constitute a representative sample of American adults. The general criticism of the Kinsey sample is that, in reality, it was not a study of the American male or female, but rather a study of a particular population sample — one biased in the direction of individuals who were from the northeastern United States, lived in urban areas, were among the more highly educated, and were willing to be interviewed.[21] Because sexual behavior for many people is seen as private, there will always be a significant number who will not give out information about themselves, and therefore it is difficult and very expensive to randomly sample broad universes in the study of sexual behavior.

What Gets Studied?

As indicated, up until recent years most of the social science research into sexuality was restricted to the sexual aspects of marriage. However, in the 1960s an interest began to develop in deviant sexual behavior. (It may be added that during the 1960s there was little new research into marital sex.) The new interest in deviant sex is closely related to the emergence of the new interest in the sociology of deviance. However, to say that some interest has developed as to the study of sexual deviance is not to say that there has been a great deal of research in this area. There have been a few studies in recent years by psychologists, anthropologists, and sociologists into homosexuality (both male and female), prostitution, pornography, and extramarital sexuality.

There are problems in *what* gets studied that overlap with those of *who* gets studied. Given the high sense of privacy and embarrassment associated with legitimate modes of sexual expression, the problems of reaching respondents may be compounded when they are involved in sexual deviance. Often here the sex research problems are complicated by the secretiveness of the behavior as well as high sensitivity. The sensitivity may be personal, ethical, social, or legal. When one studies sexual deviance, it is clearly implied that the persons being studied have engaged in some practices that are illegal or immoral or both. When an interviewer is an outsider, as is often the case, there may be a tendency in the interviewee to protect himself, to put on or put down the interviewer, or to try to use him in some way. For example, a female researcher working with one of the authors was interviewing lesbians and ran into specific problems. On some occasions the lesbians would sexually proposition the interviewer, and if she said she was "straight," they often became critical of her ability to do the study. The "straight" interviewer often unintentionally suggests to the lesbians that their behavior is somewhat "freakish" and that they are being studied as a kind of strange tribe. This often contributes to the homosexuals' being very critical of the studies done of them. The point is not that one necessarily has to be a member of a deviant group to really understand it; but rather, if the respondents believe it to be true, it may negatively affect their responses to the interviewer or influence the degree to which the interviewer is able to understand certain ingroup subleties. Basically the problem with *what* gets studied is that in deviant sex there are so many negative forces making study difficult.

Honesty of Response

One of the most common questions asked of persons who study sexual behavior through any informational approach is how do they know if people tell the truth. In an extended interview there are methods for checking conscious distortion. For example, ask the same question, worded in different ways, at different points in the interview. But what is far more difficult to control are the limitations placed by human ability to recall accurately. In general, the further that one probes into the past of an individual, the more questionable becomes the accuracy of his recall. For example, a middle-aged man asked to describe the frequency of some sexual behavior during his adolescence must go back over many years to give his answer. How much he will factually recall is bound to be limited. Over a period of time some individuals reach a point where they persuade themselves that some things happened. This often occurs in the recall of sexual experiences. Males, in particular, are often notorious liars in reference to their sexual behavior. If they tell stories long enough — to themselves or to others — they may grow to believe the events actually happened. There are some middle-aged men who believe they were sexually active during their long-past adolescence, but who in reality had very limited sexual experience. An opposite distortion of recall probably operates for some women who conveniently "forget" certain sexual experiences of the past. This suggests that recall has a built-in psychological bias that makes the sexual experiences of men and women seem more different than they are in reality.[22] So the problem of conscious or unconscious distortion about one's sexual past will bias any study and one must try to be aware of the bias and control it or account for it in the interpretation of the data.

Measuring Sexual Expression

One of the most common complaints directed at the Kinsey research was that the emphasis was too biological. The basic unit of measurement was the achievement of orgasm, and comparisons between various subdivisions were usually made on the basis of cumulation and frequency of orgasm. Orgasm has been used by Kinsey and others because people *know* when they experience it. That is, it is a much more objective measurement than any emotional interpretation could be. The same general criticism has been directed at the Masters and Johnson research. They, like Kinsey before them, are told by some critics that the emphasis on orgasm tends to rule out the significance of emotional influences. These critics ask if one can quantitatively equate an orgasm involving nothing more than purely physical and psychological aspects with one of high emotional involvement. While the point of the criticism is reasonable, there is the practical question of how one objectively studies the emotional factors related to various types of sexual release. This is a difficult methodological problem for which no one has come up with a research answer. It should also be recognized that sometimes the bias is in the critic — his bias is the belief that sexual experience *must* be significantly different according to the degree of emotional commitment in the paired relationship.[23]

The Clinical Bias

A great deal of the materials that get into the literature on sexual behavior studied by psychologists and psychiatrists is based on clinical samples. Many recognize that clinical samples are roughly representative of persons who seek out help but not of all those who engage in a particular area of behavior. This is especially true in the area of sexual deviance. For example, often the sample of homosexuals that a clinician works with may be a highly distorted segment of the total homosexual population — a population which is unknown as to number as well as social and personal characteristics. On this point the psychologist Wardell Pomeroy writes: "If my concept of homosexuality were developed from my practice, I would probably concur in thinking of it as an illness. I have seen no homosexual man or woman in that practice who was not troubled, emotionally upset, or neurotic. On the other hand, if my concept of marriage in the United States were based on my practice, I would have to conclude that marriages are all frought with strife and conflict, and that heterosexuality is an illness."[24]

Some of the points discussed in this introduction will be seen in greater detail in the readings that follow. On the broadest level the readings attempt to help in what has been a severe problem of dealing with sex — that of effective communication. In marriage there is probably no area of interpersonal involvement between the husband and the wife with more restrictions, implicit or explicit, than the failure to verbalize their sexual needs with reference to one another. The same can be said of any meaningful exchange between generations about sexual matters. But possibly even more important is that many individuals are not willing or able to learn about their own sexuality — whether it be from a book or through experimentation. This collection of readings will hopefully contribute to a better body of sexual knowledge for those who read it.

Notes

1. Kinsey, Alfred C., Wardell B. Pomeroy, Clyde E. Martin, and Paul W. Gebhard, *Sexual Behavior In The Human Female,* Philadelphia: W. B. Saunders Company, 1953, p. 9.

2. See Michael Gordon, "From an Unfortunate Necessity to a Cult of Mutual Orgasm: Sex in American Marital Education Literature, 1830–1940," in James Henslin (ed.) *Studies in the Sociology of Sex,* New York: Appleton-Century-Crofts, 1971, pp. 55–73.
3. Barber, Bernard, and Walter Hirsch, *The Sociology of Science,* New York: The Free Press of Glencoe, 1962, p. 87.
4. Merton, Robert K., *Social Theory and Social Structure,* New York: The Free Press of Glencoe, 1951, p. 299.
5. Reiss, Ira L., "Personal Values and the Scientific Study of Sex," *Advances in Sex Research,* New York: Harper and Row, Publishers, 1963, p. 6.
6. *Ibid.,* pp. 8–9.
7. Merton, *op. cit.,* p. 300.
8. See Ernest Jones, *The Life and Work of Sigmund Freud,* New York: Basic Books, 1961; and Havelock Ellis, *My Life,* Boston: Houghton, Mifflin, 1969.
9. Kinsey, Alfred C., Wardell B. Pomeroy and Clyde E. Martin, *Sexual Behavior in the Human Male,* Philadelphia: W. B. Saunders Co., 1948, p. 23.
10. Kinsey, et al, 1953, *op. cit.,* p. 298.
11. Davis, Katherine B., *Factors in the Sex Life of Twenty-Two Hundred Women,* New York: Harper and Bros., 1929.
12. Hamilton, Gilbert V., *A Research in Marriage,* New York: Albert and Charles Boni, 1929.
13. Dickinson, Robert L. and Lura Beam, *A Thousand Marriages,* New York: The Century Co., 1932.
14. Havelock Ellis in the introduction to Dickinson and Beam, *Ibid.,* p. ix.
15. Bell, Robert R., *Premarital Sex in a Changing Society,* Englewood Cliffs, New Jersey: Prentice-Hall, Inc., 1966, p. 7.
16. Lerner, Max, *America As a Civilization,* New York: Simon and Shuster, Inc., 1957, p. 680.
17. Zimmerman, Carle C., *The Family of Tomorrow,* New York: Harper and Row, 1949, p. 222.
18. Masters, William H., and Virginia E. Johnson, *Human Sexual Response,* Boston: Little, Brown and Company, 1966.
19. Masters, William H., and Virginia E. Johnson, *Human Sexual Inadequacy,* Boston: Little, Brown and Company, 1970.
20. *Newsweek,* "Response to Response," May 22, 1966, p. 94.
21. Bell, *op. cit.,* pp. 90–91.
22. Bell, *op. cit.,* pp. 91–92.
23. *Ibid.,* p. 91.
24. Pomeroy, Wardell B., "Homosexuality," in Ralph W. Weltze, *The Same Sex,* Philadelphia: Pilgrim Press, 1969, p. 13.

part two

Premarital sex

During the past three decades it has been commonly assumed that the premarital sexual experience of American girls has been steadily increasing. It has also frequently been assumed that the college girl has been at the forefront in attaining greater sexual experiences. But up until recently the studies had not shown any significant increase in premarital coital experience for unmarried girls since the 1920s. One of the authors, after an extensive look at past studies, came to the conclusion that "there is no evidence to suggest that when women born after 1900 are compared by decades of birth, there are any significant differences in their rates of premarital coitus."[1]

For a period of approximately forty years there did not appear to be much change in the behavior aspects of premarital coital experience. This may be seen by looking at some trends with regard to premarital sex that had developed up until the mid-1960s. First, Reiss has pointed out that while the Terman, Burgess and Wallin, and Kinsey studies had examined married couples from California, Chicago, and New York, the results were very much alike.[2] "All three of these major studies showed that in their sample of the people born after 1900 about 50 percent of the women entered marriage nonvirginal."[3] Reiss goes on to point out that considering the "geographical and time spans that separate these studies

16

and their respondents, such findings are indicative of high validity."[4] There was until recently no evidence to suggest that when women born after 1900 were compared by decades of birth, there were any significant differences in their rates of premarital coitus.

A second trend was that the studies indicated that being a nonvirgin at the time they were married was not an indication of extensive premarital experience with a number of different partners. For the female premartial coitus generally depended on strong emotional commitment and plans for marriage. The Terman, Burgess and Wallin, and Kinsey studies reported premartial coitus most often only with the men they eventually married.

Third, up until the mid-1960s probably the greatest behavioral change in premarital sexual experience since the 1920s was the increase in premarital petting. Winston Ehrmann wrote that "the dramatic change, or revolution, in the premarital sexual behavior of Americans in the last forty years is characterized by the marked increase in petting."[5] This meant that with their extensive petting experiences many virgins entered marriage far more sexually experienced than did virgins fifty years before.

Fourth, if the assumption of at least a temporary stabilization of premarital sexual coitus in the United States is true, it

17

means that young people have been engaging in essentially the same types of behavior for three or four decades. This suggests that the older generation had many of the same types of experiences as did the younger generation. In the 1920s the older generation was very much disturbed by the assumed premarital sexual activity of the younger generation. By contrast, the older generation today appears less upset about the younger generation. The reason may be that the parents and grandparents of the last decade were the young generation who introduced the new sexual patterns of several decades ago.

While it has been pointed out that premarital sexual behavior patterns had remained fairly constant for over a third of a century it is suggested that there is evidence that a change has been occurring with respect to the sexual experiences of college women since the mid 1960s. In a recent study by Bell and Chaskes it was found that the rates of premarital intercourse had significantly increased for a sample of coeds from 1958 to 1968, and this was true while dating, going steady, and engaged.[6] Similar evidence of change has also been found in the following study by Christensen and Gregg.[7]

There are a number of reasons as to why it is believed that the premarital coital rates among coeds have been going up since the mid 1960s. Over the past few years, even more so than before, the group primarily responsible for rebellion among the young has been the college student. While there has always been rebellion among the younger generation toward their elders, it probably never has been as great in the United States as it has been since the mid 1960s. In recent years youths not only have rebelled, but also have rejected many aspects of the major institutions in American society. Since the mid 1960s a small but highly influential proportion of college students has been deeply involved in the Civil Rights movement and then in the protest over the Vietnam War.

Many college students have come to believe that a number of the norms of adult institutions are not only wrong but also immoral. This is the view held by many college students toward the treatment of the Black, toward the war in Indochina toward American political procedures, and so forth. It therefore seems logical that if many of the norms of these institutions are viewed as wrong and immoral by large numbers of the younger generation, they are also going to be suspicious and critical about other norms in other adult controlled institutions. One social institution the younger generation is bound to view with skepticism would be that concerned with marriage and sexual behavior. There are several more specific social factors that appear to be related to changes in premarital sexual experiences.

18

One very important factor of the 1960s was the development, distribution, and general acceptance of the birth control pill. On most large university campuses the pill is available to the coed, or it is easy for her to find out where to get it in the local community. While studies have shown that fear of pregnancy has not been a very important deterrent to premarital coitus for a number of years, it now seems to have been largely removed for most college girls. Also while the "pill scare" of 1969–70 took a number of women off the pill it does not appear to have greatly influenced the college woman's use of oral contraception.

A second influence since the mid 1960s has been the legitimization of sexual candor. In part the new sexual candor has been legitimized by the Supreme Court. In recent years the young person has had access to a level of sexual expression far greater than just a few years ago. In the past year, even the most conservative of the mass media, television, has begun to show it. The new sexual candor, whatever its origin, is often seen by the rebelling younger generation as "theirs" in that it, too, critically subverts the traditional institutions. As a result the sexual candor of the early 1970s is both a manifesto and a guidebook for many in the younger generation.

It may also be suggested that the rebellion of the younger generation has been given both implicit and explicit approval by many in the older generation. Many adults want to think of themselves as part of the younger generation and its youth culture. For example, this is seen in the music and fashion of the youth culture which has had a tremendous impact on adults. It would seem that if many adults take on the values of the youth culture, this would raise questions as to the significance of many of their adult values for the youth world. In other words, the very identification of many adults with youth culture contributes to adult values having less impact on college youths. On the basis of the discussed reasons it is suggested that the social forces that developed in the mid 1960s led to a rapid increase in the rejection of many adult values, and the development of increasingly important patterns of behavior common to a general youth culture. This has led to an increased rate of premarital coitus among college girls along with fewer feelings of guilt about their experiences.

The three articles presented in this first section on premarital coitus look at the area from somewhat different perspectives. The first article, by Robert R. Bell, examines the contrasting points of view toward premarital sex as held by parents and their adolescent and young adult offspring. In the second article Ira Reiss is interested in examining the various theoretical approaches to the study of deviance and seeing how those approaches fit premarital sex as a substantive area of deviance. The final article, by Harold Christensen and Christina Gregg, examines the changing norms of sexual behavior by examining two samples in the United States and one in Denmark.

Notes

1. Bell, Robert R., *Premarital Sex In a Changing Society.* Englewood Cliffs, N. J.: Prentice-Hall, Inc., 1966, p. 68.
2. See: Ternam, L. M., *Psychological Factors in Marital Happiness,* New York: McGraw-Hill Book Co., 1938; Burgess, Ernest W., and Paul Wallin, *Engagement and Marriage,* Chicago: J. B. Lippincott Co., 1953; and, Kinsey, Alfred C., Wardell B. Pomeroy, Clyde E. Martin, and Paul H. Gebhard, *Sexual Behavior In The Human Female,* Philadelphia: W. B. Saunders Co., 1953.
3. Reiss, Ira L., *Premarital Sexual Standards In America,* New York: The Free Press of Glencoe, 1960, p. 77.
4. Reiss, *Ibid.,* p. 77.
5. Ehrmann, Winston, "Some Knowns and Unknowns In Research Into Human Sex Behavior," *Marriage and Family Living,* February, 1957, p. 19.
6. Bell, Robert R., and Jay B. Chaskes, "Premarital Sexual Experience Among Coeds, 1958 and 1968," *Journal of Marriage and The Family,* February, 1970, pp. 81–84.
7. Christensen, Harold T., and Christina F. Gregg, "Changing Sex Norms In America and Scandinavia," *Journal of Marriage and The Family,* November, 1970, pp. 616–627.

1

Parent-Child Conflict in Sexual Values

Robert R. Bell

The old cliché that as one grows older he becomes more conservative may be true, if premarital sexual values held by parents are compared with the values they held when they were younger. In this paper, the interest is in the nature of sex value conflict between parents and their unmarried late adolescent and young adult children. Our discussion will focus on values held by parents and by their unmarried children toward premarital sexual intimacy.

Conceptually, our approach focuses upon values related to a specific area of sexual behavior held by individuals from two very different role perspectives. The perspectives differ because parents and children are always at different stages in the life cycle, and while parents are highly significant in the socialization of their children, other social forces increasingly come to influence the child as he grows older. The various social values that influence the child's sexual behavior are often complementary, but they may also be contradictory. Furthermore, various types of influences on the acceptance of a given set of values may operate on the child only during a given age period. For example, the youngster at age fifteen may be influenced by his age peers to a much greater extent than he will be at age twenty.

Reprinted from *The Journal of Social Issues*, Vol. XXII, No. 2, pp. 34–44, by permission of the Society for the Psychological Study of Social Issues.

Given their different stages in the life cycle, parents and children will almost always show differences in how they define appropriate behavior for a given role. Values as to "proper" premarital sexual role behavior from the perspective of the parents are greatly influenced by the strong emotional involvement of the parent with his child. Youth, on the other hand, are going through a life cycle stage in which the actual behavior occurs, and they must relate the parent values to what they are doing or may do. There is a significant difference between defining appropriate role conduct for others to follow and defining proper role conduct to be followed by oneself. Even more important for actual behavior, there is often more than one significant group of role definers to which the young person can turn to as guides for his sex role behavior. Therefore, our discussion will focus more specifically on parent values related to premarital sexual intimacy, the peer group values of youth, and how these two different age groups as role definers, influence the sexual values and behavior of unmarried youth.

Limits of Discussion. For several reasons, our discussion will center primarily on the middle class. First, this class level has been highly significant in influencing changes in general sexual values and behavior. Second, and on a more pragmatic level, what little research has been done on parent-child conflict over sexual values has been done with middle-class groups. Third, the general values of the middle class are coming to include an increasing proportion of the American population. This also suggests that the values and behavior of college youth are of increasing importance as this group continues to expand in size and influence within the middle class.

A further limit is that our main focus is on the generational conflict between mother and daughter. The history of change in sexual values in the United States has been complexly interwoven with the attainment of greater sex equality and freedom by the female (2). Also, the relationship between the mother and daughter tends to be the closest of the possible parent-child relationships in the family socializing of the child to future adult sex roles. Furthermore, whatever the value system verbalized and/or applied by the girl, she often has more to gain or lose personally than the boy by whatever premarital sexual decisions she makes.

We also believe that any analysis of conflict over premarital sex between generations should center on *value* changes rather than *behavioral* changes. On the basis of available evidence, it appears that there have been no significant changes in the *frequency* of premarital sexual petting or coitus since the 1920s. Kinsey has pointed out that "there has been little recognition that the premarital petting and coital patterns which were established then (1920s) are still with us" (15, p. 300). Therefore, it is important to recognize that the parents and even some of the grandparents of today were the youth who introduced the new patterns of premarital sexual behavior about forty years ago.

22

Parent Values About Premarital Sex

The transmission of sexual values by parents to their children is only a small part of all parent values passed on during the family socialization process. Most parents do a more deliberate and comprehensive job of transmitting values to their children in such areas as educational attainment, career choice, religious beliefs, and so forth than they do with reference to any aspect of sexual values. Often when parents do discuss sex with their children it may be from a "clinical, physiological" perspective with overtones of parental embarrassment and a desire to get a distasteful task over with.

But perhaps more important than the formal confrontation between the parent and child in sexual matters are the informal values transmitted by the parent. In the past girls were often taught that premarital sexual deviancy was dirty and shameful, and that nonconformity to premarital sexual chastity values would mean suffering great personal and social shame. This highly negative view of premarital sex is undoubtedly less common today, but the newer, more "positive" values may also have some negative consequences. Very often today the mother continues to place great value on the daughter's virginity, and stresses to the daughter the great virtues of maintaining her virginity until marriage. But the "romantic" view of the rewards for the girl who waits for coitus until after marriage are often highly unrealistic and may sometimes create problems by leading the girl to expectations that cannot be realistically met in marital sex. Morton Hunt writes with regard to this approach that "if the woman has been assured that she will, that she ought, and she *must* see colored lights, feel like a breaking wave, or helplessly utter inarticulate cries, she is apt to consider herself or her husband at fault when these promised wonders do not appear" (13, 114). Whether or not the "romantic" view of marital sex is presented by her mother the girl often encounters it in the "approved" reading list suggested by the adult world, which tells her about the positive delights of waiting for sex until after marriage. So, though premarital sexual control may be "positive" in that it is based on rewards for waiting, it can be "negative" if the rewards are unrealistic and unobtainable.

For many parents, a major problem as their child moves through adolescence and into early adult years centers around how much independence to allow the child. Because they often recall the child's younger dependency, it may be difficult to assess the independency of the same child who is now older. Also, over the years the growing child has increasingly become involved with reference groups outside — and sometimes competing with — the family. In other words, the self-role definitions by the child and the parents' definitions of the child's role undergo constant change as the child grows older. For example, "The daughter in her younger years has her role as daughter defined to a great degree by her mother. But as she grows older

23

she is influenced by other definitions which she internalizes and applies to herself in her movement toward self-determination. The mother frequently continues to visualize the daughter's role as it was defined in the past and also attaches the same importance to her function as mother in defining her daughter's role. But given the rapid social change associated with family roles the definer, as well as the definitions, may no longer be institutionally appropriate" (5, 388).

Parents may also be biased in their definitions of their child as less mature than they, the parents, were when they were the child's age. One can not recall experiences earlier in the life cycle free from influence by the events that have occurred since. This may result in many parents' thinking of their younger selves as being more mature than they actually were. At the same time the parents' view of their child's degree of maturity may be biased by their recall of him when he was younger and less mature. Thus, from the parents' perspective they may recall themselves as youngsters within the context of what has occurred since (more mature) and may see their offspring within the context of their earlier childhood (less mature).

There also may be some symbolic significance for parents who must define their children as having reached the age when something as "adult" as sexual behavior is of relevance. In part, viewing one's children as too young for sexual involvement may contribute to the parents' feeling young, while seeing their children as old enough to be involved in sexual activity may lead to some parents feeling forced to view themselves as aging. For example, the comment about a man seen out with a young woman that "she is young enough to be his daughter" may have implications for his self-role image if the young woman *is* his daughter. We have little research data on how the aging process of parents influences their definitions of appropriate behavior for their young adult children.

In general, it is probable that most parents assume that their children, especially their daughters, accept the traditional restrictive values about premarital sexual behavior unless they are forced to do otherwise. Also, because of the great emotional involvement of parents with their own children, there is a common parental tendency to attribute sexual "immorality" to other youngsters. For many parents to face the possibility that their children do not conform to their values is to suggest some failure on the part of the parents. Often, rather than admit failure, the parents may define their children as having been forced to reject the parent values by other social influences or that their children have willfully let them down.

Youth Views About Premarital Sex

The importance of age peer group influence on the values and behavior of young people has been shown by a number of social scientists (see: 6, 9, 10, 11, 12, 14, 19, 20, 21, 22). Because youth subcultures are to some degree

24

self-developing, they often have conflict points in relation to some dominant adult values. However, the inconsistency and lack of effective adult definitions for adolescent behavior have also contributed to the emergence of youth subcultural values. That adults often view the adolescent with indecision as to appropirate behavior means that sometimes given adolescent behavior is treated one way at one time and in a different way at another time. Since the young person desires some decisiveness and precision in his role definitions, he often develops his own role prescriptions. Often when he creates his own role expectations, he demands a high degree of conformity by other adolescents as "proof" of the rightness of his definitions. It is ironical that the adolescent often thinks of himself as a social deviant. What he fails to realize is that his adolescent group deviates from the adult world, but that the requirements for conformity within his youth subculture are very strong (1, 369–74).

Youth subcultures have developed great influence over many aspects of premarital male-female interaction. The patterns of dating and courtship, appropriate behavior, success and failure are for the most part patterns defined by the youth group and not by the adult world. Yet, heterosexual relationships of youth are often based on adult role patterns, and they are therefore an important part of the youth world because they are seen by the youth as symbolizing adult status. To many young people, who are no longer defined by the adult world as children, but are not yet given full status as adults, their involvement in what they see as adult roles is important to them in seeking for adult status and recognition.

A part of the American youth subculture has been the development of new values related to premarital sexual intimacy. Reiss suggests that "It might well be that, since the 1920's, what has been occuring is a change in attitudes to match the change in behavior of that era" [premarital sexual behavior] (16, 233). The evidence suggests that for at least some college students new sex norms are emerging at the various stages of dating and courtship. One study found that "on the dating level necking is the norm for females and petting for males. During going steady and engagement, petting seems to be acceptable for both sexes. This would suggest that the young people both act and accept a higher level of intimacy than has generally been suggested by courtship norms." (3, 63).

In the past, emphasis was placed on the girl's virginity at the time of marriage; but today, many young people may only emphasize her being a virgin until she is in love, which may mean at the stage of going steady or engagement (8, Ch. 5 and 16, Ch. 6). If the girl is in love, some premarital sexual relations may be acceptable by peer group standards, although the dominant adult values — that love *and* marriage are basic prerequisites for coitus — continue. In the United States love as a prerequisite for sexual relations has long been a necessary condition for most middle-class females. The condition has not changed; rather, the point in the courtship-marriage

25

process where it may be applied to sexual involvement has shifted. Hence, the major point of parent-child conflict over premarital sex centers around the parent value that one should be in love *and* married before entering coitus and the modified value system of youth that an emotional and interpersonal commitment is important, but that this may occur before marriage.

There are two recent studies that provide some evidence on the nature of generational conflict; one study is of youth and adults in general and the other study is specifically concerned with mothers and their daughters. Reiss, in his extensive study of premarital sexual permissiveness, provides data on values held by adults as contrasted with values in a sample of high school and college students. The respondents were asked to express their beliefs about different combinations of intimacy and degree of interpersonal commitment for both unmarried males and females. Respondents were asked if they believed petting to be acceptable when the male or female is engaged. In the adult sample the belief that petting during engagement was acceptable for the engaged male was the response of 61 per cent, and for the engaged female the response was 56 per cent. Of the student responses 85 per cent approved for the engaged male and 82 per cent for the engaged female (17, 190–91); thus adult attitudes about petting during engagement were more conservative than those of the student population. It may also be noted that for both the adult and student groups there was a single standard — that is, the acceptance rates were esssentially the same for both males and females.

Reiss also asked his respondents if they believed full sexual relations to be acceptable if the male or female were engaged. Approval was the response given by 20 per cent of the adult group for males and 17 per cent for females. In the student group acceptance was given by 52 per cent for the male and 44 per cent for the female (17, 190–91). Here, as with petting, there are significant differences between the adult and the student samples, and once again both respondent groups suggest a single standard of acceptance or rejection for both males and females.

A study by Bell and Buerkle compared the attitudes of 217 coeds with those of their mothers. Both mothers and daughters were asked to respond to the question, "How important do you think it is that a girl be a virgin when she marries?" Of the mothers, 88 per cent answered "very important," 12 per cent "generally important," and 0 per cent "not important"; compared to 55 per cent, 34 per cent and 13 per cent of the daughters (4, 391). Both the mothers and daughters were also asked: "Do you think sexual intercourse during engagement is: very wrong; generally wrong, right in many situations?" The percentages for each response category were 83 per cent, 15 per cent and 2 per cent for the mothers; and 35 per cent, 48 per cent, and 17 per cent for the daughters (4, 391).

Both of the above questions show sharp differences between the value responses of the mothers and daughters with reference to premarital chastity. Many mothers were undoubtedly influenced in their responses by having a daughter in the age setting where the questions had an immediate and highly emotional application. Nevertheless, the differences in mother and daughter responses indicate that the area of premarital sexual behavior is one of potentially great conflict. One means of minimizing conflict is for the daughter not to discuss her sexual values or behavior with her mother. In the Bell and Buerkle study it was found that only 37 per cent of the daughters, in contrast with 83 per cent of the mothers, felt daughters should freely answer questions from their mothers in regard to attitudes toward sexual intimacy (4, 392).

The area of sexual values appears to be highly influenced by emotion, especially for the mother with reference to her daughter. Generational conflict with regard to premarital sexual intimacy has a variety of implications. First, the conflict in values clearly suggests that the traditional morality is often not socially effective as a meaningful determinant of behavior. Social values have behavioral influence when they emerge as social norms with significant rewards and punishments. In the case of sexual norms, however, there are rarely clearly-articulated rewards, or positive consequences, for the conforming individual. In almost all situations the effectiveness of sexual norms is dependent upon their negative sanctions, or punishments. For example, the traditional norm of female premarital chastity bases its behavioral influence primarily on negative consequences for the girl who fails to conform. This negative means of control is most commonly found as a part of the adult value system. In effect, the major sanctions over premarital chastity are based upon punishments for the girl and for her family if she deviates. Yet, in most cases the girl who has premarital coitus is not discovered by her parents or by the community. The real danger for the girl often centers around premarital pregnancy, because if that occurs and becomes known there can be no denying premarital coitus. Vincent has suggested that an important part of the negative sanction toward premarital pregnancy is not the pregnancy itself, but rather that it symbolizes premarital coitus *and* getting caught (23, Ch. 1).

The available studies indicate that fear of pregnancy is not the major deterrent for most girls (7, 344 and 15, 315). The personal values of the girl appear far more important in restricting her from engaging in premarital coitus. Yet, within the privacy of the youth world, there may operate for some girls certain values positive toward premarital coitus. For example, there may be a strong emotional desire and commitment to the boy and a positive feeling by the girl of wanting to engage in greater sexual intimacy.

There is a tendency by parents, as well as by many who give professional advice, to overlook the pleasurable aspects of sex at all ages, especially for the young who are experiencing sexual pleasure for the first time. Undoubtedly many girls engage in premarital sexual intimacy to "compensate" for some need and many may suffer some negative consequences. But it is foolish to state categorically that the "artificial" setting of premarital sex always makes it negative and unpleasant for the girl. We would be much more honest if we recognized that for many girls premarital coitus is enjoyable and the participants suffer no negative consequences. This was illustrated in the Kinsey research; it was found that "69 per cent of the still unmarried females in the sample who had had premarital coitus insisted they did not regret their experiences. Another 13 per cent recorded some minor regrets" (15, 316). Kinsey also found that "77 per cent of the married females, looking back from the vantage point of their more mature experience, saw no reason to regret their premarital coitus" (15, 316).

The Extent of Generational Conflict

With the evidence suggesting strong conflict between generations with regard to premarital sexual values, our final consideration is: how permanent is this generational conflict? We can provide some evidence on this question by examining the values of college-educated females of different ages. This appears justified because higher educated females are generally the most liberal in their views about sexual rights and expectations for women.

The evidence suggests that the premarital sexual liberalism of the college girl may be a temporary phenomenon. The coed's sexual liberalism must be seen as related to the interactional context of her being emotionally involved, and to a future commitment to an on-going paired relationship. The Bell and Buerkle study (4) found that the values of daughters toward the importance of premarital virginity were very similar to those of their mothers, until they had spent some time in college. However, at "around age 20 there emerge sharp differences between mothers and daughters in regard to premarital sexual attitudes. Behavioral studies indicate that it is at this point that sexual activity is greatly intensified, perhaps because it is at this age that college girls are entering engagement. A suggested pattern is that the college girl of 20 or 21 years of age, in her junior or senior year and engaged, has a strong 'liberal' pattern toward premarital sexual behavior and attitudes" (4, 392 and 18, 696).

We can get some indication of the persistence of premarital sexual liberalism by comparing the values of mothers by education. In the mothers' views as to the importance of premarital virginity it was found that the college educated mothers were actually as "conservative" as those mothers with lower levels of education (4, 392). It is quite possible that in the future the coeds will become as conservative as the college educated mothers. This may occur when the coed's attitudinal rationales are not related to herself, but as a mother to her own daughter. It is therefore possible that the "sexual emancipation" of the college girl exists only for a short period of time, centering mainly around the engagement years.

Yet, even if the girl becomes more conservative as she grows older, and especially with reference to her own daughter, her temporary "liberalism" probably is contributing to some shift in adult values about premarital sexual intimacy. Certainly, today's parental generation accepts greater sexual intimacy as a part of the premarital heterosexual relationship. Probably most parents assume that their adolescent and young adult children are engaging in necking and even some petting. Most parents, as long as they don't actually see the sexual intimacy, don't concern themselves about it. However, to suggest that parents may be more liberal (or tolerant) of premarital sexual intimacy does not necessarily suggest that parents are liberal if the intimacy reaches coitus.

It also appears that there has been some reduction in the severity of negative sanctions by parents if the daughter deviates and is caught. Among middle-class parents today it may be less common to reject the unwed daughter if she becomes pregnant than in the past, and more common for the parents to help her. This is not to suggest that today's parents offer any positive sanctions for premarital pregnancy, but that they may be able to adapt (often painfully) to it, rather than respond with high rejection and anger.

If our suggestion is correct (that parents take a less totally negative view of "discovered" premarital coitus), then this further suggests that traditional sexual values are being altered, since, as we have suggested, in the past the values of premarital chastity were primarily based on the negative consequences for those who deviated and were caught. If these negative consequences have been reduced, then the social force of the traditional values has been reduced as a means utilized by parents to control premarital sexual deviancy.

Conclusions

Based on the available evidence, there are several general speculations that may be made about future generational conflict over premarital sex. In general we would suggest that conflict between parents and their adolescent-young adult children with regard to premarital sexual intimacy may decrease in the future, because of several trends.

1. The trend in the United States is toward a more liberal view of sexual behavior in general. This is reflected in the generally accepted professional opinion that the woman has a right to sexual satisfaction, and that sexual satisfaction is a desirable end in itself. The trend toward a belief in a single sexual standard for both men and women, even though within the setting

29

of marriage, is bound to influence the beliefs and behavior of the unmarried. For the unmarried, there may be an increasing tendency to attach less importance to the marriage act as the arbitrary dividing line between socially approved and socially disapproved sexual intimacy.

2. Since the evidence suggests that over the past three or four generations the rates of female premarital coital experience have not changed, and since the younger generation has developed some value frameworks for its behavior, modification of traditional values and behavior may increasingly influence the values of parents to be more liberal. That is, it may become increasingly difficult for many parents to hold their children to a set of conservative values which they, the parents, did not hold to when they were younger.

3. Parents seem increasingly unwilling to strongly punish their daughters who sexually deviate and are caught. This parental reduction of punishment may be influenced by the increasing public attention directed at such social problems as illegal abortion. For example, many parents may be more willing to accept and help an unmarried pregnant daughter than take the risk of her seeking out an illegal abortion. The possible negative consequences of abortion may appear more undesirable than the premarital pregnancy.

4. Less generational conflict will occur if parents know less about the sexual activities of their children. A great part of the social activity of young people is carried out in the privacy of their age peer setting; what they do in the way of sexual intimacy is increasingly less apt to be noted by their parents. With the development and marketing of oral contraceptives, the risks of premarital pregnancy will be greatly reduced. In the future the rates of premarital coitus may remain the same, but with the chances of pregnancy reduced parents may be less aware of their children's premarital coitus.

Over time, then, the values of parents and the adult community in general may become more liberal and the conflict between generations reduced. (There seems little possibility that the opposite will occur; i.e., the younger generation's reducing the conflict by becoming more conservative.) But in the meantime, and certainly in the near future, it appears that parents and their children will continue to live with somewhat different value systems with regard to premarital sexual values. Parents will probably continue to hold to traditional values, and assume that *their* child is conforming to those values unless his actions force them to see otherwise. The youth generation will probably continue to develop their own modified value systems and keep those values to themselves, and implicitly allow their parents to believe they are behaving according to the traditional values of premarital sexual morality. For many parents and their children, the conflict about premarital sex will continue to be characterized by the parent's

30

playing ostrich and burying his head in the sand, and the youth's efforts to keep the sand from blowing away.

References

1. BELL, ROBERT R. *Marriage and Family Interaction,* Homewood, Ill.: The Dorsey Press, 1963.
2. BELL, ROBERT R. *Premarital Sex In A Changing Society,* Englewood Cliffs, N.J. Prentice Hall, (in press).
3. BELL, ROBERT R. AND LEONARD BLUMBERG. "Courtship Stages and Intimacy Attitudes," *Family Life Coordinator,* 1960, 8, 60-63.
4. BELL, ROBERT R. AND JACK V. BUERKLE. "Mother and Daughter Attitudes to Premarital Sexual Behavior," *Marriage and Family Living,* 1961, 23, 390-92.
5. BELL, ROBERT R. AND JACK V. BUERKLE. "Mother-Daughter Conflict During The 'Launching Stage,'" *Marriage and Family Living,* 1962, 24, 384-88.
6. BERNARD, JESSIE (Editor). "Teen-Age Culture," *Annals of the American Academy of Political and Social Science,* November, 1961, 338.
7. BURGESS, ERNEST and PAUL WALLIN. *Engagement and Marriage,* Chicago: J. B. Lippincott, 1953.
8. EHRMANN, WINSTON. *Premarital Dating Behavior,* New York: Henry Holt, 1959.
9. GINSBERG, ELI. *Values and Ideals of American Youth,* New York: Columbia University Press, 1962.
10. GOTTLIEB, DAVID AND CHARLES RAMSEY. *The American Adolescent,* Homewood, Ill.: The Dorsey Press, 1964.
11. GRINDER, ROBERT. *Studies in Adolescence.* New York: Macmillan, 1963.
12. HECHINGER, GRACE AND FRED. *Teen-Age Tyranny,* New York: Crest, 1962.
13. HUNT, NORTON M. *The Natural History of Love,* New York: Alfred A. Knopf, 1959.
14. KELLEY, EARL C. *In Defense of Youth,* Englewood Cliffs, N.J.: Prentice-Hall, 1962.
15. KINSEY, ALFRED C., WARDELL B. POMEROY, CLYDE E. MARTIN AND PAUL H. GEBHARD. *Sexual Behavior in the Human Female,* Philadelphia: W. B. Saunders, 1953.
16. REISS, IRA L. *Premarital Sexual Standards in America,* Glencoe, Ill.: The Free Press, 1960.
17. REISS, IRA L. "The Scaling of Premarital Sexual Permissiveness," *Journal of Marriage and the Family,* 1964, 26, 188-98.
18. REISS, IRA L. "Premarital Sexual Permissiveness Among Negroes and Whites," *American Sociological Review,* 1964, 29, 688-98.
19. REMMERS, H. H. AND D. H. RADLER. *The American Teenager,* New York: Charter, 1957.
20. SEIDMAN, JEROME. *The Adolescent,* New York: Holt, 1960.
21. SMITH, ERNEST A. *American Youth Culture,* New York: The Free Press, 1963.
22. SYMONDS, P. M. *From Adolescent to Adult,* New York: Columbia University Press, 1961.
23. VINCENT, CLARK. *Unmarried Mothers,* Glencoe, Ill.: The Free Press, 1961.

2

Premarital Sex As Deviant Behavior: An Application of Current Approaches to Deviance

Ira L. Reiss

Introduction

The last two decades have witnessed a revived interest and the development of new approaches in the area of deviant behavior. The so-called "labeling school" has come to the fore with the work of Lemert (1951, 1967), Becker (1963, 1964), Kitsuse (1964), and others. The older approaches to deviance have continued to receive emphasis during this period in the writings of Merton (1957), Cohen (1966), Parsons (1951), Clinard (1961) and others. The growth of new conceptions has led to increased controversy among those working in this area (see: Gibbs, 1966; Cohen, 1966 for some account of this).

Here, I propose: (1) to apply some of the basic propositions, both old and new, concerning deviant behavior to a substantive area that has not been heretofore so treated, and (2) to assess, in the light of this application, the relative utility of these propositions, the assumptions underlying them, their interrelations, and finally to indicate the value of this process for the development of deviant behavior theory.

Reprinted from *American Sociological Review*, February, 1970, pp. 78-87, by permission of the author and the American Sociological Association.

An earlier version of this paper was presented at the 1968 American Sociological Association meetings in Boston, Massachusetts. Special thanks to Albert Cohen, David Mechanic, James Price, John Stratton, and Robert Terry, all of whom read drafts of this paper and gave me the benefit of their comments.

Drugs, mental illness, and crime are the key areas that have been analyzed by those interested in deviance. The area of premarital sexual intercourse has been rarely, if ever, used for the subject matter of a study of deviance. Deviant behavior, by general agreement, refers to behavior which is viewed by a considerable number of people as reprehensible and beyond the tolerance limit. Premarital coitus qualifies on the basic ground that in the eyes of most adults (77% in a national sample of adults, 21 years and older; see Reiss, 1967) it is viewed as the violation of a norm, and many people hold this view with sufficient intensity to place such behavior outside their tolerance limits. The definition of deviance used here is that of Clinard (1961), which simply defines deviance as behavior "outside the community's tolerance limits." Premarital coital behavior seems to qualify as an object of deviance as much as the smoking of marijuana which Becker (1963) studied. While it is true that large numbers of today's youth participate in and normatively accept premarital coitus and marijuana smoking, it is equally true that large numbers of their parents label such behavior as outside of their tolerance limits. This appears to be a situation in which two groups differ sharply in their labeling of these forms of behavior. Using Clinard's definition of deviance, premarital coitus is a legitimate type of deviance from the perspective of the adult population, and it will afford a new area by which to examine some of the basic propositions concerning deviant behavior.

Cohen (1966:47) makes a useful distinction between psychological and sociological explanations of deviance: "... psychological inquiry is concerned with identifying variables and processes involved in the motivations of deviance and conformity, and with constructing exact theories about their interrelationships. Sociological theory is concerned with identifying the variables and processes in the larger social system that in turn shape those that are involved in motivation, and that determine their distribution within the system."

I shall not examine the relevance of psychological approaches to premarital coitus in this paper (See Cohen, 1966: Chapters 5 and 6); instead I shall examine three major sociological theories: (1) Labeling theory, (2) Anomie theory, and (3) Social and Cultural Support theory. For purposes of analysis I shall choose one representative proposition for each theory. It should be noted that a single proposition, while sufficient for my aims, cannot do justice to the full complexity of a given theory. One additional caution: the three approaches to be examined are by no means mutually exclusive. Cohen (1965) has indicated some key interrelationships, as has Cloward (1959). Such interrelations, which are neglected in specific analyses, are taken into account in the general discussion in the last part of the paper.

Labeling Theory

Let us start with a key proposition from the new labeling theory. As in any such classification of theorists, each of the men under this category is somewhat different from every other. Lemert (1951) has one of the earliest statements of this approach in his textbook *Social Pathology*, in which he makes a distinction between primary and secondary deviance and defines secondary deviance as follows: "When a person begins to employ his deviant behavior or a role based upon it as a means of defense, attack or adjustment to the overt and covert problems created by the consequent societal reaction to him, his deviation is secondary" (1951:75).

Primary deviation is less important in one's self concept as can be seen: "The deviations remain primary deviations or symptomatic and situational as long as they are rationalized or otherwise dealt with as functions of a socially acceptable role" (1951:76).

In short, primary deviations are the common everyday norm violations, whereas secondary deviations occur when one has come to think of himself differently because of his deviant behavior and thereby comes to assume the role of a deviant. To illustrate: such secondary deviation, as with delinquency, may occur because of frequent arrests and definitions by police and judges. Lemert believes that secondary deviation is more worthwhile to study. Previous researchers had stressed the search for causes within the individual to such an extent that they failed to see how accidental much of deviant behavior was and how vital the societal role was in producing secondary deviance.

Secondary deviance is, by definition, produced by societal reactions to deviant behavior, i.e., by societal attempts at controlling deviance. This is the key proposition of labeling theory. When a deviant is labeled as such, his self conception may be affected so as to start him on what Becker (1963) calls "career" deviance. Deviance by this view is created by society; it results from labeling of a deviant. Groups or "audiences" choose which acts to label as deviant, and then some of the particular individuals who are so labeled react and enter upon career deviation. The concern as Becker has put it is: "I will be less concerned with the personal and social characteristics of deviants than with the process by which they come to be thought of as outsiders and their reactions to that judgment" (1963:10).

Society chooses what rules to enforce, in what situations, on what people. Thus, Negroes may get censored for what whites can do; women censored for what men may do; certain men censored for what their friends are also doing and some may be labeled as deviants even though they haven't violated any norm but are merely so accused. Although some think that Becker has taken a completely relativistic position and defines deviance as unrelated to the act, this is not quite so: "In short, whether a given act is deviant or not depends in part on the nature of the act (that is, whether or not it violates some rule) and in part on what other people do about it" (Becker, 1963:14).

One could still study the class of acts which society sometimes labels and seeks for causes, but Becker's interest is, as noted above, in the way in which the labeling occurs and how it affects the deviants. How does the individual avoid the conforming pressures of society; how does he get caught and labeled; how does this affect his self image (Goffman, 1963)? Becker believes the public label leads to a self-fulfilling prophecy and thus actually creates the deviant career or what Lemert would call secondary deviance. In any full explanation, Becker and Lemert would surely bring to bear elements of the interactive process other than societal labeling. However, the labeling proposition (that societal labeling causes deviance) is a key one in their theoretical approach, and it is sufficient to utilize it to see how well it fits as an explanation of premarital sexual intercourse. The reader should keep in mind, however, that this overall approach stresses a variety of other ways in which the definition of others affects one's self definition.

One key characteristic of the sexual act creates difficulty with the above labeling approach. That characteristic is the low physical and normative visibility of sexual acts. The kind of premarital heterosexual activity that parents censure, such as premarital coitus, occurs under conditions that severely limit the likelihood of discovery. Kinsey *et al.* (1953:326) report discovery of six acts out of each 100,000 reported to them. The most common place for coitus is in the girl's home or the boy's home. Parents make little deliberate effort to catch their children copulating, and accidental discoveries are quite rare as noted above. Law enforcement agencies do not usually seek to carry out systematically the laws in their books against fornication (Ploscowe, 1951; Sherwin, 1966), unless some distinctly public display or more serious law violation accompanies such behavior. The chief circumstance in which there may be adult labeling of deviants occurs when the female becomes pregnant (Reiss, A. J., 1960; Vincent, 1961), and even here abortion and geographic mobility are ways of avoiding labeling. In sum, then, the situation is somewhat distinct from drug addiction, mental illness, or crime. In those situations the law enforcement agencies actively seek to find offenders of the norms, and widespread public labeling is much more difficult to avoid.

The reason for this difference is not simply a matter of greater concern on the part of the adult population with non-sexual normative offenses. Surely one could argue that many parents would be just as concerned about finding that their 16-year-old daughter has engaged in premarital coitus as that she has smoked marijuana. The difference is in part due to a more private, personal, conception of sexuality. Evidence from studies of sex

(Ehrmann, 1959; Shofield, 1965; Reiss, 1967) indicates a high level of tolerance of other people's views on proper sexuality and a strong association of sex with primary types of relationships. The greater privacy of sex behavior is thus believed to be only partly a result of the act itself but partly also due to the widespread conception of this behavior as private behavior. From infancy on, American parents bring up children with a general attempt to restrict public display of sexuality and thereby to develop a private conceptualization of sex behavior (Sears *et al.*, 1957). Public masturbation on the part of children is discouraged; a general avoidance approach is taken with attempts to avoid prolonged discussions about sex with children and with goals of distracting the child from any public display of sexuality. This is a basic element in explaining the ease with which youngsters can practice their sexuality without adult supervision. This avoidance approach helps give the peer group more power in the sexual sphere, for it restricts parental interference and it clearly lowers the adult's ability to know what is occuring.

The lack of widespread direct adult labeling of premarital coitus in interactive situations with youngsters means that the labeling approach is, to this extent, difficult to apply. However, we can see some application of it in the recent findings (Reiss, 1967:Chapter 7) of widespread guilt reactions at all levels of premarital sexual behavior. These findings indicated that the typical path of sexual development involved initial feelings of guilt at the first kiss, and then a reduction in guilt as kissing behavior continued through time. Then movement into a more advanced form of sexual intimacy such as breast or genital petting, and then guilt reactions which in turn were eliminated by repeated behavior, and so on until one either gets married or reaches the maximum level of permissiveness. One can also take these findings and see if the guilt and the tendency toward increased sexual permissiveness could be causally tied to acts of societal labeling of this behavior as deviant. As noted above, there is little data available on the direct interactive process of parental labeling of children as deviant because of premarital coitus. However, we do know that, as a group, married people are about twice as likely to favor premarital abstinence as are dating people (Reiss, 1967: Chapter 2).

This discrepancy between adult and child seems today to be more due to the demands of different role positions than to a generational difference. Parents with older children are significantly lower on acceptance of premarital coitus than parents of the same age with no children or very young children. A single person of the same age as these parents is most likely to accept premarital coitus (Reiss, 1967:Chapter 9). Thus, it seems that role position, rather than age or generation, is the key factor. The parental role demands one take responsibility for someone else, and the risks of premarital coitus are anxiety-provoking to a parent responsible for such consequences.

36

But despite the adult objection to premarital coitus, low visibility makes labeling difficult and unlikely. Also, we can explain the greater permissiveness of young people by reference to roles, as in the above analysis, without utilizing labeling theory. Cognitive dissonance theory concerning the reduction of dissonance between attitude and behavior would also help to explain the trend toward increased permissiveness without reference to labeling theory (Festinger, 1957).

We also have data indicating that dating-age children perceive some gap between themselves and their parents, although not a radical gap (Reiss, 1967:Chapter 8). One can conclude that the guilt feelings that youngsters feel in their premarital sexual activities result from an awareness of general parental opposition to sexuality even though direct parental labeling did not occur. The avoidance approach of many parents and the direct or indirect statements regarding sexuality of many others may well promote such feelings of guilt and other psychological qualms regarding sex. However, the parents were themselves more acceptant of premarital sexuality when they were single, and the basic values which go with such acceptance probably have not vanished from their makeup. The child may well perceive that a parent who stresses pleasure, affection, and autonomy would not severely condemn premarital coitus. This sense of only weak opposition from parents may well underlie the ease with which most youngsters seemed to be able to overcome their guilt reactions and may help explain why they did not, therefore, become career deviants.

The motivation for the increase in premarital sexual permissiveness, as youngsters get older, may well come in part from peer group support for the males, and from male persuasion for the females. Such group support also tends to weaken the potential effects of other group's labels and thereby lessens the relevance of labeling theory. However, there is another source of labeling which may affect premarital sexual permissiveness, and that is labeling from within the peer group. It is possible that a girl who is labeled by the boys or others in her school as an easy mark may react to this label and decide to continue or increase her sexual activities because of such a group label. That this occurs in some cases is undeniable. The real question is how much of the sexual behavior of females can be explained in this fashion? The research evidence from Kinsey et al. (1953), Ehrmann (1959) and Reiss (1967) all indicates that the vast majority of females who have permarital coitus have it with a very few partners. In short, the promiscuous female is statistically very much in the minority. Some of these promiscuous females may have been propelled into their behavior by deviant labeling, but the majority of the experienced females report that it was an intimate love relationship that led to their acceptance of premarital coitus (Ehrmann, 1959:Chapter 4; Reiss, 1967:114). Also, most females seem to accept their coital behavior as proper and show little evidence of being driven to do what they personally do not want to do (Ehrmann, 1959:Chapter 5; Reiss, 1967: Chapter 2).

What does the above discussion lead us to conclude? Shall we conclude that very little of premarital sexual permissiveness is secondary deviance, that it is largely primary deviance? It is difficult to say when using Lemert's definitions of these two types of deviance. Much of premarital sexual coitus is a repetitive phenomenon and not a rare one, and the actor does realize that there is societal opposition. There are secondary aspects in the sense that the individual develops an ideology to defend his sexual behavior and often feels distinct from the general adult culture. Also, the individual does redefine himself as a sexually "mature" person and relate this to a different self-view as a citizen with a new philosophy of life. These individuals often counter-label their opponents as "prudes." Such counter-labeling has not been well explored. Many of these young people are, to use Merton's terminology, "nonconformists" and not merely "aberrant" (Merton, 1966); that is, they want to replace the older, more restrictive sexual norms with their own — more permissiveness — norms. Here, then, is a situation where one can see that the growth of what parents would call "deviant behavior" occurs largely from support of a youth culture, the nature of our courtship institutions, the parental values and approach to sex and the low visibility of sex. The applicability of the labeling approach to such deviance is rather partial and incomplete. This is not a rejection of that approach but merely a qualification that it may well be better suited to the explanation of deviant behaviors with higher visibility and less subgroup support. The labeling proposition examined here (that societal labeling promotes deviance) implicitly assumes a high level of visibility and that the labeled persons are not a cohesive group capable of counteraction. These assumptions do not fit with the data on premarital coitus.

Anomie Theory

Another prominent sociological explanation of deviance involves anomie theory, as derived from Emile Durkheim (1964) and developed by Robert K. Merton (1938, 1957). Merton postulated that anomie was caused by a disjunction between culturally shared goals and institutionalized means for achieving them. Such a strain of goals and means leads to lowered conformity to goals and means, and thereby to anomie and deviant behavior, sometimes in the form of patterned evasions (Williams, 1960). This is the basic proposition from anomie theory that I will examine. Would this proposition fit with what we know about the causes of premarital sexual deviancy? As with labeling theory, I am not attempting to examine all facets of anomie theory but rather to select one central proposition which is sufficient for present purposes.

One may apply Merton's schema of five modes of adaptation (conformity, innovation, ritualism, retreatism and rebellion) to the area of premarital sex, historically. In his presentation of this proposition, Merton utilized the cultural goal of success which was difficult to obtain for the lower classes. One can analogously use the shared cultural goal of marriage. The means to achieve this include unchaperoned dating. One additional means, particularly in the pre-World War One period, was preservation of virginity. Now these means came into conflict, for the open dating system led to situations wherein it was difficult to preserve virginity. Also, a girl who was too intent on such preservation might be left out of the dating structure. Conversely, a girl who was too free sexually might be excluded from consideration as a marriage partner. This conflict of means led to an "innovation" (in Merton's terms) so that by the 1920's we find that discreet coitus when in love is becoming acceptable and providing an alternate courtship path to marriage. Thus, Merton's anomie notions do have some historical fit with an explanation of premarital coitus.

However, as an explanation of *present day* premarital sexual behavior and attitudes, the Merton proposition does not seem adequate. This is predominantly so because (1) the young people themselves have a high degree of tolerance for other people's sexual relationships, and thus the amount of felt strain is minimized (Ehrmann, 1959; Schofield, 1965; Reiss, 1967), and (2) the young people today have a fully developed autonomous courtship system which is shaped greatly by their own felt needs and desires. In sum, the preservation of virginity seems less important and less widespread today. (Reiss, 1967:Chapter 2). The likelihood of strain today is thus smaller than in the 1920's. Young people talk a great deal more openly about their sexual ideas and behaviors, and this too probably helps reduce strain in decision making. The strain model which anomie theory assumes is not always applicable to a courtship situation where autonomy is high and where the legitimacy of choosing one's own standard is supported by the youth culture.

In summary, evidence on young people shows adherence to the legitimacy of choosing from a variety of premarital sexual standards, rather than a condition of normlessness. The situation 50 years ago might have been one of anomie in the area of sex, but today the growth of new sexual codes together with the legitimacy of choice indicates the solution to this anomic situation rather than anomie itself. Today, the cultural value of female virginity at marriage is held much more strongly by parents than by their dating youngsters (Bell and Buerkle, 1961). Thus, it is largely the parents who define premarital coitus as deviant behavior. Anomie theory appears to be more of an adequate explanation concerning historical origins of current sex customs than an explanation of present day sexual attitudes and behavior. The assumption underlying anomie theory which posits the presence of "strain" does not seem to fit the situation present in all types of deviance. Once again the importance of making explicit the assumptions of a particular approach is made more obvious when we examine a new substantive area such as premarital coitus.

Social and Cultural Support Theory

One can invoke group support and cultural transmission factors (Cohen, 1966:Chapters 8 and 9) as the basis for deviance. This can be done in several ways. First, one can simply say that this subculture conditions people to perform behavior that some other subculture labels as deviant. The proposition here could be elaborated to state that people perform these deviant acts because their significant others, their reference groups, and their normative contacts are such as to support and reward such deviant behavior. Some people have tried to explain crime in various places by reference to such a proposition. The best known of these attempts is Sutherland's differential association theory in which interactive contact with deviant norms is used to explain deviant behavior (Sutherland, 1960). A. J. Reiss (1968) has pointed out the relevance of the social organization of vice to the study of deviance, and Vincent (1961:243–249) has elaborated upon the applicability of differential association to the area of sex. How does this key proposition of social and cultural support theory fit the situation of premarital coitus?

The data in the area of sex fit much better with this proposition than with either the labeling or the anomie proposition. A recent national study (Reiss, 1967) of group differences in premarital sexual attitudes stresses the importance of the basic setting of adult institutions, especially the family, and also the key importance of the autonomy of courtship groups.[1] The courtship group has special characteristics which promote acceptance of premarital coitus, e.g., high exposure to temptation via privacy, dancing and drinking; youth culture approval of adventure and hedonism; and approval of youth culture for the importance of affection as a basis for sexual relationships. Thus, the degree to which a society or a group gives autonomy to such a courtship system is one important determinant of the level of sexual performance and belief. The second key determinant is the outside institutional setting of adults. Youth reflect this setting in a variety of ways. It is perhaps easiest to see that despite this very high degree of autonomy sexual intercourse is not a causal, randomized matter for most young people, particularly not for females. The parental values of love, responsibility and future orientation are obviously present. Because of special circumstances the courtship group will have more permissive standards than the parental groups but the relation of those standards to adult values is still clear.

40

Thus, the answer derived from this view of deviance would be that premarital coitus results, in one sense, because it has subgroup support from the courtship groups.[2] Such support is present due to the autonomy of this group and given the basically more sexually acceptant youth culture, autonomy leads to acceptance of higher levels of sexual permissiveness. Such autonomy seems to have increased during the 20th Century. The differential association of young people puts them in contact with permissive norms. In addition, parental groups play a role in promoting the very deviant behavior which they condemn. They do this because, as has been mentioned earlier in this paper, they themselves once were more permissive than they are now, and thus they still have vestiges of basic values conducive to permissiveness which they transmit to their children. Also, they unintentionally promote premarital sexuality by stressing the value of an autonomous courtship system and by emphasizing the value of love. Love experience is one of the best predictors of which females will have premarital coitus. (Reiss, 1967: Chapter 5). This briefly is the way the social and cultural support proposition can be utilized to explain premarital coitus. This proposition does not assume high visibility or great strain and *does* assume subgroup support, and thus its assumptions seem best in line with the empirical reality of premarital coitus as we know it.

Some Implications of the Analysis

One could go beyond these three approaches to deviance and give attention to role and self theory and to the various elaborations and subtypes of these and other theories. Cohen (1965) has made the point that the dynamics of the interactive process can be best caught by the use of role and self theory. In the area of sex he has pointed out that boys may seek to seduce girls in order to fit their conception of the masculine role (Cohen, 1965:13). One could interpret this as a.variation of the cultural support proposition, for that proposition would assert that deviant behavior occurs due to accepted conceptions of roles and norms. Nevertheless, I did not intend this paper to be an exhaustive analysis of deviant theories, but rather I intended to show the value of a new substantive area such as premarital coitus for illustrating the limits of some approaches to deviance. In a very general way the three different propositions we have examined represent the basic types of sociological explanations of deviance. The labeling proposition is fundamentally social psychological since it stresses the key impact of audience definitions on self concepts. However, it has elements of a traditional sociological approach in its investigation of structure and operation of the societal agencies of treatment. The anomie and the social and cultural support propositions have some link with symbolic interaction but basically come out of a traditional sociological viewpoint that stresses the investigation of subcultures, institutional relationships, and social system analysis. Psychological and biological approaches have deliberately been omitted since my interest is in a sociological theory of deviance.

There is one prime value in the attempt to explain deviant premarital sexuality as I have in this paper: it affords an application of existing notions in a substantive area not utilized before and thereby opens up the possibility of fresh insight into an integrated sociological theory of deviant behavior. It should be clear by now that if we had examined a different substantive area, such as drugs, mental illness, or crime, the relevance of each of the three major explanatory schemata may have varied tremendously. For explaining premarital sexual deviancy, I think the social and cultural support theory fits the data best, although the labeling and anomie theories surely add something of value to this explanation.

I would suggest that in studying those behaviors lacking in subgroup support, such as perhaps mental illness, one would find the labeling approach of key value. Those deviant behaviors involving sharp subgroup conflict, as in many areas of crime, would perhaps best fit with the anomie explanation. Anomie also seems relevant as a historical explanation of deviance — deviance which today may have other quite different supports. Finally, those deviant behaviors which involve subgroup support, as well as little sharp subgroup conflict, and low visibility, like premarital coitus, may best be explained by social and cultural support propositions. Eventually, we may be able to offer propositions regarding the factors that promote one or another of these types of deviance and put forth propositions showing exactly how these three explanations link together.

Some of the interrelationships of these approaches should by now be obvious. By studying social and cultural supports, one inevitably comes across factors that explain why groups would differ in their labeling of a particular behavior pattern. For example, role position in family or courtship groups is one such explanatory factor. Relatedly, by studying labeling, one gains insight into group alignments reflected by such labeling and into how these come about. Anomie theory throws light on both these processes by showing the relevance of points of strain to both labeling and sub-cultural supports. Each theoretical approach has its own set of assumptions regarding visibility, subgroup support, strain, etc., and these assumptions need to be made explicit so that we may see to what extent they fit a particular substantive area and what interrelations exists.

I would suggest that premarital coital deviancy is a particularly fruitful area to study not only because it differs from other deviance in the relevance of the various explanatory schemata, but also because its study should aid us in understanding related deviant behavior such as prostitution, illegitimacy, and abortion. The relation of these other substantive areas of sex deviancy is clear since one must often first engage in premarital coitus before the possibility of illegitimacy, prostitution, or premarital abortion is present. Also, the relative effectiveness of heterosexual socialization should throw light on the entire area of homosexual socialization. Some homosexual behavior has been explained in terms of labeling theory by Kitsuse (1964) and Schofield (1965), in terms partially of cultural support by Albert Reiss (1964) and in terms of anomie by many popular writers. The examination of heterosexuality should cue us to utilize all three of these approaches in an effort to localize interrelations.

Ultimately the study of specific substantive areas that social groups label as deviant should lead to a general theory of deviance. Each substantive area has a possibility of contributing to such a theory and premarital sex is no exception. For example, one could take the theoretical position that autonomy of the courting group is one key factor in the acceptance of premarital coitus, and generalize this to deviant behavior per se. One could say that the greater the autonomy of one group from another, the greater the likelihood that the members of this group will perform acts that are labeled deviant by the other group. This sort of proposition is a possible contribution to a general theory of deviance and not simply to the explanation of a specific substantive behavior. I believe this sort of theory building will occur more rapidly if we explore new substantive areas of deviance and look for ways in which current approaches and propositions apply. In this way particular substantive areas will be more of a means to the growth of a general theory of deviance rather than a way of trying to make everything fit one specific theory.[3]

Another way that one could develop a general theory of deviance is to link together these three propositions into a hypothesized "career pattern" of deviance. One could assert that deviance is defined when strain occurs due to anomie or simple contact of two diverse subcultures. Audience labeling may reinforce such behavior. In time supports of subgroups may maintain such behavior even if the anomic strain and labeling are no longer causally involved. By examining the assumptions of each proposition we can become more aware of the limited application of each and of the ways they may fit together. Other writers can examine more completely the theoretical propositions of these three approaches and check out their applicability to a wider substantive area. It is well not to restrict the testing of one's theories to just those "problem" areas in which one is personally interested (Gouldner, 1968).

There are weaknesses in our current theorizing in all three of the propositions about deviance examined here. There is need for greater specificity and for different questions to be asked. While it seems true that subcultural support helps explain premarital coital behavior and anomie may explain certain types of criminality and labeling may help explain the occurrence of mental illness — this level of explanation, while valuable, is still somewhat

43

primitive. What we need to develop are additional propositions that will enable us to further specify aspects of deviant behavior. For example, we need a set of propositions that will explain why one group has greater cultural support for a greater number of deviant behaviors. This goes beyond simply stating that such support promotes deviance. Why do some groups have radically different definitions of what is deviant? Why do some groups have much greater anomic strains than others? What are the specific mechanisms that promote cultural support, labeling, or anomie related to deviant behavior? How do these mechanisms differ for non-deviant behavior?

The three propositions we have examined offer the first steps in this direction. They give us a general guideline as to why deviance occurs in human society. But they are as yet so unspecified that they each would also explain the occurrence of behavior that was not labeled deviant. Now, it is true that any theory of deviance is also in part a theory of conformity. Ultimately, deviance theory answers the basic question Thomas Hobbes raised concerning the explanation of social order. I am not detracting from the value of the three propositions discussed here. Rather, I am saying that we need to add to them and find specific propositions concerning deviance which will add further to our understanding. I believe one major pathway to such knowledge will come from the study of specific substantive areas of deviance to show us the limits of our present propositions and aid us in developing new propositions. By expanding the number of substantive areas that we are investigating and by comparing the social processes involved in them, we have an excellent opportunity to further develop deviant theory. I offer the area of premarital sex as one of several substantive areas that may help in this work.

Notes

1. I will not bother here to go into the complexities involved in distinguishing what I have called the old and new basis of permissiveness except to note here that the old permissiveness was based in good measure upon the economic hardship of the lower classes and the resultant lack of advantage of the marital state over the other states. The new permissiveness is based more upon a rational, affection oriented, contraceptively informed, view of the psychic value of sexual intimacy. The clash of parent and child in these two types of permissive social settings will naturally differ. See Reiss, 1967: Chapters 3, 4, and 10 for further discussion of these points.

2. DeLamater (1968) makes a related point by stressing the distinction between deviants whose initial socialization was conventional and those whose socialization was in terms of deviant norms.

3. The historical approach to deviance is also of considerable value in understanding the processual quality of deviance as can be seen in Erikson (1966) and O'Neill (1967).

References

Becker, Howard S.
   1963   Outsiders: Studies in the Sociology of Deviance. New York: The Free Press
          of Glencoe.
Becker, Howard S. (ed.).
   1964   The Other Side: Perspectives on Deviance. New York: The Free Press of
          Glencoe.
Bell, Robert R. and Jack V. Buerkle.
   1961   "Mother and daughter attitudes to premarital sexual behavior." Marriage and
          Family Living 23 (November):390–392.
Burgess, Ernest W. and Paul Wallin.
   1953   Engagement and Marriage. Philadelphia: W. B. Lippincott Co. Clinard,
          Marshall B.
   1961   Sociology of Deviant Behavior. New York: Holt, Rinehart & Winston.
Clinard, Marshall B. (ed.).
   1964   Anomie and Deviant Behavior. New York: The Free Press of Glencoe.
Cloward, Richard A.
   1959   "Illegitimate means, anomie and deviant behavior." American Sociological
          Review 24 (April):164–176.
Cohen, Albert K.
   1965   "The sociology of the deviant act: Anomie theory and beyond." American
          Sociological Review 30 (February):5–14.
   1966   Deviance and Control. New Jersey: Prentice-Hall Inc.
DeLamater, John.
   1968   "On the nature of deviance." Social Forces 46 (June):445–455.
Durkheim, Emile.
   1964   The Division of Labor in Society. New York: The Free Press of Glencoe.
          (First published 1893.)
Ehrmann, Winston W.
   1959   Premarital Dating Behavior. New York: Holt, Rinehart & Winston.
Erikson, Kai T.
   1966   Wayward Puritans. New York: Wiley.
Festinger, Leon.
   1957   A Theory Cognitive Dissonance. New York: Harper and Row.
Gibbs, Jack P.
   1966   "Conceptions of deviant behavior: The old and the new." Pacific Sociological
          Review 9 (Spring):9–14.
Goffman, Erving.
   1963   Stigma. Englewood Cliffs, New Jersey: Prentice-Hall.
Gouldner, Alvin W.
   1968   "The sociologist as partisan: Sociology and the welfare state." The American
          Sociologist 3 (May):103–117.
Kinsey, Alfred C., Wardell Pomeroy and Clyde Martin.
   1948   Sexual Behavior in the Human Male. Philadelphia: W. B. Saunders Co.
Kinsey, Alfred C., Wardell Pomeroy, Clyde Martin and Paul Gebhard.
   1953   Sexual Behavior in the Human Female. Philadelphia: W. B. Saunders Co.
Kitsuse, John I.
   1964   "Societal reaction to deviant behavior: Problems of theory and method."
          Pp. 87–102 in Howard S. Becker (ed.), The Other Side: Perspectives on
          Deviance. New York: The Free Press of Glencoe.

Lemert, Edwin M.
   1951   Social Pathology. New York: McGraw-Hill Book Co.
   1967   Human Deviance, Social Problems and Social Control. New Jersey: Prentice-Hall, Inc.
Mechanic, David.
   1966   "The sociology of medicine: Viewpoints and perspectives." Journal of Health and Human Behavior 7 (Winter):237–248.
Merton, Robert K.
   1938   "Social structure and anomie." American Sociological Review 3 (October): 672–682.
   1957   Social Theory and Social Structure. New York: The Free Press of Glencoe.
Merton, Robert K. and Robert A. Nesbit (eds.).
   1966   Contemporary Social Problems (2nd ed.). New York: Harcourt, Brace and World.
O'Neill, William L.
   1967   Divorce in the Progressive Era. New Haven: Yale.
Parsons, Talcott.
   1951   The Social System. New York: The Free Press of Glencoe.
Ploscowe, Morris.
   1951   Sex and the Law. New York: Prentice-Hall, Inc.
Reiss, Albert J., Jr.
   1960   "Sex offenses: The marginal status of the adolescent." Law and Contemporary Problems 25 (Spring):309–333.
   1964   "The social integration of queers and peers." Pp. 181–210 in Howard S. Becker (ed.), The Other Side: Perspectives on Deviance. New York: The Free Press of Glencoe.
   1968   "The study of deviant behavior: Where the action is." Pp. 56–67 in Mark Lefton *et al.* (eds.), Approaches to Deviance. New York: Appleton-Century-Crofts.
Reiss, Ira L.
   1960   Premarital Sexual Standards in America. New York: The Free Press of Glencoe.
   1967   The Social Context of Premarital Sexual Permissiveness. New York: Holt, Rinehart and Winston, Inc.
Schofield, Michael.
   1965   The Sexual Behavior of Young People. Boston: Little, Brown & Co.
Sears, Robert R., Eleanore Maccoby and Harry Levin.
   1957   Patterns of Child Bearing. New York: Row-Peterson Co.
Sherwin, Robert V.
   1966   "The law and sexual relationships." Journal of Social Issues 22 (April): 109–122.
Sutherland, Edwin H. and Donald R. Cressley.
   1960   Principles of Criminology. Chicago: Lippincott.
Vincent, Clark.
   1961   Unmarried Mothers. New York: The Free Press of Glencoe.
Williams, Robin.
   1960   American Society. New York: Macmillan Co.

3

Changing Sex Norms
in America and Scandinavia

Harold T. Christensen and Christina F. Gregg

It has been popular of late to claim that the so-called *Sexual Revolution* which has been sweeping America during the recent fifties and sixties is little more than a liberalization of attitudes: that there has been no real or significant increase in nonmarital sexual behavior. No one disputes the more or less obvious facts of greater tolerance with respect to the sexual behavior of others or of greater freedom and openness in discussion, in dress and manners, in public entertainment, and throughout the mass media. But when it comes to the question of whether premarital coitus — the practice itself — is undergoing much of an increase, there tends to be either uncertainty or the suggestion that it is not. Part of this may be due to wishful thinking, part to a lack of adequate data, and part to a tendency among scholars to overgeneralize from the data available. At any rate, there is need for new data and for a reexamination of the problem.

Reprinted from *Journal of Marriage and the Family*, November, 1970, pp. 616–627, by permission of the authors and the National Council on Family Relations.

The research upon which this paper is based was done in 1958 and again in 1968, permitting a trend analysis. George R. Carpenter assisted with the questionnaire part of the research in 1958. Christina F. Gregg has been responsible for carrying out the midwestern phase of the study in 1968, including the special statistical analyses of the data from that sample. The authors wish to express appreciation to Wayne Gregg, Kathryn Johnsen, Eugene Kanin, Dean Knudsen, and Carolyn C. Perrucci for critical reviews of the manuscript; but assume full responsibility themselves for any imperfections that may remain.

Terman (1938:320–323) was one of the first to present solid evidence concerning incidence and trends in premarital coitus. He compared persons born in and subsequent to 1910 with persons born before 1890 and reported increases of premarital coitus for both men and women — though at a more rapid rate for the latter, signifying an intersex convergence.

Then came Kinsey. Kinsey and associates (1953:298–302) also compared incidence of premarital coitus by decade of birth and reported virtually no trend for males but a very significant increase for females, which likewise pointed to an intersex convergence. Yet even for females there appeared to be little difference in non-virginity among those born during the first, second and third decades of the present century. But non-virginity was more than twice as great for females born in these three decades after the turn of the century as compared with those born before 1900. Since approximately twenty years are required to reach maturity, the suggestion in this finding is that the big change in the liberalization of female sexual behavior took place during the decade following World War I and that the picture has not altered much since that time. It must be noted, however, that these data are not suitable for measuring trends that may have occurred during the 1950s and 1960s.

Nevertheless, Reiss (1969) and certain other scholars (for example, Bell, 1966; Gagnon and Simon, 1970), after drawing upon the Kinsey data, have moved beyond the reach of these findings by claiming that there has been little if any increase in non-virginity over the past twenty years or so. Reiss explains the widespread *belief* concerning an increase as being due largely to the liberalizing of attitudes, which makes people more willing to talk and so increases their awareness and anxiety. In support of his position of no significant trend in premarital coitus since the 1920s, he cites several studies made during the 1950s and 1960s (Ehrmann, 1959; Freedman, 1965; Kirkendall, 1961; Reiss, 1967; Schofield, 1965) which give somewhat similar incidence percentages as those reported earlier by Kinsey. But there is a question of comparability. Although these more recent studies do not show incidence percentages greatly different from Kinsey's, they each tap different populations and employ differing methodologies — so that the no-trend conclusion may be quite spurious. Furthermore, the reported research by Reiss himself deals almost exclusively with attitudes, largely ignoring behavior. It is to his credit though, that he recognized the tenuous nature of the evidence and because of this, states his position somewhat cautiously. He said simply that the common belief that non-virginity has markedly increased of late "is not supported by the research"; and concluded: "Thus, although the evidence is surely not perfect, it does suggest that there has not been any change in the proportion of non-virginity for the past four or five decades equal to that which occurred during the 1920's" (Reiss, 1969:110).

But the message that has come across to the public and even some schol-

48

ars is that research has established that a virtually static level of premarital coitus has maintained itself since the early post World War I period. This has been the most usual interpretation given recently in the popular press, by radio and television, and in some high school and college textbooks.

Even so, not everyone has believed it. Some, like the authors of this paper, have held mental reservations, though, until recently, they have been without appropriate data to test it out. A few years ago Leslie (1967: 387–392) examined this question by classifying chronologically virtually all studies which had reported incidence of premarital coitus, starting with 1915 and ending with 1965. He observed that for both sexes percentages tend to be higher in the more recent studies. Similarly, Packard (1968: 135–204, 491–511, 517–523) took a careful look at the reported findings of over forty studies including one of his own, which elicited student responses from 21 colleges in the United States and five from other countries (Luckey and Nass, 1969). He compared these studies and their findings across time; conceding, of course, the lack of strict comparability due to differing samples and methods. His tentative general conclusion was that "... while coital experience of U.S. college males seemed comparable to that of males 15 or 20 years ago, the college females reported a quite significantly higher rate of experience" (Packard, 1968:186).

The very latest information coming to our attention is a report by Bell and Chaskes (1970) wherein the earlier no-evidence-to-support-a-trend position of Bell (1966) is modified with the statement: "The writers believe that change *has* been occurring in the sexual experience of college girls since the mid 1960's" (Bell and Chaskes, 1970:81). These authors report increases in the premarital coitus of coeds between 1958 and 1968: from 10 to 23 percent during the dating relationship, from 15 to 28 percent during the going-steady relationship, and from 31 to 39 percent during the engagement relationship. Since proportionate increase was greatest at the first two dating levels, they conclude that the commitment of engagement has become a less important condition for many coeds participating in premarital coitus. They also report significant reductions at each dating level in the guilt connected with coitus, and point to a suggestion from their data of an increase in promiscuity. Still additional findings — though ones less relevant to our present analysis — were that premarital coitus tends to be associated with non-attendance at church, starting to date at an early age, and dating or going steady with a larger than average number of boys.

The Bell and Chaskes study has an advantage over many of the previous ones in that it taps college students in the same institution with the same measuring instrument at two different points in time, which more clearly enables it to look at *trends.* It nevertheless is limited to females alone on one college campus, and so sees its conclusions as suggestive rather than conclusive of any national change. These authors argue, from what is known

49

about the youth rebellion movement of very recent years, that the increase in the premarital coitus of coeds is a phenomenon of the mid 1960s. It should be noted, however, that there is nothing in their data to establish the change as occurring at that precise point in time as against the early 1960s or even the late 1950s.

Our own research about to be reported has some of the same limitations as certain of the earlier studies (including the small size and non-random character of its samples) but there are added features which we hope will enable us to carry the analysis a little farther. We have involved behavior as well as attitudes, studied males as well as females, compared three separate cultures against each other, and measured identical phenomena in the same manner in the same populations at two different points in time. The focus of this report is to be upon the time dimension, or social change. Nevertheless, by seeing change cross-culturally and in the context of male-female interaction and attitude-behavior interrelatedness, it should be possible to better understand what actually is taking place. There is an interplay among these and possibly other factors. We feel that it is important to try to see the premarital sex phenomenon as a network and to look for interrelationships and then build toward an impirically-based theory to explain it all. Our study is but one start in that direction.

The senior author initiated his cross-cultural research on premarital sex back in 1958, at which time questionnaires were administered to college samples in three separate cultures differing on a restrictive-permissive continuum: highly restrictive Mormon culture in the Intermountain region of western United States; moderately restrictive Midwestern culture in central United States; and highly permissive Danish culture which is a part of Scandinavia (Christensen, 1960; 1966; 1969; Christensen and Carpenter, 1962a; 1962b). The 1958 study involved both record linkage and questionnaire data, but it is only the latter that are of concern in the present writing. He then repeated the study in 1968, using the same questionnaire administered in the same three universities. Every effort was made to achieve comparability across the two years. The unchanged questionnaire was administered in the same way to similar classes in the identical universities. In most instances within both years social science classes were used; the only real change being in Denmark, where large proportions of medical and psychology students were used in 1958 as against an almost exclusively sociology student sample in 1968. The repeat, of course, was chiefly for the purpose of getting at changes which may have occurred during a period of time popularly described as experiencing a sexual revolution. Although the study dealt with all levels of intimacy — necking, petting, and coitus — this report is to be limited to premarital coitus alone. Furthermore, it is limited to only selected aspects of premarital coitus. This is because our analysis of data has just begun, plus the necessity to restrict the length of a journal article.

50

table 1

PERCENTAGES[a] TAKING LIBERAL POSITIONS ON SEX QUESTIONS,
1958 AND 1968 COMPARED

Items and Years	Intermountain		Midwestern		Danish	
	Males	Females	Males	Females	Males	Females
	%	%	%	%	%	%
I. Opposition to Censorship						
1968	61	58	71	59	99	97
1958	42	54	47	51	77	81
Difference	19	4	24	8	22	16
II. Acceptance of Non-Virginity						
1968	20	26	25	44	92	92
1958	5	11	18	23	61	74
Difference	15	15	7	21	31	18
III. Approval of Premarital Coitus						
1968	38	24	55	38	100	100
1958	23	3	47	17	94	81
Difference	15	21	8	21	6	19

[a] Percentages are based on numbers answering the question. The number of cases leaving a question unanswered varied from 0 to 8 in the various groups.

Respective sample sizes involved in calculations for the statistics now to be reported were: for the Intermountain, 94 males and 74 females in 1958, and 115 and 105 respectively in 1968; for the Midwestern, 213 males and 142 females in 1958, and 245 and 238 respectively in 1968; for the Danish, 149 males and 86 females in 1958, and 134 and 61 respectively in 1968.

Some Measures of the Liberal Attitude

Three items from the questionnaire have been selected to illustrate comparisons and trends in the attitudinal component. Table 1 has been constructed to show percentages of respondents holding liberal or permissive views regarding these matters.

OPPOSING THE CENSORSHIP OF PORNOGRAPHY

Presented first are percentages of respondents who indicated agreement with the statement: "It is best not to try to prohibit erotic and obscene literature and pictures by law, but rather to leave people free to follow their own judgments and tastes in such matters." The three comparisons of interest in this analysis are as follows:

(1) As one moves from left to right — from the restrictive Intermountain culture to the permissive Danish culture — percentages taking the liberal stance by agreeing with the statement are seen to increase. This is true for both sexes and with respect to both sample years (with the single exception of the 1958 female comparison between Intermountain and Midwestern).

(2) More females than males opposed the censorship of pornography in 1958, whereas ten years later the reverse was true. Furthermore, this shift in pattern occurred consistently in each of the three cultures, suggesting that it may be something of a general phenomenon.

(3) The time trend over the decade 1958–68 was consistently in the direction of increasing opposition to this kind of censorship. The trend held for each of the three cultures and for both sexes — although females liberalized on this point in *smaller* degree than did males, which accounts for the shift in the male-female pattern mentioned in the previous paragraph.

Since (as will be shown throughout the remainder of our paper) females generally have liberalized in a proportionately *greater* degree than have males, this contrary finding on censorship requires some attempt at explanation. Our speculation is that females, with their more sheltered life, have been less knowledgeable and realistic regarding pornography and also possibly less attracted by its appeal. This might explain their greater opposition to censorship than males in 1958, not seeing pornography as particularly threatening. But the new openness of recent years undoubtedly has given them greater sophistication in these matters, and they may now better understand the reality of hardcore pornography and its differential appeal to the male; which could explain their lower opposition to censorship than males in 1968.

ACCEPTING THE NON-VIRGINITY OF A PARTNER

In the second section of Table 1 are shown percentages of those who indicated *disagreement* with the statement: "I would prefer marrying a virgin, or in other words, someone who has not had previous coitus (sexual intercourse)." As with the statement on pornography, permissive attitudes increased for both sexes and in both sample years from lows in the restrictive Intermountain to highs in the permissive Danish; and increased between 1958 and 1968, for both sexes and in each of the three cultures. These trends are shown to be without exception. The male-female comparisons show *females* to be the most *permissive*, in both sample years and in each of the cultures (with the single exception of 1968 Danish respondents, where they were equal).

Since practically every other measure in our questionnaire — as well as virtually all studies now in the literature — show females to be more conservative than males in sexual matters, one must ask "why this exception?"

Two possible reasons occur to us: in the first place, the typical female attitude may represent a realistic acceptance that more males do have premarital sex, making her chances of actually marrying a virgin somewhat smaller; and in addition, some females, with a sheltered upbringing and more limited sexual expression, may feel inadequate and hence welcome an experienced male to help show them the way. In this connection, it is interesting to note also that in the Midwestern sample — which may approximately reflect the overall situation for United States — females moved away from insistence on a virginal partner at a much more rapid rate than did males.

APPROVING COITUS AMONG THE UNMARRIED

Finally, Table 1 shows percentages of those approving premarital coitus. Respondents were asked: first, to consider an average or typical courtship "in which there is normal love development and mutual responsibility"; next, to assume that this hypothetical relationship progresses at a uniform rate of six months between the first date and the start of going steady, another six months to an engagement, and still another six months to the wedding (or a total courtship of eighteen months); and then to mark on a scale the earliest time they would approve the start of necking, then of petting, and then of coitus. The percentages shown are restricted to coitus and they represent approval at any point prior to the wedding.

This item on approval of premarital coitus is free of the kinds of irregularities mentioned for the previous two. It shows highly consistent results for all three comparisons: a movement toward greater approval from Intermountain to Midwestern to Danish, for both sexes and in both sample years; greater approval given by males than by females (except for a tie among 1968 Danish respondents where both sexes hit the ceiling), for both sample years and each of the three cultures; and a trend toward greater approval over the 1958–68 decade, for both sexes and in each of the three cultures.

In connection with this last point, it is important to note that in each of the cultures females moved toward approval more strongly than did males, which means a trend toward intersex convergence. Females still have more restrictive attitudes than males but the difference is less than formerly.

An additional observation which should not be missed is that, in both sample years, male-female percentages are closer together in Denmark than in the other two cultures. This suggests that norm permissiveness may operate to reduce differences between the sexes seen in cross-cultural comparisons as well as in liberalizing trends over time.

TREND COMPARISON WITH RELEVANT
VARIABLES CONTROLLED

As a double check on this trend pattern — and to at least partially determine whether it is real or merely the result of differing compositions of the two samples drawn ten years apart — we made a supplementary analysis of matched data. This was done for the Midwestern culture only (the most representative of American society and the most feasible for matched testing because of the larger sizes of its samples) and was further limited to data on premarital coitus (the most central in our present analysis). The matching occurred on four variables: sex of respondent, cumulative number of years in school, frequency of church attendance, and level of courtship development. This had the effect of controlling these variables across the 1958–68 period, while the time trend was being examined. Successful matching was completed for 202 pairs of respondents (127 pairs were male, 75 female).

In Table 2 we show for the Midwestern culture two measures of premarital coital approval for both matched and total samples. The first consists of average (mean) scores computed from the approval timing scale introduced earlier. The scale had ten divisions, with the first representing time of first date and the last representing time of marriage. Scores ranged from 1 to 10 according to markings on the scale, and it is *average* coital scores (means) that are shown here. The lower the score, the farther from marriage is the approved timing of first coitus. It will be observed that, by this measure, both males and females showed up more permissive in 1968 than they did in 1958 and that the trend held for the matched as well as unmatched comparisons.

The second measure is simply percent approving premarital coitus. Unmatched percentages are shown here in juxtaposition to percentages from the matched cases. But again the picture is very clear: matching has not altered the general trend; in the uncontrolled and the controlled analyses the trend was found to be toward greater approval — which is the permis-

table 2

MEASURES OF PREMARITAL COITAL APPROVAL ON MATCHED
AND TOTAL SAMPLES, MIDWESTERN CULTURE,
1958 AND 1968 COMPARED

Measures of Coital Approval	Total Sample		Matched Sample	
	Males	Females	Males	Females
I. Average Score				
1968	8.10	9.02	8.10	9.47
1958	8.58	9.69	8.63	9.67
Difference	−.48	−.67	−.53	−.20
II. Percent Approving				
1968	55.4	37.7	55.1	30.7
1958	46.7	17.4	48.0	21.3
Difference	8.7	20.3	7.1	9.4

sive stance. And this was true for males and females alike, but for the latter the trend was the stronger.

Relationship of Behavior to Attitude

Some might argue that most of our generalizations up to this point are obvious, that everyone accepts the fact that attitudes toward premarital coitus have been liberalizing in recent years. The more controversial questions have to do with trends in sexual *behavior* and with how these relate to attitude. Has incidence of premarital coitus remained virtually unchanged since the 1920's with a decline in guilt brought about by an increasing acceptance of the behavior — which is the position arrived at by Reiss (1969), or has behavior changed with attitudes regarding it?

INCIDENCE OF PREMARITAL COITUS

As a first approach to the behavioral component, we show percentages of respondents claiming the premarital coital experience (Table 3). Our percentages on incidence of premarital coitus do not, of course, give an accurate picture of total coitus before marriage but only of experience up to the time the questionnaire was administered. This fact should not influence our various comparisons, however, since all the data are the same kind and hence comparable. Percentages are given for males and females separately and for the three cultures and both sample years of our study. An added refinement in testing for a time trend is provided for the Midwestern

table 3

PERCENTAGE[a] WITH PREMARITAL COITAL EXPERIENCE,
TOTAL AND MATCHED SAMPLES

| | | Sample Culture | | | | | |
| | | Intermountain | | Midwestern | | Danish | |
Samples and Years		Males	Females	Males	Females	Males	Females
		%	%	%	%	%	%
I.	Total Samples						
	1968	37	32	50	34	95	97
	1958	39	10	51	21	64	60
	Difference	−2	22	−1	13	31	37
II.	Matched Samples						
	1968			49	32		
	1958			55	25		
	Difference			−6	7		

[a] Based upon number answering. The number who failed to answer in any one group varied from 0 to 4.

culture by means of matched cases to control for intervening variables, as was done in the case of attitudes.

Before examining the time-trend data, let it be noted that these incidence figures are (1) higher for males than females and (2) higher for the Midwestern than the Intermountain and for the Danish than the Midwestern. These generalizations are consistent for all comparisons (except the one between 1958–68 Danish males and females) and are the same as our earlier ones regarding approval of premarital coitus. Furthermore, there is, as before, the phenomenon of greater male-female similarity in Denmark than the other two cultures, suggesting that norm permissiveness may induce a leveling of gender differences.

Comparisons of 1968 with 1958 produce three additional generalizations. (1) In the two American samples, male incidence of premarital coitus remained approximately the same. Actually the figures show that it decreased slightly, but our conjecture is that this is no more than random variation. (2) On the other hand, female incidence in the two American samples rose sharply, suggesting that, as with coital approval, there is a trend toward intersex convergence. (3) The Danish sample, while showing a slightly higher rise in premarital coitus for females than for males, demonstrated a sharp rise for *both* sexes. This brought incidence figures for that country close to the ceiling. Approximately 95 percent had engaged in premarital coitus; and it will be recalled that 100 percent of both sexes there approved of such activity. It may be, of course, that at least part of the dramatic liberalization shown for Danish respondents is to be explained by the greater weighting of the 1968 Danish sample with sociology students.

The introduction of controls through matched-sample comparisons in the Midwestern culture made no appreciable change in the outcome (Table 3, part II). Although males decreased their behavior more and females increased theirs less in the matched sample as compared with the total sample, the conclusion of greater female than male liberalization and of intersex convergence during the decade seems inescapable.

THE APPROVAL-EXPERIENCE RATIO

It is important to know how approval of and experience in premarital coitus interrelate: to what extent practice corresponds with precept and what are the directions and magnitudes of discrepancies in this regard. The ratios of Table 4 have been calculated by dividing percentages approving premarital coitus (part III of Table 1 and part II of Table 2) by percentages having experienced it (Table 3). A ratio of 1.00 would mean that approval and experience coincide exactly. Ratios lower than this indicate that experience exceeds approval; and higher, that approval exceeds experience. With the sex drive as strong as it is, one may wonder how the approval-experience ratio could ever be above 1.00: why, if people approve

table 4

COMPARISONS OF APPROVAL — EXPERIENCE RATIOS,
TOTAL AND MATCHED SAMPLES

| | Sample Cultures | | | | | |
| | Intermountain | | Midwestern | | Danish | |
Samples and Years	Males	Females	Males	Females	Males	Females
I. Total Samples						
1968	1.05	.73	1.10	1.10	1.06	1.04
1958	.59	.31	.92	.84	1.48	1.35
Difference	.46	.42	.18	.26	−.42	−.31
II. Matched Samples						
1968			1.13	.96		
1958			.87	.84		
Difference			.26	.12		

premarital coitus, they don't engage in it. The primary explanation seems to be that the attitude percentages are for approval of coitus occurring *anytime prior to marriage,* and approving respondents may not be close enough to marriage to feel ready for the experience.

The following generalizations seem evident: (1) In 1958, the magnitude of the ratio varies directly with the permissiveness of the culture; which means that restrictive cultures have higher percentages of their offenders who are violating their own standards — though it must be remembered that restrictive cultures have fewer offenders to start with. (2) Except for Midwestern respondents in 1968, females showed up with lower ratios than males, which means that proportionately more of them violate their own standards when they engage in premarital coitus. However, this inter-sex difference is of large magnitude only within the highly conservative Intermountain culture. (3) The 1958–68 trend was toward a rise in the ratio for both the Intermountain and Midwestern samples, where it previously had been below 1.00, and a lowering of the ratio in Denmark where it previously had been above 1.00. Thus the time trend has been toward a leveling and balancing of the approval-experience ratios, bringing them closer to each other and to the value of 1.00. In 1968, all ratios except for Midwestern males were closer to 1.00 than was true ten years earlier, and Intermountain females represented the only group in the total sample with experience remaining greater than approval (although in the matched sample this was true for Midwestern females also). The evidence suggests that there is less of a gap today between one's values and his behavior; that, regardless of his sex or the culture he is in, a person is more likley now than formerly, to follow his own internalized norms.

Again, the matching procedure has not altered the basic conclusion. With these data, as with the total sample, the trend is seen to be toward a rising ratio. Attitudes have liberalized more rapidly than has behavior, so that the over-all pattern today seems not to be one of violating one's own value system. Some individuals do, of course, but in terms of group averages the evidence is against it.

EVIDENCES OF VALUE-BEHAVIOR DISCREPANCY
In an earlier article (Christensen and Carpenter, 1962b) the senior author has demonstrated from cross-cultural data for 1958 that — even more than the act itself — it is the discrepancy between what one values and what he then does that determines guilt, divorce, and related negative effects. The analysis was based upon both group and individual comparisons between permissiveness scores (measuring attitude) and behavioral percentages (measuring coital experience).

Here we wish to report a slightly different approach applied to the 1958 and 1968 Midwestern samples, first with the total respondents and then with the matched cases. In Table 5 are presented percentages of those with premarital experience who answered approvingly of coitus before marriage. These percentages, in other words, are based upon *individual* case-by-case comparisons between coitus and coital approval. They show the proportions of cases in which there was *no discrepancy* of this kind. By subtracting any percentage figure from 100.0, the reader can, if he prefers it that way, determine the corresponding discrepancy magnitude.

It will be observed that the trend between 1958 and 1968 was toward larger approval percentages (or less value-behavior discrepancy). This is true with respect to both sexes and for the matched as well as the total samples. It supports a similar finding based upon grouped data reported in the previous section. In both instances the evidence suggests that attitudes have been catching up with behavior and that proportionally fewer people today violate their own values when they engage in premarital coitus. Nevertheless, some individuals still show this discrepancy — perhaps as many as one-fifth of the males and two-fifths of the females.

It will be observed also that the movement of premarital coital participants toward approving what one does was greater for females than males (consistently shown in both sets of comparisons). Females in 1968 still gave evidence of greater value-behavior discrepancy than did males but the intersex difference in this regard was less than in 1958. And here too, the finding of Table 5 stands in general support of the picture for grouped data shown in Table 4.

USING ATTITUDES TO PREDICT BEHAVIOR
Since the overall evidence is that attitudes have been liberalizing at a greater rate than behavior, which is narrowing the gap between the two, it might be expected that the predictive power of attitudes is increasing.

58

table 5

PERCENTAGES WITH PREMARITAL COITUS WHO APPROVED
SUCH EXPERIENCE, MIDWESTERN CULTURE,
1958 AND 1968 COMPARED

	Total Sample		Matched Sample	
	Males	Females	Males	Females
	%	%	%	%
1968	82	78	76	58
1958	65	41	65	37
Difference	17	37	11	21

To test this out, we calculated Gammas on the interaction of two variables: approval of premarital coitus and experience with premarital coitus. The Gammas reported in Table 6 indicate that the expectation was supported: coital approval was a better predictor of coital behavior for males and females at the end of the decade than at the beginning.

The Commitment Phenomenon

Reiss (1969), largely from analyses of his attitudinal data, has concluded that America is moving toward the traditional Scandinavian pattern of "permissiveness with affection." This phrase has been used by Reiss and others to also mean *permissiveness with commitment*. Our own data should permit us to check out this claim at the behavioral level.

Two indices of affection-commitment are presented in Table 7: percent-

table 6

INCIDENCE OF PREMARITAL COITUS AS RELATED TO APPROVAL
OF PREMARITAL COITUS, MIDWESTERN SAMPLE

Incidence of Premarital Coitus	Approval of Premarital Coitus					
	Males			Females		
	Yes	No	Total	Yes	No	Total
			1968			
Yes	98	22	120	63	18	81
No	35	83	118	26	128	154
Total	133	105	238	89	146	235
	Gamma = .83			Gamma = .89		
			1958			
Yes	68	37	105	12	17	29
No	30	73	103	12	95	107
Total	98	110	208	24	112	136
	Gamma = .63			Gamma = .69		

ages (of those experienced in premarital coitus) who had confined their overall experience to one partner; and percentages whose first experience was with a steady or fiance(e). It will be noted that the cross-cultural, cross-sex, and time-trend comparisons derived from these two measures are remarkably similar. In both cases (with very minor exceptions that become evident upon close inspection) rather consistent patterns show up: more American than Danish respondents, more female than male respondents, and more 1958 than 1968 respondents confined their total premarital coital experience to one partner and *also* had their first coitus in a commitment relationship. The other side of the coin, so to speak, is that Danes appear to be more promiscuous than Americans, males more promiscuous than females, and 1968 respondents more promiscuous than 1958 respondents. The term "promiscuity" is used here in a non-evaluative sense and merely to designate the opposite of "commitment." Our measures of these two concepts are indirect and imperfect, to be sure, but undoubtedly they tell something.

Not only were the Danish generally more promiscuous than the Americans (1958 Danish males being an exception), but the shift toward greater promiscuity during the decade under study was greater for them. Apparently, Denmark may be moving away from its traditional pattern of premarital sex justified by a commitment relationship, and sexual promiscuity is coming in to take its place. But without further testing, this observation

table 7

PERCENTAGE[a] DISTRIBUTIONS OF RESPONSES TO ITEMS
SHOWING A COMMITMENT IN THE SEXUAL RELATIONSHIP

Items and Years	Sample Cultures					
	Intermountain		Midwestern		Danish	
	Males	Females	Males	Females	Males	Females
	%	%	%	%	%	%
I. Experience Confined to One Partner						
1968	28.6	43.8	39.0	70.0	20.5	25.0
1958	35.1	57.1	33.7	65.5	40.9	42.9
Difference	−6.5	−13.3	5.3	4.5	−20.4	−17.9
II. First Experience with a Steady or Fiance(e)						
1968	53.8	78.1	52.9	86.3	46.3	55.4
1958	47.2	100.0	42.8	75.9	67.8	74.5
Difference	6.6	−21.9	10.1	10.4	−21.5	−19.1

[a] Based upon number answering. The number failing to answer in any one group varied from 0 to 4.

must be regarded as highly speculative, since the two Danish samples lack strict comparability.

It also is worth noting that the Danish male-female differences in response to both of these items tended to be smaller than in either of the other two cultures, another example of the possible leveling effect of norm permissiveness.

Intermountain females also moved dramatically in the direction of greater promiscuity as indicated by these two measures, possibly because, being so near the "floor" at the beginning of the decade, there was opportunity for the general trend toward permissiveness to affect them proportionately more. Intermountain males did not change much by either measure and, with them, direction of change was inconsistent.

In two important respects Midwestern respondents stood out from the rest. In the first place, they tended to show higher proportions in a commitment relationship (1958 males being the most noticeable exception); and in the second place, this was the only culture where both sexes on both measures showed *higher* commitment percentages in 1968 than 1958 (1958 Intermountain males did on the item "first coitus with a steady or fiancé"). Could it be that a general trend toward sexual freedom, such as has occurred in recent years, encourages the development of promiscuity in *both* the commitment-oriented permissive society (such as Denmark) and the ascetic-oriented restrictive society (such as the Intermountain Mormon): the same trend but for different reasons — in the first, to escape commitment; in the second, to escape repression? The question needs further research.

At any rate, the time trend in our Midwestern culture seems clear. To the extent that our sample is representative and our measures adequate, the Reiss hypothesis is supported there. Although it must be said that the testing of this important phenomenon has only begun, it probably can be tentatively concluded that at least a major current in premarital sex trends within this country is a movement toward permissiveness with commitment.

While the emerging American pattern seems to be toward the traditional Danish norm of premarital sex justified by commitment, the emerging Danish pattern may be away from both commitment and restriction, toward free and promiscuous sex. Furthermore, in this one respect at least, the converging lines of the two cultures seem now to have passed each other. Today the Danes appear to be less committed and more promiscuous in their premarital sexual contacts than do Midwestern Americans.

Negative Accompaniments of Coitus

Considerable interest centers around the question of consequences. Does premarital coitus affect everyone the same, or do the norms of the culture and the values which the individual has incorporated into his personality make any difference? Our working hypothesis has been that values are relevant data; and following this, the consequences of premarital sex acts are to some extent relative to the alignment or misalignment of values and behavior, being most negative where the disjuncture is the greatest. In sociological circles this line of reasoning has been labeled "Theory of Cognitive Dissonance" (Festinger, 1957). Applied to the data of our present study, we would predict greater negative effects in America than Denmark, for females than males, and during 1958 as compared with 1968 since these are the categories showing disproportionately high value-behavior discrepancy.

Table 8 presents data for two negative accompaniments of premarital coitus. The first of these — yielding to force or felt obligation — means simply that there were pressures other than personal desire which were chiefly responsible for the experience. It will be observed that, in general, results turned out as expected: coitus because of pressure is seen to be higher in restrictive than permissive cultures, higher among females than males, and higher in 1958 than in 1968.

One irregularity in the patterns just noted was introduced by an unexpected increase in pressured coitus among Danish males, which also had the

table 8

PERCENTAGE[a] DISTRIBUTIONS OF RESPONSES TO ITEMS
THAT INDICATE NEGATIVE FEELINGS ACCOMPANYING
FIRST PREMARITAL COITUS

Items and Years	Sample Cultures					
	Intermountain		Midwestern		Danish	
	Males	Females	Males	Females	Males	Females
I. First Experience Either Forced or by Obligation						
1968	2.4	24.2	2.5	23.1	10.0	18.5
1958	13.5	42.9	9.3	37.9	4.4	35.6
Difference	−11.1	−18.7	−6.8	−14.8	5.6	−17.1
II. First Experience Followed Chiefly by Guilt or Remorse						
1968	7.1	9.1	6.6	11.1	1.6	0.0
1958	29.7	28.6	12.1	31.0	4.3	2.0
Difference	−22.6	−19.5	−5.5	−19.9	−2.7	−2.0

[a] In I, the percentages are based upon the number answering; the number failing to answer varying from 0 to 6.
In II, the total number of cases was used as the base of the percents.

62

effect of reversing the cross-cultural picture for 1968 males. Reasons for this reverse trend for Danish males are not known, but it will be remembered from Table 7 that it also was Danish males who showed the greatest increase in promiscuous coitus. There is at least the possibility that these two phenomena are connected.

Part II of Table 8 gives percentages of those who specified either guilt or remorse as their predominant feeling the day after first premarital coitus. Here again, the overall patterns were in expected directions: coitus followed by guilt or remorse is seen to be higher in restrictive than permissive cultures (although Midwestern females exceed the Intermountain), higher for females than males (although not uniformly and with Denmark being a major exception), and consistently higher in 1958 than 1968. Whether the exceptions noted represent anything more than random variation cannot be determined from our non-probability samples. But at least the broad patterns seem clear and the consistency between our two measures builds confidence in the general findings.

Thus, whether measured by a feeling of external pressure at the time or a subsequent feeling of guilt or remorse, the negative accompaniments of premarital coitus appear to be greatest where the sex norms are restrictive (and, significantly, also where value-behavior discrepancy is the greatest) — in the American culture as compared with the Danish, with females as compared with males, and in 1958 as compared with 1968.

Conclusion

The design of our investigation has enabled us to compare premarital sexual attitudes and behavior against each other; and to compare them separately and in combination across a restrictive-permissive continuum of cultures, across the differing worlds of males and females and across a recent decade in time. Although the primary concern of this paper has been with recent social changes in premarital sex values and practices, the additional involvement of intersex and cross-cultural variables has enabled us to see the phenomena in better perspective and to tease out certain meanings that otherwise may have remained obscure. Furthermore, we have been interested in going beyond mere description, to the discovery of relationships; and then to interconnect these relationships with each other and with relevant concepts and propositions, with theory building as the ultimate goal. To establish needed controls, we have in places made supplementary analyses of Midwestern data including the use of matched sampling techniques. Nevertheless, we regard our study as more exploratory than definitive. We feel that some significant leads have been uncovered but at the same time regard our conclusions as tentative — as plausible for the present, perhaps, but as hypotheses for future research.

We call attention to the strong suggestion from our data that values and norms serve as intervening variables *affecting the effects* of behavior. For the explaining of consequences, it would seem that even perhaps more important than the sexual act itself is the degree to which that act lines up or fails to line up with the standards set. Whether the comparisons have been between males and females, across cultures, or over time, we have demonstrated two parallel and probably interrelated patterns: value-behavior discrepancy is associated with sexual restrictiveness; and certain negative effects of premarital intimacy are associated with sexual restrictiveness. The possibility — we think probability — is that it is primarily value-behavior discrepancy that is causing the difficulty. This facet of our theory has been explored at greater length in earlier writing (Christensen, 1966; 1969).

References

Bell, Robert R.
   1966   Premarital Sex in a Changing Society. Englewood Cliffs, New Jersey: Prentice-Hall.
Bell, Robert R. and Jay B. Chaskes
   1970   "Premarital sexual experience among coeds, 1958 and 1968." Journal of Marriage and the Family 32 (February): 81-84.
Christensen, Harold T.
   1960   "Cultural relativism and premarital sex norms." American Sociological Review 25 (February): 31-39.
   1966   "Scandinavian and American sex norms: Some comparisons, with sociological implications." The Journal of Social Issues 22 (April): 60-75.
   1969   "Normative theory derived from cross-cultural family research." Journal of Marriage and the Family 31 (May): 209-222.
Christensen, Harold T. and Christina F. Gregg
   1970   "Changing Sex Norms in America and Scandinavia." Journal of Marriage and the Family 32 (November): 616-627.
Christensen, Harold T. and George R. Carpenter
   1962a "Timing patterns in the development of sexual intimacy." Marriage and Family Living 24 (February): 30-35.
   1962b "Value-behavior discrepancies regarding premarital coitus in three Western cultures." American Sociological Review 27 (February): 66-74.
Ehrmann, Winston W.
   1964   "Marital and nonmarital sexual behavior." Pp. 585-622 in Harold T. Christensen (ed.), Handbook of Marriage and the Family. Chicago: Rand McNally.
   1959   Premarital Dating Behavior. New York: Holt.
Festinger, Leon
   1957   A Theory of Cognitive Dissonance. New York: Harper and Row.
Freedman, Mervin B.
   1965   "The sexual behavior of American college women: An empirical study and

an historical survey." Merrill-Palmer Quarterly of Behavior and Development 11 (January): 33-48.

Gagnon, John H. and William Simon
   1970   "Prospects for change in American sexual patterns." Medical Aspects of Human Sexuality 4 (January): 100-117.

Kinsey, Alfred C., Wardell Pomeroy, Clyde Martin and Paul Gebbard
   1953   Sexual Behavior in the Human Female. Philadelphia: W. B. Saunders Co.,

Kirkendall, Lester A.
   1961   Premarital Intercourse and Interpersonal Relationships. New York: Julian.

Leslie, Gerald R.
   1967   The Family in Social Context. New York: Oxford University Press.

Luckey, Eleanore B. and Gilbert D. Nass
   1969   "A comparison of sexual attitudes and behavior in an international sample." Journal of Marriage and the Family 31 (May): 364-379.

Packard, Vance
   1968   The Sexual Wilderness: the Contemporary Upheaval in Male-Female Relationships. New York: David McKay Company, Inc.

Reiss, Ira L.
   1967   The Social Context of Premarital Sexual Permissiveness. New York: Holt, Rinehart and Winston.
   1969   "Premarital sexual standards." In Carlfred B. Broderick and Jessie Bernard (eds.), The Individual, Sex, and Society: A Siecus Handbook for Teachers and Counselors. Baltimore: The Johns Hopkins Press.

Schofield, Michael
   1965   The Sexual Behavior of Young People. Boston: Little Brown.

Terman, Lewis M.
   1938   Psychological Factors in Marital Happiness. New York: McGraw-Hill.

part three

Marital sexuality

In a majority of the cultures of the past marital sex has been important in two ways: first, as the means of reproduction, and second, as a means of satisfying the sexual needs of the husband. With few reliable means of controlling conception, pregnancy frequently occurred as a result of marital coitus. Historically, the result has been a large number of children, high rates of maternal mortality, and a short life span for the reproductive wife. However, in middle-class America today the traditional patriarchal beliefs about marital sex have been altered and expanded. No longer is the relationship of the sexual act and conception viewed as beyond the control of the individual. Through the development and use of birth-control methods, conception is increasingly controlled. Another change in the traditional beliefs about marital sex is today's assumption that the wife has as much right to expect sexual fulfillment in marriage as her husband. Thus, the two general social changes in regard to marital coitus have had their greatest impact on women.

What has been very important to martial sexuality, especially among the American middle class, has been the development around the rights and expectations of the wife. Today she is generally taught that when she enters marriage she has a right to sexual fulfillment; in fact, most modern marriage manuals give this attainment the highest emphasis. Such a change in expectations is closely related to the development of effective methods of birth control; these methods allow the wife to enter the sex act as an end in itself, rather than with the traditional belief that it can, on any given occasion, lead to pregnancy.

Very often today the belief is that the major problem of sexual adjustment in marriage centers around the wife's achievement of orgasm. In marriage manuals attention is directed at the need for extended foreplay so that actual coitus does not start until the wife is near her sexual peak; the couple may then together reach "the ultimate summit of mutual orgasm." The assumption usually made is that the male should control his sexual desire to make sure his wife reaches her sexual peak. Seldom is any attempt made to understand that prolongation by the male is not always susceptible to rational control. The overall assumption is that the husband is usually sexually ready and all he must do is help his wife reach the same state.

The importance that is placed on the wife achieving sexual satisfaction is for the most part characteristic of the middle class. For example, Rainwater found in his lower-lower-class sample that 67 percent of the respondents said the husband enjoyed coitus more, 7 percent said the wife, and 26 percent about equally as contrasted with the middle class where 33 percent said the husband enjoyed coitus more, 8 percent said the wife more, and 59 percent about equally.[1] Masters and Johnson found that husbands with fear of sexual performance were confined primarily to the higher educated. They found that only 14 percent of those men with no college education expressed the slightest concern with responsibility for their partner's sexual satisfaction. "These men felt that it was the female's privilege to achieve satisfaction during active coition if she could, but certainly it was not the responsibility and really not the concern of the male partner to concentrate on satisfying the woman's sexual demands."[2] By contrast, of those males with college matriculation, 82 percent of them expressed concern with coital-partner satisfaction.[3]

In general the cultural values of American society have led to different sexual concerns and fears by men and women. Increasingly for middle-class women, fears of performance concern their ability to achieve orgasm. For the male, the fears are related to attaining and keeping a penile erection; his orgasmic capacity is assumed.[4] Beyond these fears there are two major areas of physiological difference between the orgasm experience of men and women. "First, the female is capable of rapid return to orgasm immediately following an orgasmic experience, if restimulated before tensions have dropped below plateau-phase response levels. Second, the female is capable of maintaining an orgasmic experience for a relatively long period of time."[5]

Sexual adjustment in marriage calls for at least minimum satisfaction for the self and the other in sexual interaction. The sexual-role relationship is less often guided by open verbal communication than are other areas of interaction in marriage. Frequently, each partner may have to try and "read" the sexual desire of the partner. Because of the failure to communicate, one partner may mistakenly believe that the techniques and frequency of marital coitus are satisfactory to the other. Role relationship efficiency is based on the assumption of symbolic interaction and if it does not exist, the persons may feel a sense of role frustration. Because the the sex act and the marriage role are new to the young married woman, and because taboos against open sex verbalization — even after marriage — still exist, the woman may not be able psychologically to free herself for open communication. The young wife may desire greater frequency of intercourse, different methods of foreplay, or different techniques of sexual expression, but be too inhibited to let her husband know it, either by action or word. As time goes along and the wife's role as a sexual partner becomes more internally a part of her self concept, many of her inhibitions may be dropped. Over the years, most females become less inhibited and develop an interest in sexual relations which they then maintain into their sixties.[6]

The importance of sexual communication in marriage is stressed by Masters and Johnson. They suggest that "rather than following any preconceived plan for stimulating his sex partner, the male will be indefinitely more effective if he encourages vocalization on her part. The individual woman knows best the areas of her strongest sensual focus and the rapidity and intensity of manipulative technique that provides her with the greatest degree of sexual stimulation."[7] The above suggestion helps to get away from the idea that the male, in some intuitive way, is an expert on the female's sexual feelings and desires. Masters and Johnson further point out that the most unfortunate misconception in our society has been to assign to sexual functioning the assumption, held by both men and women, "that men by divine guidance and infallible instinct are able to discern exactly what a woman wants sexually and when she wants it. Probably this fallacy has interfered with natural sexual interaction as much as any other single factor."[8] On the same point, Vincent states that few young men are aware of the complex nature of sexuality because there is no place where they would have learned. This means that to learn more about human sexuality the man must admit there are some things he does not know. However, for many men to admit lack of knowledge and skill in the sexual area is seen by them as questioning their masculinity. "The majority of young husbands are 'boxed in' by their childhood indoctrination that masculinity is synonymous with knowing all about sex."[9]

Some of the above points are elaborated upon in the selections that follow. The article by Paul Gebhard describes what is known about the nature of orgasm experience in marital sexual expression. The selection by Lee Rainwater examines the values and stress placed on marital sexual expression as found in four lower-class subcultures.

Notes

1. Rainwater, Lee, *Family Design,* Chicago: Aldine Publishing Co., 1965, p. 68.
2. Masters, William H., and Virginia E. Johnson, *Human Sexual Response,* Boston: Little, Brown and Co., 1966, p. 202.
3. *Ibid.,* p. 202.
4. *Ibid.,* p. 218.
5. *Ibid.,* p. 131.
6. Kinsey, Alfred C., Wardell B. Pomeroy, Clyde E. Martin and Paul H. Gebhard, *Sexual Behavior In The Human Female,* Philadelphia: W. B. Saunders, 1953, p. 353.
7. Masters and Johnson, *Op. cit.,* p. 66.
8. *Ibid.,* p. 87.
9. Vincent, Clark E., "Sex and The Young Married," *Medical Aspects of Human Sexuality,* March, 1969, p. 17.

4

Factors in Marital Orgasm

Paul H. Gebhard

The Institute for Sex Research has in its standard schedule of questions asked of every interviewee a large number devoted to marriage and marital sexual behavior. The answers to these questions provide us with too large a body of data to be compressed into any journal article; consequently, I have chosen to select one aspect of sexuality in marriage to serve as an illustration of our studies. This aspect is one which has received much attention in marriage manuals but which has never been subjected to any large-scale empirical testing: the matter of the wife's orgasm in marital coitus.

Background

From the Victorian middle and upper class unconcern with female orgasm, we have, through the emancipation of women and the emergence of sex as a discussable subject, reached a point of intense concern with orgasm. It has become to no small degree a symbol of woman's being accepted as a human of equal stature and with her own sexual needs. Orgasm in marital coitus has become not only her goal but her due, and inability to achieve it frequently engenders feelings of personal inadequacy and failure in both the husband and wife. The pendulum has swung from unconcern to over-concern in less than a century.

Reprinted from *The Journal of Social Issues*, Vol. XXII, No. 2, pp. 88-95, by permission of the author and the Society for the Psychological Study of Social Issues.

In our culture, enchanted with technology and with a mechanistic conception of the body, the emphasis on female orgasm has produced a veritable flood of marriage manuals and similar publications which say, in essence, that the key to female orgasm is in the length of precoital foreplay and the duration of penile intromission once coitus has begun.

Reacting aginst this preoccupation with foreplay and intromission Kinsey (1953:364) (1,p.364) stated, "We are not convinced that the data demonstrate that any limitations or extensions of pre-coital petting are of primary importance in establishing the effectiveness or satisfactoriness of coitus." However, he presented no data supporting this statement. Nevertheless, the decade-of-birth data did clearly show an increase in the orgasm rates of wives and a growing use of more elaborate precoital and coital techniques. All of this could be construed to indicate more elaborate and protracted foreplay was, after all, conducive to increased female orgasm. No data were presented on duration of penile intromission.

Considering the emphasis in literature and clinical practice on the importance of female orgasm, the omissions in our prior volumes call for rectification, and this was undertaken in the study now reported in this article.

Sample

The data in this paper derive from some of the interviews conducted in the United States by the Institute for Sex Research between 1939 and 1960. The interview consists of a lengthy series of questions designed to give a comprehensive account of the individual's overt sexual behavior and some of his or her responses and attitudes from childhood to the time of the interview. The respondent's answers are recorded in code at the time and any confusion or ambiguity can be dealt with then. The interview of an adult with one marriage requires on the average about one and one-half hours. The information is, of course, subject to the reservations which accompany any recollected reported data, but by reinterviewing a number of individuals after an interim of years, we have demonstrated that the reliability of such reported data is high.

In order to minimize selective bias the Institute ordinarily chose target groups (e.g., a parent-teacher group, a classroom, a business office) where a complete list of group members could be made so that all could be solicited for interview. Where interviewing all members proved impossible, the group was not abandoned until at least three quarters of the members had been interviewed. A study of reluctant interviewees demonstrated that persons resist being interviewed for a great diversity of reasons and, therefore, they do not constitute a sexually homogeneous unit; hence the refusal rate may have little bias effect. The portion within a group who were not interviewed did not consist wholly of refusals, but included persons not

71

solicited and persons who had agreed to an interview but with whom mutually satisfactory appointments could not be made.

The Institute staff has interviewed roughly 8,000 females and a sample from these case histories was selected for this paper.

Originally the sample was to have consisted of white U.S. females with some college education who had been married for one year or more, and in the case of multiple marriage the data were to derive only from the first marriage. The data obtained from this original sample were confusing, and it became evident that this was due to an uncontrolled variable, which proved to be unhappy marriage terminating in separation or divorce. A series of tabulations revealed that greater marital happiness was associated with a higher percentage of coitus resulting in orgasm for the wife (Table 1). This was not an unexpected finding since our clinical impression has always been that separation or divorce is frequently presaged by a decline in female orgasm rate. It was also found that marriages in our original sample which terminated in separation or divorce tended to be shorter than those marriages which were intact at the time of interview (Table 2). Since we know from our prior studies that female orgasm rates increase with length of marriage (Kinsey *et al*, 1, pp. 383–384), this difference in marriage duration was clearly another analytical problem to be overcome.

Since the number of marriages which terminated in separation or divorce were not equal in the various analytical categories used in this study, one could never be sure whether or not variation was due to this fact rather than to items presumable being tested.

The simple, albeit somewhat painful, solution was to confine the sample

table 1

FEMALE ORGASM RATE AND MARITAL HAPPINESS IN INTACT MARRIAGES

Per cent of Coitus Resulting in Orgasm	Marital Happiness Rating						
	1 very happy	1–2	2 moder- ately happy	2–3	3 moder- ately unhappy	3–4	4 very unhappy
	Percent						
0	4.4	3.2	9.0	16.1	15.8		19.0
1–9	3.6	9.5	4.5	12.9	8.8		19.0
10–39	6.5	20.6	11.3	3.2	10.5	Too few to calculate	9.5
40–59	9.5	12.7	17.1	12.9	15.8		4.8
60–89	16.5	17.5	17.1	16.1	14.0		9.5
90–100	59.4	36.5	41.0	38.7	35.1		38.1
Cases	587	63	222	31	57	4	21

Too few to calculate

FEMALE ORGASM RATE AND DURATION OF MARRIAGE
IN INTACT MARRIAGES AND MARRIAGES BROKEN BY
SEPARATON OR DIVORCE

Per cent of Coitus Resulting in Orgasm	Intact Marriages		Broken Marriages	
	Median years duration	Cases	Median years duration	Cases
0	7.0	74	4.9	76
1–9	7.0	54	5.0	36
10–39	7.6	87	5.5	46
40–59	8.5	119	6.3	32
60–89	8.3	168	5.3	30
90–100	8.8	524	7.6	94

There were too few widows to merit a category.

to women whose marriages were intact at the time of interview and who expressed no intention of terminating their marriages.[1] This reduced the sample to 1,026 women. The sample size in some tables totals less than this due to interviewer failure to obtain, or to properly record, usable data.

Marital Happiness

Table 1 clearly illustrates that wives who reach orgasm in 90 to 100 per cent of their marital coitus are found more commonly (59 per cent) in very happy marriages than in any other marriages. Curiously, the five other categories of marital happiness do not differ much in terms of female orgasm: the figures for wives who reach orgasm with 90–100% frequency remain within six percentage points of one another (35 to 41 per cent) even when happy marriages are compared to very unhappy marriages, and no trend is visible. If all six of the categories had roughly the same percentages of women experiencing orgasm in all or nearly all of their coitus, one could postulate that a sexually responsive female can reach orgasm from sexual activity alone, independent of her customary feeling toward her spouse. However, this is not the case. Rather than abandon the hypothesis, perhaps one should add to it a statement that in the very happy marriages, in addition to the sexually responsive wives who would reach orgasm under most circumstances, there are a number of other women who are less responsive and who would not reach orgasm so often were it not for the happiness of the marriage.

This modified hypothesis fits well with the figures concerning wives who never reach orgasm in marital coitus: here we see a clear negative correlation between the number of such women and happiness. There are but four per cent of the very happy marriages wherein the wives fail to reach orgasm, but this figure gradually increases as marital happiness decreases until in the very unhappy marriages it reaches 19 per cent.

With wives who reach orgasm rarely (1–9%) this correlation is still visible; in the central categories (orgasm rates of 10–39% and 40–59%) it disappears; and in the 60 to 89 per cent orgasm category the small N in the very unhappy marriages prevents our assuming that the correlation reappears.

One is left with the impression that marital happiness and female orgasm do correlate but only in the extreme categories: at both ends of the orgasm scale (0 and 90–100%) and at both ends of the happiness scale (very happy and very unhappy). Perhaps the correlation is elsewhere simply obscured by other factors, including the physiological.

Duration of Marriage

As Kinsey *et al* (1, pp. 383–384) demonstrated, the percentage of coitus resulting in the wife's orgasm rises steadily with increased length of marriage. Consequently, it is not surprising to see in Table 2 that there is a distinct tendency for women with higher orgasm rates to have been married longer than women with lower orgasm rates. The differences, however, are not great: the wives without orgasm having been married an average (median) of 7 years while the wives who almost always experienced orgasm had the longest marriages, the average being 8.8 years. This same trend was noted among the marriages which ended in separation or divorce, and which were briefer than the intact marriages.

Duration of Precoital Foreplay

The sample for Table 3 was considerably reduced in size because many wives reported duration of foreplay in terms of ranges rather than averages and time considerations prevented our converting these ranges into averages. In connection with a later study, we intend to program the computer so as to make these conversions. No substantial change in the findings is anticipated since the majority of ranges appear to center about the averages reported here. In order to increase the sample size within categories, several categories were combined. Despite these handicaps it is clear from Table 3 that there is a positive correlation between duration of foreplay and wife's orgasm rate.

Where 1 to 10 minutes of foreplay were involved, two fifths of the wives reached orgasm nearly always; 15 to 20 minutes foreplay raised this percentage to half; and still longer foreplay resulted in nearly three fifths of the women achieving this high orgasm rate. Conversely, wives with lesser orgasm rates received shorter periods of foreplay, the 1–10 minutes category having the most cases.

table 3

FEMALE ORGASM RATE AND DURATION OF PRE-COITAL
FOREPLAY IN INTACT MARRIAGES

Per cent of Coitus Resulting in Orgasm	Average Duration of Foreplay in Minutes			
	0	1–10	15–20	21 plus
		Percent		
0	(2 cases)	3.9	7.6	7.7
1–39	(1 case)	19.5	12.6	7.7
40–89	(1 case)	34.6	28.9	25.6
90–100	(2 cases)	41.9	50.6	58.9
Cases	6	179	79	78

The women who never experienced orgasm in marital coitus constitute a separate phenomenon. While their number in Table 3 is small, it appears that many of their husbands (most of whom were also college educated) were protracting foreplay with the hope of inducing orgasm. The number of cases in the 15–20 minute and 21 plus minute categories are nearly twice the number in the 1–10 minute category.

One may legitimately raise the possibility that the women were unconsciously giving the interviewers biased data: that the women with lesser orgasm rates were minimizing the amount of foreplay. This possibility seems quite remote in view of the smallness of some of the differences and particularly in view of the fact that the wives without orgasm reported lengthy foreplay.

Duration of Intromission

The length of time the penis is in the vagina prior to ejaculation — after which most males soon cease pelvic movements and withdraw — is a matter accorded great importance in our folklore as well as in our marriage manuals. All females with coital experience were questioned as to duration of intromission. Their responses appear to be reasonably accurate since they agree with the time measurements from a small but growing number of cases of observed coitus. Our data here are not easy to interpret: it seems that the effect of duration of intromission is masked by other variables. It is not unlikely that lengthy foreplay with brief intromission may be as effective for female orgasm as brief foreplay and lengthy intromission; this has yet to be tested.[2] Also, the lack of strong distinctions in Table 4 may reflect the fact that most males of this upper and upper-middle socio-economic level can delay ejaculation for two minutes but seldom can delay for over seven, and hence most cases fall in our 2–3.9 minute and 4–7 minute categories. Yet another complication is the probability of the husband's adjusting

table 4

FEMALE ORGASM RATE AND DURATION OF PENILE
INTROMISSION IN INTACT MARRIAGES

Per cent of Coitus Resulting in Orgasm	Average Duration of Intromission in Minutes						
	−.9	1–1.9	2–3.9	4–7	8–11	12–15	16 plus
	Percent						
0	12.5	6.9	7.0	4.5	12.4	2.7	5.1
1–9	10.0	5.6	5.1	4.5	5.6	2.7	5.1
10–39	20.0	11.2	9.4	6.5	6.7	6.8	7.7
40–59	12.5	9.4	12.9	13.6	14.6	4.1	7.7
60–89	17.5	15.6	15.2	19.2	12.4	21.9	7.7
90–100	27.5	51.2	50.2	51.6	48.3	61.6	66.7
Cases	40	160	255	308	89	73	39

himself to the speed of his wife's response: a man with a highly responsive wife being less inclined to delay ejaculation.

Nevertheless, one can see a tendency for higher orgasm rates to be associated with lengthier duration of intromission. Note that where intromission is under one minute only slightly over one quarter of the wives achieved orgasm always or nearly always, while lengthier intromission (1 to 11 minutes) raises this proportion to roughly half, and where intromission is protracted beyond 11 minutes three fifths to two thirds of the wives reach this high orgasm rate. Conversely, the women with low orgasm rates (none, 1–9%, and 10–39%) tend to have experienced brief intromission.

The same correlation was seen, though less clearly, in calculations based on broken marriages. An unexpected fact emerged from these calculations: there was a general tendency for lesser duration of intromission in the marriages which ended in separation or divorce, and considerably fewer wives in any duration-category reached orgasm nine or more times out of ten acts of coitus. In categories 1–1.9, 2–3.9, and 4–7 minutes roughly one third of the women reached orgasm 90 to 100 per cent of the time; in these same categories based on intact marriages (as Table 4 shows) half of the wives had orgasm rates of 90 to 100 per cent.

Examination of Table 4 permits some interesting inferences. Firstly, it is clear that penile intromission of less than one minute is insufficient to cause regular orgasm in most women. Secondly, it appears that about half of the wives are capable of high (90–100%) orgasm rate with intromission ranging from one to eleven minutes. This uniformity regardless of whether intromission is 1–1.9 minutes, 2–3.9, 4–7, or 8–11 minutes is puzzling and one is tempted to hypothesize that, except for extremely brief or extremely prolonged intromission, some physiological or psychological constant is maintaining this plateau. Perhaps about half of the women are capable of this high orgasm rate although some require but one minute while others require eleven.

Extremely prolonged (i.e., about the upper ten per cent in terms of duration) intromission evidently can raise another ten to fifteen per cent of the wives to the high orgasm rate. We see that intromission of 16 minutes or more results in (the causal implication is intentional) high orgasm rate for two thirds of the wives. The remaining third are scattered so evenly throughout the other orgasm rate categories one gains the impression that these women, too, have reached their physiological ceiling. In brief, 16 or more minutes of intromission suffices to bring essentially all women to the limits of their orgasmic capacities.

Concluding Comment

There are certain neurophysiological and unconscious psychological factors which prevent female orgasm in coitus, but the degree of their influence cannot be accurately ascertained by means of the data presently available. However, there are several reasons for believing this influence is of the magnitude of five to ten percentage points:
1. In extremely happy marriages only 4.4 per cent of the wives have not experienced orgasm in marital coitus.
2. In marital coitus preceded by lengthy (21 or more minutes) foreplay only 7.7 per cent of the wives have not experienced orgasm.
3. Where penile intromission lasts 16 minutes or more only 5.1 per cent of the wives had failed to experience orgasm.

Aside from the limitations imposed by physiological and unconscious psychological factors, it is clear that there is a strong correlation between female orgasm and marital happiness (presumably causal in both directions); a definite correlation between female orgasm rate and duration of pre-coital foreplay; and a moderate (and complex) correlation between female orgasm rate and duration of penile intromission.

Notes

1. Tables 1, 3, and 4 in this paper were controlled by duration of marriage (1–3 years; 4–10 years; 11 years) to see if this variable was causally related to the results found. No alteration occurred and thus duration of marriage does not qualify any of the relations reported in these tables.

2. A check was made on the interrelation of foreplay and intromission with the finding that there generally was little relationship except at the higher orgasm rates (90–100% orgasm) wherein some synergistic effect was found and when duration of intromission was held constant, a greater amount of foreplay was conducive to a higher orgasm rate. Similarly if foreplay was held constant, longer intromission resulted in

more orgasm. But in general this control worked only in a minority of cells in the table, so that Tables 3 and 4 may stand by and large as they are.

Reference

1. KINSEY, ALFRED C., POMEROY, W. B., MARTIN, C. E., and GEBHARD, P. H. *Sexual Behavior in the Human Female.* Philadelphia, W. B. Saunders, 1953.

5

Marital Sexuality in Four Cultures of Poverty

Lee Rainwater

Oscar Lewis has asserted that "Poverty becomes a dynamic factor which affects participation in the larger national culture and creates a subculture of its own. One can speak of a culture of the poor, for it has its own modalities and distinctive social and psychological consequences for its members . . . (it) cuts across regional, rural-urban and even national boundaries." He sees similarities between his own findings about the Mexican poor and findings of others in Puerto Rico, England, and the United States. This paper deals with such similarities in one area of interpersonal relationships, namely, in the attitudes and role behaviors which characterize the sexual relationships of lower-class husbands and wives in these four countries. This paper seeks to demonstrate that, in spite of important differences in the cultural forms of these four areas, there are a number of striking similarities in the ways husbands and wives act sexually and in the ways they regard their actions. The concern is thus not with the simplest level of sexual description — "Who has intercourse with whom, how and how often?" — but with the meanings these experiences have for their participants and for the assimilation of heterosexual with other family roles.

Reprinted from *Journal of Marriage and the Family*, November, 1964, pp. 457–466, by permission of the author and the National Council on Family Relations.

This is an expanded version of a paper read at the plenary session on Sex and Culture of the annual meeting of the American Anthropological Association, Philadelphia, 1961. The writer is indebted to Marc J. Swartz for helpful comments and suggestions during the preparation of this paper.

The materials from which this comparison is drawn are rather varied. For Mexico, there is Lewis's work on Tepoztlan[1]; for Puerto Rico, J. M. Stycos' investigation of family and fertility in the northeastern area of the island[2] and David Landy's study of child-rearing in an eastern cane-raising area.[3] For England, there are several studies of English working-class life, among which those of Spinley,[4] Madeline Kerr,[5] and Slater and Woodside[6] deal specifically with sexual relations. For the United States, there are the Kinsey studies[7] and this author's exploratory work on lower-class marital sexuality.[8]

Methodologically, these studies represent two kinds of approaches: Lewis, Landy, Kerr, and Spinley depended both on anthropological field techniques and some systematic interviewing of respondents; this author's work and that of Stycos and of Slater and Woodside are based only on interviews. In none of these studies were sexual relations a primary focus of the study. Given these differences in method and focus, it is perhaps surprising that there should be as much compatibility in findings as in fact exists.

The central sexual norm: "Sex is a man's pleasure and a woman's duty."

That sexual relations exist for the pleasure of the man and that enjoyment for the woman is either optional or disapproved is specifically noted in each of these four cultures. Women are believed either not to have sexual desires at all or to have much weaker sexual needs, needs which do not readily come to the fore without stimulation from a man. In Tepoztlan, ". . . women who are passionate and 'need' men are referred to as *loca* (crazy) . . ."[9]; in the other three areas, women are likely to be regarded as immoral if they show too much interest in sexual relations with their husbands. In Gorer's study of English character,[10] one set of questionnaire items deals with the nature of women's sexuality. Gorer reports that the poor were more likely than the more affluent to agree that women "don't care much about the physical side of sex" and "don't have such an animal nature as men" and to disagree that women enjoy sex as much or more than men.

Man's nature demands sexual experience; he cannot be happy without it; and if he is not satisfied at home, it is understandable that he looks elsewhere. That the wife might look elsewhere is a common fantasy of men in these areas, but neither men nor women so often say that dissatisfaction with sexual relations is likely to lead the wife to stray. The husband's anxiety that his wife's "unnatural" impulses could lead her to look for a lover, however, is often given as a reason for not stimulating her too much or developing her sensual capacities through long or elaborated lovemaking.[11] Stycos notes that Puerto Rican men expect such more elaborated sexual experiences in their relations with prostitutes or other "bad" women.[12]

In all four areas, it is not considered appropriate for parents to devote attention to the sexual education of their children. Boys may be encouraged, either overtly or covertly, to acquire sexual experiences. This seems most fully institutionalized in Puerto Rico.[13] Elsewhere, the boy seems to be left more to his own devices. In any case, there is recognition that boys will acquire a fair amount of knowledge about sexual relations and that they probably will have intercourse with available women. In Puerto Rico and Tepoztlan, these women are seen as very much in the status of prostitutes or "loose women," and the boy feels he must be careful about approaching a more respectable girl. These lines seem more blurred in England and the United States — in these countries, in the context of group or individual dating, boys seem to feel freer about forcing their attention and less vulnerable to repercussions from the girl's family.[14] The Latin pattern of sharp separation of "loose women" and the virginal fiancée seems a highly vulnerable one in any case and quickly breaks down under the pressures of urbanization in a lower-class environment.[15]

Girls, on the other hand, are supposed not to learn of sexual relations either by conversation or experience. Mothers in all four cultures do not discuss sex with their daughters and usually do not even discuss menstruation with them. The daughter is left very much on her own in this area, with only emergency attention from the mother — e.g., when the girl proves unable to cope with the trauma of onset of menses or begins to seem too involved with boys. Later, women will say that they were completely unprepared for sexual relations in marriage, that no one had ever told them about this, and that they had only the vaguest idea of what this shrouded part of their marital responsibility involved. Girls tend to be trained to a prudish modesty in relation to their bodies (even though they may also elaborate their dress or state of undress to attract boys) — in England, for example, Spinley notes that girls will not undress in front of each other or their mothers.[16] Modesty in the two Latin cultures is, of course, highly elaborated.

The sexual stimulation that comes in all of these cultures from the close living together of children and adults is apparently systematically repressed as the child grows older. The sexual interests stimulated by these and other experiences are deflected for the boys onto objects defined as legitimate marks (loose women, careless girls, prostitutes, etc.) and for the girls are simply pushed out of awareness with a kind of hysterical defense (hysterical because of the fact that later women seem to protest their ignorance too much).

In these cultures, therefore, marriage is hardly made attractive from the point of view of providing sexual gratification. The girls are taught to fear sex and most often seem to learn to regard it in terms of the nonerotic gratifications it may offer. The boys learn that they may expect fuller sexual experiences from other, less respectable objects, and in some groups (Puerto Rico most overtly[17]), because of their identification of the wife as a "second mother," men have very potent reasons for not regarding the wife hopefully as a sexual object. Yet both boys and girls know that they will marry; the girls are anxious to do so, and the boys feign resistance more than maintain it.

For the girls, the transition to the married state often takes place via a period of high susceptibility to romantic love. The girl becomes involved with notions of falling in love with a man — this being but vaguely defined in her mind and oriented to an idealized conception of love and marriage. Stycos sees this as a "psychological mechanism intervening between ... rebellion (against the cloistered life imposed by parents) and elopement, providing the dynamism by which this radical move can be made."[18] Spinley notes that girls fall in love more with love than with their particular boy friends.[19] Arnold Green has described a similar pattern for a lower-class Polish group in the United States.[20] Lewis notes that participation in court-ship is one of the main gratifications of the adolescent period, albeit one flavored with many risks.[21] The girl is both pushed toward marriage by her desire to get away from home (where demands for work and/or support tend to be made increasingly as she gets older) and *pulled* in that direction by her knowledge that the only appropriate role for a woman in her culture is that of wife and mother, that if she does not marry soon she runs the risk of being regarded as an immoral, "loose" woman or a ridiculous old maid.

For the young man, too, marriage looms large as representing the final transition to adult status. In Tepoztlan, only married men may hold respon-sible positions; without marriage, one is still tied to one's own father. In Puerto Rico, the situation is similar, and in addition, one cannot be con-sidered truly masculine until one has fathered children, preferably sons. If one is to establish himself as an independent adult, he needs a woman to wash and cook and take care of him as his mother would. Sex, too, plays a part in the man's desire for marriage. Because in reality women of easy virtue are not as available as the norm has it, the man may want to be married to have sexual relations whenever he wants — as one American said, "It's nice to have it ready for me when I get home." Also, some American men express the desire to have a woman whom they know is "safe" and "clean," i.e., does not have a venereal disease.

But the assertion of independent adult status which marriage represents in these groups meets with considerable opposition from parents, more so for the girl than for the young man. Lewis notes that in the mid-forties as many as 50 percent of unions took place by elopement,[22] and Stycos indicates a similarly high percentage for Puerto Rico.[23] Because girls are not cloistered in the United States and England as they are in these Latin cultures, clear-cut elopement is not so much the pattern, but feigned surprise and anger are common parental responses, and it is not unusual for a premarital preg-nancy to be used as a final argument to the parents to accept the marriage of their daughter to a man whom they like to feel is "not good enough for her." The wife in particular, then, is launched into marriage during a period of overt strain in her relations with her parents. Although later relationships with relatives may come to be central to her integration socially, during this period she is often more "alone" than at any other time in her life.

The "honeymoon trauma"

The adjustment to sexual relations is observed to be difficult for many women in all four groups. Stycos notes that in a majority of cases, the wedding night was traumatic for the woman, with trembling, weeping, and speechlessness being frequently reported.[24] Several women were so frightened that they managed to delay the first intercourse for several days. Lewis reports a similar pattern for Tepoztlan,[25] although he feels that the less sheltered girls of today are less likely to be so resistant. Lewis also notes that the fact that couples often start their marriage sleeping in the same room with the husband's family imposes additional constraints. Slater and Woodside indicate that many of their English lower-class women reported unpleasant wedding nights but claimed to have overcome their initial fear and repugnance,[26] a pattern also noted in the United States.[27] It should be noted that the wife's modesty and reticence are not necessarily disapproved by her new husband; he may value them as an indication that she is still a virgin and that she is not "oversexed." Even so, he is confronted with a problem: while he does not wish his wife to be desirous independent of his initiation, he does need her cooperation, and he does not like to be made to feel guilty by her protests and fright.

Individual behavior and the norm

The effect of early socialization processes and later experiences, then, seems to be to establish the husband as the one to whom sexual relations are really important and the wife as the unwilling vehicle for his gratification. Given this cultural statement of the nature of men and women, what are the actual patterns of sexual gratification in these four cultures? For Tepoztlan, Lewis reports only what is presumably the majority pattern: ". . . much of the women's expressed attitudes toward sexual relations with their husbands dwell upon its negative aspects and reveal feelings of self-righteousness which border on martyrdom. Women speak of submitting to their husband's 'abuse' because it is their obligation to do so,"[28] For the husband's part, he reports, "Husbands do not expect their wives to be sexually demanding or passionate, nor are these viewed as desirable traits in a wife. Husbands do not complain if their wives are not eager for or do not enjoy sexual intercourse. . . . Some husbands deliberately refrain from arousing their wives sexually, because they do not want them to 'get to like it too much.' . . . Few husbands give attention to the question of their wives' sexual satisfaction. In general, sexual play is a technique men reserve for the seduction of other women." (Furthermore, a passionate wife may be considered a victim of black magic.) Perhaps some wives of Tepoztlan do enjoy sexual relations with their husbands, and the husbands do not object, but Lewis apparently did not find this pattern frequent enough to warrant comment.[29]

Stycos reports a similar pattern for Puerto Rico: most women say they do not enjoy sexual relations; for them, sex is a duty and their emotional stance a continuation of the premarital rejection of sex as an appropriate interest for a woman.[30] Women report a sense of disgust and revulsion about this necessary role, or they communicate a sense of detachment and minor irritation. Some women say they deceive the husband into believing that they enjoy sexual relations somewhat — perhaps to keep them from feeling too guilty, perhaps to allay any suspicion that they have a lover. The woman in this case seeks a balance of apparent enjoyment and reticence in which she communicates to her husband that her interest is solely due to her love for him, that her enjoyment is secondary to his right. Women use various excuses to cut down on the frequency of intercourse — they feign sleep, or illness, argue about the danger of becoming pregnant, welcome menstruation, seek to prolong postpartum abstinence — but they feel that such a course is risky because it may make the husband violent or suspect infidelity. Stycos also notes that over one-third of the women in his sample indicated real enjoyment of sexual relations, but he does not discuss how these women differ from the majority who to some extent reject sexual relations.

The patterns described by Stycos for Puerto Rico are also apparent in data from lower-class American families currently being studied by the author.[31] Table 1 presents a tabulation of wives' attitudes toward sexual relations with their husbands for 195 middle- and lower-class women. The wom-

table 1

SOCIAL CLASS AND WIFE'S ENJOYMENT OF SEXUAL RELATIONS

	Middle Class (58)	Upper-Lower Class (68)	Lower-Lower Class (69)
Highly accepting: very positive statements about enjoyment	50%	53%	20%
Moderately accepting: enjoyment not emphasized	36	16	26
Lack of acceptance: avoidant or rejecting attitudes expressed	14	31	54
	100%	100%	100%

$X^2 = 26.48$, df $= 4$, P$<$.005.

en's responses were categorized into three gross patterns: *highly accepting of sexuality* (referring to positive statements of interest in, desire for, and enjoyment of sexual relations with the husband and explicit or implicit indications that sexual relations were highly significant in the marital relationship), *moderately accepting of sexuality* (referring to positive statements about sexual relations with the husband, but without glowing testimony to the importance of, or gratification in, sexual relations, and often with an effort to place sexuality in proper perspective in relation to other activities and gratifications in marriage), and *lack of acceptance of sexuality* (in which the wife indicates that sexual relations are for the husband's gratification, not hers). In the middle class (no significant differences between upper-middles and lower-middles), only 14 per cent of the women indicate lack of acceptance of sexuality; in the upper-lower class, this proportion rises to 31 per cent; and in the lower-lower class, 54 per cent of the women do not show acceptance of themselves as sexually interested and do not indicate enjoyment of sexual relations.[32] The women who do not find sexual relations enjoyable range in their attitude toward the necessity to have intercourse: a good many try to neutralize the unpleasantness they feel, others are overtly hostile to the husband about his demands, but the latter pattern seems a difficult one to maintain since it has ready repercussions on the marital relationship, and generally the women fear their husbands will stray or desert them. Some of these women report with pride that they never directly refuse their husbands, although they use the same devices reported by Stycos to reduce the frequency of their husbands' demands. (One device reported by these women but not mentioned by Stycos is precipitating an argument with the husband so that he will go out to a tavern.)

For England, Spinley reports only that the most common pattern is for sex to be only the man's pleasure,[33] but Slater and Woodside supply some idea of the frequency of the wife's enjoyment of sexual relations. They report that only a minority of women find real gratification in sexual relations and that about half indicate that they do not participate of their own wish.[34]

Women in all of these areas sometimes justify holding back from emotional participation in sexual relations by saying that they are less likely to become pregnant if they do not have orgasm. This is perhaps related to the general tendency, observed in the English and American reports at least, for the sexual relationship to become less and less involved, more automatic, after the first few years of marriage. There is not only a decrease in frequency, but also a tendency to relegate intercourse more and more to the category of satisfying the husband's biological need, and for whatever sense of mutuality has existed to wither. Several American women who reject sex comment that earlier in marriage they had sometimes enjoyed intercourse but that now, with many children and other preoccupations, would just as soon do without it. Slater and Woodside also note that the longer-married women tend to be the more dissatisfied.[35]

Kinsey's data on educational level and sexual behavior are by and large congruent with the patterns outlined here.[36] He finds that although men of lower educational status are much more likely than men with more education to have premarital relations, women of this status are less likely to do so. He finds that for women, erotic arousal from any source is less common at the lower educational levels, that fewer of these women have ever reached orgasm, and that the frequency for those who do is lower. For men, he reports that foreplay techniques are less elaborated at the lower educational levels, most strikingly so with respect to oral techniques. In positional variations in intercourse, the lower educational levels show somewhat less versatility, but more interesting is the fact that the difference between lower and higher educational levels increases with age because variations among lower status men drop away rapidly with age, while the drop among more educated men is much less. The same pattern characterizes nudity in marital coitus.

One final aspect of marital sexuality can be considered: the prevalence of extramarital relations. As noted, the sexual norms of all of these cultures or subcultures treat extramarital relations on the part of men as understandable, sometimes to be expected, while such relations by wives are strongly disapproved. Kinsey finds that men of below college level are more likely than others to have extramarital relations, but the lowest educational level is not the most frequent participant in such relationships. Also, the differential between college and grammar-school-only men disappears with age (by the 36–40 age period, college-level-men show a slightly higher incidence than those of grammar school levels). Extramarital intercourse, except in the early married years, does not seem as highly class-bound as does premarital intercourse. Since no comparable data are available for the other three societies, it can only be said that extramarital relations by the husband — so long as there is no marked interference with the life of the couple — are not heavily condemned. Indeed, in Puerto Rico and Tepoztlan, at least, they are to be expected.

For women, considerable unclarity exists in the reports for all four areas. It is known that the partners for erring husbands are usually prostitutes or single, separated, or widowed women, but this is not always the case. It is not clear who the married women who participate in these affairs are, or whether they do so out of sexual desire or from other motives — to get even with the husband, to receive attention and presents from another man because the husband ignores them, or what. Kinsey's data indicate clearly that few lower-status women have extramarital relations and that the proportion is lower than among more educated women, especially for marriages of longer duration. It seems likely that in these lower-class groups, the concern about the wife's extramarital relations is more a manifestation of the husband's concern over her taking revenge for his domination than a prevalent pattern of deviance which he must realistically guard against.

86

Cultures mold the expression of sexual drives, the manifestations of male potency and female receptivity, in varied ways to conform to the requirements of particular social and cultural systems. Each individual in the system responds sexually not only, or even primarily, in terms of sexual drive, but in terms of the interpersonal implications which such action has.[37] What, then, are the characteristics of the social systems and processes of socialization to which the patterns of sexual behavior and attitudes outlined above represent accommodations?

In all of these lower-class subcultures, there is a pattern of highly segregated conjugal role relationships. Men and women do not have many joint relationships; the separation of man's work and woman's work is sharp, as is the separation of man's and woman's play. Stycos indicates that half of the women in his sample do not report common activities with their husbands outside the home, and many of the remaining cases report only infrequent or limited outside activities[38]; a similar pattern seems characteristic of Tepoztlan[39]; and in both groups, the necessity for respect toward the husband reduces joint activities. This has been the traditional pattern in England and the United States, although trends toward less segregation are observable.[40]

The low value placed on mutuality in sexual relations can be seen, then, as in part an extension of a more generalized pattern of separateness in the marital relationship. It is not difficult to understand that husbands and wives do not think of sexual relations as a way of relating intimately when they have so few other reasons for doing so. The role segregation of which the pattern of sexual relationships seems a part has as one consequence a considerable difficulty in communication between husbands and wives on matters not clearly defined in terms of traditional expectations. It is difficult for such couples to cope with problems which require mutual accommodation and empathy. This has been noted as one reason couples in these groups are not able to practice birth control effectively[41] and seems also to be involved in the distance husbands and wives feel with respect to sexual relations.

In these groups, then, husbands and wives tend to be fairly isolated from each other. They do not seem to be dependent on each other emotionally, though each performs important services for the other. In the traditional social systems of these groups, social integration is somewhat separate for the husband and wife. Each participates in relatively closed social networks to which he can look for a sense of stability and continuity in his life.[42] For women, social relations often are organized about relations with kin, the woman regards herself as most importantly a person embedded in a network of kin extending upward to maternal figures and downward to her children. The importance of "Mum" for the English lower class has been noted by many observers, and Mum in turn is the center of a network of kin and neighbors which absorbs many of the emotional demands of the wife.[43] In Tepoztlan, the young wife traditionally orients herself to her husband's mother or to her own at a later date. The tie with the grandmother also seems important emotionally. In the United States, this pattern of kin relating is not so sharply defined as in other areas, but some evidence exists that lower-class people maintain kin relationships more fully than do middle-class people.[44] It is not clear from the Puerto Rican data how much wives orient themselves to kin networks, but it is clear that whatever their social relationships, these do not depend on joint relating by the couple to others.[45]

The husband's social network is not as dependent on kindred as that of the wife, although his too tends to be closed in the sense that the men he relates to tend also to relate to each other. His status in the home, and among the wife's kin network, tends to be tangential. Though he may be defined as the final authority, by default he usually has less influence on what goes on from day to day than his wife or the maternal figure to whom she looks for guidance. His important social relationships are outside the home, with other men — some of whom may be relatives, others not. His performance as a husband and father is more influenced by the standards they set than by his wife's desires, just as her behavior is more influenced by the standards and expectations of her kin-based network.[46]

What all of this suggests, in short, is that in a system characterized by closed social networks, the impact in the direction of highly segregated conjugal roles makes close and mutually gratifying sexual relations difficult because neither party is accustomed to relating intimately to the other. Further, a close sexual relationship has no particular social function in such a system since the role performance of husband and wife are organized on a separate basis, and no great contribution is made by a relationship in which they might sharpen their ability for cooperation and mutual regulation.[47] It is possible that in such a system, a high degree of intimacy in the marital relationship would be antagonistic to the system since it might conflict with the demands of others in ego's social network.[48]

However, not all lower-class couples can be said to be caught up in closed social networks of the kind just discussed. Where residence is neolocal and geographical movement breaks up both kin and lifelong community relationships, the lower-class couple finds itself either isolated or participating in loose social networks in which there is not so great an opportunity for relationships with others to take up the emotional slack of a segregated relationship between husband and wife. In these situations, there is a tendency for husband and wife to be thrown more on each other for meaningful standards and emotional support, a push in the direction of joint organization and joint role relationships.[49] The impact of such a disruption of previous social networks is probably greatest on the wife. Since she does not have the work situation as a ready base for forming a new network of relationships, her network probably remains denuded for a longer period of time. This is apparent in some of the United States data[50] and can be inferred for

Puerto Rico. In this situation, the stage is set for sexual relations to assume a more important role in the couple's relationship. The wife wishes her husband to be more affectionate and to spend more time with her. She may try to overcome her resistance to sex. The outcome will depend on the husband's ability to adapt to the new situation, in which his sexual need is not the sole factor, and in which he is expected to moderate his demandingness in the service of a mutually gratifying relationship. The relationship becomes one in which, as one American woman said, "He takes and I give, but I take, too." Given the cultural norms to which such couples have been socialized, however, such a delicate accommodation is not easily achieved.[51]

The socialization experiences of husbands and wives, of course, provide the motivational basis for the role behaviors discussed above and account for some of the resistance to change which individuals show when the network of relationships changes.[52] As has been noted, girls growing up are not encouraged to internalize a role as interested sexual partner, but are taught instead a complex of modesty, reticence, and rejection of sexual interests which continues into marriage. Girls are not rewarded, either prospectively or after marriage, by the significant others in their social networks for tendencies in the direction of passionate wife. Instead, the direction of proffered goals is toward functioning as a mother to children and husband, and perhaps continuing as daughter to a maternal figure. Although during late adolescence the girl may break from this pattern via romance and elopement, she finds that her greatest security comes from a return to the fold (if it is available). Finally, since her father has not been an integrated part of the household during her childhood, she has never developed the early psychic basis for a close relationship with a man which could be transferred to her husband. (Or the relationship with the father has come to have incestuous overtones which make a transfer difficult.)

The socialization experiences of the boy make greater allowance for a sexual role, but primarily in a narcissistic way. The boy learns to regard sex as a kind of eliminative pleasure for himself, and there is little emphasis on the sexual relationship as a social relationship. The aggressive component in sex is strongly emphasized, in the form of seduction and fantasies of raping, fantasies which in England[53] and the United States[54] are sometimes acted out in sham fashion as part of individual or group "dating" behavior. The masculinity of the *macho* pattern in the Latin cultures incorporates an aggressive pride in relations with men and with women; with respect to women, it stresses both having many partners and being insistent on taking one's own pleasure in each relationship. In the English and American lower class, there is no comparable name for this pattern, but the behavior encouraged is very similar. This exaggerated masculinity may be viewed as an over-compensation for the difficulty the boy has in developing a masculine identity. His early life is spent very much in the company of women; he tends to identify more with his mother than with his father since the latter is not much in the home and tends not to interact closely with his children.[55] The heavy emphasis on man's pleasure and indifference to the woman serves to ward off feelings of inadequacy stemming both from past difficulties in identification and present marginal status in the family.[56] Given this vulnerability in his sense of masculine competence, it is not difficult to understand that the husband in these groups does not want to complicate his functioning as a sexual partner by having to take into account, or by stimulating, his wife's needs and demands. Nor does he want to feel that he has to compete with other men to keep her affections.

Thus, even though the current social situation may encourage joint role organization and greater dependence of husband and wife on each other, the legacy of socialization directed toward a system in which men and women orient themselves to different social networks and sharply segregated conjugal roles makes change difficult, and reduces the frequency with which couples develop sexual relations involving mutual gratification.

Summary

This paper began with an examination of similarities in the patterns of marital sexuality in four "cultures of the poor," all part of, or strongly dominated by, the over-all Western European culture.[57] It was shown that among the lower classes of certain communities in Mexico, Puerto Rico, England, and the United States, there are significant similarities in the sentiments expressed by husbands and wives concerning sexual experiences and in their expectations about sexual role performances by the two marital partners. The paper has concluded with an explanatory hypothesis which seems adequate to account for the data from these four cultures, but which perhaps has wider applicability.[58] It will occur to the reader, for example, that middle-class marriage according to the "Victorian" model was and is similarly marked by a lack of mutuality in sexual relations; in place of mutuality, a variety of repressive and mistress-lover patterns have developed.[59] A more general hypothesis can be advanced which very likely is relevant to these situations also. This is that *in societies where there is a high degree of segregation in the role relationships of husbands and wives, the couple will tend not to develop a close sexual relationship, and the wife will not look upon sexual relations with her husband as sexually gratifying* (although she may desire such relations as signifying the continuing stability of the relationship). This leaves open the question of whether in other cultures having such a role segregation pattern, the wife may commonly seek other relationships for sexual gratification, as on Truk,[60] nor does it take into account the complexities in societies in which polygamy is common. Should such a hypothesis have wider validity, it would represent an additional step toward understanding patterns of sexual relations in different societies as more than anthropological *curiosa*.

Notes

1. Oscar Lewis, *Life in a Mexican Village: Tepoztlan Restudied,* Urbana: U. of Illinois Press, 1951.
2. J. Mayone Stycos, *Family and Fertility in Puerto Rico: A Study of the Lower Income Group,* New York: Columbia U. Press, 1955.
3. David Landy, *Tropical Childhood: Cultural Transmission and Learning in a Rural Puerto Rican Village,* Chapel Hill: U. of North Carolina Press, 1959.
4. B. M. Spinley, *The Deprived and the Privileged: Personality Development in English Society,* London: Routledge and Kegan Paul, 1953.
5. Madeline Kerr, *The People of Ship Street,* London: Routledge and Kegan Paul, 1958.
6. Eliot Slater and Moya Woodside, *Patterns of Marriage: A Study of Marriage Relationships in the Urban Working Classes,* London: Cassell and Co., 1951.
7. Alfred C. Kinsey *et al., Sexual Behavior in the Human Male,* Philadelphia, W. B. Saunders, 1948; and *Sexual Behavior in the Human Female,* Philadelphia, W. B. Saunders, 1953.
8. Lee Rainwater, *And the Poor Get Children: Sex, Contraception and Family Planning in the Working Class,* Chicago: Quadrangle Books, 1960.
9. Lewis, *op. cit.,* p. 326.
10. Geoffrey Gorer, *Explaining English Character,* New York: Criteron Books, 1955, pp. 115–116.
11. Lewis, *op. cit.,* p. 326; Slater and Woodside, *op. cit.,* p. 172.
12. Stycos, *op. cit.,* p. 143.
13. *Ibid.,* pp. 42–43; Landy, *op. cit.,* p. 108 and pp. 159–160.
14. Spinley, *op. cit.,* p. 87.
15. Cf., Oscar Lewis, *Five Families: Mexican Case Studies in the Culture of Poverty,* New York: Basic Books, 1959; and *The Children of Sanchez: Autobiography of a Mexican Family,* New York: Random House, 1961.
16. Spinley, *op. cit.,* pp. 62–63.
17. Stycos, *op. cit.,* p. 142.
18. *Ibid.,* p. 99.
19. Spinley, *op. cit.,* p. 87.
20. Arnold W. Green, "The 'Cult of Personality' and Sexual Relations," *Psychiatry,* IV (1941), pp. 343–344.
21. Lewis, *Life in a Mexican Village, op. cit.,* 399–405.
22. *Ibid.,* p. 407.
23. Stycos, *op. cit.,* pp. 91–97.
24. *Ibid.,* pp. 134–135.
25. Lewis, *Life in a Mexican Village, op. cit.,* pp. 326–327.
26. Slater and Woodside, *op. cit.,* p. 173.
27. Rainwater, *op. cit.,* pp. 60–64.
28. Lewis, *Life in a Mexican Village, op. cit.,* p. 326.
29. Lewis's studies of urban Mexican couples suggest that a more complex sexual relationship is common (*Five Families, op. cit.; The Children of Sanchez, op. cit.*).

30. Stycos, *op. cit.*, pp. 134–142.

31. Lee Rainwater, *Family Design: Marital Sexuality, Family Size and Contraception*, Chicago: Aldine Publishing Co., 1964.

32. These data are taken from a study currently in progress concerning family size desires and family planning success based on interviews with 150 couples (husband and wife interviewed separately) and 100 individual husbands and wives. An analysis of the latter 100 interviews has been presented in Rainwater, *And the Poor Get Children, op. cit.*; the discussion of sexual relations is given on pp. 92–121. A fuller analysis, based on the total sample, of variations in sexual relations by social class status is presented in Rainwater, *Family Design, Ibid.* The lower-class sample tabulated in Table 1 includes both Negros and whites. However, at each class level, the differences in acceptance of sexual relations between Negro and white wives are very small.

33. Spinley, *op. cit.*, p. 61.

34. Slater and Woodside, *op. cit.*, pp. 168–169.

35. Slater and Woodside *(Ibid.)* note that women frequently shift from "he" to "they" when discussing sexual relationships with the husband, a usage apparent also in the American interviews. Apparently, a good many women find it difficult in connection with sex to think of the husband as other than a representative of demanding men as a type.

36. The Kinsey data *(op. cit.)* suggest that late in marriage (36–40 age period) at the lowest educational level, men have extramarital relations four times as often as women; at the intermediate level slightly more than twice as often; and at the highest educational level, only 50 per cent more often.

37. Margaret Mead, *Male and Female*, New York: William Morrow, 1949, pp. 201–222.

38. Stycos, *op. cit.*, p. 149.

39. Lewis, *Life in a Mexican Village, op. cit.*, pp. 319–325.

40. The literature on the English and American working class is quite extensive: in addition to the works cited in the discussion of sexual relations, there are several English studies (Raymond Firth, *Two Studies of Kinship in London*, London: Athlone Press, 1956; J. M. Mogey, *Family and Neighborhood*, London: Oxford U. Press, 1956; Richard Hoggart, *The Uses of Literacy*, London: Chatto and Windus, 1957; Michael Young and Peter Willmott, *Family and Kinship in East London*, London: Routledge and Kegan Paul, 1957; Peter Willmott and Michael Young, *Family and Class in a London Suburb*, New York: Humanities Press, 1961) and several American studies (Allison Davis, Burleigh B. Gardner, and Mary R. Gardner, *Deep South: A Social and Anthropological Study of Caste and Class*, Chicago: U. of Chicago Press, 1941; Allison Davis and Robert J. Havighurst, *Father of the Man*, New York: Houghton Mifflin, 1947; Allison Davis, *Social Class Influences Upon Learning*, Cambridge; Harvard U. Press, 1952; Martin B. Loeb, *Social Class as Evaluated Behavior*, unpublished Ph.D. dissertation, University of Chicago, 1957; Lee Rainwater, Gerald Handel, Richard P. Coleman, *Workingman's Wife: Her Personality, World and Life Style*, New York: Oceana Publications, 1959; Jerome K. Myers and Bertram H. Roberts, *Family and Class Dynamics in Mental Illness*, New York: John Wiley, 1959; Bennett M. Berger, *Working Class Suburb: A Study of Auto Workers in Suburbia*, Berkeley: U. of California Press, 1960; Herbert Gans, *Urban Villagers*, Glencoe Ill.: Free Press, 1962) which discuss family relationships in a way pertinent to this paper.

41. Reuben Hill, J. M. Stycos, and Kurt W. Back, *The Family and Population Control*, Chapel Hill: U. of North Carolina Press, 1959.

42. Elizabeth Bott, *Family and Social Network*, London: Tavistock Publications, 1957.

43. Kerr, *op. cit.*, Firth, *op. cit.*; Young and Willmott, *op. cit.*

44. Davis and Gardner, *op. cit.;* Rainwater, Handel, and Coleman, *op. cit.*

45. Various Puerto Rican sources (Stycos, *op. cit.; The People of Puerto Rico,* ed. by Julian Steward, Urbana: U. of Illinois Press, 1956; Landy, *op. cit.*) suggest that there is some tendency for the wife to retain a tie with a maternal figure after marriage, but not in the same organized way that is traditional in Tepoztlan or common with the "Mum" system in England.

46. Elizabeth Bott *(op. cit.),* from a sample not confined to the lower class, finds a correlation between the value placed by a couple on sexual relations and the degree of joint organization in their role relationships and "looseness" of their social network. She notes, in the one case of a highly segregated conjugal role relationship associated with a closed network, that the wife "felt physical sexuality was an intrusion on a peaceful domestic relationship . . . as if sexuality was felt to be basically violent and disruptive" (p. 73). Among families having a joint conjugal role relationship associated with a loose-knit network, ". . . a successful sexual relationship was felt . . . to be very important for a happy marriage . . . to prove that all was well with the joint relationship, whereas unsatisfactory relations were indicative of a failure in the total relationship" (p. 83). And among couples with intermediate segregation of role relationships and medium-knit networks, "In general, the greater the importance attached to joint organization and shared interests, the greater the importance attached to sexual relations" (p. 88). In the present author's current research on American lower-class couples referred to above, a similar pattern emerges. Among lower-class wives with highly segregated role relationships, 60 per cent indicated a lack of acceptance of sexual relations; among those with less segregated role relationships, only 28 per cent indicated such a lack of acceptance. Phrased another way, 77 per cent of the wives in highly segregated role relationships indicated less enjoyment of sexual relationships than did their husbands; among wives in less segregated relationships, only 36 per cent were less interested in, or enjoyed sex less than, their husbands.

47. Erik Erikson, *Childhood and Society,* New York: W. W. Norton, 1950.

48. See the closely related discussion by William J. Goode ["The Theoretical Importance of Love," *American Sociological Review,* 24 (1959), pp. 38–47] and by Max Gluckman *(Custom and Conflict in Africa,* Oxford: Basil Blackwell, 1955) in which these authors argue that romantic love between a couple tends to interfere with other important solidarities in a society and that therefore societies tend to operate in ways that keep love from disrupting existing social arrangements. While the efforts of society to control love are clearest in connection with mate selection, these efforts continue after marriage also and have some bearing on the kind of sexual relationship that commonly exists among couples in a society.

49. Bott, *op. cit.*

50. Rainwater *et al., op. cit.*

51. In a study of Detroit wives' feeling about their marriages, Robert O. Blood and Donald M. Wolfe *(Husbands and Wives: The Dynamics of Married Living,* Chicago: Free Press, 1960, pp. 221–235), it was found that the wife's satisfaction with the "love and affection" she receives from her husband increases steadily with social status. This seems related to the fact that there is a greater degree of sharing, communication, and joint participation in social relations at the higher- than on the lower-status levels.

52. Melford Spiro, "Social Systems, Personality and Functional Analysis," in *Studying Personality Cross-Culturally,* ed. by Bert Kaplan, Evanston: Row and Peterson, 1961.

53. Spinley, *op. cit.,* p. 87.

54. Green, *op. cit.,* pp. 343–344.

55. Spinley, *op. cit.,* pp. 81–82.

56. Kerr, *op. cit.,* p. 88.

57. Jamaica represents a fifth "culture of poverty" that has been the subject of a number of studies which touch on sexual life (Judith Blake, *Family Structure in Jamaica: The Social Context of Reproduction*, Glencoe, Ill.: Free Press, 1961; Fernando Henriques, *Family and Colour in Jamaica*, London: Eyre and Spottiswoode, 1953; Yehudi A. Cohen, *Social Structure and Personality: A Casebook*, New York: Holt, Rinehardt, and Winston, 1961, pp. 71–81 and 167–181). However, the specific discussion of attitudes and feelings toward sexuality is both conflicting and somewhat offhand. None of the studies contains the detail of the references for the four subcultures discussed in this paper. On balance, the Jamaican studies suggest that marital sexuality there has much in common with the pattern outlined here, but this can be asserted only very tentatively.

58. Cf. Margaret Meade's *Growing Up in New Guinea* (New York: New American Library, 1930, pp. 101–102) for a description of marital sexual relations among the Manus: "Unrelieved by romantic fictions or conventions of wooing, untouched by tenderness, unbulwarked by cooperativeness and good feelings as between partners, unhelped by playfulness, preliminary play or intimacy, sex is conceived as something bad, inherently shameful, something to be relegated to the darkness of the night.... Most women welcome children because it gives their husbands a new interest and diverts their unwelcome attentions from themselves." The pattern of rejection of her sexual role by a wife can be viewed as a rather extreme case of the lack of *attachment* to a social role in spite of *commitment* to it, a commitment which, in Erving Goffman's sense, has fateful consequences for the performer. As Goffman notes (*Encounters: Two Studies in the Sociology of Interaction*, Indianapolis: Bobbs-Merrill, 1961, pp. 88–89), social scientists have tended to "neglect the many roles that persons play with detachment, shame or resentment."

59. Richard Lewinsohn, *A History of Sexual Customs*, London: Longmans, Green and Co., 1958. Also see Joseph A. Banks's *Prosperity and Parenthood: A Study of Family Planning Among the Victorian Middle Classes*, London: Routledge and Kegan Paul, 1954), in which the discussion is congruent with the view presented here, although without the desirable empirical detail. Clellan S. Ford and Frank A. Beach's *Patterns of Sexual Behavior* (New York: Harper, 1951) is a cross-cultural study of sexual behavior which unfortunately contains almost nothing about the particular aspect of sexual behavior under discussion here, being instead concerned mainly with sexual techniques, rules for sexual mateships and liaisons, and prevalence of particular kinds of sexual behavior.

60. Marc J. Swartz, "Sexuality and Aggression on Romonum, Truk," *American Anthropologist*, 60:3 (June 1958), pp. 467–486.

part four

Extramarital sex

While all sexual relations outside of marriage in the United States are morally condemned, the negative views towards extramarital coitus are generally even stronger than those directed at premarital sexual intercourse. This is the result of two beliefs: first, that with marriage there is an approved sexual partner and therefore the individual has the opportunity of having his sexual needs met; and second, that any extramarital sexual involvement threatens the highly valued relationship of marriage. In the past, the American male could often discreetly indulge in sexual relations outside of marriage, but under no circumstances was the wife allowed any such sexual outlet. For many Americans the traditional double-standard values have been altered to the extent that both partners are expected to restrict their sexual needs to marriage, and, if the husband has any extramarital "rights," then it is believed that the same "rights" should also exist for the woman.

Adultery is legally punishable in the United States, but actual prosecution is rare and in most states the penalties are mild. Adultery has its greatest importance as legal grounds for divorce, since it is the only legal grounds for divorce recognized by all legal jurisdictions of the United States. The anthropological evidence points out that all known societies have placed some limitations on extramarital coitus and have developed some means for enforcing the restrictions. However, the nature of the restrictions and the means to effectively control them vary widely between societies, and often within a given society over time. The reason for the restrictions on most preliterate groups, ancient societies, and even recent civilizations has not been because of sexual restrictions *per se* or even because of morality. Rather, "adultery has most often been considered a threat to the economic stability of society; most specifically, male property rights."[1]

It is clear that in the United States extramarital sex may follow a number of different patterns. One writer has suggested that today the two extremes are the new open and accepted affair and the old secret and guilt ridden one.[2] The variation as well as the changing nature of extramarital sex is reflected in what they are called. Not too many years ago it was *cheating,* but now it's an *affair.* In fact it is increasingly getting to be that only the lower-middle and lower classes call it cheating. In fact, adultery is getting to sound old fashioned and almost quaint.[3]

It must be remembered that many Americans probably never have any sexual experiences outside their marriages. For most of these people the traditional controls over sexual morality will continue to be strong. But for more and more, especially among the young, the views about sexual morality are changing. In fact today many people who engage in extramarital sexual relationships suffer little or no social criticism if their behavior is discreet. Generally, extramartial sex is seen by many as a personal concern unless it becomes general knowledge. "Even then no legal action is likely unless the adultery, left unpunished, is thought to set a bad moral example for youth or otherwise to encourage wrongdoing."[4]

As has recently happened in many areas of deviancy, a number of persons who are involved have moved from a defensive to an offensive point of view. Put another way, they have often shifted from rationalizing their behavior to proselytizing it. For example, the Sexual Freedom League believes "that sexual expression, in whatever form agreed upon between consenting persons of either sex, should be considered an inalienable right. . . . Sex without guilt and restriction is good, pleasurable, relaxing, and promotes a spirit of human closeness, compassion and good will. We believe that sexual activity . . . has a wealth of potential for making life livable and enjoyable."[5]

In the past the belief existed that extramarital sexual involvement would destroy a marriage, which it often did because the belief was so strong, even though there may have been no other logical reason for ending the marriage. However, there is no reason to believe that people, if they chose, cannot invent ways to reduce or remove the social conditions that make extramarital coitus hazardous for happily married people.

Whatever changes do occur will be part of the new sexual morality that argues for equal rights of sexual expression for both men and women. This means that women will increasingly demand the same sexual rights for themselves as do men, whether in or out of marriage. As Love points out, "No matter what the outcome of the academic and ethical debates, women are going to continue to demand equal time and equal rights to erotic pleasure, to self-realization, to self-respect — and if they can't find these qualities within marriage, they will quietly go on seeking them elsewhere."[6]

It is also of interest to see that the new sexual morality places great importance on the woman's achieving sexual satisfaction. It is believed by many that she has greater freedom to enjoy sex in the same way that men have always enjoyed it. But the irony of this liberation is that a woman may have greater apprehension if she doesn't fully enjoy the sexual experience. She knows she has a right to orgasm, and, if she is not getting it with the frequency or intensity she believes she should, she may begin to wonder what is wrong. At the same time the man who accepts the new morality may wonder what is wrong with himself if his mate doesn't reach full sexual fulfillment. These kinds of concerns are important whether in or out of marriage. But in one sense they may be most important outside of marriage where the affair is essentially sexual and any sexual failure undermines the limited tie of the relationship.

In the reading by Harold Christensen there is a view of modern cultural variations with regard to extramarital sexual activity. The article by John Cuber and Peggy Harroff examines some new dimensions to the old phenomena of the man and mistress relationship. The third article, by Duane Denfield and Michael Gordon, looks at the development of a single standard type of extramarital sexual activity — that of mate swapping or "swinging."

Notes

1. Harper, Robert A., "Extramarital Sex Relations," in Albert Ellis and Albert Abarbanel, *Encyclopedia of Sexual Behavior,* New York: Hawthorne Books, Inc., 1961, p. 384.
2. Love, Nancy, "The '70's Woman and the Now Marriage," *Philadelphia Magazine,* February, 1970, p. 56.
3. *Ibid.*
4. Harper, *op. cit.,* p. 387.
5. Lind, Jack, "The Sexual Freedom League," in Walt Anderson, *The Age of Protest,* Pacific Palisades, Calif.: Goodyear Publishing Co., Inc., 1969, p. 184.
6. Love, *op. cit.,* p. 63.

6

A Cross-Cultural Comparison of Attitudes Toward Marital Infidelity

Harold T. Christensen

This is one in a series of articles[1] comparing sexual intimacy within and across three modern western societies. The societies involved are: Denmark, with its relatively liberal or permissive sex norms; Midwestern United States, with its somewhat typical or average sex culture for the country of which it is a part; and Intermountain United States, with its rather conservative or restrictive sex norms due to Mormon influence.[2]

Some generalizations from the earlier reports, which are relevant to our cross-cultural emphasis, are as follows: Every statistical measure that was used showed the Danish culture to be the most permissive and the Intermountain culture the most restrictive regarding premarital intimacy, with the Midwestern culture in between though generally closer to the Intermountain than to the Danish. With respect to *attitudes*, Danish respondents more frequently approved of premarital coitus, approved of earlier starts in relation to marriage of each level of intimacy (necking, petting and coitus), thought in terms of a more rapid progression from the beginning of intimacy in necking to its completion in coitus, and favored a longer period of coital activity prior to marriage. With respect to *behavior*, many more persons in the Danish sample actually engaged in premarital coitus and the incidences of both illegitimacy, and premarital pregnancy followed by marriage, were substantially higher there. With respect to *effects or consequences*, pre-

Reprinted from *International Journal of Comparative Sociology*, September, 1962, pp. 124–137, by permission of the author and the publisher.

marital coitus among respondents in the Danish sample was more likely to occur because of desire and to have pleasant feelings associated with it, accompanied by a lower level of guilt; in addition, Danish respondents who were involved in a premarital pregnancy were less likely to hurry up the wedding or to terminate their marriage by divorce. In all of these things[3], Denmark stood off by itself, so to speak; the great gap was between it and the two American cultures — which were quite similar to each other, though with the Intermountain almost always showing up as the most restrictive.

Thus, there is a certain amount of evidence that the more permissive the culture regarding premarital sexual intimacy, the higher will be the actual occurrence of such intimacy but the lower will be any negative effects deriving therefrom. And, conversely, the more restrictive the culture, the lower will be the actual occurrence but the higher will be the negative effects. Apparently negative consequences are more likely when behavior is out of line with the surrounding value system.

Problem and Procedure

Whereas the earlier publications discussed above have dealt with certain attitudes, behaviors, and consequences of *premarital* sexual intimacy, this report is to focus solely upon *attitudes* regarding *marital* infidelity, or, in other words, adultery. As will be explained below, data limitations will prevent us from dealing with either behavior or the consequences of behavior here. Nevertheless, the same three cultures will be examined and the cross-cultural theme will be maintained. Furthermore, by describing attitudes toward marital infidelity, we hope further to complete the overall picture in our three cultures of patterns of sexual intimacy outside of marriage, and by this indirection to add to an understanding of the roles of married mates.

RELATED LITERATURE

Generally speaking, societies regard premarital intimacy as much less of a problem than they do marital infidelity, for while the former does not usually involve deception, and may in some cases actually prepare for marriage, the latter usually does involve deception and hence makes a mockery of the marriage contract. Virtually all societies recognize this difference. Murdock, for example, working from the Human Relations Area Files at Yale University, reports that non-incestuous premarital relations are permitted by about 70 percent of the 158 societies for which information on this point is available. But regarding adulterous relations he says:

> Taboos on adultery are extremely widespread, though sometimes more honored in the breach than in the observance. They appear in 120 of the 148 societies in our sample for which data are available. In 4 of the remaining 28, adultery is socially disap-

101

proved though not strictly forbidden; it is conditionally permitted in 19 and freely allowed in 5. It should be pointed out, however, that these figures apply only to sex relations with an unrelated or distantly related person. A substantial majority of all societies . . . permit extramarital relations with certain affinal relatives.[4]

In reviewing the legal side of sex offenses within the United States, Ploscowe makes the point that adultery is much more widely prohibited among the states, and the penalties are much more severe, than is true for fornication (premarital coitus).[5]

Kinsey and associates included this topic within their study of American sexual behavior. Important among their conclusions are the following: Historically and cross-culturally considered, extra-marital intercourse has more often been a matter for regulation than has intercourse before marriage, and has been more heavily prohibited for the female than for the male. In the American culture, approximately half of the males as compared with slightly more than one-fourth of the females, have sexual intercourse with someone other than the married partner at some time while they are married. Incidence rates for females who have engaged in extra-marital intercourse become higher with advancing age; are higher in the present than with earlier generations; are higher with the religiously inactive than the religiously active; and are higher for those who had previously experienced premarital coitus than for those who had not. (Some of these relationships may be presumed to hold for the male also, though apparently all of them were not tested.) Extra-marital intercourse is believed to have contributed to a substantial number of the divorces which had occurred among the subjects of this study; furthermore, "the males rated their wives' extra-marital activities as prime factors in their divorces twice as often as the wives made such evaluations of their husbands' activities."[6]

Two more recent studies will be briefly cited here for whatever light they may throw on the subject at hand. One took place in England and the other in France. Both of these were conducted via the questionnaire method and dealt with attitudes, whereas the Kinsey research used the interview approach and focused upon behavior. (1) Chesser, in a rather extensive survey of the family attitudes of over 6,000 English women, included a few questions on extra-marital sexual intercourse. He found that most of his female subjects claimed never to have had a desire for extra-marital intercourse; but that the proportion experiencing such a desire was highest with wives who got the least sexual satisfaction from their husbands and were least happy in their marriages; and that one-third or more of the married women believed that *most* men would like to have extra-marital intercourse even though they were happily married.[7] (2) In an extensive survey of the sex attitudes of French women, the French Institute of Public Opinion reported the following on the subject of adultery: Almost half of those interviewed believed that "nearly all men" or "many men" deceive their wives in this way, whereas only about one-fifth of them believed that "many women" deceive their husbands; belief in adultery as common was found to be greater for urban than rural, single than married, and, of the single, greater for the older and experienced respondents; majority belief was that adultery is equally serious for both sexes, but of those who had contrary views 32 percent believed it to be more serious when committed by the wife as against only 3 percent when committed by the husband; half of the respondents believed that it is excusable for a man to have a short and casual affair with another woman, but the more serious affair was not excused since this implies a loss of love and confidence and a breakdown of the marital relationship.[8]

RESEARCH DESIGN

It should be evident from the above that, though each of the studies cited throws important light upon the culture of its focus, they do not "add up" cross-culturally. This is because each has its own frame of reference and method of investigation; since questions are posed in different ways, there is difficulty in seeing how the answers to one compare with those of another. In order to avoid this difficulty we sought, in our research, to apply the same concepts and procedures in a consistent manner to the several cultures studied.

Cultural relativism was our central concern. We were interested in knowing to what extent the value norms of a given culture affect its behavior patterns and also affect the consequences of this behavior. Sexual intimacy was chosen as the substantive area to be investigated, since it was believed that the strong views and feelings which people have concerning sex would cause intercultural differences to stand out. Denmark, Midwestern United States, and "Mormon Country" of Intermountain United States were selected as the populations for cross-cultural investigation, primarily because this offered a convenient testing range for our problem — extending from rather permissive sex norms at the one end to relatively restrictive sex norms at the other end.

The three cultures were then studied by means of both the "record linkage" method and a questionnaire survey; however, only the latter of these is used in the present paper. Three universities were selected, one from each of the cultures, and during the Spring of 1958 students in certain of the classes were invited to fill out questionnaires and to hand them in without signature.[9] Almost one-hundred percent returns were received and the numbers of incomplete or inconsistent returns which later had to be discarded were small.

It is recognized, of course that these university samples are not entirely representative of the broad cultures of which they are a part, since they were not drawn randomly to reflect cross-sections of the populations. It is believed, however, that they represent similar segments of the respective populations and that they therefore may be safely used for purposes of cross-cultural comparison.[10] Though cross-sectional samples would have been preferable, they would have been more difficult to work with in an intimate study of this kind. Since the investigators were laboring under rather severe limitations in time and resources, and since cross-cultural research at best presents some unusual difficulties, it was decided to stay with university students where cooperation could be most expected.

But in settling for these kinds of samples, we limited ourselves in the kinds of data that could be obtained. Since relatively few university students are married, there was virtually no opportunity to obtain data on adulterous practices. Therefore, when we report on marital infidelity, as is to be done below, it is necessary that we confine ourselves to beliefs or attitudes concerning such behavior — rather than the behavior itself.

In building the questionnaire, every effort was made to avoid ambiguity and to insure identical meanings in each of the populations. Professional persons familiar with each of the cultures were consulted and several pretests were run on both sides of the Atlantic, with revisions made on the basis of each experience. Danish translations were used for both the pretests and the final administration of the questionnaire in that culture. As a final check, the near-ready Danish questionnaire was translated back into English, by a person not previously connected with the study, and then compared with the near-ready English questionnaire for discrepancies.

Marital infidelity, or adultery, which is the subject of this paper, has been approached by means of one set of questions in the larger questionnaire just described. Readers desiring information on other aspects of the study should consult the sources listed in the first footnote.

Intra-Cultural Comparisons

Tables 1 and 2 present the basic data with which we are concerned. The plan is to comment first upon the phenomenon as such, as seen separately within each of the cultures; and then, in the following section, to focus upon the cross-cultural comparisons.

Students were asked, "Under which of the following circumstances would you approve of coitus (sexual intercourse) before marriage?", and then the same for "sexual infidelity after marriage?" In both instances answer categories started out with "Never under any circumstances," followed by a number of specified circumstances for which approval could be checked. Table 1 gives data for this first category concerning both premarital coitus and marital infidelity. Table 2 gives data for the alternate approval categories concerning just marital infidelity.

table 1

PERCENTAGES DISAPPROVING NONMARITAL COITUS UNDER ANY CIRCUMSTANCES FOR BOTH PREMARITAL AND POSTWEDDING SITUATIONS BY SEX AND CULTURE

Classification	Danish Sample (N = 149M, 86F)	Midwestern Sample (N = 213M, 142F)	Intermountain Sample (N = 94M, 74F)
I. Premarital Coital Experience			
A. Disapprove for Females Only[a]			
(1) Males	1.3	10.8	6.4
(2) Females	5.8	16.9	18.9
B. Disapprove for Both Sexes			
(3) Males	4.7	25.8	55.3
(4) Females	11.6	48.6	70.3
II. Postwedding Infidelity			
C. Disapprove for Females Only[a]			
(5) Males	2.0	7.5	3.2
(6) Females	3.5	5.6	16.2
D. Disapprove for Both Sexes			
(7) Males	37.6	61.0	73.4
(8) Females	41.9	71.8	78.4

[a] Indicates a double standard of morality wherein greater sexual freedom is permitted males than females. Merely 6 and 12 persons disapproved "for *males* only" in the respective premarital and postwedding categories; since these numbers are so small, they are eliminated from the table and ignored in the analysis.

SINGLE VERSUS DOUBLE STANDARD

First to be noted is the rather strong picture of a *single standard* of sexual morality, in contrast to the double standard. From Table 1 it can be seen that, when sex outside of marriage was disapproved, it was generally disapproved for *both* males and females rather than for the latter only.[11] This was true in the answers of both males and females, in all three cultures, and for both premarital and marital categories (A compared with B, and C compared with D). All intra-cultural differences, with sex categories combined, were found to be statistically significant.[12]

The double standard finds less acceptance when applied to adultery than when applied to premarital coitus (C compared with A). With the exception of Danish males, this relationship was suggested for both sexes in all three cultures. Intra-cultural differences, with sex categories combined, were found to be statistically significant in the Midwestern sample but not in the Danish or Intermountain samples.

Another major observation is that disapproval of adulterous relationships increases, and approval decreases, with each advance in level of involvement and/or commitment. From Table 1 we see that across-the-board disapproval is considerably higher when marital infidelity is being considered than when premarital coitus is being considered (D compared with B). This was true for both sexes and within all three cultures. All three intra-cultural differences, with sex categories combined, were found to be statistically significant. From Table 2 we see that approval of marital infidelity is highest when it is viewed as a temporary expedient during periods of absence from spouse (Stage I), that approval rates go down when the element of love between the offending party and the paramour is added (Stage II), and that they go down even farther when the paramour is also a married person (Stage III). With a few minor exceptions, these differences can be seen to hold true for both males and females and within all three of the cultures. But here, intra-cultural differences, with sex categories combined, were not significant. They, nevertheless, approached significance in both the Danish (.07 level) and the Midwestern (.08 level) but not in the Intermountain.

To recapitulate, our data show approval of non-marital coitus to be highest when both parties to the act are unmarried (Table 1), lower when

table 2

PERCENTAGES[a] APPROVING SEXUAL INFIDELITY DURING MARRIAGE UNDER SPECIFIED CIRCUMSTANCES BY SEX AND CULTURE

Classification	Danish Sample (N = 122M, 69F)	Midwestern Sample (N = 163M, 114F)	Intermountain Sample (N = 73M, 62F)
I. If he or she feels the need for sexual release (with prostitutes or others) during long absence from spouse.			
(1) Males	41.0	12.3	5.5
(2) Females	36.2	5.3	—
II. If he or she has fallen in love with an unmarried person.			
(3) Males	32.8	8.6	1.4
(4) Females	34.8	1.8	—
III. If he or she has fallen in love with another married person.			
(5) Males	27.0	6.7	1.4
(6) Females	29.0	1.8	1.6

[a] Percentages were derived by using total cases that were answered and were free from ambiguity and contradiction as the denominator (given at top of column headings), and the number approving for *both* men and women as the numerator.

one is unmarried and there is no love or permanence involved (Table 2—I), still lower when one is unmarried but there is love between them (Table 2—II), and lowest of all when there is love between them and both are married to other persons (Table 2—III). Though there are minor exceptions to this within some of the sub-categories and though certain of the tests do not reach statistical significance by rigorous standards, the general consistency in direction of difference, plus the fact that most of the tests at least approach significance, tend to give confidence in the generalization. There is the strong suggestion of a negative relationship between the degree of involvement in the affair and/or commitment to another marriage on the one hand, and the willingness of respondents to approve adulterous experiences on the other hand.

In contrast to the point just made, Christensen and Carpenter earlier reported a positive relationship between approval of *premarital* coitus and level of involvement and/or commitment between the persons.[13] The explanation, however, seems obvious: prior to the wedding, each advance in involvement and/or commitment seems to justify greater intimacy since marriage may be the assumed end; whereas after the wedding, involvement with *another* person is likely to work against the marriage — and where two married persons are involved, two marriages might be broken up.

MALE-FEMALE DIFFERENCES

The well accepted fact that females tend to be more conservative than males regarding non-marital sex is supported by the data of this study. In all but one of the twelve comparisons of Table 1 (C in the Midwestern sample), females showed proportionately greater disapproval than did males; and in all but three of the nine comparisons of Table 2 (II in the Danish sample and III in the Danish and Intermountain samples), females showed proportionately lesser approval than did males. Table 3 indicates that only nine of the twenty-one tests between male and female responses showed statistical significance. Nevertheless, since three others approached significance, as will be seen from Table 3, and since there was general consistency in direction of difference as explained a few sentences above, there is a suggestion of support for the conclusion of greater female conservativeness.

In this connection, it is interesting to note that proportionately more females than males adhere to the double standard of sexual morality (A and C of Table 1), even though this standard discriminates against their own sex. Two of the six comparisons in this regard are statistically significant and two others approach significance (Table 3). It may also be noted from Tables 1 and 3 that male-female differences regarding the double standard are greater for premarital than for marital behavior; when adultery is being considered, both sexes converge on the single standard.

107

table 3

SIGNIFICANCE LEVELS BETWEEN MALE AND FEMALE RESPONSES[a]

Comparisons	Danish Sample	Midwestern Sample	Intermountain Sample
From Table 1			
Lines 1 & 2 compared	(.06)	(.10)	.02
Lines 3 & 4 compared	.05	.01	.01
Lines 5 & 6 compared	—	—	.01
Lines 7 & 8 compared	—	.05	—
From Table 2			
Lines 1 & 2 compared	—	.05	(.07)
Lines 3 & 4 compared	—	.02	—
Lines 5 & 6 compared	—	.05	—

[a] Based upon Chi-Square tests. Significance levels for 5 percent and above are shown. (Levels between 10 and 5 percent are shown also but are set off with parentheses.)

OTHER VARIABLES

There was an attempt to determine how ten additional factors are related to the phenomenon under study. These factors, together with significance levels for differences among the internal breakdowns, with sex categories combined, are shown in Table 4. No consistent directions of difference were found for *age, education,* or *residence;* except in the Danish sample, where disapproval showed greatest for farm residence (significant) and highest educational level (approached significance). As for *social class,* more of the upper than lower class respondents disapproved (significant in the Midwestern sample only). Similarly for *church attendance* and for *parental happiness;* the tendency was for the most frequent church attenders to give the greatest disapproval (significant in the Danish and Midwestern samples), and for those with the most happy parents to give the greatest disapproval of adultery (significant in the Danish sample). *Source of sex education* showed little consistency, except for a slight tendency for those whose chief source was other than "friends" to disapprove more (significance approached in the Midwestern sample). In regard to *courtship status,* it was those who were engaged or going steady who, in all three samples, showed greatest disapproval of adultery (significant in the Danish and Midwestern samples). Similarly, in all three samples, it was those who were most *satisfied* with their present status who most frequently disapproved of adultery (significant in the Danish and Intermountain samples and significance approached in the Midwestern sample). Finally, the non-permissive, as measured by a special *attitude scale,* were the ones who gave greatest disapproval of adultery. This was true in all three samples, though the difference was significant in only the Danish and Midwestern.[14]

Despite some irregularities in direction of difference, and the lack of sta-

table 4

SIGNIFICANCE LEVELS AMONG RESPONSES IN VARIOUS FACTOR BREAKDOWNS[a]

Factors[b]	Danish Sample	Midwestern Sample	Intermountain Sample
Age	—	—	—
Education	(.09)	—	—
Residence	.05	—	—
Social Class	—	.01	—
Church Attendance	.01	.01	—
Parents' Happiness	.01	—	—
Source of Sex Education	—	(.08)	—
Courtship Status	.05	.02	—
Courtship Satisfaction	.02	(.07)	.01
Permissiveness Scale	.01	.01	—

[a] Based upon Chi-Square tests. Significance levels for 5 percent and above are shown. (Levels between 10 and 5 percent are shown also but are set off with parentheses.)

[b] For all tests reported here, only cases with unambiguous answers to disapproval of adultery "under any circumstances" were used. Factor breakdow.ıs were as follows: age — 20 or under, 21–23, 24–29; education — 1st year college, 2nd or 3rd year, 4th year or higher; residence — farm, city under 10,000, city with 10,000 or more; social class — working class and lower middle class combined, upper middle and upper class combined; church attendance — less than once a month, once a month or more; parents' happiness — very happy in marriage, other categories combined; source of sex education — family members, friends, reading or schooling; courtship status — random or casual dates, going steady or engaged, married; satisfaction with courtship status — very satisfied, other categories combined; and permissiveness scale — 0–5 (non-permissive), 6–10 (permissive).

tistical significance in many of the differences, there is evidence in Table 4 to suggest that disapproval of adultery is frequently associated with such factors as: residence on a farm, advanced educational training, high social status, frequent church attendance, happiness of the parental home, sex education derived from sources other than friends, a going steady or engaged relationship between the sexes, satisfaction over one's level of interaction with the opposite sex, and a restrictive attitude toward sexual matters generally. However, as will be stressed below, these tentatively suggested relationships do not apply equally across the three cultures studied.

Inter-Cultural Comparisons

Though cross-cultural analysis is the central concern of this paper, the reader already will have surmised the general picture in this regard, and hence a brief pointing up of findings is all that should be necessary here.

OVERALL ATTITUDE PATTERN

The most consistent and significant differences found in our entire study were those extending across the three cultures. A re-examination of Tables

1 and 2 will make quite clear that the Danish respondents were always the most permissive and the Intermountain respondents generally[15] the most restrictive in attitudes regarding adultery. All inter-cultural differences from these two tables, with sex categories combined, were found to be statistically significant.[16]

More specifically, it can be said from the data presented that Danish college students, as compared with American college students, hold significantly closer to the single standard of sexual morality[17] and are more liberal or permissive regarding both premarital coital experience and marital sexual infidelity — in general and under each of the circumstances specified.

It may also be observed from Tables 1 and 2 that, though the Midwestern answers are generally intermediate, they are usually closer to the Intermountain than to the Danish.

HOMOGENEITY OF ATTITUDE

Though the Danish and Intermountain are at opposite ends of our permissiveness-restrictiveness continuum, they both seem to be characterized by cultures that are relatively homogeneous. In regard to religion, for example, nine-tenths of the Danish population belonged to some church denomination which is Lutheran in tradition; the Intermountain population has the largest proportion belonging to a single church (about three-fourths is Mormon) of any other region in the United States; whereas the Midwestern population is more distributed among various church and non-member groups, without any one having a clear majority.[18]

When the focus was brought down to attitudes regarding premarital sexual intimacy the picture was generally the same; that is, the Danish showed up as homogeneously permissive, the Midwestern as heterogeneously moderate, and the Intermountain as homogeneously restrictive. In one test, average deviations of individual scores from mean scores on an Intimacy Permissiveness Scale were calculated for each sex in each of the three cultures. These average deviations for males and females respectively, were 1.29 and 1.83 for the Danish, 2.13 and 1.93 for the Midwestern, and 1.63 and 1.38 for the Intermountain — showing the first and last named to have the most homogeneous attitudes, and especially the males of the former and the females of the latter.[19] In another test, mean Intimacy Permissiveness Scores were compared between males and females within each of the cultures. Intersex differences were found to be lowest in the Danish, next lowest in the Intermountain, and highest in the Midwestern. Furthermore, it was only in the Midwestern that the male-female differences showed up as being statistically significant.[20]

What about attitudes regarding marital infidelity? Here too there is the strong suggestion of intersex homogeneity in both the Danish and Intermountain and of intersex heterogeneity in the Midwestern. This may be

110

loosely observed in Tables 1 and 2 and it becomes even clearer in Table 3. There (when the first two lines are omitted so as to compare for attitudes toward adultery only), it will be noted that none of the intersex differences were statistically significant in the Danish sample, only one was significant at the five percent level or above in the Intermountain sample, but four of the five differences were significant in the Midwestern sample.

But, when Table 4 is examined for cross-cultural differences in homogeneity regarding other factors almost the reverse of this picture is obtained. Whereas the Danish sample showed fewer significant male-female differences (Table 3), it now shows a larger number of significant differences for these ten additional factors — six, compared with four for the Midwestern and only one for the Intermountain. Apparently, sexual permissiveness, as it exists in Denmark, tends to level male and female attitudes regarding adultery while at the same time failing to level out many other differences within the sub-cultures; and, on the other hand, sexual restrictiveness, as it exists in the Mormon culture of Intermountain United States, seemingly tends to level most factors, including to some extent the male-female factor.

Conclusions

By means of questionnaire data from three university samples, we have been able to make both intra- and inter-cultural comparisons on attitudes toward marital infidelity. The three cultures under investigation were: sexually permissive Denmark; Midwestern United States with its somewhat typical or average sex norms; and sexually restrictive "Mormon Country" in the Intermountain region of the United States.

Major *intra-cultural* tendencies observed were: an overwhelming acceptance of the single standard of sexual morality, especially as applied to adultery; a decrease in approval of extra-marital sexual relationships with each advance in assumed level of involvement and/or commitment; and the suggestion of an association of disapproval concerning adultery with such factors as being a female, residing on a farm, being well advanced in college studies, having high social status, attending church frequently, having parents who are happily married, obtaining most of one's sex education from sources other than friends, carrying on either a going steady or engaged relationship with the opposite sex, being satisfied with one's level of interaction with the opposite sex, and having restrictive attitudes toward sexual matters generally. It must remembered, however, that the suggested associations of these last named ten factors with attitude toward adultery have not been fully established, since only some of the differences tested out as being statistically significant (see Tables 3 and 4).

Major *inter-cultural* observations were: a universal tendency for Danish respondents to be the most liberal or permissive of the three in their atti-

111

tudes toward sex; a tendency for Intermountain respondents to be the most conservative or restrictive in their sex attitudes, with Midwestern respondents in between but closer to the Intermountain than to the Danish; a greater tendency for Danish respondents to adhere to the single standard of sexual morality than for those in the other two cultures, with the Intermountain being second in this respect; a greater intersex homogeneity in attitude in the two extreme cultures, Danish and Intermountain (Table 3); and a paralleling homogeneity regarding other sub-cultural factors in the Intermountain, contrasted with the greatest heterogeneity, regarding these factors in the Danish (Table 4).

Apparently, the extremes of permissiveness (Denmark) and restrictiveness (Intermountain) *both* lead to a convergence of male and female attitudes regarding adultery — the former by freeing the female and the latter by restricting the male. Thus male-female heterogeneity in this regard is found to be greatest where the attitudes are most moderate (Midwestern).

But why is the most restrictive culture (Intermountain) also extremely homogeneous regarding additional factors, while the most permissive culture (Danish) shifts to the other extreme of heterogeneity? Though tentative, the following explanation seems plausible: In a sexually restrictive culture, such as the Mormon of the Intermountain region of the United States, morality tends to be rigidly fixed; things are regarded as either black or white, good or bad; in judging an act, little allowance is made for conditions or circumstances; hence a thing that is considered wrong, is wrong — period! This results in a narrow range of tolerance and discourages deviation and the development of sub-cultures. On the other hand, in a sexually permissive culture, such as the Danish of Scandinavia, morality is more flexible and hence more variable. Since the range of tolerance is greater in such a culture, it can be expected that sub-cultures will play a greater role.[21]

Nevertheless, at this stage in our theory building, these explanations are largely speculations. Their verification must await further cross-cultural research.

Notes

1. Previous publications include: Christensen, "Value Variables in Pregnancy Timing: Some Intercultural Comparisons," in Nels Anderson, editor, *Studies of the Family*, Göttingen, Germany: Vandenhoeck & Ruprecht, 1958, Vol. 3, pp. 29–45; Christensen, "Cultural Relativism and Premarital Sex Norms," *American Sociological Review*, Vol. 25, No. 1, February, 1960, pp. 31–39; Christensen, "Selected Aspects of Child Spacing in Denmark," *Acta Sociologica*, Vol. 4, No. 2, about August, 1959, pp. 35–45; Christensen and George R. Carpenter, "Timing Patterns in Premarital Sexual Intimacy: An Attitudinal Report on Three Modern Western Societies," *Marriage and*

Family Living, Vol. 24, No. 1, February, 1962, pp. 30–35; Christensen and George R. Carpenter, "Value-Behavior Discrepancies Regarding Premarital Coitus in Three Western Cultures," *American Sociological Review,* Vol. 27, No. 1, February, 1962, pp. 66–74.

2. The contrasting sex norms of these three cultures are described in the previous articles just cited. For the sake of anonymity, the three samples will be referred to throughout this paper simply as "Danish," "Midwestern," and "Intermountain."

3. Except that divorce comparisons were between the Danish and Midwestern only, since data were lacking for the Intermountain.

4. George Peter Murdock, *Social Structure* (New York: Macmillan, 1949), p. 265.

5. Morris Ploscowe, "Sex Offenses: The American Legal Context," *Law and Contemporary Problems,* Vol. 25, No. 2, Spring 1960, p. 219.

6. Alfred C. Kinsey *et al, Sexual Behavior in the Human Male.* (Philadelphia: W. B. Saunders Co., 1948), Chapter 19, "Extra-Marital Intercourse," pp. 583–594; *Sexual Behavior in the Human Female.* (Philadelphia: W. B. Saunders Co., 1953), Chapter 10, "Extra-Marital Coitus," pp. 409–445. Quotation from the latter volume, p. 436.

7. Eustace Chesser, *The Sexual, Marital and Family Relationships of the English Woman* (Watford: Hutchinson's Medical Publications Limited, 1956), pp. 441–2, 451–2; 516–9.

8. French Institute of Public Opinion, *Patterns of Sex and Love: A Study of the French Woman and Her Morals* (New York: Crown Publishers, Inc., 1961), "Adultery," pp. 179–194.

9. The author conducted this survey in Denmark while there on a Fulbright Research Fellowship during 1957–58. He was assisted on the American side by George R. Carpenter. Carpenter helped with the building of the questionnaire and administered it in the two American universities. His work was compiled into a Ph.D. dissertation filed at Purdue University in June, 1960.

10. On the other hand, these samples may not be *strictly* comparable, since a smaller and more selective proportion of the population attends a university in Denmark, as compared with the United States. The age and sex composition of all three samples are roughly equivalent, except for a slightly higher proportion in the upper ages in the Danish sample.

11. As stated in footnote *a*, p. 105, disapproval for *males* only was almost non-existent and hence, for practical purposes, can be disregarded.

12. Unless otherwise noted, significance tests throughout this paper are based upon Chi-Square analyses, with the .5 percent level of confidence used as the minimum acceptable standard.

13. Christensen and Carpenter, *loc. cit.;* see the article on timing Patterns. Approval of pre-marital coitus was shown to be lowest where the persons were dating randomly and casually, next where they were in love and going steady; and highest where they were in love and formerly engaged to be married.

14. Construction of the Intimacy Permissiveness Scale is explained in Christensen and Carpenter, *loc. cit.;* see the article on value-behavior discrepancies. None of the items used in the scale are the same as those reported in the present paper; yet, a correlation between the two, whereby the least permissive according to the scale give greatest disapproval of adultery, is entirely in line with expectation.

15. The only exception is where Midwestern males show up as being more accepting of a double standard of morality than Intermountain males (A of Table 1).

16. Furthermore, significance was at the 0.1 level in six of the tests and at the .05 level in only one (C of Table 1).

17. Additional evidence of greater adherence to the single standard in Denmark was provided by another part of the questionnaire. Ninety-four percent of the Danish respondents, as compared with 71 and 80 percent respectively, of Midwestern and Intermountain respondents, agreed with the statement: "Society should be no more critical of an unmarried woman's sexual behavior than of an unmarried man's sexual behavior; the same standard should apply to both."

18. Though both the Danish and Intermountain are homogeneous in regards to religion, the sexual permissiveness of the former may be due partly to the purely nominal nature of much of the church membership there, with little individual participation; and the sexual restrictiveness of the latter may be due partly to the vigorous program of the Mormon church, which involves considerable lay participation.

19. See George R. Carpenter, "Cross-Cultural Values as a Factor in Premarital Intimacy," Ph. D. dissertation, Purdue University, 1960, p. 96.

20. Christensen and Carpenter, *loc. cit.;* see the article on value-behavior discrepancies, especially Table 1.

In this same publication it was noted that, though intersex homogeneity regarding *attitude* was high for both Danish and Intermountain, when *behavior* was being considered only the Danish showed intersex homogeneity while the Intermountain showed the largest intersex *heterogeneity* of the three samples. Thus — though in all three cultures relatively more males than females (1) engaged in premarital coitus, (2) were promiscuous in their coital contacts, (3) experienced pleasant feeling the day following first coitus, and (4) behaved in accordance with their value systems when they engaged in premarital coitus — intersex *differences* in all of these things were found to be lowest in the Danish and highest in the Intermountain. Apparently sexual restrictiveness tends to converge male and female attitudes (in common with sexual permissiveness) but to diverge male and female behavior (in contrast with sexual permissiveness, which converges the behavior also).

All of this pertains to *premarital* sex, where data are available for both attitudes and behavior. Since the present article is limited to attitudes alone, this matter cannot be pursued further here.

21. At some future time, the author hopes to further pursue this lead concerning a possible relationship between cultural permissiveness-restrictiveness on the one hand and normative heterogeneity-homogeneity on the other hand; and, in turn, to relate what is found to the respective behavioral systems under study so as to get closer to an undestanding of what makes for cultural cohesion.

A highly suggestive analysis along these lines may be found in Ephraim H. Mizruchi and Robert Perrucci, "Norm Qualities and Differential Effects of Deviant Behavior: An Exploratory Analysis," scheduled for publication in a forthcoming issue of the *American Sociological Review.* These authors hold that the strain which follows deviant behavior is primarily the result of the quality of the normative order — essentially, whether this order is prescriptive or proscriptive (with the latter being productive of the greatest disorganization). This formulation may prove to be a reinforcing complement to our own previously reported theory regarding "value-behavior discrepancies."

7

Other Involvements

John F. Cuber and Peggy B. Harroff

The Significant Americans associate with one another for long and important periods at the office, studio, or laboratory. They come from the Utilitarian Marriages and from Intrinsic Marriages. Some are conscious of being mismated and are lonely in varying degree; some have an active sense of well-being where men and women are concerned. Some wish to put sexual matters as completely out of their minds as they can; others look upon the world of work as another hunting ground. Despite their intentions and often even promises to keep the personal and professional parts of life distinct, practically everyone acknowledges that it is difficult to pull off. Etiquette and morality aside, Eros asserts himself at the office.

Reference to the office is figurative. The Upper-Middle-Class man's office fans out on a large and diffuse stage. He works at airports and on trains, at cocktail parties and at the offices of his associates. He goes or is sent almost anywhere in the world for reasons of business or profession. He works any time of the day or night — on any day of the week. It is difficult, if not impossible, for him to draw a sharp line between work and private life.

His work force is made up of both sexes and he often works very closely with women. This atmosphere of diffuse sexuality opens up opportunities and fosters relationships which many find it difficult to limit to the legitimate purpose. And others don't even remotely intend to. Thus, any realistic account of relationships of men and women in the Upper Middle Class should include not only marriage relationships but also those which are formed and carried on in the broader context.

The Significant American's wife meanwhile typically has little intimate knowledge of the subtle and important aspects of his work world. Even in those cases where he would like to share his world with his wife, he often finds it hard to bridge the chasm fostered by specialized language and the technical activities, but most of all by the strange values which pervade the enterprise. Some men have said that they feel they suffer the consequences of an inability to communicate adequately with their wives about career matters of enormous importance.

> How do you go about explaining, without sounding like a sniveling coward, that you are *not* going to get that promotion, when your friend, who hasn't been there half as long gets his . . . How can you get her to understand what a snakepit this echelon of the corporation has become — and it won't get better for years. If she worked there, like my secretary, she'd know all about it almost before I do.

What knowledge of her husband's work world the wife has is usually fragmentary and stereotyped. It comes chiefly through secondary, symbolic evidences — income, promotions, changed titles, and miscellaneous feedback at the cocktail party or the protocol dinner.

Meanwhile the man's work associate very often is a woman, who is involved physically and emotionally in practically everything he does. She is a partner, a helpmate; her activities and efforts and attitudes must, if she is to be effective, dovetail neatly with his. A mutuality, if not identity, of purpose evolves. There is shared satisfaction when things go well, shared frustrations when they do not. Particularly where the relationship is enduring, it tends to take on a wifelike emotional and protective quality.

We use the phrase *office wife* for this widespread relationship with some hesitancy, since it conveys sexual meanings which the facts do not always justify. The office wife is usually a woman of superior intelligence and training who occupies a position of trust and responsibility as some important man's "Girl Friday." But it "says" much neater than it stays. A typical analysis came from a fifty-year-old executive secretary:

> You do get fond of him — almost in spite of yourself. At first you're a sort of chore girl, but as you learn the job better, you're entrusted with responsibility and get to know more and more about his worries, his humiliations, the ways his white hopes are dashed on the rocks of "policy." A decent human being cares, not in any impassioned way at first, but cares what happens to people

116

she works with closely in this way. . . . If he looks a little worn, you bring him a cup of coffee with just the right amount of cream and no sugar. . . . And you check his briefcase before the important conferences so that if he's forgotten an important paper in his harassment, you can spare him some embarrassment.

They say there is a gratifying sense of accomplishment in this, and that "if we do move into further involvement, particularly when there is reciprocation, it should be no surprise." The "further involvement" sometimes does and sometimes does not mean strictly sexual involvement. We made no attempt to take a census of either, although both admissions of sexual involvement and assurances to the contrary were frequently made.

There often is tacit, if not overt, reciprocation by the men. Men told us that they'd shared their private thoughts and fears and even hopes more with their office wives than they did with their wives at home. Repeatedly the phrase, "she understands better" came up. It seemed to us too, as we talked both with the wives and the office wives, that the latter do know more, and not merely more about the technical aspects of the enterprise. The claim of several office wives that "we know more about the deep, inner feelings of men than do their wives" was acknowledged as correct by many of the men. Why? Is it simply exposure, the many hours spent together, the mutual dependency? Or is there an acceleration of intimacy when the partner has continuing, important and common experience? Or is it the other side of the watershed of misalliance? Or the "unflattering polyeroticism of the species?"

One kind of answer came from a serious, forty-year-old scientist's assistant:

> We *do* have an advantage over the wives at home. If I help him draft a proposal that comes through with flying colors, I can really feel overjoyed at our mutual success, can feel that I have been a real part of it. But if the proposal falls through, I'm the one closest to his disappointment and I find deep comfort myself in my efforts to comfort him. . . . I haven't lost any status through his serious failures, as the wife at home often does. I have the advantage of understanding his feelings and knowing, after a time, better than anyone else how to take his mind off the slip-ups. Not just by patting him on the shoulder or smoothing his thinning locks, but by asking for his competent advice on the charts that are being worked out for the next proposal, or by reminding him of the tremendous reception his last speech had, and wondering aloud if that main theme shouldn't be worked into the next prospectus. The wife at home (and I'm one too) suffers by her distance from a very important part of her man's life. The woman at the office shares deep satisfactions whether the day goes well or not — she is needed and appreciated and she knows it.

And so the team is formed, solidified, and there is reported to be a deep personalization in working this way, for both.

Meanwhile the boss and the Girl Friday are both likely to be married — and not to each other. Kindnesses and considerations and carings of the sort which frequently develop are, by conventional definition, disloyalties to the spouse who has prior and superior rights. One must be secretive as a rule about the deeper meanings and sharings of the office partnership. This causes the relationship to become closer than it may intrinsically need to be, "because we share the secret knowledge that one or both of us must be protected from exposure at home."

Even when the husband is "understanding, broad-minded, emancipated, and all the rest," more than a little strain is created at home when the wife's work hours are not totally predictable, when in some occasional excited way she allows it to be known that the job is not so onerous after all, and when she shows defensiveness if some ungenerous observation is made about her employer. Such are the telltale marks of the office wife; "and even if they seem to tell things that are not true, the real-wife side of the total woman often knows when the office side has been exposed."

It is not always the case, however, that the office wife or her male counterpart is forced to play peek-a-boo with the spouse at home. Occasionally we found that this mode is understood and accepted. One wife, formerly a career woman herself, who is generally liberal in her views and self-consciously philosophical about serious matters, characterized the situation as:

> . . . not only inevitable but an altogether sensible way in which to work out a life in this crazy, fragmentized world. . . . What if she *is* a little more meaningful to him than interacting with a business machine? . . . In another time it would have been some other arrangement.

In addition to the close relationships in the office there are the various opportunities which present themselves when a Significant American travels. Much of the time he is "entertained" on his trips or does some semi-official entertaining himself. Variations cover a wide range, from activities appropriate for the local Sunday School picnic to a binge of wining and dining and call girls suggestive of the Roman holiday.

In the course of our conversations we came across several instances of "total entertainment." For example, one of the top men in a branch office of one of America's largest corporations keeps a small locked box in his office containing a card file of the important men who come to town with some regularity. Only he and his private secretary have access to the box. This file contains information on whether and what each man drinks and whether a girl is to be made available during his stay on company business. Many of our informants said that it is simply taken for granted that entertaining will include the privileges of bed as well as board, and both in some form suitable to the status of the guest. This is, as a public relations man put it, merely:

> ... the time-honored tradition of proper respect for the traveler away from home. If the corporation provides a fifty-dollar-a-night call girl (by another name of course) instead of the host's wife for the night, as among the Eskimo, the difference is trivial.

When the entertainment is not provided by the host, or when one is en route or has an evening to himself, invitations "to play a little" are said to be hard to avoid.

> Wherever you go — to the cocktail lounge for a nightcap, to the theatre or concert, or just drop off in the lobby to scan a paper — there are other unattached people, you strike up a conversation, and bingo!

Sometimes these friendships are brief; they may or may not have an open sexual element, but the opportunities are there and the rationalizations to capitalize on them come easily. Over and over, from both men and women, we heard the same explanation. As one woman said:

> After all, we're a broad-minded group of people, both the guys and the gals, and not stuffy about the old-fashioned notions. And besides, a fellow or a girl needs to have some fun once in a while, to let off steam and to raise a little hell.

The whole routine reminds some of them of earlier days when they were "civilian servicemen" (and women). Said a writer:

> About the only difference is that today's "girls" (always a "nice girl" who is somebody's best friend) are the camp girls a little better put up and a little more expensive. Even if you don't care too much for that kind of a night, it's practically taken for granted. If someone else supplies the girls and the liquor and the hotel room — it's sort of a package deal. So why not?

These practices have passed the stage of being naughty oddities which only a few people know about. They are somewhat standardized, understood, almost institutional. Everyone in this group knows what they are and uses a consistent terminology for them, like the "pickup" which is described in many subtypes. Even those who profess to take no part personally are mostly not condemnatory or only mildly so.

Actual participation in these opportunities, of course, varies. Some men and women "have no part of it," either because they are "well taken care of at home" or because they profess "moral standards which do not condone such behavior under *any* circumstances." Others participate freely, but they do so on the fringes of their lives. A consulting engineer who rose rapidly to an executive vice-presidency, who called himself a "family man with a nice place in the country," described the practice of "living a little off the land":

> So you pick up a cute piece once in a while at an office party or when you're on the coast. She knows what she's doing and she likes it too. So what? I'm not at home, so I can't do the old girl any good anyway.... No, there's no continuity. Hell, I don't even know their names if I should want to look them up again.

Sometimes, however, there *is* continuity, especially where the object of sexual attraction is more continually available.

> Sure, I sleep off and on with Ross' secretary. It's not really an affair. Neither of us is exclusive about it. We just like each other that way.... Every once in a while we look at each other and sort of know it's about that time again. . . .

Other men and women have moved clearly beyond the mere business-related opportunities for expressing free-floating sexuality. Married or not, they acknowledge that they "live and date like single people."

For the married middle-aged of either sex, the date may lead to sex thrill or to an intellectual companionship at a lecture on nuclear physics. It may be cast in a romantic atmosphere, or it may simply be a somewhat longer than necessary ride home from some essential activity "like choir practice or having to work late at the office." The erotic element, the amount of secrecy, the amount of love involvement — all these and everything else they told us about the pairing is essentially parallel to the customary behavior of single people.

One of these married women is now in her late forties. Her husband is a prominent professional with a national reputation, highly respected in the metropolis where he works. They have two children — successful in school and immensely talented.

> When I tell you that I feel quite happy, I don't mean that I am happy just with my marriage — or any other one I can imagine having. My happiness is due to my wit and luck in working out a good life. . . .
> First of all, I escape home through a job. It pays pretty well but, don't tell my boss, I'd work for nothing — just to have something interesting and challenging to do and to be around interesting people — chiefly, I suppose, men. . . . Then too, my husband and I live very independent lives — work and play — and you might as well know — sex too. When I tell you this, don't get the idea that we sleep around promiscuously whenever a chance comes along. . . . We just live more or less like single people — when something interesting comes along, for either of us, we pursue it. There may be satisfactions, mediocrity, or even

120

disappointment at the end of the rainbow. But it's usually a nice trip. . . . And this doesn't mean we have separate rooms at home — or even beds. Far from it! Probably half of the time — you see what I mean — it's us together. And the rest of the time we're wherever luck takes us. . . . It's all kinds — one-night thrills, affairs that have lasted a year or two, a couple (of the affairs) have drifted apart and then been reactivated, so to speak. . . . Yes, I'd say my husband and I love each other — we just don't own each other.

It's hard to say how we got into this pattern. . . . One outgrows adolescence slowly and the one-and-only-and-forever routine is sort of for kids, don't you think? . . .

Gosh no, we're not unique. We know dozens of couples like us. The details are different — sometimes only one of the couple wants freedom — sometimes they're not as open about it as we are. Sometimes they seem to feel less sure of themselves than we do — but it amounts to the same thing. . . . I'd say that this (pattern) may be present from the very start of a marriage — a straight continuation of the single stage. Or it may start later. . . . I suppose it could end, but I don't know anyone who has given it up. Of course, none of our friends are really *old* yet.

A single woman, forty-seven, a former university professor, is now employed in a high-ranking governmental position. She explains the role from the viewpoint of the unmarried woman. She has never married, but says:

I prefer to date married men because they have a more natural attitude toward sex — single men are so self-conscious about it. . . . The best men *are* married but they also are quite available.

She has tried continued relationships with the same man.

. . . but it tends to get dull, or else gets too serious. I have a very married kind of attitude toward sex in relation to the rest of life — I want neither too much nor too little emphasis on it. I want it only in a larger relationship and in perspective. . . . I wear a diaphragm on every date. I don't always need it; and I insist that the rewards of the date do not depend on a sexual climax. . . . No, there's no problem around here in finding as good a milieu as married people have. No one cares any more, if you don't go out of your way to offend — well, like arriving without luggage, or being overdressed, oh, you know. . . .

Yes, I'd say the pattern is common in Washington and other places in the East where I spend most of my time. . . .

She spends several weekends a year with men at homes of friends, some married and some not, who know about the arrangements, even though many of them do not practice such. She does not drink. She has had two pregnancies: "No regrets — except that I wasn't too bright at first and got pregnant when I didn't need to."

She averages two dates per week, with "about, oh, I'd say, every other weekend spent somewhere as a pair."

A man in his early fifties, holding a distinguished position in the communications industry, makes his point more philosophically:

> Marriage is simply an institutional arrangement for the immature — for the people who can't stand the strain of regulating their lives themselves — who need laws and public opinion and the Church to tell them what to do and what not to do. So, I'm all for marriage for the country and for most of the people. But not for me. . . . To do my best work, I need to be unencumbered — and even with the most ideal marriage I've ever seen, there is a lot of simple encumbrance. . . . You're probably wondering about sex. Well, I'm no eunuch — just disgustingly average, by Kinsey's tables, for my age and educational level. Now, there's no problem of finding good — in fact, I'd say excellent — sex partners wherever I've been — and that's all over the world. Before long you learn how to look for it and then it comes to meet you.
>
> That doesn't mean that all my sex life is a binge sort of thing. I have two sort of steady girls I have known and slept with off and on for twenty years — one is married; the other one isn't. I see them about as often as some of the career military men and State Department attachés see their wives.
>
> I have one son — eighteen now — a freshman at ———— (an Ivy League college). He was brought up by his mother and I see them both a great deal — only socially the past two or three years. Neither of us wanted to marry and, being Catholic, we just couldn't condone abortion, so she just decided to see it through. There was less social difficulty than we expected. . . .

Despite the well-known hazards purported to beset them, a rather high incidence of relatively enduring affairs was acknowledged by the men and women we spoke to. They vary widely from one another not only in details, but also with respect to the purpose they are said by the participants to fulfill. While sometimes they compensate for admittedly bad marriages which are held together for the sake of children or respectability or religion, at other times they involve people who say their marriages are fundamentally good. There seems to be a growing tolerance of the idea that some men and women need or want enduring sexual as well as platonic relationships with more than one person concurrently. Many who tolerate, or even approve, this kind of relationship admit that they wish the facts were otherwise, but "given human nature as it is and the world as it is, it just cannot be any other way."

122

Condonement of such relationships seems to come from a variety of motives. Sometimes, as in the following account by a wife, it comes more from resignation and empathy than from clear commitment to the practice.

> Well, I've been a party to an affair for almost ten years now. . . . No, I said I was a party, not that I *had* the affair. You see, it all started this way. About ten years ago I noticed that my husband and the woman next door discovered a compelling interest in trimming the roses and the hedge between our two houses. They had practically trimmed all the leaves off. She's a fine person and I guessed they would like to know each other better. I knew they both liked bowling and I suggested they go bowling together. Her husband was away so I baby-sat with her kids. Since then, on two nights a week my husband and this woman go bowling together. . . . They usually come home about two. We don't say much about it, although everything is perfectly clear to all four of us directly concerned. . . . The neighbors? Well, by now they largely ignore it — at least we're not ostracized at any of the neighborhood social affairs. They may gossip about it, but there's so much else to gossip about that I don't suppose we get more than our fair share. A few years ago one woman did mention it to me and I quietly assured her that I knew all about it. That closed the case.
>
> I would say that I am in love with my husband and the woman next door is in love with hers. Also, of course, she and my husband are in love with each other. . . . I don't think this has had any effect on our sex life as far as I can see. Of course, it's hard to say how things would be if they were different, but right from the start, I must admit that I thought it would either improve or worsen our intimate relations but it didn't do either.
>
> No, I have not had an affair myself, simply for the reason that no good prospect came along. I am willing, but not eager. I can wait, but I won't fight it if it should come. . . . There are many designs for living. This one is ours. If it's not ideal, it's better than a lot I've seen, and whose business is it anyway?

Sometimes the "other involvement" was explained as demonstrably beneficial to both husband and wife. In one case the private secretary of a high state official (appointed) often travels with him and when at home serves as his hostess on virtually all protocol occasions. Her charm and poise are obviously appreciated by the man, and she herself enjoys the role. Whether or not there is sexual involvement we do not know, but the wife seemed untroubled by the possibility; she gave us this explanation:

> Bill does half his work over dinner or cocktails — he just *has* to do a lot of entertaining. . . . I'm sure he'd rather use our home, but I just can't do it. We tried — and I'm just not the hostess

type. I'm a wife and mother and that's all I want to be. Bill's different when he's home with me and the children — he's relaxed and fun. But when we entertained here at home, he was like a different person — all charged up, critical of me — I was always scared to death I'd do the wrong thing. I would get sick for days before an important dinner. . . . I'd get in such a state of nerves I didn't even recognize myself. I just can't try to be something I'm not. . . .

I don't really understand Jane (the secretary) — but in a way I admire her — and Bill certainly needs her. I don't see how she can be so efficient — and she always looks right and says the right thing, never forgets names or faces — and everyone likes her. That's important. . . .

Bill's practically taken over one of the private dining rooms at the ——— Hotel for business and I can't tell you what a relief that is to me. . . . When he's home now we can just be a family — and I know he loves me and the children. He's a good man — and I'm a very happy woman. (They live in the country in a rambling nineteenth-century house so that she can "indulge in the good old-fashioned homemaking arts." She gardens, bakes, and sews, and cheerfully supervises their six children.)

In still other instances, the affairs are almost quasi marriages. A financier, who called himself "a fifteen-year veteran of a love affair" was one of several who do not link love and marriage in a conventional manner.

Frankly, I'm through with marriage. I've had it! Aside from the practical conveniences it brings, I can't see any advantages at all. We don't plan children at our age; we love and trust each other, and when we're together we both know it's because it's what we want more than anything else. When I go to her I do so knowing that this is what I want — it's not out of a sense of duty or convenience or because it's what everyone expects of me. The only thing that holds us together is our love for each other and that's the way it ought to be for a man and woman. In marriage everything goes stale. That hasn't happened to us in all these years. Why should we marry? It's more risk than it's worth.

Where the arrangement is more clearly a compromise, the man and woman in such a pair sometimes see it differently. The circumstances, of course, may be more difficult for one than for the other. We have heard a great deal of impassioned resentment concerning the hard compromise.

We live constantly in a state of suspension. I never doubt that he loves me, but sometimes it just doesn't make sense that he's still married to someone else. I know in his profession it's risky to have a divorce on your record, but there are risks this way too. What if people would find out about us? What would happen to

124

his career then? It's such a strain to be covering up all the time — worrying about being seen where we shouldn't be, worrying about an apartment being "bugged," waiting for something to hit the newspapers. I don't know if I have the courage to go on like this indefinitely. We have so few times when we can both get away, when we can find an atmosphere of freedom. They're the times that sustain me. But must it *always* be this way? I feel as if we're living with something tragic hanging over our heads. And I can see no hope for any change. Do other people live out their loves this way?

In other instances habituation to conditions at first considered to be compromise brought an awareness that "one fits the role better than he at first thought."

At first we talked a lot about getting married when we could both get free. But you know, I don't think it would really work. We're both such forceful people, I'm not sure we could stand being together all the time. When we meet now it's violent and passionate and wonderful — and when we part, it's with a deep tearing at our insides. But we've gotten used to this — and when we're apart, we're both more productive than we've ever been before. Her latest shows have been her greatest successes and I've never had things more in hand. Knowing and loving her is the biggest thing in my life. She has sharpened my sensibilities, my creativity — I think I would collapse without her. We've had to work out an elaborate intrigue, but our life is full of crescendos — we do more real living in the hours we spend together than most people do in a lifetime. But maybe the living would be too rich for a steady diet. We both have commitments to other lives and maybe it's best that we do.

Another concluded casually:

It's like anything else in life. You try to balance out pluses and minuses and come up with something which is the best you can have under the circumstances. Nothing's ideal. But, all things considered, this is a pretty darn good arrangement for two people in love.

It is difficult, we found, to draw a line between enduring affairs such as these and arrangements which border so close on marriage that to call them "affairs" is to use a misnomer. Except for the legalities, the relationship is like that in marriage — the man (already legally married to someone else) assumes financial responsibility, spends as much time as he can with his "real wife," feels in love, and is identified as "father" by the children of this mating. The first marriage is the only legal one, of course, and that wife the recognized "status" wife in the formal community. The younger of the two relationships, although not necessarily involving a younger woman, must necessarily exist *sub rosa*, which is apparently not impossible to do in New York City or Chicago or San Francisco — and even in smaller places, we found.

These persons offered varied reasons for their conduct:

> Now you tell me, what is a man supposed to do when his Church tells him he can't divorce and remarry, even though he and his so-called wife haven't really been man and wife for eleven years. We have nothing in common, not even spunk enough to fight, and both want nothing more than to be free of each other. I'm not taking that dictate like a slob — I've done something about it. . . . Sure, I'd rather have it clean and neat and honorable — especially for Helen. It's harder for her and for Chris too. Could be real bad some day. But Helen and I were in love and that love wasn't the kind of thing you get in motels and Caribbean cruises — it was whole love and that means a place called home and a kid — to see yourself and her in another human life. It's worth taking the risks for — and God, I know they're big risks.

A similar situation occurred in several cases in which the wife refused to give a divorce. It should not be assumed that spite or other negative sentiments necessarily underlie such refusals. Sometimes we found that the considerations involved saving public face or protecting a family name or fortune.

A case in point involves a physician who has built a successful and highly lucrative partnership in a private clinic with a small group of other doctors. Almost all of his wealth is tied up in the clinic — real estate, equipment, and so on — and in order to make a reasonable financial settlement with his estranged wife, he says it would be necessary to dissolve the clinic partnership. This would be embarrassing professionally, he fears, as well as financially.

So he and his wife have worked out a private agreement under the terms of which he maintains his home as before and spends some time there, and also maintains another home in a nearby city with his "real wife" and their two children with whom he spends considerable time, but not so openly as with the "status family." "In one way it's a hell of a life and in another, I feel so lucky that I'm not inclined to complain much." Both his wife and his "wife" confirmed the accuracy of the facts he gave us.

In other instances the motivations for refusing divorce are not strictly emotional ones. A few wives said that they even cooperate with their husband's maintenance of coexistent "marriages" because they recognize the legitimacy of the second relationship and yet do not wish to terminate their present marriages, which they still find somewhat satisfactory. It is not quite resignation — there is sometimes clear empathy for the second relationship, even though the wife nevertheless intends to retain her nominal marital

126

status. One wife, estranged from her husband for almost ten years, prefers to maintain the form of the marriage, even though she gets no intrinsic benefits.

> Of course I can see that they have the same right to happiness that anyone else does. I'd even go so far as to say that they have the *moral* right to it. . . . But why should *I* tear up *my* life — live as a divorcee, run the risk of financial problems later on when I'm older. . . . So, we worked it out like this. I'm sure he'd rather be free, and she too, and I feel for them. But I'm not sacrificial enough to go the whole way. . . . It's worked pretty well now for eight years.

They go on with these arrangements as the best they can work out for the psychological realities at hand, although they are quite aware that such patterns are not condoned by most people, even in their own somewhat practical and liberal class.

We discussed these relationships with an attorney in order to secure information relative to their legal status. He said that he had several clients who have evolved patterns of this type. He also confirmed our findings that the second "marriage" did not originate necessarily because of any manifest failure of the first marriage or necessarily from a refusal of the first spouse to agree to a divorce. The principals involved simply recognize "either that certain personalities cannot be encompassed in any one relationship or that compelling relationships between adults can arise after marriage as well as before." They honor the latter as they did the former ones as "being morally valid." As a rule, the first wife maintains the fiction publicly that she does not know about the second "marriage." Since she is likely to be in Russell Lynes' sense an "upper bohemian" rather than a true one, she finds it necessary to do so in order to pay homage to the public sanction system.

This is all not as unrewarding for the first wife, some said, as it might at first seem. She finds that freeing her husband from the restrictions of monogamy frees her too, and she may express her freedom in playing the role as if single, or in an affair of her own. Or she may do neither of these; she may simply continue to participate in a less than one hundred per cent relationship with her husband. Said one wife: "Having half of my husband is worth more to me than having one hundred per cent of any other man I have ever known." This was said uncomplainingly and without pretense that she would not prefer it otherwise. It was simply an acknowledgment of the status quo and a candid recognition that "life cannot always be fashioned from the maxims of the schoolgirl's copybook."

A clergyman in a large, predominantly Upper-Middle-Class congregation told us that he was aware of numerous such arrangements and had observed that

> . . . these always seem to be extremely vital and energetic people — people who have the capacity and the desire to live unusually fully. They seem to want to live two lifetimes in one life span.

And it does seem as if a few of them are able to achieve such an ambition with more vigor than other people can muster for one mating.

All is not rosy for the people with these *de facto* "marriages." Sometimes the problems and dilemmas are practical — insufficient money, how to divide one's leisure time, what to tell the children and when, and since the man is usually an important one, what to do if there is public exposure. They told us that they have discovered long since that one must stand ready to pay if one chooses to dine. Sometimes they "may misjudge the size of the check and may have to wash the dishes for a long time to pay off the bill." But typically this doesn't happen. They seem to move through life about as inconspicuously as anyone else — whether more totally fulfilled or not, one cannot objectively say.

The moralistic interpretation of all this would seem to some that these men and women are irresponsible and "sex mad" and that we have here presented an outline of their sordid sins. What such an interpretation misses may be the nub of the matter however. As we have pointed out previously, there is a pervasive loneliness for many of these people where man-and-woman matters are concerned. There is often a deep and serious lack of communication between many married pairs. This inability to share undermines the monogamous commitment. Couples may, and typically do, share various superficials, but these are not enough to dissipate the overwhelming awareness for so many that their spouses are "like different breeds." The strictly sexual stresses are there too, but mostly they are only outward symptoms of more encompassing loneliness, of desertion, or of felt need for a fuller participation than has yet been attained. Much research has documented the fact that men and women vary enormously in the amount and kind of sexual expression they need and desire. Often they are very unequally yoked in marriage in this respect, and yet do not wish — or one of them doesn't — to dissolve the marriage so that each may try again.

It should be clear, however, that these modes of adaptation are not necessarily or exclusively sexual with respect to the satisfactions which they are said to bring. The patterns, we were told repeatedly, are typically established to relieve more total stress. The enduring affairs and much of the dating too, have a low sexual component as measured by frequency or centrality of sex. While short on sex, they are said by the participants to be long on understanding and empathy. Yet there is no denying that the sexual valence is there. Typically, it is not there as sex per se; it is more an emergence of human totality. "After all, we are male and female," said one, "and I suppose sex is the ultimate means of communication between people who care."

This may all seem to be a scandalously amoral dismissal of a serious matter. How about higher motivations, good example, and responsible citizenship? To say nothing about proper respect for the proscriptions of the Deity. Is personal satisfaction all there is to it? Is a self-focused hedonism the appropriate end for human conduct? The Significant Americans whose relationships have provided the substance for this chapter find such "cosmic considerations" largely irrelevant and immaterial. The deviants are rarely, if ever, troubled by such matters. Obviously, they don't enjoy the acrimonious remarks about themselves, but they mostly shrug their shoulders and go on their way, convinced that they have the *right* to seek love and happiness in their own way. Said a doctor, "I have examined my conscience in the matter and I feel anything but guilty." While hardly a definitive discourse on morality, his remarks do reflect what these people think about their own situations. On the whole they are neither troubled nor self-consciously philosophical about what they are doing. They are simply making the best of the opportunities presented by a confused and contradictory societal context in order to satisfy their deeply human needs.

8

The Sociology of Mate Swapping: Or the Family that Swings Together Clings Together

Duane Denfeld and Michael Gordon

In the early decades of this century, and to a certain extent still today, social scientists equated deviant behavior with disease and set about to find the cures. The tone of this early perspective is nicely illustrated by the following excerpt:

> The study of social pathology is undertaken not to breed pessimism but to furnish a rational ground for faith in the future of the world. The diseases of society, like the diseases of the human body, are to be studied so that remedies may be found for them where they exist, but most of all, that by a larger wisdom the number of diseases may be reduced to the lowest terms and we may set ourselves to social tasks with the ideal of conquering them altogether (Smith, 1911).

So firm a commitment to the extirpation of "social pathology" obviously precluded consideration of any contributions its phenomena might make to the social order.

More recently there has been a reappraisal of the role of deviant behavior in society. Albert Cohen (1959), for one, has admonished his colleagues for equating deviance with social disorganization, and other sociologists have begun to focus their attention on deviance as a societal process rather than

---

Reprinted with permission of the editor from the *Journal of Sex Research*, Vol. 6, No. 2, May 1971, pp. 85–100.

as a social disease. Howard Becker, a leading proponent of this new position has argued:

> We ought not to view it [deviant behavior] as something special, as depraved or in some magical way better than other kinds of behavior. We ought to see it simply as a kind of behavior some disapprove of and others value, studying the processes by which either or both perspectives are built up and maintained (Becker, 1963).

Perhaps of greater significance for the viewpoint of this paper are the opinions of the students of deviance who claim that deviance may support, not undermine, social order; among the most eloquent of these is Kai Erikson:

> ... Deviant behavior is not a simple kind of leakage which occurs when the machinery of society is in poor working order, but may be, in controlled quantities, an important condition for preserving the stability of social life. Deviant forms of behavior, by marking the outer edges of group life, give the inner structure its special character and thus supply the framework within which the people of the group develop an orderly sense of their own cultural identity (Erikson, 1966).

We shall maintain that only from the perspectives found in the writings of Becker, Erikson, and their associates can the social scientist understand mate swapping and the role it plays in American society.

In this country there has been a tradition of great ideological commitment to the importance of confining sexual behavior in general, but sexual intercourse in particular, to the sanctity of the marital bed. Concomitantly there has also been a rich history of institutionalized nonmarital sex. One of the foremost historians of Colonial family life has noted that "the cases of premarital fornication [in Colonial New England] by husband and wife were evidently numerous" (Calhoun, 1960). Further, prostitution never appears to have been completely absent from these shores. However, it was not until the second half of the nineteenth century that sexual morality and prostitution especially became a national concern. David Pivar in his history of the Social Purity Movement in the United States claims that

> during the nineteenth century many social evils existed, but *the* Social Evil was prostitution.
>
> Prostitution, its development and spread, constituted the primary element in the moral crisis that shook Western civilization in the latter decades of the nineteenth century. A premonition that traditional morality was failing permeated the fabric of American life, and reformers increasingly expressed alarm over

a general decay in morality. Religionists and moralists found decay manifestly evident in official life, but most strikingly in the man-woman relationship (Pivar, 1965).

Attention to the destructive effects of prostitution did not cease with the coming of the new century, or even with the moral revolutions supposedly wrought by World War I; in a very much milder form it is present still.

Nevertheless, in 1937 Kingsley Davis published a paper that was to cause many social scientists, at least, to reappraise this great "Social Evil." He advanced what has since come to be known as the "safety-valve" model of deviance, developing with great insight and much cogency the idea that

> ... the attempt of society to control sexual expression, to tie it to social requirements, especially the attempt to tie it to the durable relation of marriage and the rearing of children, or to attach men to a celibate order, or to base sexual expression on love, creates the opportunity for prostitution. It is analogous to the black market, which is the illegal but inevitable response to an attempt to fully control the economy. The craving for sexual variety, for perverse satisfaction, for novel and provocative surroundings, for ready and cheap release, for intercourse free from entangling cares and civilized pretense — all can be demanded from the woman whose interest lies solely in price (Davis, 1966).

A further point implicit in Davis' argument is that since the prostitute by "virtue" of her profession is, for the most part, excluded from the ranks of potential spouses, the risk of romantic involvement which may threaten a man's marriage is greatly reduced.

Let us stop at this point to look more closely at the underlying assumption of this "safety-valve" model of deviance: a society may provide certain institutionalized outlets for forms of behavior which are condemned by the prevailing legal and/or moral system. This is not to say that in every society all deviants will find some structured way of satisfying their proclivities with minimal danger of running afoul of the law. A good case in point here would be pedophilia. With the virtual disappearance of child brothels, the pedophile must, if he wishes to gratify his need, engage in acts which almost certainly will result in a confrontation with the police; in contrast is the man who frequents house of prostitution for some unusual form of sexual activity. Therefore, the "safety-valve" model does not assume that *all* forms of deviant behavior will be provided with outlets, but rather that *some* of those forms for which "frustration and discontent may lead to an attack on the rules themselves and on the social institutions they support" (Cohen, 1966) will be provided with outlets. So, then, in the case of prostitution (or any other form of deviance), the "safety-valve" model does not explain why it exists, but why it is tolerated: presumably it is supportive of monogamous marriage. It should be emphasized that this idea is best thought of as an

132

hypothesis, not as a law. Interestingly enough, one of the few other convincing applications of the "safety-valve" model also applies to sexual behavior.

Ned Polsky recently applied Davis' ideas concerning prostitution to pornography, and claimed that the latter was a functional alternative to the former:

> In saying that prostitution and pornography are, at least in modern societies, functional alternatives, I mean that they are different roads to the same desired social ends. Both provide for the discharge of what the society labels antisocial sex, i.e., impersonal, nonmarital sex: prostitution provides this via real intercourse with a real sex object, and pornography provides it via masturbatory, imagined intercourse with a fantasy object (Polsky, 1967).

He places particular emphasis on a point which Davis mentions but does not elaborate, viz., that prostitution and pornography cater to a considerable amount of what, in the parlance of the prostitute, is known as "kinky" sex — oral, anal, masochistic, fetishistic, etc. To this extent pornography, more than prostitution, provides a safety valve for those sexual inclinations for which no institutionalized behavioral outlets exist, e.g., pedophilia, which we have already mentioned.

In both the Davis and Polsky papers the focus is almost exclusively, if not exclusively, on *male* non-marital sex. Males prostituting themselves for females has never been common, perhaps merely because, apart from their economic positions, males are constitutionally less suited for frequent and prolonged intercourse. Drawing largely on the Kinsey studies, Polsky argues that pornography is largely produced for, and consumed by, males. Kinsey found that relatively few women are aroused by pornography, and even fewer use it as grist for the masturbatory fantasy mill (Kinsey, 1953). While no reliable systematic data are available, there is some indication that at least one form of pornography, the "stag" film, is migrating from the fraternity house and VFW lodges — though not abandoning them altogether — to the suburban home, i.e., it is now being viewed by heterosexual audiences (Knight and Alpert, 1967). A replication now of the section of the Kinsey study dealing with female response to pornography might yield some surprising results.

If, in fact, pornography is now becoming more of a heterosexual item — and we must emphasize again that this is by no means documented — it provides support for the main argument of this paper: mate swapping (we will use the terms "mate swapping" and "swinging" synonymously) is an outgrowth of the dramatic changes that have taken place in this century in the position of women in American society and, more crucially, changes that have taken place in the conceptions of female sexuality and female sexual

133

rights. While the contention that women are now seeing and enjoying pornography more than was so previously cannot be proved, there is no lack of documentation for the larger changes noted above. Evidence can be found both in the realm of sexual ideology and behavior.

One of the most vivid indicators of the degree to which American women have come into their own sexually since 1900 is the marriage manual. Michael Gordon [1971] has recently completed an extensive study of American marital education literature for the period 1830 to 1940. Perhaps the most striking finding to emerge from his work is that the transformation in the prevailing conception of female sexuality, and marital sex in general, took place in the first four decades of this century. The following passage is based on the Gordon article.

Throughout most of the nineteenth century the commonly held attitude toward sexual intercourse was that it was, unhappily, required for the perpetuation of the species. Not only was it an unfortunate necessity, but also a dangerous one at that. Frequent indulgence by the male in the pleasures of the flesh could lead to an enervating loss of the "vital fluids" contained in the sperm; for the female it could result in nervous and constitutional disorders. In short, sex was a seriously debilitating business. As the century drew to a close we begin to get rumblings of acceptance of marital sex as something which, apart from its procreative function, was beneficial to the marriage, but such views are very much in the minority even in the 1890's.

With the first decade of the twentieth century, however, and reaching — if the reader will pardon the expression — its climax in the 1930's, there is a growing belief not only in the fact that women experience sexual desire (which in its own way is held to be as strong as that of men), but also that this desire should be satisfied, most appropriately in intercourse resulting in simultaneous orgasm. What we observe in these decades, then, is sex moving, ideologically, from an act whose prime purpose is procreation to one whose prime purpose is recreation, a shift which has been commented on by others (Foote, 1948; Sprey, 1969). Because this development has been extensively documented in the article by Gordon, there is no need to explore it further. Let it suffice to say that by 1930 the concern with marital sex, its "artistry" and technique has reached such proportions as to allow characterization of the authors of marriage manuals of the time as proponents of a "cult of mutual orgasm."

The increasing acceptance of the pleasures of marital sex seems to have had an impact on a number of areas relevant to the theme of this paper; possibly the most important of these is prostitution. To the best of our knowledge there are no data available which support the contention that since 1900 prostitution has been a declining profession. However, it has been claimed (Kinsie, 1967) that there has been a reduction in the number of brothels in American cities; furthermore, there is good evidence on which

134

to base the opinion that premarital intercourse with prostitutes is declining:

> The frequencies of premarital sexual relations with prostitutes are more or less constantly lower in the younger generations of all educational levels. . . . In most cases the average frequencies of intercourse with prostitutes are down to two-thirds or even one-half of what they were in the generation that was most active 22 years ago (Kinsey, 1948).

This, it could be reasoned, may well be related to a finding reported in the second Kinsey volume:

> Among the females in the sample who were born before 1900, less than half as many had had the pre-marital coitus as among the females born in any subsequent decade. . . . For instance, among those who were still unmarried by age twenty-five, 14 per cent of the older generation had had coitus, and 36 per cent of those born in the next decade. This increase in the incidence of premarital coitus, and the similar increase in the incidence of premarital petting, constitute the greatest changes which we have found between the patterns of sexual behavior in the older and younger generations of American females (Kinsey, 1953).

It should be noted by way of qualification, that Kinsey also found that most women who did have premarital intercourse had it exclusively with the men they eventually married. These two phenomena — the decreasing amount of premarital contact with prostitutes for males and the increasing amount of premarital sex for women — give credence to our argument that the acceptance of female sexuality and the pleasures of marital sex has grown in this century. It is unusual now to find a man saying he has intercourse with prostitutes because his idealized wife-mother image of his spouse prevents him from carrying out the act with her (Winick, 1962). Furthermore, there are also attitudinal data on the breakdown of the double standard in this country (Reiss, 1967).

It is implicit in our thesis that shifts in attitudes toward female sexuality, premarital sex, and, especially, marital sex, which we have been discussing, are crucial to the understanding of mate swapping as an institutionalized form of extramarital sex. Another factor which has undoubtedly also made a contribution to the development of mate swapping, or at least has facilitated its growth, is the revolution in contraceptive techniques that has occurred in the past decade. A study done in 1960, based on a national probability sample, found the following order of frequency for contraceptive techniques: condom, 50%; diaphragm, 38%; rhythm, 35%; douche, 24%; withdrawal, 17%, and others in small percentages. (The total exceeds 100% because many couples used more than one method (Whelpton, *et al.*, 1966)). Similar studies are yet to be made for the last years of the 1960's, but some comparative data are available. Tietze (1968) estimated that as of mid-1967 there were 6½ million women in this country on the pill, and somewhere between one and two million using the IUD. A recent Gallup poll estimated that 8½ million American women were on the pill (Newsweek, February 9, 1970). Figures such as these allow us to estimate that about 10% of the fecund American women take the pill and another 1% use the IUD.

The emergence of chemical and intra-uterine birth control methods is of significance on several counts. One, they are considerably more reliable than the previously available techniques, and thus, one would assume, dramatically reduce anxiety over unwanted pregnancy. Two, and the importance of this cannot be minimized, they separate the act of prevention from the act of sex. While the new methods insure against pregnancy resulting from failure to take contraceptive measures in the heat of spontaneous passion, they also improve what could be termed the aesthetics of sex, i.e., there need be no hasty retreat to insert a diaphragm or roll on a "safe" (to use an antiquated but charming term). All in all, then, the new contraceptives allow sex to be indulged in with less apprehension and more pleasure.

We shall now try to summarize and more explicitly state the argument contained in what we have written up to this point. The current conception of female sexuality as legitimate and gratifying coupled with enlarged opportunities for women to pursue sex without unwanted pregnancies is likely to have greatly increased the incentive for women to seek — as men have always done — sexual variety outside marriage. Among the available ways for both husbands *and* wives to find such variety, mate swapping is the least threatening and the one most compatible with monogamy.

Of the alternatives to mate swapping, the one which comes to mind immediately is what might be called "bilateral prostitution" (a term suggested to us by Albert Cohen). We have already pointed out that constitutionally males seem less suited than females for prostitution, although there may be some homosexual hustlers who can turn "tricks" at a surprising rate, but nothing that compares with that of their female counterparts. There are, however, economic problems associated with bilateral prostitution. It might place a greater drain on the family's financial resources than swinging, and, more significantly, create conflict over budgeting for the extramarital sexual expression of the husband and wife, i.e., how is the decision on allotment of funds to be made? Perhaps of greater concern is that it would separate the husband and wife for recreation at a time when a great deal of emphasis is placed on "familistic" activity, especially of the recreational variety, e.g., couples play bridge together, bowl together, boat together, and so on. That is to say, bilateral prostitution would enlarge their private worlds at the expense of their common world.

Given such considerations, the advantages of mate swapping as a solution to the problem of marital sexual monotony become obvious, though in all fairness we must note that many of the points we are going to make cannot be fully appreciated until the reader has completed our description of mate swapping himself. To begin with, the cost is probably less than that of bilateral prostitution, and is much more easily integrated into the normal recreational or entertainment budget. Second, it keeps the couple together, or at least in the same house. But further, it is an activity which involves common planning and preparation, and provides subject matter for conversation before and after, thus it could further consolidate the marriage. Finally, the sexual activity that takes place is, to a greater or lesser extent, under the surveillance of each; this means that each exercises control over the extramarital activity of the other, and the danger that the sexual relationship will become a romantic relationship is minimized. This, of course, is also facilitated by the brief and segmented nature of the relationship.

In summary, then, for the couple committed to the marital relationship and for whom it still perfoms important functions for which no other relationship exists, mate swapping may relieve sexual monotony without undermining the marriage.

The Study of Swinging

Swinging, or mate swapping, has been a subject that sells "adult reading" paperbacks, but few social scientists have analyzed it. Fortunately, there are a handful of serious studies of the swinging scene. This is not to maintain that we know all we need to know; the analyses available must be viewed as tentative. The findings of the research are problematic because designs have not been employed which allow generalization. Furthermore, some crucial aspects of the phenomenon have been neglected, e.g., what are the characteristics of those who drop out of swinging? We say this not by way of criticism of the research of our colleagues; they are pioneering in an area that involves great technical as well as ethical problems. Our statements are merely intended to qualify what we have to say in the rest of the paper.

Despite the problems cited above, there are studies, some of which are included in this issue, which provide excellent descriptive data based on participant observation and interviewing (G. Bartell, 1969; J. and L. Smith, 1969; W. and J. Breedlove, 1964; C. Symonds, 1968). We will use these ground-breaking papers to test the model presented earlier. It is hoped that the important contributions of Symonds, Bartell, the Smiths, and the Breedloves will encourage further research in this area. Before evaluating our model it is necessary to specify the term "swinging," to discuss the emergence and extent of swinging, and the swingers themselves.

Swinging

One definition of "swinging" is "having sexual relations (as a couple) with at least one other individual" (Bartell, 1969). Another definition, and

137

more appropriate for our purposes, is that "swinging" is a husband and wife's "willingness to swap sexual partners with a couple with whom they are not acquainted and/or to go to a swinging party and be willing for both he and his mate to have sexual intercourse with strangers" (Symonds, 1968). The latter definition directs our attention to swinging as a husband-wife activity. The accepted term among mate-sharing couples is "swinging"; the term "wife swapping" is objectionable, as it implies sexual inequality, i.e., that wives are the property of husbands.

Swingers, according to Symonds, are not of one mold; she distinguishes "recreational" from "Utopian" swingers. The recreational swinger is some-one "who uses swinging as a form of recreation"; he does not want to change the social order or to fight the Establishment. He is, in Merton's typology of deviance, an "aberrant." The recreational swinger violates norms but accepts them as legitimate. The Utopian swinger is "noncon-formist," publicizing his opposition to societal norms.

> He also tries to change them. He is generally acknowledged by the general society to be doing this for a cause rather than for personal gain. (Merton, 1966).

Swinging, for the Utopian, is part of a new life style that emphasizes communal living. The proportion of Utopians within the swinging scene has not been determined. Symonds feels that their number is small. She found the Utopians more interesting

> because of their more deviant and encompassing view concerning the life that they desire to live if it ever becomes possible. In some respects, they fall close to the philosophy of some hippies in that they would like to retreat from the society at large and live in a community of their own kind (Symonds, 1968).

In societal terms, the recreational swinger is a defender of the status quo; the Utopian swinger is one who wants to build a new order.

We are most interested in the recreational swingers, because their devi-ation is limited to the sharing of partners; in other areas they adhere to societal norms. Couples who engage in recreational swinging say they do so in order to support or improve their marriage. They favor monogamy and want to maintain it.

The Swinger

The swingers who advertise and attend swinging parties do not conform to the stereotypical image of the deviant. They have higher levels of edu-cation than the general population; 80% of one study attended college, 50% were graduates, and 12% were still students. They are disproportionately found in professional and white-collar occupations (J. and L. Smith, 1969). They tend to be conservative and very straight.

> They do not represent a high order of deviance. In fact, this is the single area of deviation from the norms of contemporary society. The mores, the fears, that plague our generation are evidenced as strongly in swingers as in any random sampling from suburbia. (Bartell, 1969).

Every study we looked at emphasized the overall normality, conventionality, and respectability of recreational swingers.

Extent of Swinging

The number of couples engaged in swinging can at best be roughly estimated. The Breedloves developed, on the basis of their research, an estimate of eight million couples. Their figure was based on a sample of 407 couples. They found that less than four per cent of them placed or replied to advertisements in swinging publications, and in the year prior to publication (1962–1963) of their study "almost 70,000 couples either replied to, or placed ads as swinging couples" (W. and J. Breedlove, 1964). With this figure as a base they arrived at their estimate of the number of couples who have at one time or another sexually exchanged partners. They further concluded that, conservatively, 2½ million couples exchange partners on a somewhat *regular* basis (three or more times a year).

Getting Together

The "swap" or Swingers club is an institutionalized route to other swingers, but it is not the only method of locating potential partners. Bartell suggests four ways: (1) swingers' bars, (2) personal reference, (3) personal recruitment, and (4) advertisement (Bartell, 1970). The last method deserves special attention.

Advertisements are placed in underground papers and more frequently in swingers' magazines. The swingers' publications, it has been claimed, emerged following an article in *MR.* magazine in 1956.

> Everett Meyers, the editor of *MR.*, later claimed that it was this article which touched off a flood of similar articles on wife-swapping, or mate-swapping. In any event, *MR.* followed up its original article with a regular monthly correspondence column filled with alleged letters from readers reporting their own mate-swapping accounts (Brecher, 1969).

Publications began to appear with advertisements from "modern marrieds" or swingers who wished to meet other swingers. *La Plume*, established about 1955, has boasted in print that it was the first swingers' magazine. A recent issue of *Select*, probably the largest swingers' publication, had 3,500 advertisements, over 40 per cent from married couples. *Select* and *Kindred Spirits* co-sponsored "Super Bash '70'" on April 11, 1970. It was advertised to be "the BIGGEST SWINGDING yet," and featured dancing, buffet supper, go go girls, and a luxurious intimate ballroom. Clubs such as Select, Kindred Spirits, Mixers, and Swingers Life have moved beyond the swingers' party to hayrides and vacation trips.

> There are at least a couple of hundred organizations like Select throughout the country. Many of them are very small, some with only a few members, and many of them are fly-by-night rackets run by schlock guys less interested in providing a service than in making a quick buck. Most however, are legitimate and, as such, very successful. They have been a major factor influencing the acceleration of the swapping scene (Fonzi and Riggio, 1969).

Our review of the swinging club and magazine market located approximately fifty nationally-sold publications. The "couple of hundred" figure reported above may include some lonely hearts, nudist directories, homosexual, and transvestite organizations, some of which serve the same purpose as swingers' publications. They bring together persons with the same sociosexual interests.

A person's first attendance at a swingers' party can be a difficult situation. He must learn the ideologies, rationalizations, and rules of swinging. These rules place swinging in a context that enables it to support the institution of the family. We turn to these rules in the next section.

Rules of the Game

Our model views swinging as a strategy to revitalize marriage, to bolster a sagging partnership. This strategy can be seen in the following findings of the empirical research. Evidence to support the model is divided into four parts: (1) the perception of limitation of sex to the marital bond, (2) paternity, (3) discretion, and (4) marital supportive rules.

1. "Consensual adultery": the perception that sex is limited to the marital bond. — Swingers have developed rules that serve to define the sexual relationship of marriage as one of love, of emotion. Some of the Smiths' respondents would answer "no" to questions pertaining to "extra-marital sexual experience," but would answer "yes" to questions pertaining to "mate-sharing or co-marital relations" (J. and L. Smith, 1969). Sharing, for the swingers, means that the marriage partners are not "cheating." Swingers believe that the damaging aspects in extramarital sex is the lying and cheating, and if this is removed extramarital sex is beneficial to the marital bond.

140

In other words, "those who swing together stay together" (Brecher, 1969). Swingers establish rules such as not allowing one of a couple to attend a group meeting without the other. Unmarried couples are kept out of some groups, because they "have less regard for the marital responsibilities" (W. and J. Breedlove, 1964). Guests who fail to conform to rules are asked "to leave a party when their behavior is not appropriate."

> For one group of recreational swingers, it is important that there be no telephone contact with the opposite sex between functions. Another group of recreational swingers always has telephone contact with people they swing with, although they have no sexual contact between functions (Symonds, 1968).

2. *Swinging and children* — "Recreational swingers are occasionally known to drop out of swinging, at least temporarily, while the wife gets pregnant" (Symonds, 1968). By not swinging, the couple can be assured that the husband is the father of the child; unknown or other parentage is considered taboo. This reflects a traditional, middle-class view about the conception and rearing of children.

Swinging couples consider themselves to be sexually avant-garde, but many retain their puritan attitudes with respect to sex socialization. They hide from their children their swinging publications. Swingers lock their children's bedrooms during parties or send them to relatives.

3. *Discretion* — A common word in the swingers' vocabulary is discretion. Swingers desire to keep their sexual play a secret from their non-swinging or "square" friends. They want to protect their position in the community, and an effort is made to limit participation to couples of similar status or "respectability."

> Parties in suburbia include evenly numbered couples only. In the area of our research, singles, male or female, are discriminated against. Blacks are universally excluded. If the party is a closed party, there are rules, very definitely established and generally reinforced by the organizer as well as other swingers . . . stag films are generally not shown. Music is low key fox trot, not infrequently Glenn Miller, and lighting is definitely not psychedelic. Usually nothing more than a few red or blue lightbulbs. Marijuana and speed are not permitted (Bartell, 1969).

The swinging suburban party differs, then, from the conventional cocktail party only in that it revolves around the sexual exchange of mates.

4. *Swingers' rules* — We suggest that the above rules on sex and paternity are strategies to make swinging an adjunct to marriage rather than an alternative. Another set of rules or strategies that is relevant is that dealing with jealousy. Swingers recognize the potentially disruptive consequences of jealousy, and are surprisingly successful in minimizing it. The Smiths

141

found that only 34 per cent of the females and 27 per cent of the males reported feelings of jealousy. Some of the controls on jealousy are: (1) that the marriage commands paramount loyalty, (2) that there is physical but not emotional interest in other partners, (3) that single persons are avoided, and (4) that there be no concealment of sexual activities. The sharing couples

> reassure one another on this score by means of verbal statements and by actively demonstrating in large ways and small that the marriage still does command their paramount loyalty. Willingness to forego an attractive swinging opportunity because the spouse or lover is uninterested or opposed is one example of such a demonstration (Brecher, 1969).

Developing a set of rules to control potential jealousies demonstrates the swingers' commitment to marriage.

Conclusion

In this paper we have attempted to account for a new form of extra-marital sexual behavior in terms of a sociological model of deviance. We have contended that swinging may support rather than disrupt monogamous marriage as it exists in this society. A review of the volumes of the *Reader's Guide to Periodical Literature* and *The New York Times Index* failed to reveal any articles dealing with this phenomenon in the United States. This would suggest that swinging has not as yet been defined as a social problem in the traditional sense of the word. Thus swinging, like prostitution, despite its violation of the social and, in many cases, legal norms is permitted a degree of tolerance which would appear to demonstrate the appropriateness of our model.

Finally, it should be said that we make no pretense to having touched upon all the changes that have played a role in the emergence of swinging. Restrictions of space prevented our looking at the larger societal trends that may have been at work here, e.g., feminism, the changing occupational position of women, suburbanization, and so on. Nevertheless, we do feel that we have delineated those issues which are most directly related to it. The validity of our model will be tested by time.

References

BARTELL, GILBERT D. "Group Sex Among the Mid-Americans." Paper presented at the Twelfth Annual Conference of the Scientific Study of Sex, November 1, 1969, New York. *Jl. of Sex Research*, 6: 2, Aug. 1970.

BECKER, HOWARD S. *Outsiders.* Glencoe, Ill.: The Free Press, 1963.

BRECHER, EDWARD M. *The Sex Researchers.* Boston: Little Brown and Co., 1969.

BREEDLOVE, WILLIAM AND JERRYE. *Swap Clubs.* Los Angeles: Sherbourne Press, 1964.

CALHOUN, ARTHUR W. *A Social History of the American Family.* Vol. I. New York: Barnes and Noble, 1960.

COHEN, ALBERT K. The Study of Social Organization and Deviant Behavior, in R. K. Merton, *et al.* (eds.). *Sociology Today.* New York: Basic Books, Inc., 1959.

COHEN, ALBERT K. *Deviance and Control.* Englewood Cliffs, N.J.: Prentice-Hall, Inc., 1966.

DAVIS, KINGSLEY. Sexual Behavior, in R. K. Merton and R. A. Nisbet (eds.). *Contemporary Social Problems.* New York: Harcourt, Brace, and World, 1966.

ERIKSON, KAI T. *Wayward Puritans.* New York: John Wiley, 1966.

FARBER, BERNARD. *Family: Organization and Interaction.* San Francisco: Chandler Publishing, 1964.

FONZI, GAELON, AND JAMES RIGGIO. Modern Couple Seeks Like-Minded Couples. Utmost Discretion. *Philadelphia, 60:* 9, 76–89, 1969.

FOOTE, NELSON N. Sex As Play, in E. Larabee and R. Neyersohn (eds.). *Mass Leisure.* Glencoe, Ill.: The Free Press, 1948.

GORDON, MICHAEL. From a Functional Necessity to a Cult of Mutual Orgasm: Sex in American Marital Education Literature, 1830–1940, in James Henslin (ed.). *The Sociology of Sex.* New York: Appleton-Century-Crofts, forthcoming.

KINSEY, A. C., W. B. POMEROY, AND C. E. MARTIN. *Sexual Behavior in the Human Male.* Philadelphia: W. B. Saunders Company, 1948.

KINSEY, A. C., W. B. POMEROY, C. E. MARTIN, AND P. H. GEBHARD. *Sexual Behavior in the Human Female.* Philadelphia: W. B. Saunders Company, 1953.

KINSIE, PAUL. Her Honor Pushes Legalized Prostitution. *Social Health News,* February 1967.

KNIGHT, ARTHUR, AND HOLLIS ALPERT. The History of Sex in the Cinema. Part 17: The Stag Film. *Playboy,* November, 1967.

MERTON, ROBERT K. Social Problems and Sociological Theory, in R. K. Merton and R. A. Nisbet (eds.). *Contemporary Social Problems.* New York: Harcourt, Brace and World, 1966.

PIVAR, DAVID J. The New Abolitionism: The Quest for Social Purity. Unpublished Ph.D. dissertation, University of Pennsylvania, 1965.

POLSKY, NED. *Hustlers, Beats and Others.* Chicago: Aldine, 1967.

REISS, IRA L. *The Social Context of Premarital Sexual Permissiveness.* New York: Holt, Rinehart and Winston, 1967.

SMITH, JAMES R., AND LYNN G. Co-Marital Sex and the Sexual Freedom Movement, presented at the Twelfth Annual Conference of the Society for the Scientific Study of Sex, November 1, 1969, New York. *Jl. of Sex Research, 6:* 2, Aug. 1970.

SMITH, SAMUEL G. *Social Pathology.* New York: The Macmillan Company, 1911.

SPREY, JETSE. On the Institutionalization of Sex. *J. Marriage and Family, 31:* 3. 432–440, 1969.

SYMONDS, CAROLYN. Pilot Study of the Peripheral Behavior of Sexual Mate Swappers. Unpublished Master's thesis, University of California, Riverside, 1968.

TIETZE, CHRISTOPHER. Oral and Intrauterine Contraception: Effectiveness and Safety. *International Journal of Fertility, 13:* 4, 377–384, 1968.

WHELPTON, P. K., A. A. CAMPBELL, AND J. E. PATTERSON. Fertility and Family Planning in the United States. Princeton: Princeton University Press, 1966.

WINICK, CHARLES. Prostitutes' Clients' Perception of the Prostitutes and of Themselves. *The International Journal of Social Psychiatry, 8:* 4, 289–297, 1962.

part five

Female sexuality and the liberated woman

Some may wonder why this book contains a section on female sexuality but not one on male sexuality. This is a reflection of the fact that over the years men have interpreted women's sexuality in various ways, while keeping a fairly constant view of their own sexuality. Now that women have begun to define for themselves the nature of their sexuality, it becomes especially important to look at these new definitions and emerging expectations.

Throughout most of the 19th century, women were told that sex was something alien to them.

As a general rule, a modest woman seldom desires any sexual gratification for herself. She submits to her husband, but only to please him; and, but for the desire of maternity, would far rather be relieved of his attention. The married woman has no desire to be treated as a mistress.[1]

In the early decades of this century women were portrayed as being capable of sexual desire but only under special circumstances — namely, in a love relationship — in contrast to men, whose capacity to respond was supposedly ever ready. Even with love present, it was felt necessary for the male to cultivate and call forth this desire, thus making female sexuality a male creation.

144

More recently, differences in the sexuality of men and women have been played down, but women continue to be frequently described as creatures whose sexuality is less imperious than that of men and tied to the emotions to a much greater extent. Furthermore, normal women have been generally thought to be satisfied with one orgasm as is evidenced by what Gordon has called "the cult of mutual orgasm," i.e., the view characteristic of many sex manuals published in this century that saw the ultimate in sexual experience being coitus culminating in simultaneous orgasm.[2]

Among the developments which have made it increasingly difficult to maintain such traditional views of female sexuality is the now famous research of Masters and Johnson. They found that many women when allowed to stimulate themselves digitally or mechanically experienced several orgasms.

If there is no psychosocial distraction to repress sexual tensions, many well-adjusted women enjoy a minimum of three or four orgasmic experiences before they reach apparent satiation.[3]

In contrast, very few men were found capable of repeated orgasm without going through a recovery period between each ejaculation. In point of fact, multi-orgasmic capacity is one of the two significant differences in the sexual response cycles of men and women, the other being the longer duration of female orgasm.

This was not the only misconception toppled by their research. While others before them had questioned the distinction between vaginal and clitoral orgasms it was not until their work was published that this distinction was widely abandoned in professional circles. By making it evident that the clitoris was the seat of sexual sensation for the woman, irrespective of the area of the body stimulated, they undercut the prevailing Freudian notion that for the sexually mature women sensation was centered in the vagina, what Koedt has called "the myth of the vaginal orgasm."[4]

All of this would seem to suggest that our notions about the sexual capacities of men and women require considerable rethinking. While for years men have been told of their supposedly superior libidinous interests and abilities, we now see that the observed differences in this realm may be more a product of culture than physiology. In fact there are those, the psychiatrist Mary Jane Sherfey, for example, who claim that women are potentially insatiable sexually, and that the form their sexuality currently takes is a result of men having suppressed women's impulses to meet the demands of sedentary societies.[5]

The implications of Masters and Johnson's research have yet to be fully appreciated outside of radical Feminist circles. Susan Lydon, in one of the papers included in this section, focuses on what she describes as "the politics of orgasm," and does deal with this. Writers of a more conservative bent, however, generally discuss the Masters and Johnson research without any consideration of its meaning for the broader relations between the sexes.

The findings of Masters and Johnson have done a great deal to dispel some important sexual mythology, but the creation of a climate favorable to the reception of their data was a product of a number of other factors among which birth control technology probably figures importantly. Recent breakthroughs in contraceptive technology, such as the pill and the IUD, are important for a variety of reasons. For one thing, they place the responsibility for birth control in the hands of women in contrast to most earlier techniques such as the condom and withdrawal. Of equal importance is the fact they separate contraception from copulation, which was not the case even with a technique of feminine initiative such as the diaphragm; that is to say, sexual arousal need not be interrupted by any precautionary measure. Finally, the failure rate, especially for the pill, is negligible in contrast to sizeable failure rates for other techniques. In consort these factors serve to reduce the anxiety of an unwanted pregnancy and allow women to take greater pleasure in sexual relations.

We see objective evidence of women now asserting their sexuality in a variety of places. Among them are marital expectations. Bell, in one of the papers that follows, reports that 25 per cent of the married women in his sample expressed dissatisfaction because of coital infrequency. When these findings are compared to those of earlier studies there is reason to believe that the number of women reporting such dissatisfaction is now higher than in the early decades of the century. These findings convey the extent to which we have moved from the older image of the sexually acquiescent wife and the overly demanding husband.

In so brief a space one can only touch upon some of the themes relevant to the subject of emerging patterns of female sexuality. We must realize, as writers such as Kate Millett and Germaine Greer have noted, that coitus may be thought of as a microcosm of broader social relations between the sexes.[6] Patriarchal societies have been very loath to grant women equality in the sexual sphere and the fact that women are now *beginning* to achieve this has to be seen as an indication of gains they are making in other avenues of life. Only when women do not have to depend on men for their social and economic positions will we see sexual equality emerge in every sense of the term.

Notes

1. Hayes, A., *Sexual Physiology of Women*, Boston: Peabody Medical Institute, 1869, p. 227.
2. Gordon, Michael, "From an Unfortunate Necessity to a Cult of Mutual Orgasm: Sex in American Marital Education Literature, 1830–1940," in James Henslin (ed.) *Studies in the Sociology of Sex*, New York: Appleton-Century-Crofts, 1971, pp. 55–73.
3. Masters, William H., and Virginia E. Johnson, *Human Sexual Response*, Boston: Little, Brown, and Company, 1966, p. 65.
4. Koedt, Ann, "The Myth of the Vaginal Orgasm," *Notes From the Second Year: Women's Liberation*, 1970, pp. 37–41.
5. Sherfey, Mary Jane, "The Evolution and Nature of Female Sexuality in Relation to Psychoanalytic Theory," *Journal of the American Psychoanalytic Association*, January, 1966, pp. 28–127.
6. Millet, Kate, *Sexual Politics*, New York: Doubleday, 1970; and Germaine Greer, *The Female Eunuch*, New York: McGraw Hill, 1971.

9

The Female Orgasm

William H. Masters and Virginia E. Johnson

For the human female, orgasm is a psychophysiologic experience occurring within, and made meaningful by, a context of psychosocial influence. Physiologically, it is a brief episode of physical release from the vasocongestive and myotonic increment developed in response to sexual stimuli. Psychologically, it is subjective perception of a peak of physical reaction to sexual stimuli. The cycle of sexual response, with orgasm as the ultimate point in progression, generally is believed to develop from a drive of biologic-behavioral origin deeply integrated into the condition of human existence.

Where possible, material presented reflects consideration of three interacting areas of influence upon female orgasmic attainment previously recognized in attempts to understand and to interpret female sexual response: (1) physiologic (characteristic physical conditions and reactions during the peak of sex tension increment); (2) psychologic (psychosexual orientation and receptivity to orgasmic attainment); and (3) sociologic (cultural, environmental, and social factors influencing orgasmic incidence or ability). The quantitative and qualitative relationship of these factors appears totally variable between one woman's orgasmic experiences, and orgasm as it occurs in other women. Only baseline physiologic reactions and occasional individually characteristic modes of expression remain consistent from or-

Reprinted from *Human Sexual Response,* Boston: Little, Brown and Company, 1966, pp. 127–140, by permission of the publisher.

148

gasm to orgasm, reflecting the human female's apparent tendency toward orientation of sexual expression to psychosocial demand.

Factual data pertaining to orgasm may be more meaningful when placed in clinical context. However, in order to provide a point of departure for nonsubjective interpretation of female orgasmic response, most of the material will be related to recognizable baselines of physiologic response and psychosocial patterns of sexual expression which can be duplicated within investigative context. General impression rather than statistical data will be reflected owing to the selected quality of the population and the research atmosphere to which the female study subjects have been exposed.

Physiologic Factors of Orgasm

Female orgasmic experience can be visually identified as well as recorded by acceptable physiologic techniques. The primary requirement in objective identification of female orgasm is the knowledge that it is a total-body response with marked variation in reactive intensity and timing sequence. Previously, other observers have recognized and interpreted much of the reactive physiology of female orgasm. However, definition and correlation of these reactions into an identifying pattern of orgasm per se has not been established.

At orgasm, the grimace and contortion of a woman's face graphically express the increment of myotonic tension throughout her entire body. The muscles of the neck and the long muscles of the arms and legs usually contract into involuntary spasm. During coition in supine position the female's hands and feet voluntarily may be grasping her sexual partner. With absence of clutching interest or opportunity during coition or in solitary response to automanipulative techniques, the extremities may reflect involuntary carpopedal spasm. The striated muscles of the abdomen and the buttocks frequently are contracted voluntarily by women in conscious effort to elevate sexual tensions, particularly in an effort to break through from high plateau to orgasmic attainment.

The physiologic onset of orgasm is signaled by contractions of the target organs, starting with the orgasmic platform in the outer third of the vagina. This platform, created involuntarily by localized vasocongestion and myotonia, contracts with recordable rhythmicity as the tension increment is released. The intercontractile intervals recur at 0.8 second for the first three to six contractions, corresponding in timing sequence to the first few ejaculatory contractions (male orgasm) of the penis. The longer contractions continue, the more extended the intercontractile intervals. The number and intensity of orgasmic-platform contractions are direct measures of subjective severity and objective duration of the particular orgasmic experience. The correlation between platform contractions and subjective experience at or-

149

gasm has been corroborated by study subjects during thousands of cycles. Vaginal spasm and penile grasping reactions have been described many times in the clinical and nonprofessional literature. Orgasmic-platform contractility provides an adequate physiologic explanation for these subjective concepts.

Contractions of the orgasmic platform provide visible manifestation of female orgasmic experience. To date, the precise mechanism whereby cortical, hormonal, or any unidentified influence may activate this and other orgasmic reactions has not been determined (perhaps by creating a triggerpoint level of vasocongestive and myotonic increment).

Orgasmic contractions of the uterus have been recorded by both intrauterine and abdominally placed electrodes. Both techniques indicate that uterine contractions may have onset almost simultaneously with those of the orgasmic platform, but the contractive intensity of the uterine musculature is accumulated slowly and contractions are too irregular in recurrence and duration to allow pattern definition. Uterine contractions start in the fundus and work through the midzone to terminate in the lower uterine segment. With the exception of the factor of contractile excursion (indication of intensity), physiologic tracings of uterine orgasmic contractions resemble the patterns of first-stage labor contractions. Uterine contractile intensity and duration vary widely from orgasm to orgasm. However, there is some early indication that both factors have a positive relation to the parity of the individual and the prior extent of her orgasmic experience, both incidental and cumulative.

Involuntary contractions of the external rectal sphincter also may develop during orgasm, although many women experience orgasm without evidencing sphincter contraction. When the contractions do occur, they parallel in timing sequence the initial intercontractile intervals of the orgasmic platform. The rectal-sphincter contractions usually terminate before those of the orgasmic platform.

The external urethral sphincter also may contract two or three times in an involuntary expression of orgasmic tension release. The contractions are without recordable rhythmicity and usually are confined to nulliparous premenopausal women.

The breasts evidence no specific response to the immediacy of orgasm. However, detumescence of the areolae immediately subsequent to orgasm is so rapid that its arbitrary assignment purely as a resolution-phase reaction has been cause for investigative concern. Often areolar detumescence is evident shortly after subjective report of orgasmic onset and usually develops simultaneously with the terminal contractions of the orgasmic platform. As a final stage of the rapid detumescent reaction, the areolae constrict into a corrugated state. The nipples remain erect and are turgid and quite rigid (the false-erection reaction).

Rapid detumescence of the vasocongested areolae, resulting in a constricted, corrugated appearance, occurs only with orgasm and is an obvious physical manifestation that provides for visual identification of female orgasmic experience. If orgasm does not occur areolar detumescence is a much slower process, corrugation does not develop, and the false-erection reaction of the nipples usually is reduced in intensity.

The sex flush, a maculopapular rash distributed superficially over the body surfaces, achieves its greatest intensity and its widest distribution at the moment of orgasmic expression. Subsequent to orgasmic experience, the sex flush disappears more rapidly than when resolving from plateau-phase levels of erotic tension.

From a cardiorespiratory point of view, orgasm is reflected by hyperventilation, with respiratory rates occasionally over 40 per minute. Tachycardia is a constant accompaniment of orgasmic experience, with cardiac rates running from 110 to beyond 180 beats per minute. Hypertension also is a constant finding. The systolic pressures are elevated by 30–80 mm. and diastolic pressures by 20–40 mm. Hg.

The clitoris, Bartholin's glands, and the major and minor labia are target organs for which no specific physiologic reactions to orgasmic-phase levels of sexual tension have been established.

Aside from ejaculation, there are two major areas of physiologic difference between female and male orgasmic expression. First, the female is capable of rapid return to orgasm immediately following an orgasmic experience, if restimulated before tensions have dropped below plateau-phase response levels. Second, the female is capable of maintaining an orgasmic experience for a relatively long period of time.

A rare reaction in the total of female orgasmic expression, but one that has been reduplicated in the laboratory on numerous occasions, has been termed status orgasmus. This physiologic state of stress is created either by a series of rapidly recurrent orgasmic experiences between which no recordable plateau-phase intervals can be demonstrated, or by a single, long-continued orgasmic episode. Subjective report, together with visual impression of involuntary variation in peripheral myotonia, suggests that the woman actually is ranging with extreme rapidity between successive orgasmic peaks and a baseline of advanced plateau-phase tension. Status orgasmus may last from 20 to more than 60 seconds. The severe tachycardia (more than 180 per minute) and the long-maintained (43 seconds), rapidly recurring contractile patterns of the orgasmic platform are identified easily.

Of interest from both physiologic and psychologic points of view is the recorded evidence of an initial involuntary spasm of the orgasmic platform, developing before the regularly recurring contractions of orgasmic expression. The study subject identified the onset of orgasm and vocalized this subjective experience before the onset of regularly recurrent contractions of the orgasmic platform. However, the initial spasm of the orgasmic platform developed parallel in timing sequence with the subjective identification of the orgasmic experience. To date, preliminary spasm of the orgasmic platform has been recorded only in situations of severe tension increment.

It is investigative impression that the inability to record initial spasm of the orgasmic platform in all orgasmic experiences well may reflect lack of effective experimental technique rather than unimpeachable physiologic fact. Subjectively, the identification of initial spasm of the orgasmic platform is a constant factor in any full orgasmic experience. The subjective and objective correlation of orgasmic experience will be discussed later in the chapter.

No preliminary spastic contraction of the uterine musculature comparable to the initial spasm of the orgasmic platform has been recorded to date. However, the work is in its infancy, and such a preliminary spasm before onset of the regular, expulsive, fundal contractions may, in fact, exist and be recorded in the future.

The subjective identification of orgasmic expression by the human female simultaneously with the initial spasm of the orgasmic platform, but 2 to 4 seconds prior to onset of its regular recurrent contractions, draws an interesting parallel with the human male's ejaculatory experience. When the secondary organs of reproduction contract, the male feels the ejaculation coming and can no longer control it, but there still is a 2- to 4-second interval before the seminal fluid appears at the urethral meatus under the pressure developed by penile expulsive contractions. Thus the male's psychosensory expression of ejaculatory inevitability may have counterpart in the female's subjective identification of orgasmic onset. The initial spasm of the orgasmic platform, before the platform and the uterus contract with regularity, may parallel the contractions of the prostate and, questionably, contractions of the seminal vesicles before onset of the regularly recurrent expulsive contractions of the penis.

Understandably, the maximum physiologic intensity of orgasmic response subjectively reported or objectively recorded has been achieved by self-regulated mechanical or automanipulative techniques. The next highest level of erotic intensity has resulted from partner manipulation, again with established or self-regulated methods, and the lowest intensity of target-organ response was achieved during coition.

While variations in the orgasmic intensity and duration of target-organ response have been recorded and related to modes of stimulation, there have been no recorded alterations in the basic orgasmic physiology. This finding lends support, at least in part, to many earlier concepts of orgasmic response. The fundamental physiology of orgasmic response remains the same whether the mode of stimulation is heterosexual or artificial coition or mechanical or automanipulative stimulation of the clitoral area, the breast, or any other selected erogenous zone. It follows that orgasm resulting from fantasy also would produce the same basic physiologic response patterns, although a woman capable of fantasying to orgasm has not been available for inclusion in the research population. The ability of women to fantasy to orgasm has been reported by other investigators.

With the specific anatomy of orgasmic-phase physiology reasonably established, the age-old practice of the human female of dissimulating has been made pointless. The obvious, rapid detumescence and corrugation of the areolae of the breasts and the definable contractions of the orgasmic platform in the outer third of the vagina remove any doubt as to whether the woman is pretending or experiencing orgasm. The severe vasocongestive reactions reflecting higher levels of sexual tension cannot be developed other than during involuntary response to sexual stimulation. For example, the transitory but obvious increase in nulliparous breast size, the sex flush, and the minor-labial sex skin reactions are all plateau-phase phenomena that develop only in response to effective sexual stimulation.

Psychologic Factors of Orgasm

It is well to restate from time to time the necessity for maintaining a concept of total involvement when any facet of human sexuality is to be considered. This is equally true when the study is directed to areas of psychologic influence upon orgasmic achievement.

Female orgasm, whether it is attained within the context of an interpersonal relationship (either heterosexual or homosexual) or by means of any combination of erotically stimulative activity and/or fantasy, remains a potpourri of psychophysiologic conditions and social influence. Many theoretical as well as individually graphic accounts of the female experience at orgasm have been offered in the professional literature of many disciplines and are even more widespread in general publications. This vast amount of published quasiauthority depicts both objective and subjective female reaction to orgasm with almost every possible degree of accuracy and inaccuracy.

Without referring to the prior literature, a description of subjective response to orgasmic incidence has been compiled from reports of 487 women, given in the laboratory in the immediacy of the postorgasmic period, obtained through interview only, or developed from a combination of both sources. This composite is offered as a baseline for a concept of the psychologic aspects of the human female's orgasmic experience.

The consensus drawn from the multiple descriptions has established three distinct stages of woman's subjective progression through orgasm.

STAGE I

Orgasm has its onset with a sensation of suspension or stoppage. Lasting only an instant, the sensation is accompanied or followed immediately by an isolated thrust of intense sensual awareness, clitorally oriented, but radiating upward into the pelvis. Intensity ranging in degree from mild to shock level has been reported by many women within the context of their personal experience. A simultaneous loss of overall sensory acuity has been described as paralleling in degree the intensity and duration of the particular orgasmic episode. Loss of sensory acuity has been reviewed frequently in the literature.

During the first stage of subjective progression in orgasm, the sensation of intense clitoral-pelvic awareness has been described by a number of women as occurring concomitantly with a sense of bearing down or expelling. Often a feeling of receptive opening was expressed. This last sensation was reported only by parous study subjects, a small number of whom expressed some concept of having an actual fluid emission or of expending in some concrete fashion. Previous male interpretation of these subjective reports may have resulted in the erroneous but widespread concept that female ejaculation is an integral part of female orgasmic expression.

Twelve women, all of whom have delivered babies on at least one occasion without anesthesia or analgesia, reported that during the second stage of labor they experienced a grossly intensified version of the sensations identified with this first stage of subjective progression through orgasm. Reports of this concept also have appeared from time to time in the literature.

STAGE II

As the second stage of subjective progression through orgasm, a sensation of "suffusion of warmth," specifically pervading the pelvic area first and then spreading progressively throughout the body, was described by almost every woman with orgasmic experience.

STAGE III

Finally, as the third stage of subjective progression, a feeling of involuntary contraction with a specific focus in the vagina or lower pelvis was mentioned consistently. Frequently, the sensation was described as that of "pelvic throbbing."

Women with the facility to express sensate awareness frequently separated this final stage of subjective progression into two phases. The initial phase was expressed as contractile, followed immediately by a throbbing phase, with both sensations experienced as separate entities. The initial contractile feeling was described as localized vaginally, subsequently merging with the throbbing sensation which, though initially concentrated in the pelvis, was felt throughout the body. The "pelvic throbbing" sensation often was depicted as continuing until it became one with a sense of the pulse or heartbeat.

Only the two phases of this third stage of subjective progression during orgasm afforded positive correlation between subjective response and objective reaction. This correlation has been developed from a composite return of direct interrogation of female study subjects during investigative sessions. The phase of contractile sensation has been identified as paralleling in time sequence the recorded initial spasm of the orgasmic platform.

Regularly recurring orgasmic-platform contractions were appreciated subjectively as pulsating or throbbing sensations of the vagina. Although second-phase sensations of pulsation coincided with observable vaginal-platform contractions, consciousness of a pulsating sensation frequently continued beyond observable platform contractions. Finally this pelvic-throbbing sensation became one with a subjective awareness of tachycardia described frequently as feeling the heartbeat vaginally. Subjective awareness of orgasmic duration was somewhat dependent upon the degree of intensity of the specific orgasm.

Rectal-sphincter contraction also was described by some anatomically oriented or hypersensitive women as a specific entity during intense orgasmic response.

Observation supported by subjective report indicates that a relative norm of orgasmic intensity and duration is reflected by approximately five to eight vigorous contractions of the orgasmic platform. A level of eight to twelve contractions would be considered by observer and subject to be an intense physiologic experience. An orgasmic expression reflected by three to five contractions usually is reported by the responding female as being a "mild experience" unless the woman is postmenopausal. These physiologically recordable levels of orgasmic intensity never must be presumed arbitrarily to be a full or consistent measure of the subjective pleasure derived from individual orgasmic attainment.

Pregnancy (particularly during the second and, at times, the third trimester) has been noted to increase general sensitivity to the overall sensate effects of orgasm. To date, an increase in contractile intensity of the pregnant woman's orgasmic platform as compared to that in her nonpregnant state has not been corroborated by physiologic tracings. Orgasmic contractions of the uterus recorded during the second and third trimesters consistently have been reported as subjectively more intense sensations than those of nonpregnant response patterns. Of interest from an objective point of view is the fact that tonic spasm of the uterus develops in response to orgasmic stimulation and has been recorded during the third trimester of pregnancy.

Sociologic Factors in Orgasm

In our culture, the human female's orgasmic attainment never has achieved the undeniable status afforded the male's ejaculation. While male orgasm (ejaculation) has the reproductive role in support of its perpetual acceptance, a comparable regard for female orgasm is still in limbo. Why has female orgasmic expression not been considered to be a reinforcement of woman's role as sexual partner and reproductive necessity? Neither totem, taboo, nor religious assignment seems to account completely for the force with which female orgasmic experience often is negated as a naturally occurring psychophysiologic response.

With orgasmic physiology established, the human female now has an undeniable opportunity to develop realistically her own sexual response levels. Disseminating this information enables the male partner to contribute to this development in support of an effective sexual relationship within the marital unit. The female's age-old foible of orgasmic pretense has been predicated upon the established concept that obvious female response increases the male's subjective pleasure during coital opportunity. With need for pretense removed, a sexually responding woman can stimulate effectively the interaction upon which both the man's and woman's psychosocial requirements are culturally so dependent for orgasmic facility.

Impression formed from eleven years of controlled observation suggests that psychosocially oriented patterns of sexual expression evolve specifically in response to developing social and life cycle demands. When continuity of study-subject cooperation permitted long-range observation and interrogation, it was noted that major changes in social baseline were accompanied by actual changes in sexual expression. For the female study subjects, changes involving social or life-cycle demands frequently resulted in a reorientation of sexual focus. This was manifest in alterations in desired areas of stimulation, preferred actions of partner, and reported fantasy. Often variations in coital and masturbatory techniques were observed.

These alterations usually appeared gradually, although, depending upon the impact of the social change involved, there were occasions of sudden onset. To date, physiologically measurable intensity in orgasmic response has shown no specific parallel to onset or presence of these psychosocial influences. This may indicate that physiologic capacity, as influenced by purely biologic variations, remains a dominant factor in orgasmic intensity and facility. Reported levels of subjective pleasure in orgasm did, of course, parallel reports of desirable or undesirable social change.

It became evident that laboratory environment was not the determining factor in the success or failure of female study subjects' orgasmic attainment. Rather it was from previously established levels of sexual response that the individual female was able to cope with and adapt to a laboratory situation.

There were no particular personality trends toward high- or low-dominance individuals among the participating female research group. The women's personalities varied from the very shy through the agreeably in-

156

dependent, and histories reflected sexual-partner experience ranging from single to many. The ability to achieve orgasm in response to effective sexual stimulation was the only constant factor demonstrated by all active female participants. This observation might be considered to support the concept that sexual response to orgasm is the physiologic prerogative of most women, but its achievement in our culture may be more dependent upon psychosocial acceptance of sexuality than overtly aggressive behavior.

Many existing psychologic theories find support in the physiologic data emerging from this study. However, it must be recalled that these data have been presented primarily as impression, due to the selectivity of the research group and, in many instances, the absence of a statistically significant number of recorded reactions. There always is great temptation to connect theory to considered fact, when subjective reports of the research population are placed as an overlay on the observed and recorded physiologic reactions. If recall by interrogated subjects of early sexual feeling and of manipulative activity, often to a remembered peak of experience, is to be given credence, sexual response well may be viewed as an instinctual activity arising from an undifferentiated sexual state. Although molded and transmitted genetically, sexual response, in this concept, would be subject to both immediate and continued learning processes.

Unreported observations suggest that an infant sexual response as an undifferentiated state is not beyond possibility. Certainly, elaboration of sexual behavior in early childhood of less restricted cultures has been reported. The development of sexual responsiveness to orgasmic level, identifiable subjectively, must be a cumulative result of interaction between the individual female's hereditary endowment and the psychosocial influence to which it is exposed. The element of time must be assumed to be a finally determining factor, as it accrues the experience of social and psychosexual maturation.

A detailed psychosocial study of the research population cannot be presented within the framework of this text. Yet neither this book nor this chapter can be considered complete without emphasizing an acute awareness of the vital, certainly the primary influence, exerted by psychosocial factors upon human sexuality, particularly that of orgasmic attainment of the female. Although the basic physiology of female orgasm never would have evolved from behavioral theory or sociologic concept, it equally is obvious that physiologic detail is of value only when considered in relation to these theories and concepts. When completed, psychosocial evaluation of the study-subject population will be published in another book.

10

Some emerging sexual expectations among women

Robert R. Bell

In recent years interest in the changing role of the middle-class woman has caused a proliferation of books, articles, and television programs ranging from the academic to the sensational. In this paper, the interest is in one aspect of possible change in the modern woman's role — that of sexual satisfaction in marriage. An increasingly common middle-class belief in regard to marital coitus places great importance on the "rights and obligations" of the wife, and probably most middle-class young women today grow up with the belief that when they enter marriage they have a right to expect personal sexual fulfillment and satisfaction.

"Scientific" attitudes of the past

A brief look at some past professional attitudes toward marital sex for the woman provides a vivid contrast with present-day values. Up through the 19th century, both moral and "scientific criticisms were directed at the women who achieved sexual satisfaction in marriage. In a standard text on the reproductive system, William Acton wrote that the belief that women have a sexual appetite was a "vile aspersion." William Hammond, a surgeon-general of the United States, asserted that "nine-tenths of the time decent women feel not the slightest pleasure in intercourse." And at the University

Reprinted from *Medical Aspects of Human Sexuality*, October, 1967, pp. 65–67, 72, by permission of Hospital Publications, Inc.

of Basel, an eminent gynecologist named Fahling labeled sexual desire in the young woman as "pathological."[1]

In 1839, a highly successful English marriage manual written by a physician named Michael Ryan warned that female sterility was due, among other causes, to "excessive ardor of desire" or "passion strongly excited," and declared: "It is well known that complaisance, tranquility, silence, and secrecy are necessary for a prolific coition."[1]

In the past, the belief that female sexual satisfaction was achieved only by the "depraved" prostitute was shared by many poets, physicians, and moralists.

Contemporary views of the wife's sexual role

Old attitudes about the restricted sexual rights of the married woman have drastically changed. In fact, it would be next to impossible to find any reputable writers in the United States today voicing the old double-standard values.

A common view today is expressed in Maxine Davis's statement that "to serve as the cornerstone of happy marriage, sexual intercourse must be welcome and delighting not to the husband alone but to the wife as well."[2] The same writer says, "It is necessary that she [the wife] share the grandeur of the topmost heights with him [the husband] — orgasm, the sexual climax — or else the enterprise becomes meaningless for both." Sexual satisfaction is usually presented today as being of primary importance not only to the personal satisfaction of the wife but also to the overall marriage relationship.

In addition to rejecting the old patriarchal values, a number of the modern writers take a highly romantic view of marital sex which implies not only sexual "rights" for the wife, but a set of highly idealistic expectations about marital coitus. Another quotation from a best-selling book on the sexual role of the modern American woman[2] illustrates this point:

> In concrete terms women might compare sexual love with a mountainside which she and her husband climb together because they want to share the adventure along the upward path and the superb view from the summit — they adjust their pace to each other, ascend the last steep slope side by side, and share the sudden beauty of the valleys and skies at the moment they reach their peak.

Such "romantic" expectations may create a problem by leading to female expectations that cannot be realistically met. As Hunt[3] points out, "If a woman has been assured that she will, should, and must see colored lights, feel like a breaking wave, or helplessly utter inarticulate cries, then she is apt to consider herself or her husband at fault when these promised wonders do not appear."

These attitudes and values that seem to be new do not always replace the old values, but rather, for many middle-class women, they exist alongside them. Such a coexistence of new and old values creates a sexual dilemma for some middle-class wives who intellectually accept the idea that they should expect and achieve sexual satisfaction in their marriage even though emotionally many are still conditioned to be sexually frigid.[4]

Sexual emancipation of college-educated wives

The modern belief in personal sexual satisfaction is probably found most often among more highly educated wives. In a study of less educated wives, Rainwater[5] found that "both husbands and wives feel that sexual gratification for the wife is much less important than for the husband." The greater personal sex interest of the college-educated wife indicates that old beliefs, values, and fears have been altered or replaced by new beliefs and values stressing the personal importance of sex in marriage. Thus there is reason to believe that the "emancipated" sexual values have been greatest for the more highly educated wife.

There is also some evidence that the more highly educated wife achieves greater sexual satisfaction in marriage. For example, Kinsey found that "the number of females reaching orgasm within any five year period was rather distinctly higher among those with upper educational backgrounds."[6]

With these thoughts in mind, a study was carried out with a group of women who were four-year college graduates and had been married not more than ten years. The respondents were asked to privately answer a questionnaire and place it in a sealed envelope. In this way 196 usable questionnaires were acquired. The respondents were all married and living with their husbands. They had a median age of 26.2 years and a median length of marriage of 4.2 years. By religion the sample was 51% Jewish, 38% Protestant, and 11% Catholic.

We were interested in whether their attitudes about the importance of sex had changed since these women entered marriage. We asked them to contrast the present importance of sex in their marriage with the attitudes about marital sex that they had taken into marriage. Most (58%) said it was about what they had estimated, but 20% said they had overestimated its importance and 13% that they had underestimated it. Of course, their recollection of the view they initially took into marriage was influenced by the experiences they had had since marriage, and their memory of earlier beliefs was often altered by actual marital experiences. But for a significant minority, there is a stated belief that premarital estimates of marital sex had proved to be inaccurate.

The wives were also asked to asses their own feelings and their husband's feelings about the present sexual adjustment of their marriages. The wives reported their own feelings about their sexual adjustment as follows: 79% "very good" or "good"; 17% "fair"; and 4% "poor" or "very poor." Their assessments of their husband's feelings were almost exactly the same: 78% "very good" and "good"; 18% "fair"; and 4% "poor" and "very poor."

For many wives there is undoubtedly a "halo" effect in their evaluations. They do not usually have a scale or model with which to measure their sexual adjustment. But as far as their personal definitions of satisfaction are concerned, the fact that if compared to some objective standard they might not be rated as sexually well adjusted is beside the point.

Our college-educated women indicate a much higher satisfaction with marital sex than did Rainwater's less educated group. Only about one-fourth of the wives in Rainwater's sample gave any indication of mutual enjoyment in their marital coitus.[5]

Attitudes toward frequency of intercourse

The college-educated wives were also asked how they felt about the frequency of sexual relations in their marriage. This question was intended to provide some information on the impact of the "emancipated" belief that the woman has a right to expect personal sexual satisfaction in her marriage. If she feels that intercourse is either too frequent or too infrequent, this may be taken as an indication that she feels some dissatisfaction as to how her personal sexual needs are being met.

In our sample, 69% said the frequency of intercourse was "about right"; 6% said it was "too frequent"; and 25% said it was "too infrequent." The small "too frequent" percentage indicates a change from the traditional view that marital sex is primarily centered around the husband's needs.

More significantly, the fact that one out of four wives said "too infrequent" suggests that a large number of wives may feel their sexual needs are not being satisfied by their husbands. However, these answers do not always represent a personal criticism of the husbands, because sexual infrequency may be due to a variety of demands on a couple that restrict their sexual opportunities in a way that is not directly the fault of either spouse. For example, the demands on the wife by children or activities outside the home and on the husband by occupational and community involvements may physically or psychologically reduce their sexual activity.

When our findings are contrasted with other studies, some changes in wives' feelings can be seen. In the 1920's, K. B. Davis[7] found that two out of three married women said they had a less intense and less frequent desire for sex than did their husbands. Very few gave any indication of a desire for sex that was greater than that of the husband. The Burgess and Wallin study carried out in the early 1940's reported that 64% of the wives were satisfied with the frequency of marital coitus while 16% said it was too frequent and 20% too infrequent.[4] These findings are essentially the same as ours except that the wives more often said that marital coitus was "too frequent" than did those in our sample.

Influence of length of marriage on sexual attitudes

We divided our sample into three groups by length of marriage: less than three years, three to six years, and seven to ten years. Analysis of the data did not indicate any differences among these groups in the assessment of the original notions taken into marriage. This may be the result of original attitudes remaining fairly constant over time, or of the recollections of initial beliefs being changed in the individual's recall.

The wives' assessment of their own adjustments to sex in marriage did not differ by length of marriage. However, there was some evidence that in the longer marriage, less satisfaction was attributed to the husband. The husband's feelings about sexual adjustment were described as "fair," "poor," or "very poor" by 14% of the wives whose marriage duration was less than three years. From three to six years the figure was 26%, and from seven to ten years it was 30%.

In the wives' evaluations of the frequency of sexual relations, no really significant differences were found by length of marriage, although there is some slight evidence that with greater length of marriage the wife may be more apt to define sexual relations as "too frequent" (12% in the seven-to-ten-year group as compared to 4% for those married less than three years and 2% in the three-to-six-year group). The "too infrequent" response remained relatively constant for the three groups (26%, 23%, and 27%).

Early in marriage romantic idealism often operates because there is limited experience with which individuals can make comparisons. With length of marriage, disillusionment may increase. In some cases where feelings of sexual maladjustment were severe, marriages would have ended through divorce. Therefore, the older group would include some women who were sexually dissatisfied, but not enough to have actually ended their marriages. Furthermore, the "traditional" view of the woman's sexual rights would in some cases be a part of a "traditional" view of marriage held by those less apt to turn to divorce.

The evidence is somewhat confusing on the relationship of length of marriage and sexual satisfaction. Early marriage may be a period where there would be high sexual satisfaction because of high personal anticipation by many young women. But the adjustment to the new wifely role and the reassessment of romantic beliefs about sex may sometimes create a feeling of frustration or lack of sexual satisfaction early in marriage. As length of marriage increases, the sexual aspects of marriage often become more realistically defined and natural for the wife. But at the same time other role demands, personal interests, or changes in the husband's sexual desires may cut down the wife's sexual satisfactions. So for many wives a variety of influences at different periods may negatively influence their sexual satisfactions.

Implications for the future

This study had as its primary purpose the delineation of some stated attitudes of college-educated wives as to how they perceive some aspects of sex in their marriages. There seems little doubt that the traditional values that minimized the feelings of personal sexual satisfaction for wives have been greatly altered. Future research should examine these changes in much greater detail.

We believe, however, that this study and others indicate that the college-educated wife is not only expecting, but also demanding, greater personal sexual satisfaction in marriage. This points to what may be an increasingly important problem area. Not only may women increasingly be achieving personal sexual satisfactions in marriage, but they may also be increasingly conscious of any self-defined lack of achievement.

One implied assumption of many writers has been that once the double-standard restrictions on marital coitus are removed for the wife, she will catch up to the husband in sexual desire and they will then be sexually equal in their desires and interests. But what has generally been overlooked is that a number of women may pass their husbands in sexual interest and desire.

The social and psychological sexual liberation of the modern woman has led some women to shed many past restrictions and inhibitions and emerge in their marriages with greater sexual interest than their husbands. As our data indicate, about one in four wives studied stated they were not satisfied with the frequency of coitus in their marriages. This is probably a new personal response for wives that carries important implications for many marriages.

Increasing importance of the biological difference in sexual capacity

The data on frequency of sexual relations point to an important difference between the male and the female. As more and more restrictions are removed from the woman and she is encouraged to achieve personal sexual satisfaction, it seems logical that she will increasingly desire greater frequency of sexual intercourse. This is confirmed by empirical evidence.[4,6]

Biologically, there is little to restrict the frequency with which women can indulge in sexual intercourse. She continues to be partially inhibited by social and psychological influences, but as these influences are altered or removed her sexual interests and desires may further expand. By contrast, most males are already free of many of the psychological and social restrictions about coitus (in and out of marriage) that operate for the woman. If women, through the loss or modification of inhibiting values, are moving in a less restricted direction of desiring personal sex satisfaction, then the biological differences between the male and the female in regard to sexual frequency are becoming of increasing importance.

A number of married couples may find that the sexual interests and desires of the wife have increased to a point greater than that of the husband. But because of biological limitations on the male he cannot normally function as a sex partner without some sexual interest (as women can and often do). While this is probably not an important problem early in marriage, it may become one as the couple grows older if the sexual interests of the woman increase because of the reduction of inhibitions, especially since the male's sexual drive and interest often decrease with age. Therefore the older wife may increasingly desire more frequent sexual activity while her husband is neither physically nor psychologically capable of satisfying her needs. This could have great significance for many aspects of the marriage relationship and the sense of personal role fulfillment for both husband and wife.

It is possible that in the near future there will be an increasing number of problems in marriage centering around the lack of sexual satisfaction by the wife. This is an ironic switch from the patriarchal past, but it is not merely an equivalent reversal of the past situation. The basic differences required of the male and the female for sexual intercourse may make the results far more serious for the sexually inadequate or uninterested male than they were for the personally unfulfilled female of the past.

Conclusion

If agreement as to frequency is taken as an indication of sexual balance in marriage, when one partner feels unfulfilled it is still most apt to be the husband. However, the limited evidence now available seems to support the speculative suggestion that the number of wives who are sexually frustrated in their marriages may increase in the future.

First, the extension of higher education to more women will probably lead more to accept the "emancipated" belief in sexual rights for wives. They will be more apt than the less educated women to enter marriage expecting and desiring personal sexual fulfillment, and hence more likely to feel some personal frustrations if their expectations are not met. Second, earlier age at marriage and longer life expectancy both increase the years of marriage during which sexual satisfaction is important.

References

1. Hunt, M. M.: The Natural History of Love (New York: Alfred A. Knopf, 1959), p. 319.
2. Davis, M.: The Sexual Responsibility of Women (New York: Permabooks, 1954), pp. 23, 24, 95.
3. Hunt, M. M.: Her Infinite Variety (New York: Harper & Row, 1962), p. 114.
4. Burgess, E. W., and Wallin, P.: Engagement and Marriage (Philadelphia: J. B. Lippincott Co., 1953), pp. 666, 697; chap. 20.
5. Rainwater, L.: And the Poor Get Children (Chicago: Quadrangle Books, 1960), p. 94.
6. Kinsey, A. C., Pomeroy, W. B., Martin, C. E., and Gebhard, P. H.: Sexual Behavior in the Human Female (Philadelphia: W. B. Saunders, 1953), p. 378; chap. 9.
7. Davis, K. B.: Factors in the Sex Life of Twenty-Two Hundred Women (New York: Harper & Brothers, 1929), pp. 73, 74.

11

The Politics of Orgasm

Susan Lydon

Tiresias, who had been both man and woman, was asked, as Ovid's legend goes, to mediate in a dispute between Jove and Juno as to which sex got more pleasure from lovemaking. Tiresias unhesitatingly answered that women did. Yet in the intervening 2,000 years between Ovid's time and our own, a mythology has been built up which not only holds the opposite to be true, but has made this belief an unswerving ideology dictating the quality of relations between the sexes. Woman's sexuality, defined by men to benefit men, has been down graded and preverted, repressed and channeled, denied and abused until women themselves, thoroughly convinced of their sexual inferiority to men, would probably be dumfounded to learn that there is scientific proof that Tiresias was indeed right.

The myth was codified by Freud, as much as by anyone else. In *Three Essays on the Theory of Sexuality*, Freud formulated his basic ideas concerning feminine sexuality: for little girls, the leading erogenous zone in their bodies is the clitoris; in order for the transition to womanhood to be successful, the clitoris must abandon its sexual primacy to the vagina; women in whom this transition has not been complete remain clitorally-oriented, or "sexually anaesthetic" and "psychosexually immature."

> The fact that women change their leading erotogenic zone in this way, (Freud wrote) together with the wave of repression at

Reprinted from Robin Morgan *Sisterhood is Powerful*, New York: Vintage Press, 1970, pp. 197–205, by permission of Susan Lydon, c/o International Famous Agency. Copyright © 1970 by Susan Lydon.

puberty, which, as it were, puts aside their childish masculinity, are the chief determinants of the greater proneness of women to neurosis and especially to hysteria. These determinants, therefore, are intimately related to the essence of femininity.

In the context of Freud's total psychoanalytic view of women — that they are not whole human beings but mutilated males who long all their lives for a penis and must struggle to reconcile themselves to its lack — the requirement of a transfer of erotic sensation from clitoris to vagina became a prima facie case for their inevitable sexual (and moral) inferiority. In Freud's logic, those who struggle to become what they are not must be inferior to that to which they aspire.

Freud wrote that he could not "escape the notion (though I hesitate to give it expression) that for women the level of what is ethically normal is different from what it is in men. . . . We must not allow ourselves to be deflected from such conclusions by the denials of the feminists, who are anxious to force us to regard the two sexes as completely equal in position and worth."

Freud himself admitted near the end of his life that his knowledge of women was inadequate. "If you want to know more about femininity, you must interrogate your own experience, or turn to the poets, or wait until science can give you more information," he said; he also expressed the hope that the female psychoanalysts who followed him would be able to find out more. But the post-Freudians adhered rigidly to the doctrine of the master, and, as in most of his work, what Freud hoped would be taken as a thesis for future study became instead a kind of canon law.

While the neo-Freudians haggled over the correct reading of the Freudian bible, watered-down Freudianism was wending its way into the cultural mythology via Broadway plays, novelists, popular magazines, social scientists, marriage counselors, and experts of various kinds who found it useful in projecting desired images of women. The superiority of the vaginal over the clitoral orgasm was particularly useful as a theory, since it provided a convenient basis for categorization: clitoral women were deemed immature, neurotic, bitchy, and masculine; women who had vaginal orgasms were maternal, feminine, mature, and normal. Though frigidity should technically be defined as total inability to achieve orgasm, the orthodox Freudians (and pseudo-Freudians) preferred to define it as inability to achieve vaginal orgasm, by which definition, in 1944, Edmond Bergler adjudged between 70 and 80 percent of all women frigid. The clitoral vs. vaginal debate raged hot and heavy among the sexologists — although Kinsey's writings stressed the importance of the clitoris to female orgasm and contradicted Bergler's statistics — but it became clear that there was something indispensable to the society in the Freudian view which allowed it to remain unchallenged in the public consciousness.

In 1966, Dr. William H. Masters and Mrs. Virginia E. Johnson published

Human Sexual Response, a massive clinical study of the physiology of sex. Briefly and simply, the Masters and Johnson conclusions about the female orgasm, based on observation and interviews with 487 women, were these:

1) That the dichotomy of vaginal and clitoral orgasms is entirely false. Anatomically, all orgasms are centered in the clitoris, whether they result from direct manual pressure applied to the clitoris, indirect pressure resulting from the thrusting of penis during intercourse, or generalized sexual stimulation of other erogenous zones like the breasts.

2) That women are naturally multi-orgasmic; that is, if a woman is immediately stimulated following orgasm, she is likely to experience several orgasms in rapid succession. This is not an exceptional occurrence, but one of which most women are capable.

3) That while women's orgasms do not vary in kind, they vary in intensity. The most intense orgasms experienced by the research subjects were by masturbatory manual stimulation, followed in intensity by manual stimulation by the partner; the least intense orgasms were experienced by women during intercourse.

4) That the female orgasm is as real and identifiable a physiological entity as the male's; it follows the same pattern of erection and detumescence of the clitoris, which may be seen as the female equivalent of the penis.

5) That there is an "infinite variety of female sexual response" as regards intensity and duration of orgasms.

To anyone acquainted with the body of existing knowledge of feminine sexuality, the Masters and Johnson findings were truly revolutionary and liberating in the extent to which they demolished the established myths. Yet four years after the study was published, it seems hardly to have made much of an impact at all. Certainly it is not for lack of information that the myths persist; *Human Sexual Response,* despite its weighty scientific language, was an immediate best-seller, and popular paperbacks explicated it to millions of people in simpler language and at a cheaper price. The mythology remains intact because a male-dominated American culture has a vested interest in its continuance.

Dr. William Masters had searched for a woman co-worker for his research because, as he said, "No male really understands female sexuality." Before Masters and Johnson, female sexuality had been objectively defined and described by men; the subjective experience of women had had no part in defining their own sexuality. And men defined feminine sexuality in a way as favorable to themselves as possible. If woman's pleasure was obtained through the vagina, then she was totally dependent on the man's erect penis to achieve orgasm; she would receive her satisfaction only as a concomitant of man's seeking his. With the clitoral orgasm, woman's sexual pleasure was independent of the male's, and she could seek her satisfaction as aggressively as the man sought his, a prospect which didn't appeal to too many men. The definition of normal feminine sexuality as vaginal, in other words, was a part of keeping women down, of making them sexually, as well as economically, socially, and politically subservient.

In retrospect, particularly with the additional perspective of our own time, Freud's theory of feminine sexuality appears an historical rationalization for the realities of Victorian society. Culture-bound in the Victorian ethos, Freud had to play the role of pater familias. Serving the ethos, he developed a psychology that robbed Victorian women of possible politics. In Freud's theory of penis envy, the penis functioned as the unalterable determinant of maleness which women could symbolically envy instead of the power and prestige given men by the society. It was a refusal to grant women acknowledgment that they had been wronged by their culture and their times; according to Freud, women's lower status had not been conferred upon her by men, but by God, who had created her without a penis.

Freud's insistence on the superiority of the vaginal orgasm seems almost a demonic determination on his part to finalize the Victorian's repression of feminine eroticism, to stigmatize the remaining vestiges of pleasure felt by women, and thus make them unacceptable to the women themselves. For there were still women whose sexuality hadn't been completely destroyed, as evidenced by one Dr. Isaac Brown Baker, a surgeon who performed numerous clitoridectomies on women to prevent the sexual excitement which, he was convinced, caused "insanities," "catalepsy," "hysteria," "epilepsy," and other diseases. The Victorians had needed to repress sexuality for the success of Western industrialized society; in particular, the total repression of woman's sexuality was crucial to ensure her subjugation. So the Victorians honored only the male ejaculation, that aspect of sexuality which was necessary to the survival of the species; the male ejaculation made women submissive to sex by creating a mystique of the sanctity of motherhood; and, supported by Freud, passed on to us the heritage of the double standard.

When Kinsey laid to rest the part of the double standard that maintained women got no pleasure at all from sex, everyone cried out that there was a sexual revolution afoot. But such talk, as usual, was deceptive. Morality, outside the marriage bed, remained the same, and children were socialized as though Kinsey had never described what they would be like when they grew up. Boys were taught that they should get their sex where they could find it, "go as far" as they could. On the old assumption that women were asexual creatures, girls were taught that since they needed sex less than boys did, it was up to them to impose sexual restraints. In whatever sex education adolescents did manage to receive, they were told that men had penises and women vaginas; the existence of the clitoris was not mentioned, and pleasure in sex was never discussed at all.

Adolescent boys growing up begging for sexual crumbs from girls frightened for their "reputations" — a situation that remains unchanged to this day — hardly constitutes the vanguard of a sexual revolution. However, the marriage-manual craze that followed Kinsey assumed that a lifetime of psychological destruction could, with the aid of a little booklet, be abandoned after marriage, and that husband and wife should be able to make sure that the wife was not robbed of her sexual birthright to orgasm, just so long as it was vaginal (though the marriage manuals did rather reluctantly admit that since the clitoris was the most sexually sensitive organ in the female body, a little clitoral stimulation in foreplay was in order), and so long as their orgasms were simultaneous.

The effect of the marriage manuals of course ran counter to their ostensible purpose. Under the guise of frankness and sexual liberation, they dictated prudery and restraint. Sex was made so mechanized, detached, and intellectual that it was robbed of its sensuality. Man became a spectator of his own sexual experience. And the marriage manuals put new pressure on women. The swing was from repression to preoccupation with the orgasm. Men took the marriage manuals to mean that their sexuality would be enhanced by bringing women to orgasm and, again co-opting feminine sexuality for their own ends, they put pressure on women to perform. The endorsement by the marriage manuals of the desirability of vaginal orgasm insured that women would be asked not only, "Did you come?," but also, "Did you conform to Freud's conception of a psychosexually mature woman, and thereby validate my masculinity?"

Rather than being revolutionary, the present sexual situation is tragic. Appearances notwithstanding, the age-old taboos against conversation about personal sexual experience still haven't broken down. This reticence has allowed the mind-manipulators of the media to create myths of sexual supermen and superwomen. So the bed becomes a competitive arena, where men and women measure themselves against these mythical rivals, while simultaneously trying to live up to the ecstasies promised them by the marriage manuals and the fantasies of the media ("If the earth doesn't move for me, I must be missing something," the reasoning goes.) Our society treats sex as a sport, with its record-breakers, its judges, its rules, and its spectators.

As anthropologists have shown, women's sexual response is culturally conditioned; historically, women defer to whatever model of their sexuality is offered by men. So the sad thing for women is that they have participated in the destruction of their own eroticism. Women have helped make the vaginal orgasm into a status symbol in a male-dictated system of values. A woman would now perceive her preference for clitoral orgasm as a "secret shame," ignominious in the eyes of other women as well as those of men.

This internalization can be seen in the literature: Mary McCarthy's and Doris Lessing's writings on orgasm do not differ substantially from D. H. Lawrence's and Ernest Hemingway's, and even Simone de Beauvoir, in *The Second Sex*, refers to vaginal orgasm as the only "normal satisfaction."

Rather than working to alleviate the pressure on them, women have increased it. Feeling themselves insecure in a competitive situation, they are afraid to admit their own imagined inadequacies, and lie to other women about their sexual experiences. With their men, they often fake orgasm to appear "good in bed" and thus place an intolerable physical burden on themselves and a psychological burden on the men unlucky enough to see through the ruse.

One factor that has made this unfortunate situation possible is ignorance: the more subtle and delicate aspects of human sexuality are still not fully understood. For example, a woman's ability to attain orgasm seems to be conditioned as much by her emotions as by physiology and sociology. Masters and Johnson proved that the orgasm experienced during intercourse, the misnamed vaginal orgasm, did not differ anatomically from the clitoral orgasm. But this should not be seen as their most significant contribution to the sexual emancipation of women. A difference remains in the subjective experience of orgasm during intercourse and orgasm apart from intercourse. In the complex of emotional factors affecting feminine sexuality, there is a whole panoply of pleasures: the pleasure of being penetrated and filled by a man, the pleasure of sexual communication, the pleasure of affording a man his orgasm, the erotic pleasure that exists even when sex is not terminated by orgasmic release. Masters and Johnson's real contribution was to stress an "infinite variety of female sexual response." One should be able to appreciate the differences, rather than impose value judgments on them.

There is no doubt that Masters and Johnson were fully aware of the implications of their study to the sexual liberation of women. As they wrote, "With orgasmic physiology established, the human female now has an undeniable opportunity to develop realistically her own sexual response levels." Two years later this statement seems naive and entirely too optimistic. Certainly the sexual problems of our society will never be solved until there is real and unfeigned equality between men and women. This idea is usually misconstrued: sexual liberation for women is wrongly understood to mean that women will adopt all the forms of masculine sexuality. As in the whole issue of women's liberation, that's really not the point. Women don't aspire to imitate the mistakes of men in sexual matters, to view sexual experiences as conquest and ego-enhancement, to use other people to serve their own ends. But if the Masters and Johnson material is allowed to filter into the public consciousness, hopefully to replace the enshrined Freudian myths, then woman at long last will be allowed to take the first step toward her emancipation, to define and enjoy the forms of her own sexuality.

part six

Homosexuality

Homosexuality in our society is so surrounded with a haze of myth, ignorance, and emotionalism that any discussion of it must begin with an attempt to clear away the more noxious elements of this haze. One of the most fundamental and widespread misconceptions about homosexuality is that it is an either-or phenomenon. That is, a sexual interest in one's own sex precludes a similar interest in members of the opposite sex. Nothing could be further from the truth! For many, the most startling findings of the Kinsey study were those concerning the incidence of homosexuality in the general population. Thirty-seven per cent of the male population and 13 per cent of the female population had had some homosexual response to the point of orgasm since adolescence and only 4 per cent of the males and 2 per cent of the females were exclusively homosexual during this period.[1] As Mary McIntosh suggests, in an article included in this section, there is some reason to believe the figures would be higher if it were not for the fact that homosexuality is so stigmatized in Western societies. In any case, the Kinsey findings make it clear that "homosexuality" is something which informs the sexual experience of many people, most of whom very probably don't think of themselves as homosexuals.

What may account for a good part of the confusion surrounding homosexuality is the failure of professionals and

172

laymen alike to distinguish between the concepts of "gender" and "sexual taste." Gender, which is believed to be established by age five, refers to social-sexual role and includes general cultural expectations regarding the way in which one sex or the other should talk, use body language, express emotion, and so on. In other words, it is what we are responding to when we describe someone as "masculine" or "feminine." While it is true that there is generally congruence between gender and sexual taste this is not always the case. Even those individuals whose sexual tastes are exclusively homosexual are for the most part unidentifiable in terms of appearance or mannerisms. Interestingly enough a recent study of married, male transvestites (men who occasionally dress as women) by H. Taylor Buckner found them to have engaged in very little actual homosexual behavior.[2] So we see homosexual experiences are not only common, but those who have had them frequently do not externally convey their sexual predilections.

A great many words have been expended trying to explain the "causes" of homosexuality. Most of these "explanations" have started with the assumption that homosexuality is an illness, generally a mental illness. This is not surprising since today we fall back on psychopathology to explain deviance in the same way our forebears used witchcraft. Frequently the

173

roots of this "disorder" are seen as lying in early childhood experience in the context of the family. Psychoanalysts such as Irving Beiber, see male homosexuals, for example, as products of homes with overbearing mothers and weak ineffectual fathers.[3] Not only are etiological explanations such as this one devoid of convincing evidence, but they also reflect a rather parochial view of human sexuality. By condemning those who engage in homosexual behavior to the ranks of the mentally ill, a dubious category in itself, we preclude a detached consideration of how sexual tastes develop, something we know little about.

Completing the circle is the illegal status of homosexuality. While homosexuality *per se* is not a crime, in the vast majority of states modes of sexual expression such as oral-genital and anal-genital contact are felonies (serious criminal offenses), in some cases punishable by life sentences. To the extent that these acts involve consenting adults, there is no victim in the sense in which this term is generally understood and thus these acts must be viewed as crimes against "public morality." Legislating morality is a sensitive matter, especially in a highly diverse society such as our own, and therefore it has been argued that the laws governing homosexual acts as well as other forms of noncoital sexual activity between consenting adults should be struck down. This has already been done by two states (Illinois and Connecticut), and before this decade ends other states undoubtedly will join their ranks.

Since the vast majority of homosexual acts take place in privacy between adults (the alleged longing of male homosexuals for boys is without empirical support), such new laws will not have much direct impact on homosexuals nor will they, as some fear, encourage homosexuality. Most arrests are made in public places such as bathrooms and steamrooms, common places for homosexual encounters, and these arrests will continue to be made under "outrageous conduct" and "lewd behavior" statutes. The importance of the Illinois and Connecticut legislation is that it has removed the stigma of criminality from those who engage in homosexual acts. By doing this much of the rationale used by various agencies to deny homosexuals employment are at least partially undermined, and furthermore the fear of blackmail is reduced. This is not to say legislation will completely or even greatly alter the pariah position of homosexuals; people will still use the term "fag" with disdain and derision and certain avenues to vocational opportunities may still be closed.

Something which, however, may go a long way toward enabling those who identify themselves as homosexuals to cope

174

with the discrimination and disdain they encounter is the homophile movement, especially in its recent posture. Many minority groups have benefited from the experiences of the Civil Rights movement and the more militant organizations it bred. The strategies adopted by Blacks have been taken over by Feminists and homophile groups as well. This represents a marked departure from the previous tactics of the latter. The homophile movement which was founded in the 1950s functioned in that decade largely as a public education and mutual support organization for homosexuals. In the 1960s, as Laud Humphries has noted, such organizations with the aid of the American Civil Liberties Union began to fight for legislative change.[4] As the sixties came to a close, the movement became increasingly radicalized and student homophile organizations surfaced on many campuses. We now see Gay Liberation demonstrations in which marchers carry banners with slogans such as "Gay Power" and "Gay is Beautiful." These developments have enabled many young and not so young homosexuals to — in their words — "come out of the closet" and come to grips with homosexual inclination without shame, disgust, or guilt.

For the most part in this introduction we have tried to cover aspects of homosexuality that are not specifically dealt with in the articles that follow. The latter have been chosen to convey that what is labeled homosexuality is not a monolithic entity; quite the contrary it is characterized by great diversity. Taken together this introduction and the articles should serve to give the reader an appreciation of the complexity and diversity of what is often unfortunately dismissed as an abberation without a consideration of how this behavior articulates with more conventional forms of sexual expression.

Notes

1. Kinsey, Alfred C., Wardell B. Pomeroy, Clyde Martin, and Paul W. Gebhard, *Sexual Behavior in The Human Female,* Philadelphia: W. B. Saunders Company, 1953, pp. 474–475.
2. Buckner, H. Taylor, "The Transvetic Career Path," *Psychiatry,* August, 1970, pp. 381–389.
3. Beiber, Irving, *et al., Homosexuality, A Psychoanalytic Study,* New York: Vintage Books, 1962.
4. Humphreys, Laud, "New Styles in Homosexual Manliness," *Transaction,* March/April, 1971, pp. 38–46+64–66.

12

The Homosexual Role

Mary McIntosh

Recent advances in the sociology of deviant behavior have not yet affected the study of homosexuality, which is still commonly seen as a condition characterizing certain persons in the way that birthplace or deformity might characterize them. The limitations of this view can best be understood if we examine some of its implications. In the first place, if homosexuality is a condition, then people either have it or do not have it. Many scientists and ordinary people assume that there are two kinds of people in the world: homosexuals and heterosexuals. Some of them recognize that homosexual feelings and behavior are not confined to the persons they would like to call "homosexuals" and that some of these persons do not actually engage in homosexual behavior. This should pose a crucial problem; but they evade the crux by retaining their assumption and puzzling over the question of how to tell whether someone is "really" homosexual or not. Lay people too will discuss whether a certain person is "queer" in much the same way as they might question whether a certain pain indicated cancer. And in much the same way they will often turn to scientists or to medical men for a surer diagnosis. The scientists, for their part, feel it incumbent on them to seek criteria for diagnosis.

Thus one psychiatrist, discussing the definitions of homosexuality, has written:

Reprinted from *Social Problems*, Vol. 16, No. 2, Fall, 1968, pp. 182–192, by permission of The Society for the Study of Social Problems and the author.

> ... I do not diagnose patients as homosexual unless they have
> engaged in overt homosexual behavior. Those who also engage in
> heterosexual activity are diagnosed as bisexual. An isolated ex-
> perience may not warrant the diagnosis, but repetetive (sic)
> homosexual behavior in adulthood, whether sporadic or continu-
> ous, designates a homosexual.[1]

Along with many other writers, he introduces the notion of a third type
of person, the "bisexual" to handle the fact that behavior patterns cannot be
conveniently dichotomized into heterosexual and homosexual. But this does
not solve the conceptual problem, since bisexuality too is seen as a condition (unless as a passing response to unusual situations such as confinement
in a one-sex prison). In any case there is no extended discussion of bisexuality; the topic is usually given a brief mention in order to clear the ground
for the consideration of "true homosexuality."

To cover the cases where the symptoms of behavior or of felt attractions
do not match the diagnosis, other writers have referred to an adolescent
homosexual phase or have used such terms as "latent homosexual" or
"pseudo homosexual." Indeed one of the earliest studies of the subject, by
Krafft-Ebing, was concerned with making a distinction between the "invert"
who is congenitally homosexual and others who, although they behave in
the same way, are not true inverts.[2]

A second result of the conceptualization of homosexuality as a condition
is that the major research task has been seen as the study of its etiology.
There has been much debate as to whether the condition is innate or acquired. The first step in such research has commonly been to find a sample
of "homosexuals" in the same way that a medical researcher might find a
sample of diabetics if he wanted to study that disease. Yet, after a long history of such studies, the results are sadly inconclusive and the answer is
still as much a matter of opinion as it was when Havelock Ellis published
Sexual Inversion[3] seventy years ago. The failure of research to answer the
question has not been due to lack of scientific rigor or to any inadequacy of
the available evidence; it results rather from the fact that the wrong question
has been asked. One might as well try to trace the etiology of committee-
chairmanship" or "Seventh-Day Adventism" as of "homosexuality."

The vantage-point of comparative sociology enables us to see that the
conception of homosexuality as a condition is, in itself, a possible object of
study. This conception and the behavior it supports operate as a form of
social control in a society in which homosexuality is condemned. Furthermore, the uncritical acceptance of the conception by social scientists can be
traced to their concern with homosexuality as a social problem. They have
tended to accept the popular definition of what the problem is and they
have been implicated in the process of social control.

The practice of the social labeling of persons as deviant operates in two ways as a mechanism of social control.[4] In the first place it helps to provide a clear-cut, publicized, and recognizable threshold between permissible and impermissible behavior. This means that people cannot so easily drift into deviant behavior. Their first moves in a deviant direction immediately raise the question of a total move into a deviant role with all the sanctions that this is likely to elicit. Secondly, the labeling serves to segregate the deviants from others and this means that their deviant practices and their self-justifications for these practices are contained within a relatively narrow group. The creation of a specialized, despised, and punished role of homosexual keeps the bulk of society pure in rather the same way that the similar treatment of some kinds of criminals helps keep the rest of society law-abiding.

However, the disadvantage of this practice as a technique of social control is that there may be a tendency for people to become fixed in their deviance once they have become labeled. This, too, is a process that has become well-recognized in discussions of other forms of deviant behavior such as juvenile delinquency and drug taking and, indeed, of other kinds of social labeling such as streaming in schools and racial distinctions. One might expect social categorizations of this sort to be to some extent self-fulfilling prophecies: if the culture defines people as falling into distinct types — black and white, criminal and non-criminal, homosexual and normal — then these types will tend to become polarized, highly differentiated from each other. Later in this paper I shall discuss whether this is so in the case of homosexuals and "normals" in the United States today.

It is interesting to notice that homosexuals themselves welcome and support the notion that homosexuality is a condition. For just as the rigid categorization deters people from drifting into deviancy, so it appears to foreclose on the possibility of drifting back into normality and thus removes the element of anxious choice. It appears to justify the deviant behavior of the homosexual as being appropriate for him as a member of the homosexual category. The deviancy can thus be seen as legitimate for him and he can continue in it without rejecting the norms of the society.[5]

The way in which people become labeled as homosexual can now be seen as an important social process connected with mechanisms of social control. It is important, therefore, that sociologists should examine this process objectively and not lend themselves to participation in it, particularly since, as we have seen, psychologists and psychiatrists on the whole have not retained their objectivity but become involved as diagnostic agents in the process of social labeling.[6]

It is proposed that the homosexual should be seen as playing a social role rather than as having a condition. The role of "homosexual," however, does not simply describe a sexual behavior pattern. If it did, the idea of a role would be no more useful than that of a condition. For the purpose of introducing the term "role" is to enable us to handle the fact that behavior in this sphere does not match popular beliefs: that sexual behavior patterns cannot be dichotomized in the way that the social roles of homosexual and heterosexual can.

It may seem rather odd to distinguish in this way between role and behavior, but if we accept a definition of role in terms of expectations (which may or may not be fulfilled), then the distinction is both legitimate and useful. In modern societies where a separate homosexual role is recognized, the expectation, on behalf of those who play the role and of others, is that a homosexual will be exclusively or very predominantly homosexual in his feelings and behavior. In addition, there are other expectations that frequently exist, especially on the part of nonhomosexuals, but affecting the self-conception of anyone who sees himself as homosexual. These are: the expectation that he will be effeminate in manner, personality, or preferred sexual activity; the expectation that sexuality will play a part of some kind in all his relations with other men; and the expectation that he will be attracted to boys and very young men and probably willing to seduce them. The existence of a social expectation, of course, commonly helps to produce its own fulfillment. But the question of how far it is fulfilled is a matter for empirical investigation rather than a priori pronouncement. Some of the empirical evidence about the chief expectation — that homosexuality precludes heterosexuality — in relation to the homosexual role in America is examined in the final section of this paper.[7]

In order to clarify the nature of the role and demonstrate that it exists only in certain societies, we shall present the cross-cultural and historical evidence available. This raises awkward problems of method because the material has hitherto usually been collected and analyzed in terms of culturally specific modern western conceptions.

The Homosexual Role in Various Societies

To study homosexuality in the past or other societies we usually have to rely on secondary evidence rather than on direct observation. The reliability and the validity of such evidence is open to question because what the original observers reported may have been distorted by their disapproval of homosexuality and by their definition of it, which may be different from the one we wish to adopt.

For example, Marc Daniel tries to refute accusations of homosexuality against Pope Julian II by producing four arguments: the Pope had many enemies who might wish to blacken his name; he and his supposed lover, Alidosi, both had mistresses; neither of them was at all effeminate; and the Pope had other men friends about whom no similar accusations were made.[8] In other words Daniel is trying to fit an early sixteenth century Pope to the

179

modern conception of the homosexual as effeminate, exclusively homosexual, and sexual in relation to all men. The fact that he does not fit is, of course, no evidence, as Daniel would have it, that his relationship with Alidosi was not a sexual one.

Anthropologists too can fall into this trap. Marvin Opler, summarizing anthropological evidence on the subject, says:

> Actually, no society, save perhaps Ancient Greece, pre-Meiji Japan, certain top echelons in Nazi Germany, and the scattered examples of such special status groups as the berdaches, Nata slaves, and one category of Chuckchee shamans, has lent sanction in any real sense to homosexuality.[9]

Yet he goes on to discuss societies in which there are reports of sanctioned adolescent and other occasional "experimentation." Of the Cubeo of the North West Amazon, for instance, he says, "*true* homosexuality among the Cubeo is rare if not absent," giving as evidence the fact that no males with persistent homosexual patterns are reported.[10]

Allowing for such weaknesses, the Human Relations Area Files are the best single source of comparative information. Their evidence on homosexuality has been summarized by Ford and Beach,[11] who identify two broad types of accepted patterns: the institutionalized homosexual role and the liaison between men or boys who are otherwise heterosexual.

The recognition of a distinct role of *berdache* or transvestite is, they say, "the commonest form of institutionalized homosexuality." This form shows a marked similarity to that in our own society, though in some ways it is even more extreme. The Mohave Indians of California and Arizona, for example,[12] recognized both an *alyhā*, a male transvestite who took the role of the woman in sexual intercourse, and a *hwamē*, a female homosexual who took the role of the male. People were believed to be born as *alyhā* or *hwamē*, hints of their future proclivities occurring in their mothers' dreams during pregnancy. If a young boy began to behave like a girl and take an interest in women's things instead of men's, there was an initiation ceremony in which he would become an *alyhā*. After that he would dress and act like a woman, would be referred to as "she" and could take "husbands."

But the Mohave pattern differs from ours in that although the *alyhā* was considered regrettable and amusing, he was not condemned and was given public recognition. The attitude was that "he was an *alyhā*, he could not help it." But the "husband" of an *alyhā* was an ordinary man who happened to have chosen an *alyhā*, perhaps because they were good housekeepers or because they were believed to be "lucky in love," and he would be the butt of endless teasing and joking.

This radical distinction between the feminine passive homosexual and his masculine active partner is one which is not made very much in our own society,[13] but which is very important in the Middle East. There, however, neither is thought of as being a "born" homosexual, although the passive partner, who demeans himself by his feminine submission, is despised and ridiculed, while the active one is not. In most of the ancient Middle East, including among the Jews until the return from the Babylonian exile, there were male temple prostitutes.[14] Thus even cultures that recognize a separate homosexual role may not define it in the same way as our culture does.

Many other societies accept or approve of homosexual liaisons as part of a variegated sexual pattern. Usually these are confined to a particular stage in the individual's life. Among the Aranda of Central Australia, for instance, there are long-standing relationships of several years' duration, between unmarried men and young boys, starting at the age of ten to twelve.[15] This is rather similar to the well-known situation in classical Greece, but there, of course, the older man could have a wife as well. Sometimes, however, as among the Siwans of North Africa,[16] all men and boys can and are expected to engage in homosexual activities, apparently at every stage of life. In all of these societies there may be much homosexual behavior, but there are no "homosexuals."

The Development of the Homosexual Role in England

The problem of method is even more acute in dealing with historical material than with anthropological, for history is usually concerned with "great events" rather than with recurrent patterns. There are some records of attempts to curb sodomy among minor churchmen during the medieval period,[17] which seem to indicate that it was common. At least they suggest that laymen feared on behalf of their sons that it was common. The term "catamite" meaning "boy kept for immoral purposes," was first used in 1593, again suggesting that this practice was common then. But most of the historical references to homosexuality relate either to great men or to great scandals. However, over the last seventy years or so various scholars have tried to trace the history of sex,[18] and it is possible to glean a good deal from what they have found and also from what they have failed to establish.

Their studies of English history before the seventeenth century consist usually of inconclusive speculation as to whether certain men, such as Edward II, Christopher Marlowe, William Shakespeare, were or were not homosexual. Yet the disputes are inconclusive not because of lack of evidence but because none of these men fits the modern stereotype of the homosexual.

It is not until the end of the seventeenth century that other kinds of information become available and it is possible to move from speculations about individuals to descriptions of homosexual life. At this period references to homosexuals as a type and to a rudimentary homosexual subculture, mainly in London, begin to appear. But the earliest descriptions of homosexuals do not coincide exactly with the modern conception. There is much more stress on effeminacy and in particular in transvestism, to such an extent that there seems to be no distinction at first between transvestism and homosexuality.[19] The terms emerging at this period to describe homosexuals — Molly, Nancy-boy, Madge-cull — emphasize effeminacy. In contrast the modern terms — like fag, queer, gay, bent — do not have this implication.[20]

By the end of the seventeenth century, homosexual transvestites were a distinct enough group to be able to form their own clubs in London.[21] Edward Ward's *History of the London Clubs*, published in 1709, describes one called "The Mollies' Club" which met "in a certain tavern in the City" for "parties and regular gatherings." The members "adopt(ed) all the small vanities natural to the feminine sex to such an extent that they try to speak, walk, chatter, shriek and scold as women do, aping them as well in other respects." The other respects apparently included the enactment of marriages and child-birth. The club was discovered and broken up by agents of the Reform Society.[22] There were a number of similar scandals during the course of the eighteenth century as various homosexual coteries were exposed.

A writer in 1729 describes the widespread homosexual life of the period:

> They also have their Walks and Appointments, to meet and pick up one another, and their particular Houses of Resort to go to, because they dare not trust themselves in an open Tavern. About twenty of these sort of Houses have been discovered, besides the Nocturnal Assemblies of great numbers of the like vile Persons, what they call the *Markets*, which are the Royal Exchange, Lincoln's Inn, Bog Houses, the south side of St. James's Park, the Piazzas in Covent Garden, St. Clement's Churchyard, etc.
>
> It would be a pretty scene to behold them in their clubs and cabals, how they assume the air and affect the name of Madam or Miss, Betty or Molly, with a chuck under the chin, and "Oh, you bold pullet, I'll break your eggs," and then frisk and walk away.[23]

The notion of exclusive homosexuality became well-established during this period. When "two Englishmen, Leith and Drew, were accused of paederasty. . . . The evidence given by the plaintiffs was, as was generally the case in these trials, very imperfect. On the other hand the defendants denied the accusation, and produced witnesses to prove their predeliction for women. They were in consequence acquitted."[24] This could only have

182

been an effective argument in a society that perceived homosexual behavior as incompatible with heterosexual tastes.

During the nineteenth century there are further reports of raided clubs and homosexual brothels. However, by this time the element of transvestism had diminished in importance. Even the male prostitutes are described as being of masculine build and there is more stress upon sexual license and less upon dressing up and play-acting.

THE HOMOSEXUAL ROLE AND HOMOSEXUAL BEHAVIOR

Thus, a distinct, separate, specialized role of "homosexual" emerged in England at the end of the seventeenth century and the conception of homosexuality as a condition which characterizes certain individuals and not others is now firmly established in our society. The term role is, of course, a form of shorthand. It refers not only to a cultural conception or set of ideas but also to a complex of institutional arrangements which depend upon and reinforce these ideas. These arrangements include all the forms of heterosexual activity, courtship, and marriage as well as the labeling processes — gossip, ridicule, psychiatric diagnosis, criminal conviction — and the groups and networks of the homosexual subculture. For simplicity we shall simply say that a specialized role exists.

How does the existence of this social role affect actual behavior? And, in particular, does the behavior of individuals conform to the cultural conception in the sense that most people are either exclusively heterosexual or exclusively homosexual? It is difficult to answer these questions on the basis of available evidence because so many researchers have worked with the preconception that homosexuality is a condition, so that in order to study the behavior they have first found a group of people who could be identified as "homosexuals." Homosexual behavior should be studied independently of social roles, if the connection between the two is to be revealed.

This may not sound like a particularly novel program to those who are familiar with Kinsey's contribution to the field.[25] He, after all, set out to study "sexual behavior;" he rejected the assumptions of scientists and laymen:

> that there are persons who are "heterosexual" and persons who are "homosexual", that these two types represent antitheses in the sexual world and that there is only an insignificant class of "bisexuals" who occupy an intermediate position between the other groups . . . that every individual is innately — inherently — either heterosexual or homosexual . . . (and) that from the time of birth one is fated to be one thing or the other . . .[26]

But, although some of Kinsey's ideas are often referred to, particularly in polemical writings, surprisingly little use has been made of his actual data. Most of Kinsey's chapter on the "Homosexual Outlet"[27] centers on his "heterosexual-homosexual rating scale." His subjects were rated on this scale according to the proportion of their "psychologic reactions and overt experience" that was homosexual in any given period of their lives. It is interesting, and unfortunate for our purposes, that this is one of the few places in the book where Kinsey abandons his behavioristic approach to some extent. However, "psychologic reactions" may well be expected to be affected by the existence of a social role in the same way as overt behavior. Another problem with using Kinsey's material is that although he gives very full information about sexual behavior, the other characteristics of the people he interviewed are only given in a very bald form.[28] But Kinsey's study is undoubtedly the fullest description there is of sexual behavior in any society and as such it is the safest basis for generalizations to other Western societies.

The ideal way to trace the effects on behavior of the existence of a homosexual role would be to compare societies in which the role exists with societies in which it does not. But as there are no adequate descriptions of homosexual behavior in societies where there is no homosexual role, we shall have to substitute comparisons within American society.

(1) POLARIZATION

If the existence of a social role were reflected in people's behavior, we should expect to find that relatively few people would engage in bisexual behavior. The problem about investigating this empirically is to know what is meant by "relatively few." The categories of Kinsey's rating scale are, of course, completely arbitrary. He has five bisexual categories, but he might just as well have had more or less, in which case the number falling into each would have been smaller or larger. The fact that the distribution of his scale is U-shaped, then, is in itself meaningless. (See Table 1).

It is impossible to get direct evidence of a polarization between the homosexual and the heterosexual pattern, though we may note the suggestive evidence to the contrary that at every age far more men have bisexual than exclusively homosexual patterns. However, by making comparisons between one age group and another and between men and women, it should be possible to see some of the effects of the role.

(2) AGE COMPARISON

As they grow older, more and more men take up exclusively heterosexual patterns, as Table 1, Column 2 shows. The table also shows that *each* of the bisexual and homosexual categories, columns 3–8, contains fewer men as time goes by after the age of 20. The greatest losses are from the fifth bisexual category, column 7, with responses that are "almost entirely homosexual." It is a fairly small group to begin with, but by the age of 45 it has almost entirely disappeared. On the other hand the first bisexual category,

table 1

HETEROSEXUAL-HOMOSEXUAL RATING:
ACTIVE INCIDENCE BY AGE*

	Percent of each age group of male population having each rating								
Age	(1) X	(2) 0	(3) 1	(4) 2	(5) 3	(6) 4	(7) 5	(8) 6	(9) 1–6
15	23.6	48.4	3.6	6.0	4.7	3.7	2.6	7.4	28.0
20	3.3	69.3	4.4	7.4	4.4	2.9	3.4	4.9	27.4
25	1.0	79.2	3.9	5.1	3.2	2.4	2.3	2.9	19.8
30	0.5	83.1	4.0	3.4	2.1	3.0	1.3	2.6	16.4
35	0.4	86.7	2.4	3.4	1.9	1.7	0.9	2.6	12.9
40	1.3	86.8	3.0	3.6	2.0	0.7	0.3	2.3	11.9
45	2.7	88.8	2.3	2.0	1.3	0.9	0.2	1.8	8.5

* Based on Kinsey (1948) p. 652, Table 148.
X = unresponsive to either sex; 0 = entirely heterosexual; 1 = largely heterosexual, but
with incidental homosexual history; 2 = largely heterosexual but with a distinct homosexual
history; 3 = equally heterosexual and homosexual; 4 = largely homosexual but with distinct heterosexual history; 5 = largely homosexual but with incidental heterosexual history;
6 = entirely homosexual.

column 3, with only "incidental homosexual histories" has its numbers not
even halved by the age of 45. Yet at all ages the first bisexual category represents a much smaller proportion of those who are almost entirely homosexual (columns 2 and 3) than the fifth category represents of those who are
almost entirely homosexual (columns 7 and 8). In everyday language, it
seems that proportionately more "homosexuals" dabble in heterosexual activity than "heterosexuals" dabble in homosexual activity and such dabbling
is particularly common in the younger age groups of 20 to 30. This indicates
that the existence of the despised role operates at all ages to inhibit people
from engaging in occasional homosexual behavior, but does not have the effect of making the behavior of many "homosexuals" exclusively homosexual.

On the other hand, the overall reduction in the amount of homosexual
behavior with age can be attributed in part to the fact that more and more
men become married. While the active incidence of homosexual behavior is
high and increases with age among single men, among married men it is
low and decreases only slightly with age. Unfortunately the Kinsey figures
do not enable us to compare the incidence of homosexuality among single
men who later marry and those who do not.

(3) COMPARISON OF MEN AND WOMEN

The notion of a separate homosexual role is much less well-developed for
women than it is for men and so too are the attendant techniques of social
control and the deviant subculture and organization. So a comparison with

185

women's sexual behavior should tell us something about the effects of the social role on men's behavior

Fewer women than men engage in homosexual behavior. By the time they are 45, 26 percent of women have had *some* homosexual experience, whereas about 50 percent of men have But this is probably a cause rather than an effect of the difference in the extent to which the homosexual role is crystallized, for women engage in less non-marital sexual activity of any kind than men. For instance, by the time they marry 50 percent of women have had some pre-marital heterosexual experience to orgasm, whereas as many as 90 percent of men have.

The most revealing contrast is between the male and female distributions on the Kinsey rating scale, shown in Table 2. The distributions for women follow a smooth J-shaped pattern, while those for men are uneven with an increase in numbers at the exclusively homosexual end. The distributions for women are the shape that one would expect on the assumption that homosexual and heterosexual acts are randomly distributed in a ratio of 1 to 18.[29] The men are relatively more concentrated in the exclusively homosexual category. This appears to confirm the hypothesis that the existence of the role is reflected in behavior.

Finally, it is interesting to notice that although at the age of 20 far more men than women have homosexual and bisexual patterns (27 percent as against 11 percent), by the age of 35 the figures are both the same (13 percent). Women seem to broaden their sexual experience as they get older whereas more men become narrower and more specialized.

None of this however, should obscure the fact that in terms of behavior, the polarization between the heterosexual man and the homosexual man is

table 2

COMPARISON OF MALE AND FEMALE HETEROSEXUAL-HOMOSEXUAL RATINGS: ACTIVE INCIDENCE AT SELECTED AGES*

	Age	Percent of each age group having each rating								
		(1) X	(2) 0	(3) 1	(4) 2	(5) 3	(6) 4	(7) 5	(8) 6	(9) 1–6
Male	20	3.3	69.3	4.4	7.4	4.4	2.9	3.4	4.9	27.4
Female		15	74	5	2	1	1	1	1	11
Male	35	0.4	86.7	2.4	3.4	1.9	1.7	0.9	2.6	12.9
Female		7	80	7	2	1	1	1	1	13

* Based on Kinsey (1948) p. 652, Table 148 and Kinsey (1953) p. 499, Table 142. For explanation of the ratings see Table 1.

far from complete in our society. Some polarization does seem to have occurred, but many men manage to follow patterns of sexual behavior that are between the two, in spite of our cultural preconceptions and institutional arrangements.

Conclusion

This paper has dealt with only one small aspect of the sociology of homosexuality. It is, nevertheless, a fundamental one. For it is not until he sees homosexuals as a social category, rather than a medical or psychiatric one, that the sociologist can begin to ask the right questions about the specific content of the homosexual role and about the organization and functions of homosexual groups.[30] All that has been done here is to indicate that the role does not exist in many societies, that it only emerged in England towards the end of the seventeenth century, and that, although the existence of the role in modern America appears to have some effect on the distribution of homosexual behavior, such behavior is far from being monopolized by persons who play the role of homosexual.

Notes

[1] Irving Bieber, "Clinical Aspects of Male Homosexuality," in Judd Marmor, editor, *Sexual Inversion*, New York: Basic Books, 1965, p. 248; this is but one example among many.

[2] R. von Krafft-Ebing, *Psychopathia Sexualis*, 1889.

[3] Later published in H. Ellis, *Studies in the Psychology of Sex*, Vol. 2, New York: Random House, 1936.

[4] This is a grossly simplified account. Edwin Lemert provides a far more subtle and detailed analysis in *Social Pathology*, New York: McGraw-Hill, 1951, ch. 4, "Sociopathic Individuation."

[5] For discussion of situations in which deviants can lay claim to legitimacy, see Talcott Parsons, *The Social System*, New York: Free Press, 1951, pp. 292-293.

[6] The position taken here is similar to that of Erving Goffman in his discussion of becoming a mental patient; *Asylums*, Garden City, N.Y.: Doubleday-Anchor, 1961, pp. 128-146.

[7] For evidence that many self-confessed homosexuals in England are not effeminate and many are not interested in boys, see Michael Schofield, *Sociological Aspects of Homosexuality*, London: Longmans, 1965.

[8] Marc Daniel, "Essai de méthodologie pour l'étude des aspects homosexuels de l'histoire," *Arcadie*, 133 (January, 1965), pp. 31-37.

[9] Marvin Opler, "Anthropological and Cross-Cultural Aspects of Homosexuality," in Marmor, editor, *op. cit.*, p. 174.

[10] *Ibid.*, p. 117.

[11] C. S. Ford and F. A. Beach, *Patterns of Sexual Behavior*, New York: Harper, 1951, ch. 7.

[12] George Devereux, "Institutionalized Homosexuality of the Mohave Indians,"

Human Biology, Vol. 9, 1937, pp. 498-527; reprinted in Hendrik M. Ruitenbeek, editor, *The Problem of Homosexuality in Modern Society,* New York: Dutton, 1963.

[13] The lack of cultural distinction is reflected in behavior; Gordon Westwood found that only a small proportion of his sample of British homosexuals engaged in anal intercourse and many of these had been both active and passive and did not have a clear preference. See *A Minority,* London: Longmans, 1960, pp. 127-134.

[14] Gordan Rattray Taylor, "Historical and Mythological Aspects of Homosexuality," in Marmor, *op cit.;* Fernando Henriques, *Prostitution and Society,* Vol. 1, London: MacGibbon and Kee, 1962, pp. 341-343.

[15] Ford and Beach, *op. cit.,* p. 132.

[16] *Ibid.,* pp. 131-132.

[17] Geoffrey May, *Social Control of Sex Expression,* London: Allen and Unwin, 1930, pp. 65 and 101.

[18] Especially Havelock Ellis, *Sexual Inversion,* London: Wilson and Macmillan, 1897, Iwan Bloch (E. Dühren, pseud.), *Sexual Life in England Past and Present,* English translation, London: Francis Aldor, 1938; German edition, Charlottenberg, Berlin, 1901-03; Gordon Rattray Taylor, *Sex in History,* London: Thames and Hudson, 1953; Noel I. Garde, *Jonathan to Gide: The Homosexual in History,* New York: Vantage, 1964.

[19] Dr. Evelyn Hooker has suggested that in a period when homosexual grouping and a homosexual subculture have not yet become institutionalized, homosexuals are likely to behave in a more distinctive and conspicuous manner because other means of making contact are not available. This is confirmed by the fact that lesbians are more conspicuous than male homosexuals in our society, but does not seem to fit the 17th century, where the groups are already described as "clubs."

[20] However, "fairy" and "pansy," the commonest slang terms used by non-homosexuals, have the same meaning of effeminate as the earlier terms.

[21] Bloch, *op. cit.,* p. 328, gives several examples, but attributes their emergence to the fact that "the number of homosexuals increased."

[22] Quoted in *Ibid.,* pp. 328-329.

[23] Anon, *Hell upon Earth: or the Town in an Uproar,* London, 1729, quoted by G. R. Taylor in Marmot, editor, *op. cit.,* p. 142.

[24] Bloch, *op. cit.,* p. 334.

[25] Alfred C. Kinsey *et al., Sexual Behavior in the Human Male,* Philadelphia and London: Saunders, 1948; and Kinsey *et al., Sexual Behavior in the Human Female,* Philadelphia and London: Saunders, 1953.

[26] Kinsey *et al., Sexual Behavior in the Human Male,* pp. 636-37.

[27] *Ibid.,* ch. 21, pp. 610-666.

[28] The more general drawbacks of Kinsey's data, particularly the problem of the representatives of his sample, have been thoroughly canvassed in a number of places; see especially William G. Cochran *et al., Statistical Problems of the Kinsey Report on Sexual Behavior in the Human Male,* Washington: American Statistical Society, 1954.

[29] This cannot be taken in a rigorously statistical sense, since the categories are arbitrary and do not refer to numbers, or even proportions, of actual sexual acts.

[30] But an interesting beginning has been made by Evelyn Hooker in "The Homosexual community," *Proc. XIVth Int. Congr. Appl. Psychol. Personality Research,* Vol. 2, Copenhagen, Munksgaard, 1962; and "Male Homosexuals and their Worlds," Marmor, editor, *op. cit.,* pp. 83-107; there is much valuable descriptive material in Donald Webster Cory, *The Homosexual in America,* New York: Greenberg, 1951; and in Gordon Westwood, *A Minority: A Report on the Life of the Male Homosexual in Great Britain,* London: Longmans, 1960, as well as elsewhere.

13

Social Roles in a Prison for Women

Rose Giallombardo

A neglected area in deviance studies of the adult prison setting concerns
female forms of deviation. The study of deviance in the prison setting has
typically been concerned with male forms of deviation. Indeed, with the
exception of Harper's analysis of the "fringer" role[1] and the recently de-
ported study of a women's prison by Ward and Kassebaum[2] which describes
the homosexual adaptation of female inmates, scientific description and
analysis of the informal organization of the adult female prison have been
overlooked.[3] In the present paper, inmate social roles and social organization in a women's prison will be described in some detail; comparisons of
this informal social structure will be made with relevant literature on the
social roles assumed by male prisoners; and the social structure inside the
prison setting will be viewed in relation to the external environment.

Previous accounts of the male prison have taken the view that the most
important features of the inmate culture emerge as a response to the conditions of imprisonment. The features of this system are well-known and
need not be repeated here.[4] The point to be stressed, however, is that the

Reprinted from *Social Problems*, Vol. 13, No. 3, Winter, 1966, pp. 268–288, by permission of The Society for the Study of Social Problems and the author.

The complete study is reported in *Society of Women: A Study of a Women's Prison*,
New York: John Wiley and Sons, 1966. The writer is indebted to Richard D. Schwartz
and Paul J. Bohannan for their critical reading and comments of an earlier version of
this paper. Acknowledgment is also made to Eliot Freidson for his constructive criticism and invaluable suggestions.

functional interpretation which is made for the emergence of the inmate system typically views the culture that forms within the prison as a response to the problems found in the internal world of the prison and the crucial ways in which it differs from the external world. It is argued that while the prisoner cannot completely eliminate the pains of imprisonment, a cohesive inmate system which has group allegiance as its dominant value provides the inmate with a meaningful reference group that may reinstate the inmate's self image, or in some sense neutralize the deleterious effects of its loss. This formulation derives from case studies of single institutions, and, therefore, it is extremely difficult to ascertain the validity of the conclusions drawn as previous writers have not explored systematically the interaction of the external culture with the conditions for survival faced by the prison aggregate. Nor has anyone assessed several adult prisons simultaneously so that a comparative analysis could be made.[5] I think we are just beginning to understand the variability of one prison from another as they are affected by organizational goals, the composition of staff and inmates. Indeed, recent systematic studies of socialization in the male prison by Wheeler and Garabedian call into question the solidary opposition model of inmate culture even within single institutions, as these scholars found that prisoners varied in their support of the inmate culture over time and according to type of prisoner.[6]

Moreover, Irwin and Cressey have advanced the thesis that there are three subcultures in the prison which they maintain reflect the presence of different types of prisoners. These differences presumably are a reflection of the values and attitudes particular inmates bring into the prison and are related to latent identities.[7] Similarly, Schrag attempts to account for inmate deviants with respect to internalization of inmate culture and support of the inmate code in terms of their preprison characteristics and identities.[8] Thus, the developing theoretical considerations tend to emphasize values and attitudes learned by inmates prior to entering the prison.

The present findings from a case study of a women's prison bear on this matter. In the adult female prison which the writer studied, it was found that in order to cope with the major problems of institutional living, the female inmates have also labeled the reactions of prisoners according to the mode of response exhibited by the inmate to the prison situation and the quality of the inmate's interaction with other inmates and staff. However, although the deprivations of imprisonment were present and felt keenly by the female prisoners, the female argot roles differ in structural form and in the sentiment attached to them from the roles assumed by male prisoners. In addition, it should be pointed out that homosexual dyads cast into marriage alliances, family groups, and other kinship ties formed by the inmates integrate the inmates into a meaningful social system and represent an attempt to create a substitute universe within the prison.[9]

190

The empirical evidence to be presented supports the thesis that differences in the informal social structure in male and female communities can be understood in terms of the differential cultural definitions ascribed to male and female roles in American society. More specifically, it is suggested that the prison structure incorporates and reflects the *total* external social structure in that the differential cultural definitions ascribed to male and female roles in the external world influence the definitions made within the prison, and function to determine the direction and focus of the inmate cultural system.

CULTURAL EXPECTATIONS OF MALE AND FEMALE ROLES

Are sex roles so sharply differentiated in American society that we would expect wide variations in behavior patterns to be found in the two prison communities? There are a number of areas in which American society differentiates male and female roles. In the main, it may be said that in contrast to the male, who is expected to prepare for an occupational role, and whose prestige rank is established by the nature of his life work, the female's life goal is achieved through marriage and child-rearing. Although the "career woman" is an important social type,[10] the percentage of women who pursue uninterrupted careers is very small in our society. So long as women bear children, there must be some social arrangement to ensure that the functions of nurturing and training during the period of dependency are fulfilled.

And we may point to other areas in which American culture tends further to differentiate male and female roles. It does not discourage and accepts a public display of affection between two women such as the use of terms of endearment, embracing, holding hands, and kissing. Such behavior on the part of the male, however, would immediately be defined as homosexual. Moreover, women are said to be more dependent, emotional, less aggressive, and less prone to violence than men. It is said that women generally show less initiative in openly defying authority, whereas men have been defined as independent, violent, and aggressive.[11] This *generalized popular culture* persists for women on another level — the woman-to-woman popular culture. In this vein, the mass media perpetuate the stereotype that a "woman's worst enemy is another woman." Because of the female's orientation to the marriage market, it is argued that she tends to see other women as rivals.[12] This view finds its significance and signature underscored in the highly stylized type of the best friend "betrayed." A similar theme is operative when we find that working women state preferences for male supervisors rather than female supervisors.

To the extent that this generalized popular culture persists in the prison setting, a situation of calculated solidarity may be said to obtain between the female inmates. Calculated solidarity is defined as a social unity based not upon automatic conformity to a set of common norms perceived to be morally binding, but, rather, a unity which is subject to constant interpretation by the inmate as she perceives each situation from the point of view of her own interests. Common responsibility in any particular situation, then, exists only to the extent that the individual perceives her own interests to be served.[13] Unless the formal organization can supply the inmates with all of their wants, then perforce inmates must turn to one another for the satisfaction of those needs which are attractive and agreeable to them, and which cannot be fulfilled by the formal organization. Clemmer's finding is relevant here. In response to questionnaire items, seventy per cent of his subjects concluded that "friendships in prison result from the mutual help man can give man rather than because of some admired trait."[14] However, if the popular culture on the woman-to-woman level is imported into the prison environment, then we would expect that violations of much tabooed behavior may not be severely punished, or may be overlooked, as the very nature of the case implies that expectations of behavior cannot be consistent. Possible latent dysfunctions of the popular culture, then, would be to neutralize deviant acts.

METHOD OF STUDY

I was fortunate to have the opportunity to undertake field work for a period of one year in a large women's prison in a correctional system generally regarded as one of the most progressive. Data were gathered by personal observation of the inmates as they participated in formally scheduled inmate activities: work assignments, vocational and avocational classes, group counseling sessions, academic educational classes, recreational and religious activities. At all inmate functions, the observer sat with the inmates. Other sources of data were obtained by personal observation of informal interaction patterns in the cottage units and on the grounds. During the year it was possible to get to know all the inmates who were at the prison when the study began, approximately 650, and, also, many of the inmates who were committed during the course of the year as well. Interviews of one hour to three hours in length were held with these inmates. These interviews provided basic information on the nature and meaning of the cultural experiences and activities of the group, as well as the social values attached to them. The sociological characteristics of the inmate population were obtained by an examination of the record files of 653 inmates who were confined at the same time.

Other data were obtained by attendance at classification and subclassification meetings; the disciplinary court; meeings of the lieutenants and correctional officers; and other scheduled staff meetings. Informal interviews with correctional officers, prison administrators, and other staff members provided additional data. During the last week of the study, an anonymous questionnaire was administered to all the correctional officers to obtain data

192

on the sociological characteristics of the correctional officers and perceptions of their role function.

THE DEPRIVATIONS OF IMPRISONMENT

Sykes has noted in his study of the Trenton prison that the pains of imprisonment for the modern prisoner are not rooted in physical brutality, but rather may be seen as attacks on the psychological level.[15] The "residue of apparently less acute hurts," he argues, such as the deprivation of liberty, goods and services, heterosexual relations, autonomy and security, "may indeed be the acceptable or unavoidable implications of imprisonment, but we must recognize the fact that they can be just as painful as the physical maltreatment which they have replaced."[16]

What would constitute deprivations for women? Interview data revealed that although the perception of the female inmates vary from one another in this regard depending upon the stage of the inmate's prison career, one's former commitment history,[17] and/or the relative ease with which the individual may adjust to the inmate social system, there is nevertheless a "hard core of consensus" among the female prisoners that prison life *is* depriving and frustrating.

In the female institution studied, it is quite true that in some areas the deprivations of imprisonment are less harsh. The physical surroundings are certainly more pleasant; the cottages although starkly simple are clean and provide the inmate with adequate physical living conditions; with some ingenuity and mutual aid, the inmates enjoy limited opportunity for variety in the matter of dress.[18] The list could doubtless be expanded.

In spite of the mitigation of the pains of imprisonment, however, the differences cited are merely peripheral to the major concerns of prison life. The problems to be solved by the female inmate in this institution are the same conditions for survival as those which the male prisoner has found it necessary to provide solutions in order to survive psychically in the prison environment. These problems have their basis in the disorientation resulting from the abrupt termination of the individual's freedom: the lack of opportunity for heterosexual relations — the fracturing of every influence favorable to the cultivation of emotional reciprocity as a result of being cut off from family and friends; withholding of material goods; attacks on the self through the humiliating experiences incidental to a prison commitment; the loss of autonomy and responsibility to which life in a prison inevitably leads; and the lack of security and privacy.

The loss of liberty and autonomy are among the most uniformly felt deprivations among the female inmates. Restraints on the inmate's freedom are keenly felt, and the transition from liberty to rigidly restricted movement is a matter with which the female must come to terms in order to survive psychically in the prison world.

Whatever the material circumstances may have been for the individual inmate in civil society, the punishing aspect of denying the inmate ownership of personal goods in prison is that it removes the last resource the inmate possesses to express individuality, and, therefore, the abrupt removal of personal effects tends to destroy the inmate's self-image. The stripping and mortifying process[19] occurs immediately after the inmate's entrance into the prison; the personal clothing and other possessions of the inmate are replaced by the prison issue which is fairly uniform, certain to have been worn by generations of prisoners, and to be either sizes too large or sizes too small. When one recalls that it is always open season on women's fashions, it is not surprising to learn that the attack on the individual's self-image with reference to clothing is particularly acute for the female inmate. The strategies employed by some of the inmates in the admission and orientation unit to individualize the prison issue by monograms, embroidery, or the strategic placement of pleats on a surplus WAC jacket in an attempt to make them "more like free world clothes" are all evidence of the subtlety of deprivation.

For the male prisoner, it has been pointed out that lack of heterosexual intercourse is frustrating and depriving, and the evidence indicates that the same holds true for the great majority of the female inmates. Most inmates have enjoyed the company of men outside, and sex constitutes a major problem of adjustment for almost every inmate. Women do not choose to live their lives entirely apart from men, and the necessity of doing so in prison is frustrating for the individual.[20] Indeed the situation for the imprisoned female may, perhaps, be seen to be more serious than for the male. "[American] culture," writes Jules Henry, "gives women no firm role except an erotic one."[21] In this regard, Parsons has discussed three broad categories of adjustment for the American female: 1) the "good companion" role; 2) the "glamor girl" role; and 3) the "domestic" role.[22] Thus, with the closing of the prison gate, the female prisoner finds herself cut off from the structure of American society conducive to the cultivation of a female role which is the avenue through which she achieves self-respect and status.

The evidence, however, suggests that the other major deprivation suffered by the male prisoner, namely, the loss of security, [23] occurs on another level of experience for the female inmate, which is consistent with the popular culture. In the words of the inmates: "The hardest part of living in a prison is to live with other *women*." Commonly expressed attitudes of the nature of women are: "You can't trust another woman"; "Every woman is a sneaking lying bitch." Hence, it is not so much the constant fear of violence or sexual exploitation such as is the case for the male prisoner which creates a hardship for the female inmates, but, rather, the strain involved in being in the forced company of women who are believed to be untrustworthy, capable of predatory tactics. Thus, the female inmate is apt to fear the consequences of aroused jealousy transformed into vitriolic verbal attacks;[24] and she suffers acute insecurity in confronting and handling the frequent

194

attacks of *penitentiary darby* — gossip which takes place at all times and on all sides within the prison. Moreover, there is enough differentiation among the inmates so that some women experience insecurity in adjusting to living in the forced company of others whom they consider to be socially inferior; some of the white women, for example, find living in close proximity with Negroes to be distasteful; others feel repulsion at having to associate with prostitutes, women who are untidy in their personal habits, or who use vulgar language.[25]

As does the male prisoner, the female prisoner soon discovers that escape routes in prison are few. Psychological and physical withdrawal are not significant modes of adaptation to mitigate the pains of imprisonment for the inmates in this institution. What follows now is a description of the informal social structure which provides a complex of clearly defined social roles for the female prisoners and sets the limits of mutual accommodation.

The Social Roles

SNITCHERS AND INMATE COPS OR LIEUTENANTS

Communication across caste lines is strictly forbidden in the female prison studied except for matters of urgent business, and all such interaction is expected to be handled with swift dispatch. Indeed, to violate the ban placed on legitimate communication flowing from inmates and staff is considered to be a very serious matter. The female inmates argue that no inmate should jeopardize the successful execution of activities based upon the common interests of the inmates in connection with the performance of illegal functions to relieve the pains of imprisonment; and secondly, supplying information to officials may result in the withdrawal of privileges or other forms of punishment, thereby adding to the pains of imprisonment for the inmate.

In the female prison, the role of the *snitcher* is the female counterpart to the "rat" in the male prison. To accuse an inmate of snitching is the most serious accusation which one inmate may hurl at another because it clearly signifies the division of loyalty between the staff and the inmates. The importance placed upon the "no snitching" norm is apparent as it covers every range of behavior and is put in the imperative to the new inmate or the deviant: "See and see nothing! Hear and hear nothing!"

Although the female prisoners agree that inmates should never give any information concerning an inmate to the staff, any prisoner according to the female inmates may occasionally engage in snitching when it is believed to serve the individual's interest. Moreover, the female's self-orientation and the tendency to see one another as rivals both function to decrease general expectations of rigid alliance from one another. Consequently, the female inmate rarely expresses any surprise when she suspects another inmate of deviating from the norm prohibiting communication of inmate affairs across

195

caste lines — only a kind of bitterness that the status of inmate is not sufficient to bind and solidify the inmates completely into a cohesive group. The popular culture, then, in connection with the extent to which any female may be trusted, functions to neutralize many deviant acts in the prison. As a result, many deviant acts are overlooked, or are not severely punished; in contrast to the situation in the male prison, we find that violation of the "no snitching" norm does not often result in violence. In the words of one prisoner: "A lot is said about what will be done if you catch a snitch, but you know women! They talk loud, draw a crowd, and that's as far as it goes. When it comes to a showdown, they chicken out." This does not mean, however, that negative sanctions are not imposed. Panning and signifying are common modes of punishment to control behavior in the female inmate community.

Panning is general derogatory gossip about an inmate when the inmate is not physically present. *Signifying*, on the other hand, is a more compelling negative sanction because the offending inmate is physically present. A group of inmates will discuss a deviant act in considerable detail with biting sarcasm, scorn, and mimicry; the inmate's name is not at any time mentioned, but little doubt is left as to the inmate's identity. Both panning and signifying are extremely effective modes of social control. But sanctions need not always be so obvious to be effective. The fact that the prison is isolated,[26] of course, makes the prisoners extremely dependent upon one another for emotional reciprocity, and this in itself serves to check much continued deviant behavior. In the words of an inmate: "It's rough when the group ignores you." Inflection in one's voice, then, pretense that one has not seen another, and turning the head to avoid a greeting, can be exquisite punishment in the prison community, and can often be quite as devastating as the more pointed panning and signifying.

Inmates who violate the ban on communication are watched closely and pertinent information concerning their activities is circulated quickly to other inmates. The snitcher, in short, is *persona non grata* in the prison community, and any common cause with an inmate assuming this role would in all certainty hurt one's reputation and close off interaction with the great majority of inmates. Th snitcher is condemned by the female inmates because she denies the cohesion of the inmate community and jeopardizes the successful execution of the many illegal activities that take place in the prison to mitigate the pains of imprisonment. And the fact that the snitcher is disloyal to the inmate group adds to the burden of imprisonment.

The behavior subsumed under "center man" in the male prison finds expression in the role of *inmate cop* or *lieutenant*. The inmate cop is a prisoner who is in a position of authority over other inmates, and in the process of executing her work function will issue orders to other inmates or report infractions of rules in connection with work. The prison experience is considered to be the "great equalizer"[27] and inmates resent taking orders from other inmates. As one prisoner said contemptuously: "She tries to act just like an officer. She forgets that she came through that gate and she's got five numbers across her chest just like the rest of us. She's an officer without a uniform, and she tries to tell another inmate what to do. They're always in the officer's face. . . ." The inmate cop or lieutenant in effect takes the role of the officer and thereby violates an important tenet of the inmate code: she denies the egalitarian ethos of the inmates.

The inmate cop's disloyalty is despised not only because it is open to view, but also because it is often flaunted in the face of other inmates. Here is an open and shut case of identification with staff values, and the inmate cop's actions deny the solidarity of the inmate body and weaken the bonds of interdependence which bind them together. Moreover, the inmate cop is apt to rationalize her actions in terms of noncriminal values which according to the inmate code have no place in the prison. Unless this inmate can be persuaded to "see the light" through socialization into the inmate culture, she cannot be reasoned with or bought. In this sense she poses a real threat to the inmate community, because the inmate cop is an added bulwark to the staff's forces, and the fact that an inmate is adding to the pains of imprisonment by joining forces with the staff makes her doubly despised.

SQUARES AND JIVE BITCHES

Along with the snitchers and the inmate cops, the *squares* are truly the pariahs of the inmate community. "Square" is a derisive label pinned on inmates who are considered to be accidental criminals. The behavior of the square in the prison community clearly betrays her alien status, as she is oriented to the prison administration and tends to possess "anti-criminal" loyalties. Degrees of "squareness" are recognized by the female inmates ranging from the inmate who is said to be "so square that she's a cube" to the inmate designated as a "hip square." The "cube square" is very definitely oriented to societal values and the prison administration, whereas the "hip square" tends to sympathize with the inmate code and adheres to some of its principles, sometimes going so far as to *pin* — act as a lookout — for other inmates. Her sympathy tends to take the form of stated tolerance for inmate activites. The distinguishing characteristic of the "hip square," however, is that she does not engage in homosexual activity, as well as the fact that she is oriented to the administration and societal values. In the female prison studied, it should be pointed out that anyone who does not engage in homosexual activities in the prison in one form or another is automatically labeled a square.

Not only are *squares* outside the main stream of inmate activities — excluded and ostracized by the inmate population — but more important for the inmate social system, squares are pitied. It is said that squares "don't know any better," and, further, it is widely believed that the square is not "woman enough" to commit a crime. "They're suckers and fools — gullible without even knowing it." And herein lies the key to understanding the threat that the square poses for the inmate community. Like the inmate cop or lieutenant, the square tends to identify with the institutional officials. In the case of squares, however, association is considered to be doubly hazardous, for in their presumed gullibility squares may unwittingly divulge information to the officials. It is for this reason that squares are apt to be "fed with a long-handled spoon," that is, information concerning inmate activities is carefully sifted and censored.

While the deviance of the square is often the consequence of an artless simplicity — and presumably leaves open the possibility that induction into the inmate culture may remedy the situation, (Indeed, the pressures applied are so great that this frequently does occur.) — the deviance of the *jive bitch,* on the other hand, is a deliberate, calculated strategy to cause conflict. In short, the *jive bitch* is a troublemaker whose strategy often involves a distortion of the facts, as in the case, for example, when she is interested in breaking up an established homosexual relationship: she will often volunteer information about *kites* (prison letters) and illicit rendezvous to the injured party who, in many cases, would prefer not to be the recipient of such information — as it will mean that ignorance is no longer bliss — and who may be goaded into terminating an affair, which although perceived not to be perfect may be felt to be better than none.

Moreover, the jive bitch can't be trusted to keep her word when she gives it, indicating her disloyalty to the inmate group. Although female inmates claim that women are not trustworthy, it is normatively demanded that once you give your word to a prisoner, you should keep it — particularly in connection with matters concerning mutual aid. An example of a jive bitch supplied by an inmate follows:

> You're out of cigarettes, and you go to a girl and say, "Look, I'm out of cigarettes, and I won't have any money until next week. When you go to Commissary, would you buy me a carton, and I'll pay you back next week?" She says, "Sure, baby, sure. I'll get them for you on Friday." When Friday comes, you go to her house to get the cigarettes and when you say, "Did you get the cigarettes?" she opens her mouth like she's surprised and maybe slaps her cheek and she looks at you and says, "Oh, baby, I forgot all about it. I'm sorry, baby, honest!" That's a jive bitch 'cause she had no intention of getting you those cigarettes in the first place.

The jive bitch, in short, is an example *par excellence* of the woman-to-woman popular culture translated into role behavior. And the fact that she cannot be depended upon weakens even the bonds of calculated solidarity which exist among the female inmates.

While no inmate trusts another woman completely — "you pick your people and even then you only go so far." — within the limitations imposed by this definition of the situation, an inmate may single out another prisoner as a special friend. She is one with whom an inmate can converse easily, and, further, assume reasonably that the conversation will be mutually binding as secret. Any two people who find one another compatible in this way may become *rap buddies* to one another. This relationship is dissolved if the expectations concerning the relationship are not honored by either of the incumbents of the rap buddy role; or if the relationship develops into a homosexual relationship, the inmates become a "couple" and assume the obligations relevant to a homosexual relationship.

The *homey* role is probably as close to "blood" relationship that one comes to in the female prison, and the relationship holds a special place in the lexicon of the inmates. Technically speaking, even if conflict ensues between homeys, the relationship still holds. The homey is the inmate who is from another inmate's home town or nearby community. Homeys may or may not have known one another before incarceration; but whatever the case, within the prison these inmates become homeys to one another. Contact is made as soon as the presence of a homey becomes known; information is usually obtained from inmate orientation helpers or inmate office workers. Inquiries as to whether a homey's needs in the orientation unit have been met are immediately made: cigarettes, soap, toothpaste, facial tissues, and any other commissary items which she needs will somehow be routed to her. The special bond of reciprocity which is established between homeys is of a vastly different degree of intensity than that between rap buddies, and is expected to cover a wide range of behavior; homeys have the right to turn to one another when material need arises, and the further expectation exists that if economically possible, the merchandise is to be returned at a later date.

Although superficially the rap buddy and homey roles may appear to be quite similar, the basis for the allocation of these roles and functions is quite different. What is the basis for allocation of functions with respect to the homey role? While there is a special relationship that exists between homeys, significantly the homey relationship excludes homosexuality. Indeed, an inmate will express great indignation if the suggestion — however lightly veiled — is made that a homosexual relationship exists between her and a homey. "That's my homey. I wouldn't do that to her," certainly suggests the exploitative evaluation many inmates have of the homosexual

199

relationship. But when we examine other aspects of the role this explanation adds little to our understanding of the function the role plays in the lives of the female inmates.

A significant aspect of the homey relationship lies in the fact that inmates sharing this status address and refer to one another by the term "homey," emphasizing to the incumbents of the role and the inmate community alike the nature of the special relationship involved. Indeed, a novitiate who calls a homey by her given name is promptly corrected by other inmates. One is quite reasonably led to ask why it is that mutual aid and mode of address are patterned between homeys and not, for example, between rap buddies. Does the answer lie in the fact that they are from the same geographical area? Given the self-orientation of the female, it is not very likely that this would seem to be a plausible explanation. Actually the occupants of the homey role are, as it were, buying insurance for the future. The extension of mutual cooperation between homeys insures both role occupants that the possibility will not arise that a homey will "read" her — that is, speak derogatively of her behavior in prison to anyone in civil society. Presumably, the inmate who resides in the same geographical area would most likely be in a favored position to do so.

The homey relationship is a splendid example of the refinement in social roles which takes place in the female community to solve the special problems of the inmates stemming from the cultural definition females have of one another.

CONNECTS AND BOOSTERS

The fifteen dollars which inmates are permitted to spend per month at the commissary store is not a large sum when one takes into account that it covers almost all purchases, including cigarettes.[28] Furthermore, even this modest sum is beyond the reach of most inmates. Few legitimate channels are open to the female inmates to improve their economic lot in the prison. Like the male prisoners, the female inmates also find it necessary to exploit the environment in order to improve their material circumstances. Here it takes the form of stealing from institutional supplies. Significantly, a role based upon aggressive physical tactics such as the "gorilla" reported by Sykes who takes what he wants from other inmates by force does not emerge in the female inmate community. By contrast, in the female prison the *connect* is any inmate with a "good job" who will cooperate in the procurement of scarce goods and/or information. Connects are also those inmates who are in a position to negotiate with other inmates to obtain information or goods, that is, acting both as middleman and distributor. Thus, this role includes the procurement of both goods and services.

In this connection, the inmates draw a sharp line between the connect who often takes a dual role, and the *booster* whose exploitation of the environment consists solely of stealing from official stores and carries on a successful business enterprise. Of course, it should be made clear that stealing from the officials is universal at the prison. Even inmates designated by sister inmates as squares and inmate cops declare they will sometimes take a pot of coffee out of the dining room "on principle." Inmates, however, make a clear distinction between the petty boosting which is engaged in by all the inmates — say a few teaspoonfuls of sugar placed in a napkin, a sandwich, and the like, while in the dining room — and the stealing engaged in by the booster. The difference lies mainly in the source of supply, the regularity with which the goods may be procured, and the purpose for which the items are stolen. Items stolen sporadically for individual consumption tend to be classified under the category petty boosting. The booster is the inmate who is in a position to steal desired objects regularly and in fairly large quantities.

Now in the male prison, regardless of the source of supply, giving and sharing is normatively demanded by the inmate code — especially if the materials have been stolen from the officials. The "pedlar" or "merchant" has been described as "a man so alienated from other prisoners, so selfish in his pursuit of material advantage, that he is willing to thrive on the misery of his companions. He places his own well-being above the well-being of the inmates as a whole. He does not share the goods in short supply but exploits, instead, the needs of others."[29] Interestingly, the same behavior for which the "merchant" is despised in the male prison is that which receives words of praise from female inmates. To "get a good thing going," that is, to engage in a successful enterprise is to draw forth admiration from the inmates. It is held: "If you can get a little racket going, more power to you." And yet at the same time inmates rationalize many of their actions by saying, "If I don't get there first, someone else will," which clearly indicates the self-orientation of the inmates. In a real sense, boosters are inmates who have "gotten there first," and for this feat there is admiration — albeit tinged with not a little envy. In addition, inmates tend to feel gratitude to the booster, for it is recognized that the booster's role involves a certain amount of risk. Whatever recompense is necessary to enjoy the pleasure of making a cup of coffee at odd hours of the day is thought to be well worth the price. The inmates will gladly exchange a carton of cigarettes for a pound of coffee,[30] and if this transaction can be made a weekly matter, prison life is made more tolerable.

In contrast to the male prisoner, no sharp line is made by the female inmates between selling and giving, except between *homeys*, inmates participating in a homosexual marriage, and other "family" members. Who are the inmates that become the clients for the supply of illicit goods? All prisoners do not have an opportunity to enjoy these luxury items, regardless of their financial situation. Low caste inmates, such as snitchers, squares, and inmate cops or lieutenants, of course, lie outside the boundary of legitimate giving, as these inmates have deviated from the inmate code and, therefore, have roped themselves off from the privilege of sharing in the scarce goods that circulate about the prison. They are in the same boat as "rats," "center men," "weaklings," and "fish" in the male prison. Apart from the pariahs in the female prison, mutual aid is greater near the locus of high intensity of emotional reciprocity. As intensity of emotional reciprocity decreases, mutual aid decreases proportionately.

PINNERS

Since complete elimination of detection is never possible in the performance of many illicit activities, the female inmates find it necessary to minimize the risk of being detected by the prison officials. For this reason, the role of *pinner* is very crucial in the prison.

The pinner in the female prison is a lookout, stationed as a sentry to prevent a surprise attack upon inmates engaging in illicit activities from all unauthorized persons — whether they be staff or inmates. With discovery always imminent and punishment a certainty, the pinner's role is not one to allocate to amateurs or to inmates whose loyalty is in doubt. The pinner must be an inmate who can be trusted, stand up under pressure, and she must be "in the know." Depending upon the task at hand, sometimes the female inmates find it necessary to mobilize a team of pinners — each of whom must share the responsibility that the task at hand be carried out successfully. The interdependence of the inmates requires the cooperation of other inmates in order to carry out their activities successfully. In the words of an inmate:

> Even if you wanted to go it alone, it's almost impossible to do. The situation is such that you need the help of other inmates. For example, if you're makin' it with someone, you need a pinner. This means initiating the aid of a third party — maybe more. And you might be called up to help two other people in the same situation. . . . The way pinning works is this — maybe I've got two friends who are involved with each other. O.K., well, I'll go into the office and keep the officer busy for an hour talking about a problem I have or I make one up. She can't be in two places at one time, so usually this is a safe procedure. Or a girl will stand at the foot of the stairs with a tin can in her hands. If the officer or a person known to be a snitcher goes up the stairs, she drops the can, or she whistles loudly. These signals are understood.

Now while it is important to the female inmates that the pains of imprisonment be mitigated, it is also imperative that in the process of doing so their deviant actions do not result in disciplinary action which will increase the burden of punishment. The pinner, therefore, is a valued individual, as

202

she imparts a measure of reasonable security to the inmates that their deviant performances will not result in loss of days or other forms of punishment.

The problems and concerns of the female inmates in adjusting to deprivation of heterosexual relationships are revealed by the number of roles channeled into homosexual behavior. Moreover, the female inmate's *role refinement* with respect to the categories of homosexual activity illustrates its function as both a motivating force in the lives of the inmates and as an organizing principle of social organization.

The inmates apply a number of labels to homosexual behavior in the prison depending upon the specific role assumed, the adeptness with which the assumed role is played, or the motivation for the behavior. Broadly speaking, the inmates differentiate between penitentiary turnouts and lesbians. The *penitentiary turnout* is the prisoner who resorts to homosexuality in the prison because heterosexual relationships are not available; in contrast, the *lesbian prefers* homosexual relations in the free community. In this respect she resembles the "fag" in the male prison. The *lesbian* is labeled as a sick person by the inmates because it is argued that the preference and selection of homosexual relations in a situation where choice is possible clearly constitute a true perversion. It is only in the penitentiary world where men are unavailable that the values and norms regarding homosexual behavior are redefined by the inmates and — within the limits imposed by this definition — accepted as a temporary substitute for heterosexual relations.

Stylized symbolic devices make it possible for the female inmates to attach new meanings to a culturally defined sex *role* representation seen as a variation of a sex *type* based upon biological attributes. The institutionalized character of the differential sex roles orders the behavior of the inmates and defines the limits of permissible behavior and regulates the interaction between the inmates.

The *femme*[31] or *mommy* is the inmate who plays the female role in a homosexual relationship. The femme role is a highly sought-after role in the prison because most of the inmates want to continue to play the feminine role in a meaningful way in the prison. Cast in the context of a "marital" relationship, the femme continues to act out many of the functions assigned to the role of wife in civil society. The complementary role to the femme is the *stud broad*[32] or *daddy* who assumes the male role. The stud broad is accorded much prestige by other inmates for these reasons: first, the stud is said to provide the prison with the male image; secondly, the role is con-

203

sidered to be a more difficult one for an inmate to assume and sustain over a period of time, because it is thought to be "unnatural" for a female to assume the guises of the male. Moreover, the role is considered to be difficult because studs not only assume certain external symbols of sex differentiation, but in addition are expected to incorporate into role behavior the many social expectations of the male role.

As far as homosexual relations are concerned, the evidence is consistent with that reported by Ward and Kassebaum; that is, homosexual relations are established voluntarily between the principals involved. No physical coercion is applied in obtaining a homosexual partner.[33] In seeking a solution to the problem engendered by the lack of heterosexual relations, interpersonal relations in connection with homosexuality play a major part in the lives of the female inmates. Cast in the context of a "marital" relationship, the homosexual dyad is viewed by the inmates as a meaningful personal and social relationship. From the mass of interview data it is clear, however, that this mode of adjustment (with the exception of homosexuals who practice homosexuality in the free community) would be repugnant for most prisoners, but the uniqueness of the prison situation compels the inmate to redefine and attach new meanings to this behavior within the prison structure.[34]

The inmates are not able to resolve their sense of isolation within the formal organization, and, therefore, develop relationships and behavior patterns within an informal structure. For the vast majority of the inmates, adjustment to the prison world is made by establishing a homosexual alliance with a compatible partner as a marriage unit. Although we cannot discuss the dynamics of mate selection, courtship, and marriage in this paper, it should be pointed out that when a stud and femme have established a homosexual alliance, they are said to be "makin' it" or to be "tight"; that is to say, they are socially recognized as constituting a legitimate married pair. Since one of the important goals in establishing a homosexual marriage alliance is to strive for what is referred to as a "sincere" relationship, which is translated to mean a stable relationship and one based upon romantic love, the *trick* is held in low esteem by the inmates because she allows herself to be exploited, rather than to develop a relationship that is sincere. And the trick permits exploitation in a variety of ways — usually economically and as a source of labor. Any individual who allows herself to be exploited in this manner is considered "weak." Moreover, tricks are regarded as "suckers" and "fools" because they may be kept dangling with promises.

Who are the inmates who utilize exploitative tactics? The *commissary hustler* is so labeled as an individual who establishes a single homosexual alliance with an inmate who lives in the same cottage, but in addition establishes relationships with one or more inmates in other cottages for economic purposes. This is called "mating for commissary reasons," and any femme other than the inmate who lives in the stud's cottage is labeled as a trick in the relationship. The commissary hustler presents a commissary list to the tricks scattered throughout the prison, and they, in turn, supply the commissary hustler with needed material items. The function of all the tricks in this "polygynous" system is an economic one. The "wife" in the cottage takes precedence over all others. She shares in the bounty and usually knows of the existence of other femmes, i.e., tricks. Indeed, if the "couple" is in serious economic difficulty, she may suggest to her stud that this role be assumed. Or the stud may consult the femme in arriving at a decision to "work a few tricks."

So long as the "wife" shares the same household as the stud, the existence of other femmes (tricks) in the relationship is tolerable. As the inmates put it: "The nearest is the dearest, and the closest gets the mostest." In addition, it should be pointed out that the "wife" who lives in the same household as the stud also derives security from the public recognition of the relationship as legitimate. They are recognized as a "couple." The additional wife (or wives) merely serves an economic function. One would be well advised to ask why an inmate enters into a trick role. The stud population is outnumbered by the femme population, and competition for studs is very keen. Actually, each trick in this situation anticipates and plans for the day when the relationship will become a permanent one; each trick anticipates displacing the cottage "wife" in the affections of the stud. And since the trick is, after all, an inmate with a commissary account, the possibility that this might occur is a good one. While it is more or less understood that she wait for an invitation to move to the stud's cottage, sometimes a trick may lose patience and forego prison etiquette. Such cottage moves present complicating triangular situations, often leading to violence.

The role of commissary hustler is one which requires a certain amount of adroitness to carry out successfully. The inmates argue that in the free community, the commissary hustler would tend to exploit men, but since there are no men in prison, they exploit women. Although there may be individual personality factors involved, there are structural features in the prison which precipitate this role. Every inmate is not compensated for work performed in the prison, and the role of commissary hustler provides an avenue whereby an inmate may solve her economic needs.

The dyad configuration cast into the framework of a marital relationship covers a wide range of behavioral expectations. The commissary hustler, although in some respects exploitative, nevertheless does maintain a stable and sincere relationship with the femme who shares the same cottage. However, when the individual exploits *each* situation with a partner for its unique possibilities, whether it be sexual gratification or material, the inmate is said to occupy a *chippie* role. This role differs from the commissary hustler in a very important way. Although the commissary hustler actually

205

establishes one sincere relationship and exploits other inmates in order to provide for the femme in the relationship, the chippie establishes no single relationship of this type. Chippies are said to be "makin' it," but not to be "in love" with any individual. The chippie, in the inmates' eyes, is the prison prostitute. The inmate who "chippies from one bed to another" — i.e. terminates affairs too quickly — is held in scorn by the inmates, as her behavior is held to be promiscuous. This behavior draws forth words of scorn from the inmates because the ideal cultural pattern in the prison is to establish a permanent relationship. The chippie clearly deviates from the ideal pattern, as the affairs of this inmate are characterized by their striking temporary quality.

The female inmates distinguish clearly between homosexual activity that is considered to be promiscuous and that which is engaged in solely for sexual gratification. Although *kick partners* are also not involved as "lovers," there is, nevertheless, a predictable permanence in the relationships maintained between kick partners, but the motivation for entering into the partnership is clearly understood to be solely for physical gratification. There is usually no economic exchange in this relationship, and the inmates exhibit no jealousy. An inmate is apt to enter such a relationship when she does not wish to assume the responsibilities that a more permanent tie would entail. The object of this relationship is to release sexual tension. Kick partners sometimes consist of a group of several women among whom partners are exchanged and friendly relations exist between all members concerned. To the extent that kick partners are "discreet," the behavior is not looked down upon by the inmates.

Every society has a reserve of members from which potential mates may be obtained. When resources are limited, or because of cultural prescriptions, mates may be drawn from other groups. In the female prison, the kick partner is an individual who may be drawn into a permanent tie. And there is also the possibility that the square will in time come to "see the light" and enter into the inmate social organization. But there is one category of inmates in prison, namely, those labeled *cherries,* who constitute an uncommitted sizeable reserve for potential mates, as they are the inmates who have never been "turned out" — initiated into homosexual practices. Cherries, however, are not squares. Often they are young and first offenders, and they are usually initiated by older women. Cherries in this context are "hep" individuals, i.e., know what the score is from the point of view of the prisoners, but for one reason or another have not engaged in homosexuality. Sometimes a short sentence may be the deciding factor; a preference not to become emotionally involved; or it may be that the individual decides that this mode of adjustment may not be desirable.

One who assumes a false part or assumes a character other than the real is despised for his hypocrisy both within and without the prison gates.

Within the female prison, the *punk* is despised for pretense and deceit. In the male prison, it will be recalled that the "punk" is an inmate who plays the submissive part in a homosexual relationship because he is coerced into doing so. In this respect it is said that "punks" differ and may be distinguished from "fags," who it is said are "born" not "made." In a sense, "fags" resemble the lesbians for it is said by the inmates that they are "born that way," or "something happened to them in their childhood."

The punk in the female prison, on the other hand, is the inmate so designated because she acts like a female, that is, takes on the coquettish mannerisms of a woman when the expected behavior is that of the male. The behavior of the punk elicits a combination of anger and ridicule from the inmates. The tendency is to heap blame upon the punk, because the punk's "impotence" is not a constitutional failure, but, rather, is due to incomplete role learning. Responsibility, therefore, is placed upon the individual. Punks are, as it were, self-proclaimed studs without substance — unconvincing sexual deviates. The punk is despised and ridiculed by the inmates.

While the punk is guilty of incomplete role learning, the *turnabout,* on the other hand, claims expertise at playing both male and female roles. As a matter of fact, she not only describes herself glowingly in terms of her versatility, that is, "good either way," but stands ready to put her boasted skill to the test. Such protean versatility, however, is viewed with amused contempt by the inmates. As a prisoner put it, "There's a lot of talk, but not the right kind of talk. She should know what she is and stay that way. And we tell them, 'Get yourself together and find out what you are!' "

The female inmates prefer a structured situation in their prison world, and inmates playing male roles one day and female roles the next confuse the issue greatly, especially for the inmate who may be planning a strategy of conquest. In addition, anything which tends to decrease the "male" population in the prison is apt to be alarming to the inmates. It is not surprising, therefore, that the turnabout is held in low esteem.

Conclusion

The social roles as distinguished and labeled by the female inmates constitute the basic structure of social relationships formed by the inmates in response to the problems of a prison commitment. While it is apparent from the previous discussion that some argot roles are mutually exclusive, other roles clearly are not. Furthermore, an inmate may assume one role soon after commitment, for example, such as square, but may assume many other roles at a later point in time if drawn into the inmate social organization.

In addition to the comparisons with the male prison community that have already been made, there are other important differences that may be pointed out at this time. Consistent with the cultural definition of the female as nonaggressive, the roles of violence that emerge in the male prison, namely, those of "wolf," "tough," "gorilla," "hipster," and "ball buster," are notably absent among the female inmates. Also significant is the fact that a role resembling the structure of the "right guy" who is such a dominant figure in the male prison does not emerge in the female prison. Concepts such as "fair play," "courage," and the like — which are consistent with the concepts of edurance, loyalty, and dignity associated with the "right guy" — are not meaningful to the female. Although it is true that the norm of inmate loyalty exists in the prison world, the popular culture of women as untrustworthy is imported into the prison world and serves both to neutralize many deviant acts and to furnish the rationale for their commitment.

The need to assert or defend one's femininity, in the same way that the male inmate must prove his masculinity in the group if his manhood is called into question, clearly does not arise for the female inmate. This is a reflection of the self-orientation of the female, and the fact that the female validates her femininity by proving she can attract men. In other words, it appears that general features of American society in connection with the cultural definitions ascribed to male and female roles are imported into the prison and are reflected in the structure of social relationships formed by the inmates. Nowhere is this more dramatically revealed than in the extraordinary function of the homey role with its extended implications for the re-entry of the inmate into civil society. From the same vantage point, we saw that the function of the pinner's role serves to control the physical distance between inmates engaging in illicit activities on the one hand, and the snitcher on the other, in order to make it possible for the female inmates to avoid discovery and punishment.

The number of roles clustered about homosexual behavior clearly reveals the problems and concerns of the female inmates in connection with adjustment to deprivation of heterosexual relationships. Moreover, the distinctions made by the inmates as to motivation, role assumed, adeptness with which the assumed role is played, and so on, indicate the values and expectations of the inmates with respect to this behavior. But the rights and obligations attached to a legitimate "marital" relationship automatically close off much interaction among the inmates, as inmates assuming this type of relationship must account for all of their contacts with members of the "opposite sex." As the inmates move closer to legitimate relationships in the prison, then, the refinement of roles becomes necessary in order to control and to account for the behavior of every inmate in the system.

The cultural orientation of males, however, precludes legitimate marriage and family groupings as a feasible alternative solution for the male prisoners, as the serious adoption of a female role is contrary to the definition of the male role as masculine. Hence, family groups do not emerge in the male prison. It is noteworthy that in the male prison the "fags" and "punks" are both held in derision by the vast majority of male inmates as it is felt that they have sacrificed their manhood, but the homosexuality of "wolves" is looked upon as a temporary adjustment to sexual tensions generated by the prison setting. The absence of sentiment and the aggressive behavior of the "wolf" is consistent with the cultural definition of the *masculine* role, and thus homosexuality loses the taint of femininity in the prison that male homosexuality tends to carry in civil society. In addition, the cultural orientation of the male role with respect to demonstrations of affection toward another member of the same sex clearly precludes the adoption of legitimate feminine roles by male inmates in informal kinship groupings such as those found among the female inmates. The ease with which women may demonstrate acts of affection, both verbally and physically, toward members of the same sex, perhaps may provide a *predisposition* to widespread homosexuality and its ready acceptance under the extreme conditions of isolation in the prison setting. This fact alone, however, is not enough to account for the emergence of the female inmate social system.

Why do these remarkable differences in inmate culture emerge in the two prison communities? Two theoretical positions have already been posed. The first of these is the typical structural-functional analysis of total institutions which asserts that behavior systems of various types of inmates are a result of the conditions of imprisonment. However, when we consider that the deprivations of imprisonment were found to be present in the female prison studied and keenly felt by the female prisoners — yet the typical cultural system which emerges in the adult male prison is not present — we must conclude that the differences in structural form found in the two prison communities are inadequately explained by current functional analysis *solely* as a response to the deprivations of imprisonment. The deprivations may provide necessary conditions for the emergence of an inmate system, but they are not in themselves sufficient to account for the structural *form* that the inmate social system assumes in the male and female prison communities.

The second interpretation views inmate culture as somehow imported into the prison world from the external world by the inmates who compose that culture, through the particular attitudes and values which inmates learned prior to entering the prison. This position has been most forcibly suggested by Schrag, Irwin, and Cressey, and calls our attention to the thesis that the behavior patterning of inmates is influenced by pre-prison experiences, social identities, and cultural background. Simply stated, the behavior patterns in the prison are the result of the inmates' relations in the external world; however, the external world is important only in providing the particular cultural elements that the inmates learn. Inasmuch as the individuals who enter the prison world are not a random sample of the population, the values and attitudes brought into the prison do not comprise a random sample of elements of outside culture; hence, prison culture differs — especially by the presence of increased hostility, violence, and traffic in illicit goods. The three sub-culture groups (thief, convict, and legitimate) in Irwin and Cressey's typology presumably demonstrate this thesis,[35] as these authors maintain that their three subculture groups share learned behaviors which are common and peculiar to them in or out of prison. Elsewhere, it has been cogently pointed out that Irwin and Cressey do not demonstrate that this is so.[36] Nevertheless, they have called attention to the important thesis that the behavior patterning of inmates may be influenced by social identities and cultural backgrounds.

We suggest, rather, that the culture that forms within the prison by males and females can be understood in these terms: the prison inmate social system is not an intrinsic response to the deprivations of imprisonment, although the deprivations of imprisonment may be important in precipitating inmate culture; nor can inmate culture be viewed as a mere reflection of the values and attitudes inmates bring into the prison world. The evidence presented here suggests that the male and female inmate cultures *are* a response to the deprivations of prison life, but the nature of the response in both prison communities is influenced by the differential participation of males and females in the external culture. The culture that emerges within the prison structure may be seen to incorporate and reflect the total external social structure; that is, the way in which roles are defined in the external world influence the definitions made within the prison. General features of American society with respect to the cultural definitions and content of male and female roles are brought into the prison setting and they function to determine the direction and focus of the inmate cultural system. These general features I have suggested are those concerned with the orientation of life goals for males and females; second, cultural definitions with respect to dimensions of passivity and aggression; third, acceptability of public expression of affection displayed toward a member of the same sex; and, finally, perception of the same sex with respect to what I have called the popular culture.

It is the *system* of roles and statuses that is imported into the prison setting, and not merely the values and attitudes of the individuals who enter the prison world. It is in these terms that the importance attached to the female role, marriage ties, and family groups can be understood as salient elements of prison culture in the female prison community, but not in the male prison community. It would seem, then, that there is greater unity between the inner and outer worlds than has heretofore been thought. Accordingly, greater understanding of the prison communities may be accomplished by focusing our attention on the relationship of the external and internal cultures rather than trying to understand the prison as an institution isolated from the larger society.

210

Notes

[1] Ida Harper, "The Role of the 'Fringer' in a State Prison for Women," *Social Forces,* 31 (October, 1952), pp. 53-60.

[2] David A. Ward and Gene G. Kassebaum, "Lesbian Liaisons," *Transaction,* 1 (January, 1964), pp. 28-32. Also David A. Ward and Gene G. Kassebaum, "Homosexuality: A Mode of Adaptation in a Prison for Women," *Social Problems,* 12 (Fall, 1964), pp. 159-177. In this institution, the authors found little evidence of the differentiated social types or of inmate solidarity that is typical of the male prison.

[3] In this connection, it should be pointed out that in addition to the aforementioned studies of the adult women's prison, there are several reports of institutions for juvenile girls which reveal homosexual practices and/or the presence of "family" groups among the delinquent girls. These reports are unsystematic investigations and impressionistic reports. See, for example, Charles A. Ford, "Homosexual Practices of Institutionalized Females," *Journal of Abnormal and Social Psychology,* 23 (January-March, 1929), pp. 442-444; Margaret Otis, "A Perversion Not Commonly Noted," *Journal of Abnormal Psychology,* 8 (June-July, 1913), pp. 112-114; Lowell S. Selling, "The Pseudo Family," *The American Journal of Sociology,* 37 (September, 1931), pp. 247-253; Seymour L. Halleck and Marvin Hersko, "Homosexual Behavior in a Correctional Institution for Adolescent Girls," *American Journal of Orthopsychiatry,* 32 (October, 1962), pp. 911-917; Sidney Kosofsky and Albert Ellis, "Illegal Communication Among Institutionalized Female Delinquents," *The Journal of Social Psychology,* 48 (August, 1958), pp. 155-160; Romolo Toigo, "Illegitimate and Legitimate Cultures in a Training School for Girls," *Proceedings of the Rip Van Winkle Clinic,* 13 (Summer, 1962), pp. 3-29. Ward and Kassebaum, however, reported that there were no indications of family groups in the prison they studied; *Social Problems, op. cit.*

[4] See esp. Gresham M. Sykes and Sheldon L. Messinger, "The Inmate Social System" in *Theoretical Studies in Social Organization of the Prison,* New York: Social Science Research Council, March, 1960, pp. 5-19; Gresham M. Sykes, *The Society of Captives,* Princeton, New Jersey: Princeton University Press, 1958; Erving Goffman, "On the Characteristics of Total Institutions: Staff-Inmate Relations," in Donald R. Cressey (ed.), *The Prison: Studies in Institutional Organization and Change,* New York: Holt, Rinehart and Winston, 1961, chs. 1 and 2; Richard A. Cloward, "Social Control in the Prison," *Theoretical Studies in the Social Organization of the Prison, op. cit.,* pp. 20-48. See also Donald Clemmer, *The Prison Community,* New York: Holt, Rinehart and Winston, 1958 (reissue of the 1940 edition); Morris G. Caldwell, "Group Dynamics in the Prison Community," *Journal of Criminal Law, Criminology and Police Science,* 46 (January-February, 1956), pp. 648-657; Norman S. Hayner, "Washington State Correctional Institutions as Communities," *Social Forces,* 21 (1943), pp. 316-322; Norman S. Hayner and Ellis Ash, "The Prison as a Community," *American Sociological Review,* 5 (August, 1940), pp. 577-583; Hans Reimer, "Socialization in the Prison Community," *Proceedings of the American Prison Association,* 1937, pp. 151-155.

[5] It is interesting that an analysis of variations in organizational goals and an examination of data on the inmates of several juvenile correctional institutions for boys call into question the "solidary opposition" model of the inmate group. See David Street, "The Inmate Group in Custodial and Treatment Settings," *American Sociological Review,* 30 (February, 1965), pp. 40-55.

[5] Stanton Wheeler, "Socialization in Correctional Communities," *American Sociological Review,* 26 (October, 1961), pp. 696-712; Peter C. Garabedian, "Social Roles and Processes of Socialization in the Prison Community," *Social Problems,* 11 (Fall, 1963), pp. 139-152.

211

[7] John Irwin and Donald R. Cressey, "Thieves, Convicts, and the Inmate Culture," *Social Problems*, 10 (Fall, 1962), pp. 142–155.

[8] Clarence Schrag, "Some Foundations for a Theory of Correction," in Donald R. Cressey (ed.), *The Prison: Studies in Institutional Organization and Change*, New York: Holt, Rinehart and Winston, 1961, pp. 309-357.

[9] Marriage, family, and kinship in the female prison will be discussed in a forthcoming paper. However, in this context it might be worthwhile pointing out that the differentiation of sex roles is crucial as it structures at the outset many other roles which the inmate may legitimately play. Once an inmate has adopted a sex role, it automatically closes off some family roles, while at the same time it opens up legitimate avenues for other roles.

[10] Robin M. Williams, Jr., *American Society* (rev. ed.), New York: Alfred A. Knopf, 1960, pp. 64-65. Although many married women at one time or another do some kind of work outside the home for which they earn a salary, marriage and family are the primary goals for most American women. Indeed, despite the marked increase in the number of married women in the labor market, the worker role of women continues to be regarded by society as secondary to the traditional role of women as mothers and homemakers.

[11] Indeed, the architecture of the male prison has been historically oriented upon the general belief that the male criminal is aggressive and dangerous.

[12] Simone de Beauvoir, *The Second Sex*, trans. and ed. by H. M. Parshley, New York: Bantam Books, 1961, p. 514. She argues that the marriage market from one age period to another is very unstable for the female. Consequently, the process of acquiring a husband becomes an urgent matter, and this concern is often destructive of feminine friendships, for the young girl sees rivals rather than allies in her companions. In this connection, Jules Henry has stated that the self-orientation of the female begins at an early age; see *Culture Against Man*, New York: Random House, 1963, pp. 150-155.

[13] As Malinowski has cogently pointed out, however, automatic conformity does not exist empirically. But we may conceive of automatic conformity and lawlessness as ideal types with the prison approximating calculated solidarity. See Bronislaw Malinowski, *Crime and Custom in Savage Society*, New York: Harcourt, Brace, 1932, esp. chs. 3, 4, and 5.

[14] Donald Clemmer, *The Prison Community, op. cit.*, p. 123.

[15] Gresham M. Sykes, *The Society of Captives, op. cit.*, p. 64.

[16] *Ibid.*, p. 64.

[17] On a selected day the records revealed that 52.1 per cent had been previously jailed or imprisoned. The commitment age of the inmates ranged from fifteen to sixty-seven years, with a mean of 32.2 and a median of 30.5. Fifty-six per cent of the inmate population were white and forty-four per cent were Negro. The marital status of the inmates indicated that 27.1 per cent were single; 31.5 per cent were married; 20.7 per cent were separated; 16.4 per cent were divorced and slightly over 4 per cent were widows.

[18] Yarn may be purchased at the commissary store. Knitted items such as socks and sweaters provide another means by which the loss of goods may be mitigated.

[19] Stripping and mortifying practices are discussed in Erving Goffman, *Asylums*, New York: Doubleday, 1961; see esp. pp. 14-25. In the prison, no clothing may be kept by the inmates except girdles (if they are not the panty type), brassieres and shoes of simple (relatively low-heeled) closed styles. Medals, simple style earrings and wedding rings which are not studded with precious or semi-precious stones may be kept by the inmate, as well as wrist watches which are valued under fifteen dollars.

[20] The obvious exceptions to this, of course, are the homosexuals who have practiced

homosexuality in the free community. Approximately 5 per cent of the inmate population falls into this category. For this group, it cannot be said that this aspect of imprisonment is depriving. In a sense, the imprisonment of the homosexual — whether male or female — is ironical, for the loss of liberty, except in a few countries, is always accompanied by the denial of contact with the opposite sex so as to increase the burden of punishment. The homosexual in prison, however, is actually in a favored position, because the competition of the opposite sex has been excluded.

[21] Jules Henry, *op. cit.*, p. 61; also cf. Margaret Park Redfield, "The American Family: Consensus and Freedom," *The American Journal of Sociology*, 52 (November, 1946), p. 182. "Beyond the roles of glamor girl and nursemaid, the part to be played by women is but vaguely defined in our society."

[22] Talcott Parsons, "Age and Sex in the Social Structure of the United States," *American Sociological Review*, 7 (October, 1942), pp. 610–613.

[23] Sykes, *op. cit.*, p. 78.

[24] This is not to say, however, that there are no fights which take place among the inmates, but the real violence that occurs in the prison, however, tends to be in connection with a homosexual triangle. And in this connection the great fear is not so much for one's life as the fear of *disfigurement* — the fear that an inmate "out to get" another will use razor or scissors to disfigure one's face. It is worthwhile noting that the prison officials issued scissors to each inmate; the blades are fairly blunt, but, nevertheless, this indicates the widely held belief of women as nonaggressive types.

[25] Types of contaminative exposures have been discussed by Erving Goffman in *Asylums, op. cit.*, pp. 25–35.

[26] Most women, as a matter of fact, serve their entire sentence without a visit from the outside world. In the year 1962, for example, an examination of the records revealed that 79 inmates or about twelve per cent of the inmate population received visits during the entire year.

[27] Cf. Judge M. Murtagh and Sara Harris, *Cast the First Stone*, New York: Cardinal, 1958, p. 244.

[28] It is possible to make special withdrawals for yarn purchases.

[29] Sykes, *op. cit.*, p. 94.

[30] Cigarettes are the most important nexus of exchange among the inmates.

[31] This role is also reported in Ward and Kassebaum, *op. cit.*, p. 169.

[32] Cf. the role of the butch in Ward and Kassebaum, *ibid.*, pp. 168–169.

[33] Ward and Kassebaum, *ibid.*, p. 171.

[34] Estimates of the number of inmates who are involved in homosexuality vary. Inmates who are very much involved in this phase of inmate culture place the figure at ninety or ninety-five per cent. The Associate Warden (treatment) estimated that eighty per cent of the inmates were involved in homosexual relations. Correctional officers tended to set the figure at fifty or seventy-five per cent which agrees with the usual estimates I obtained from squares. Some officers and other staff members set the figure at one hundred per cent. At one point in the study, I made a cottage count of inmates assuming the male role, and the studs totaled 215 inmates. The number of "males" in the prison tends to vary slightly from day to day depending upon inmate releases and individual role choice. And the same is equally true of the inmates playing the femme role. At this time, there were 336 femmes out of a total of 639 inmates. At any rate, it is apparent that femmes are competing for a scarce commodity.

[35] Irwin and Cressey, *op. cit.*, esp. pp. 148–153.

[36] Julian Roebuck, "A Critique of 'Thieves, Convicts, and the Inmate Culture,'" *Social Problems*, 11 (Fall, 1963), pp. 193–200. It should be pointed out that Schrag's analysis also remains unclear, for at one point he comments: "Juxtaposed with the

official organization of the prison is an unofficial social system originating within the institution and regulating inmate conduct with respect to focal issues, such as length of sentence, relations among prisoners, contacts with staff members and other civilians, food, sex, and health, among other things." This suggests that all inmates face a number of common problems of adjustment as a result of incarceration and that social organization develops to provide solutions. See Clarence Schrag, "Some Foundations for a Theory of Correction" in Cressey (ed.), *The Prison, op. cit.,* p. 342.

14

The Ethnography of Male Homosexual Relationships

David Sonenschein

This work has largely come about because of a dissatisfaction with previous psychological approaches and some of the recent sociological research on male homosexuality. It has been pointed out (Sonenschein, 1966) that psychology has furnished us with most of our data and methodological viewpoints of homosexuality; most of this research and rhetoric has dealt excessively with the definition, origin and operation of etiologic behaviors. Simon and Gagnon (1967) have more explicitly pointed out, however, that this approach has resulted in an extremely "simplistic and homogeneous" conception of homosexual individuals and groups; their lives are characterized in much of the literature by bizarre case histories of personal, social and sexual pathology. On the other hand, such people as Evelyn Hooker (1956, 1962), Maurice Leznoff and W. A. Westley (1956) and Albert Reiss (1961) have formed the basis of what is essentially an ethnographic tradition in the description and functional analysis of the homosexual community. Others such as Nancy Achilles (1967) have done more specifically anthropological work in the analysis of what is called in this paper the "cultural system" of the homosexual world. This paper hopes to contribute to

Reprinted with the permission of the editor from *The Journal of Sex Research,* Vol. IV, No. 2, May, 1968, and with the permission of the author.

A revised version of a paper read before the Central States Anthropological Society, Chicago, Illinois, April, 1967. I am indebted to the following people for their critical reviews of earlier drafts of this paper: Louis A. Zurcher, Jr., S. Stansfeld Sargent, John H. Gagnon, James E. Elias, Paul H. Gebhard, William T. Tucker and M. Isaac Much.

this area of objective description, and also to the newly developing sociological approach, in that certain variables are suggested which if adequately measured, may reveal a much more systematic picture of the varieties of homosexual relationships.

In other words, what the newer social approaches to homosexuality mean to do is: firstly, anthropologically describe and analyze the synchronic particular social and sexual subculture that a given homosexual both finds himself in and structures for himself, and, secondly, to sociologically describe and analyze various modes of relation and interaction of homosexuals with society as a whole (cf. Simon and Gagnon 1967). Basically, the kinds of answers one seeks then now center around the question: "given a homosexual individual, what does he do about it, what does he do with it, and what happens to him as a result?" This writer feels that this is a much more immediately important and crucial approach — to the homosexual and heterosexual alike — rather than what seems to be at this time, the unanswerable question of etiology.

The data used in this paper come from observations and interviews of informants of a homosexual community in the Southwestern United States; as a check on these initial data, subsequent brief observations were made in five other cities around the country. The subject community was roughly divided into (1) an "upper status" homosexual group composed of individuals in the higher socioeconomic brackets of the city; (2) a "lower status" homosexual group composed of the city's middle and lower class members, students and military men; and (3) an unstructured body of "marginals" composed of such individuals as transients, homosexuals who did not identify with either of the two main groups and "hustlers" or male prostitutes. Most of the observations were made of the lower status group. While it was impossible to estimate the total homosexual population in the city, observed groups ranged in size from three individuals to approximately 100. The age range of the subjects was from 16 to 57, the modal age falling roughly in the middle 20s.

The introduction into this community was a result of personal friendship and professional affiliation rather than being based on any research design.[1] Actual observations did not begin until about six months after the initial introduction in 1961. The period of association with the subject community as a heterosexual friend then lasted for about 1½ years until 1963; at no time did the members of the community know observations were being made. The directions that the ethnographic work followed included considerations of (1) the position of the homosexual community in relation to the city, (2) the social and cultural structure of the homosexual community itself, (3) the special language of homosexuality in relation to the group and, (4) the nature and structure of the interaction of individuals within their groups. This paper is a partial report on the latter set of observations and analysis of interpersonal relations.

216

table 1

TYPOLOGY OF MALE HOMOSEXUAL RELATIONSHIPS IN THE SUBJECT COMMUNITY

	Duration	
Sexuality	Permanent	Non-permanent
Social	First order friendships (I)	Second order friendships (II)
Sexual	Extended encounters (III)	Brief encounters (IV)
Sociosexual	Mateships (V)	Circumstantial encounters (VI)

Table I, then, is an attempt at a systematization of the dyadic relationships as were seen in the subject community. The organizing variables are those that were the most important in the relationships, those of sexuality and duration; the cells of the table are thus a function of the relative saliency of these variables to the participants.

I. Permanent Social Relationships

These are what may be called first order friendships and included individuals that the subjects described as their "best and closest friends." The individuals who described each other in this manner were usually found within the same clique structure and were in constant face-to-face interaction. These cliques held members who were much alike in interests, intellects, occupations, general social and sexual status-roles and attitudes.[2] Members felt strongly committed to each other in three main areas: social, psychologically (in terms of constant association, confidence in intimate matters and behavioral reinforcement), economically (such as loans of money, job placements, etc.) and materially (loans or gifts of clothes, personal items, etc.). Based on these kinds of bonds, these friendships were mutually maintained over time and distance. Most subjects claimed that they had anywhere from two to five "really close friends" with whom they always kept in contact regardless of how far apart they were.

II. Non-permanent Social Relationships

What are here called second order friendships describe those individuals that were spoken of as "good friends" but were usually found outside of an individual's clique. The sociometric choice or labeling of friendships in this case need not be reciprocal or equal; that is, A may call B his "good friend" while B may not think of A as such (cf. Lundberg and Lawsing 1937). A lesser degree of congruence of attitudes and expectations was called for in second order friendships than in those of the first order. Second order friendships did not call for continued contact over distance; a moving away of one

217

member of the dyad usually meant an end to the relationship until such time as face-to-face contact was reestablished. Even still, communication was maintained as long as the individuals were in the same community.

It is to be noticed that first and second order friendships were seen to be entirely social and non-sexual in nature. Members were fairly explicit in their statements regarding the possible sexual desirability of good or close friends. Most cited reasons were: "knowing them too well to have sex" and/or that sexual needs were amply satisfied from other sources. However, whether or not such statements come before or after the fact is not clear at this point. In other words, whether the category of "friends" is really a residual category of individuals who did not work out as sexual partners or whether there are differential expectations through which individuals are initially screened to become either "friends" or "partners" is a matter now set for future research. Leznoff and Westley (1956) discuss the question of friendships briefly in functional terms indicating that there are a few individuals that are selected specifically to form the basis of some kind of "primary group cohesiveness" which is pitted against a category of "all-others," i.e., sexual partners. The observational data from the subject community suggest that in reality both processes may operate due to the fact that many homosexuals had friends with whom they had never attempted to have sex as well as friends who were once sexual partners but had since moved into a non-sexual friendship category. There were, in addition, a few individuals who were both sexual and social partners, depending on the social situation and needs of the individuals. They will be discussed below in more detail as third order friendships under cell VI of the typology, but it is important to note at this point that this very category seems to indicate a process of "trial and selection" whereby certain individuals who may not succeed as sexual partners may still be retained as a certain class of "friends."

Where both friends and sexual partners must be drawn from the same sex, the processes involved seem to particularly depend upon sociocultural factors as well as the psychological ones. For example, while genital relations between first and second order friends were extremely rare, sex play was very common. There seemed to be a rather definite joking relationship among these individuals that allowed on the one hand for affectionate behavior and on the other, more hostile verbal behavior of teasing and chiding. A. J. M. Sykes (1966) has noted similar relationships in heterosexual groups, where it helps to define and differentiate between sexual and non-sexual partners. The operation of this kind of relationship may prove significant not only with regard to processes of selection but even with regard to the management of friends and sexual partners in interpersonal interaction. It was interesting to note that in the subject community as members became socialized into their proper status group and clique, they shared with the others a kind of group cohesiveness which presented a relatively homogeneous social and sexual front to other groups. On the other hand members within each group became more competitive with each other for social and sexual partners. This many times resulted in a good deal of tension in the confrontations in the context of the homosexual institutions. The strains on the relationships seemed to be both manifested and managed in such ways as (1) gossip, and extremely constant and common activity, (2) humor, containing unusually high amounts of self-mockery and the projection of homosexuality onto heterosexuals, and (3) "campy" or effeminate behavior, the sporadic nature of which will be discussed below.

As an initial step to analysis, Table 2, while being minimally descriptive of the subject community, suggests an approach to more quantitatively define the three classes of friendship as indicated by the observational data. It is suggested that the variable "degree of interaction," when broken into several indices, will yield the "strength of relationships" in clusters which correspond to the three categories of friendship as held by the subjects.

Before leaving cell II of the typology, there is one further important example of a non-permanent social relationship which is here simply called the roommate relation. It has been previously assumed that if two homosexuals were living together, they were sexual partners and may even be included in that vague class of "homosexual marrieds." Upon a closer examination however, it can be seen that there are several types of living arrangements, each with its special form and content. The roommate relation is a case where friends live together for varying lengths of time, usually for reasons of economics (not being able to afford a place alone) or for social psychological reasons (loneliness, wanting to be at the centers of social and sexual action, and other reasons as mentioned above). The emotional involvement between roommates was as between first and second order friends; most of the roommates in the subject community were members of the same clique.

table 2

DISCRIMINATION OF FRIENDSHIP RELATIONS

	Strength of relationship		
Degree of interaction	Best friends	Good friends	Acquaintances
Maintains face-to-face contact in social situations	yes	yes	yes
Seeks contact within the community	yes	yes	no
Maintains relationship over time within the community	yes	may or may not	no
Maintains relationship over distances	yes	no	no

Although Hauser's *The Homosexual Society* (1962) is the only study to discuss the non-sexual living arrangement, he makes a series of statements that are entirely unsupported by the present data. First of all, he sees the roommate relationship solely as a degenerated form of a love or sex relationship. This paper proposes the contrary: that the category of non-sexually involved housemates is an extension and function of a greater realm of asexual friendship relations. Secondly, Hauser suggests that this kind of arrangement can exist only between what he calls "two similarly sex-oriented" individuals, that is, two homosexuals equally masculine or equally feminine. Too many exceptions to this were observed in the subject community and others for this statement to hold true. Implicit in this is the assumption that Hauser and others make which says that instances of effeminate behavior are valid indicators of a consistent role and self-conception that is essentially feminine. While there are indeed some individuals who consistently occupy very masculine or very feminine sociosexual roles both in and out of the homosexual community, there is a good deal of evidence that most of the obvious effeminate behavior is situational-specific; that is, sporadic, circumstantial and usually satirical. In other words, much of this behavior is a function of sociocultural structure: the intersection of time and place within the homosexual community and a homosexual's idea of what he has to do to fit into the group. In short, there is doubt at this point as to whether or not a given instance of behavior does in fact indicate any sort of consistent and/or conceptualized role within the community.

Returning to the subject community and the roommates within it, it was noted that for the most part, the division of labor in terms of household duties was a matter of personal choice rather than any function of so-called masculine or feminine roles. The breaking of the roommate relation was due sometimes, as Hauser insists (1962), to some form of jealously but in the subject community, it was due more often to matters of more mundane affairs such as financial irresponsibility, conflict over the maintenance of the house, moving away and the usual assortment of "personality clashes." It is this often less interesting realm of activities and events of managing a day-to-day life that previous accounts have neglected but when they are taken into account, they prove significant in the recharacterization of the homosexual and his life.

III. Permanent Sexual Relationships

This form included what was called "being kept." Because the basis of this relationship was materialistic and sexual, the explanation of it, as a relationship, varied as to an individual's attitude toward and involvement in the dyad. The homosexual who is being "kept" is in the role of a mistress; the "kept boy" was a younger individual whose interest in the relationship was primarily materialistic and monetary and whose emotional involvement with his partner was superficial and exploitative. He did not usually enter into such a relationship unless there was a high probability of a stable income of goods and money; his role was to produce a stable output of sexual services. This individual then conceived of the relationship as "permanent" in the sense of "as long as the money holds out."

This younger individual was "kept" by an older, more well-to-do homosexual whose physical appearance and/or aging had tended to move him out of the system of competition for partners in the homosexual community. The older homosexual had greater expectations of "permanence" involving a hope or fantasy of actual emotional involvement, but he would not have committed himself to this kind of relationship unless he could have kept up a constant output of money and goods; this he realized he must do in order to "keep" (in both senses) his partner.

Group participation by these individuals was low due on the one hand to the fear on the part of the older man that his "boy" would be stolen from him, and on the other hand, to the fact that the other members of the group held a rather low opinion of such a relationship and the individuals involved in it. The "kept boy" however apparently served a social function to his "keeper" in that the older homosexual liked to occasionally "show off" his partner and the manner in which he could "keep" him to the rest of the community. Despite the expectations of permanence in this relationship, it was very unstable, the biggest factor of breakup being the infidelity of the "kept boy."

IV. Non-permanent Sexual Relationships

This cell in the Table contains two main examples: the "one night stand" and the "affair." The two tend to separate out by considering the relative duration of the interactions and the content of the relationships.

The "one night stand" is perhaps the homosexual's most frequent sexual relationship yet surprisingly little is known of its forms and even less of its dynamics and content. There were two rather distinct types of relationships under this rubric, differentiated from each other again by using the criteria of the duration of the brief encounter and the relative degree of social interaction with the partner. Both types were extremely depersonalized, the sole basis of the relationship being the purpose of sexual activity and orgasm. The briefest and most superficial of the two was known as the "quicky" and may be consummated in anywhere from a few hours of activity to the few minutes it takes to reach orgasm. This form involved the highest degree of anonymity; it seemed to be the most popular form of sex for those homosexuals with a good deal of social rank and for those who were tremendously committed to sexuality. In this activity, the partners usually had never seen one another before and usually never saw each other again.

The other type of the "one night stand" was a more prolonged relationship such as for a whole night or a weekend. Here participants were more likely to learn at least each other's name and a few mutual interests. Much like the above however, the relationship was entered into and departed from in an entirely non-committal manner.

The variety called an "affair" was defined by the subject group as a primarily sexual relationship lasting over an indefinite period of time; it may or may not involve what the participants called "love," even though the participants were seen as "lovers" by the rest of the group. Duration varied in terms of weeks or months. It would be distorting to impose an arbitrary time criterion here for definition as does Schofield (1960) when he suggests an affair last over a year. What is important is the conception of the relationship by the participants themselves; it was seen in the subject community that relationships lasting a year or more were spoken about and conceived of in entirely different terms. Participants rarely lived together in affairs. They acknowledged a relative instability in the relationship and an uncertainty of the depth of the emotional involvement. Thus for some, an affair was a trial relationship, a prelude to a more committal one and a testing of mutual emotional and sexual adjustments in terms of the individual's relations to each other and their relation to the community as a couple.

For others however, it was a kind of "going steady," referred to as a kind of young puppy love that was frequently indulged in many times during one's life and may or may not be intended as a "test" of a future mate at all. In this case, a couple may spend a varying amount of time in intense association with the implicit knowledge that the affair will end when the novelty wears off or in some cases when the risk of discovery becomes too great. Finally, for still others, the affair was merely an intensely physical relationship with another, ending when both partners were sexually satiated.

The "fear of discovery" leads to another aspect of the affair that characterized it in the subject community. Pressures of exposure were both external (the police, one's employer) and internal (other group members) to the community. To the participants however, the latter was the more important. The affair was often spoken of with illicit overtones indicating either that a homosexual was involved in a clandestine relationship with a respected and/or heterosexually married man in the city, or, more usually, that one was involved with another homosexual who was the partner of a third party. In this latter sense, "extra-marital" affairs were common in the subject group.

It is this modal category of the depersonalized sexual relationship, and more particularly the "one night stand," that has attracted the most attention from the psychological field but opinion here has largely overlooked its sociocultural context. It has been implied and stated in the psychiatric literature that all homosexual sexual encounters were of the "one night stand" variety and due in reality to a searching for the ultimate and permanent partner, or, alternately, that it was due simply to "the neurotic basis of homosexuality" (Harper 1963; cf. Hauser 1962, Schofield 1960). In the subject community however it was clearly evident that there were differential expectations operating in the formation of the various sexual relationships discussed here. Very simply, the partner desired for a "one night stand" was usually not the one a homosexual saw as a good bet for a more permanent partner. One acted very differently with a purely sexual partner than with a sociosexual partner.

It is in this connection then that one is stimulated to look to the sociocultural contexts of the behaviors involved in the relationships. It was seen that there were two major systems in the homosexual community that directly influenced interpersonal behavior: the "cultural system" and the "social system."[3] The major part of the cultural system in the subject community was a series of institutions that served the needs of its members. Places such as bars (cf. Achilles 1967), steam baths, parties and even the streets provided backdrops that were more conducive to one kind of expected relationship than another. For example, one would walk the streets or "cruise" (look for partners) the public restrooms as well as go to the bars if one wanted a purely sexual partner. On the other hand, one may have looked more in some bars, gone to parties or depended upon personal introductions by friends if one wanted a partner for a more lasting relationship, social or sexual. Even within the system of bars, there were differences; some may be more of a social rather than a sexual "market place" to paraphrase Hooker (1965). Just then as there was a difference of role behaviors as a function of the sociocultural situation, so too was there a difference in the relationships that took place in and grew out of the institutions of the homosexual subculture.

In addition to this, there was the social system of the subject community which directly involved the structure and behavior of groups and the individuals in them. One aspect of this was the status differentiation found in the community. This was very similar to what Leznoff and Westley (1956) found but although severe social distance was maintained, the separation of sexual interaction was not as great. Members of the subject community preferred and sought sexual partners from opposing groups and cliques. Based on the intention of action, the graph in Figure 1 is a representation of the tendency in the subject community for social choice to vary inversely with sexual choice. In other words, male homosexuals in the subject community tend to separate and keep separated those individuals who served their social needs from those who served their sexual needs. Also in Figure 1, the relationships from the typology are shown in the directions that they tended to distribute themselves.

It must be mentioned again however that many times these relationships are a function of the sociocultural structure of the community; the variables

223

Figure 1

RELATIONSHIP BETWEEN SEXUAL VERSUS SOCIAL CHOICE
OF PARTNERS IN THE SUBJECT COMMUNITY AND
CLUSTERING OF RELATIONSHIPS

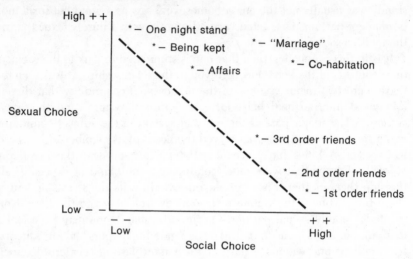

may tend to merge as the range is narrowed by the opportunity structure of any given community. For example, in a community small in numbers of members, there would be more repetitive sexual relationships with given individuals. The direction of alternatives in this case would either be to limit the numbers of members in the social and sexual categories or to tend to combine them into a more unified category.

V. Permanent Sociosexual Relationships

To find a permanent partner was certainly a common goal of many homosexuals in the subject group but it was not as universal, as constant or as compulsive as the psychological literature would have us believe. Most of the younger individuals were more intent upon the satisfaction of the moment or having partners in extended encounters rather than questing after a permanent mate. It was usually only after "aging" set in (about age 30) that finding a steadier mate became a significant concern.[4]

The psychological conception of the so-called homosexual marriage has been simplistic and misleading. It has assumed that all homosexuals living together were to be construed as being "married" in some rather homogeneous way and has defined both the form and content of this category as pathological. Thus previous conceptions of the relationship have been too inclusive[5] and have not distinguished the forms of paired relationships we have even thus far covered in this paper.

224

Yet there is a category of homosexual relationships that is indeed in many aspects much like a heterosexual marriage. But within this concept, there appeared in the subject community two rather separable patterns of behavior that so-called "married" couples exhibited.

The first form, for which the term "marriage" (in quotes) will be reserved, was characterized by the following complex of traits: (1) some sort of ritual, usually in imitation of the heterosexual marriage ceremony; (2) a material demarcation of the union as in the exchange and wearing of wedding rings; (3) a value system of the participants, based on a romantic conception of ideally unending love; and (4) a tendency to dichotomize social roles. It is this form that is the most obvious and most closely approaches the psychological characterization.

It has been commonly thought that role dichotomization was a "natural" and automatic event in homosexual marriages: one man stays home in an essentially feminine and domestic role and is called the "wife" and the other partner assumes the occupational responsibilities and the more masculine domestic chores and is called the "husband" (Hauser 1962; Bergler 1956). This also was supposed to correspond to the gender role identification and sexual behavior of the partners: one is effeminate, conceives of himself as a "woman trapped in a man's body" and is "passive" in sex; the other is more masculine in appearance and behavior, sees himself as a man and is "active" in sex. In actuality however, it was seen in the subject community and in other homosexual communities that these kinds of gender and role distinctions were typical only of a minority and special type of paired homosexual partners.

The second kind of mateship was less formalized, often the only event being a personal exchange of rings and/or the setting up of a household. It too was based on a conception of love but the relationship was less predominately sexual as was the previous variety; there was a more conscious attempt by the individuals involved to aim at a congruence of values and interests. This kind of stable pairing may be called simply "co-habitation" to differentiate it from the actual homosexual "marriage."

The first variety of the permanent relationship was less stable than the second variety. It seemed that in fact, the ritual, rather than being an attempt to cement the relationship, was more of an excuse for the ever-present and ever-needed party. It seemed in a sense to reintegrate the group in terms of its own values, particularly those that mock the heterosexual world. The pairing off into permanent mateships became, through the mock marriage, a group event in contrast to the private event of pairing for the co-habitants.

The relative publicness or privateness of interpersonal relations in the homosexual community profoundly affected their stability and duration. It was continually observed in the subject community that as soon as any two individuals entered into sexual or sociosexual relationship that was hoped to last for any period of time, these individuals rapidly withdrew from the activity of the community and decreased their participation in group affairs, regardless of how active or popular they had been before; the institutions that were more conductive to sexual interaction, and hence more competitive, were particularly avoided. This applies not only to permanent mateships but also to the relationship of "being kept" as above.

VI. Non-permanent Sociosexual Relationships

In this final cell are included situational face-to-face contacts. They were between individuals who considered themselves "friends" but also potential sexual partners. These may be called third order friendships and comprise individuals whom ego might call an "acquaintance" or speak of as "just a friend." Social encounters seemed to occur before sexual activity with these individuals in contrast to those in cell IV, where sexual interaction usually preceded social acquaintance.

It seemed in the subject community that although there were people who might fall into this category, they were relatively rare. Individuals were pointed out as to whether they were sexual partners or social partners; only rarely could they be both. As mentioned earlier, given the hypothesis of the separation of sexual from social partners, this category might then represent a category of selection rather than a static unit. It might be here that a homosexual makes the decision as to whether an individual becomes a friend of a higher order or a sexual partner.

Notes

[1] Pomeroy (1963) and Hooker (1963) discuss the problems of sex research and research on homosexuality respectively. Honigmann (1954) provides some anthropological perspectives on the Kinsey reports and sex research in general.

[2] This is similar to Lazarsfeld's concept of "homophily" (1954).

[3] This distinction is somewhat forced as both systems are aspects of a unified phenomenon. The "cultural system" focuses not only on the tangibles such as artifacts and dress but also on such intangibles as overriding value orientations, language and communication and so on (Parsons and Shils 1951). The "social system" focuses upon the structuring and relationships of groups. Communication mediates this relation of values and behaviors (Parsons 1961). Institutions become then in this sense situations or environments in time and space in which a number of fairly specific and sanctioned behaviors occur (Sheldon 1951). These are exemplified in the text of this paper.

[4] Observations outside the subject community indicate that this concern may be in part a variant of the social structure in which a homosexual has to operate in the sense that it is a function of the kind of opportunity structure in his society that allows for the presentation of potential partners plus the community's system of values that may define him as a potential partner.

[5] Robbins (1943) defines a homosexual marriage as "an essentially monogamous,

relatively durable intimacy existing between members of the same sex;" it is also defined as inherently pathological. Other definitions are by Leznoff and Westley (1956): "a stable social and sexual relationship between two homosexuals . . ." and by Hauser (1962): "only the homosexuals who have a lasting affair and are faithful to one another will be considered 'married.'"

References

ACHILLES, N. B. The Development of the Homosexual Bar as an Institution. In *Sexual Deviance* (ed. Gagnon, J. H. and Simon, W.) New York: Harper and Row, 228–244, 1967.

BERGLER, E. *Homosexuality: Disease or Way of Life?* New York: Hill and Wang, 1956.

HARPER, R. A. Psychological Aspects of Homosexuality. In *Advances in Sex Research* (ed. Beigel, H. G.) New York: Hoeber-Harper, 187–197, 1963.

HAUSER, R. *The Homosexual Society.* London: Bodley Head, 1962.

HONIGMANN, J. J. An Anthropological Approach to Sex. *Social Problems* 2: 7–16, 1954.

HOOKER, E. A Preliminary Analysis of the Group Behavior of Homosexuals. *J. Psych.* 42: 217–225, 1956.

HOOKER, E. The Homosexual Community. In *Proceedings of the XIV International Congress of Applied Psychology.* Copenhagen: Nielson, 40–59 (Vol. II), 1962.

HOOKER, E. Male Homosexuality. In *Taboo Topics* (ed. Farberow, N.) New York: Atherton, 44–55, 1963.

HOOKER, E. Male Homosexuals and Their "Worlds." In *Sexual Inversion* (ed. Marmor, J.) New York: Basic Books, 83–107, 1965.

LAZARSFELD, P. F. AND MERTON, R. K. Friendship as a Social Process: a Substantive and Methodological Analysis. In *Freedom and Control in Modern Society* (ed. Berger, M., Abel, T., and Page, C. H.) New York: Nostrand, 18–66, 1954.

LEZNOFF, M. AND WESTLEY, W. A. The Homosexual Community. *Social Problems* 3: 257–263, 1956.

LUNDBERG, G. A. AND LAWSING, M. The Sociology of Some Community Relations. *Amer. Soc. Rev.* 2: 318–335, 1937.

PARSONS, T. Introduction. In *Theories of Society* (ed. Parsons, T., *et al.*) Glencoe, Ill.: Free Press, 963–993 (Vol. II), 1961.

PARSONS, T. AND SHILS, E. A. (Eds.) *Toward a General Theory of Action.* New York: Harper Torchbooks, 1951.

POMEROY, W. Human Sexual Behavior. In *Taboo Topics* (ed. Farberow, N.) New York: Atherton, 22–32, 1963.

REISS, A. J. JR. The Social Integration of Peers and Queers. *Social Problems* 9: 102–120, 1961.

ROBBINS, B. S. Psychological Implications of the Male Homosexual "Marriage." *Psychoanalytic Rev.* 30: 428–437, 1943.

SCHOFIELD, M. G. (pseud. Westwood, G.) *A Minority.* London: Longmans, 1960.

SHELDON, R. C. Some observations on theory in the social sciences. In *Parsons and Shils* 1951, 30–44.

SIMON, W. AND GAGNON, J. H. Homosexuality: the Development of a Sociological Perspective. *J. Health and Soc. Beh.* 8: 177–185, 1967.

SONENSCHEIN, D. Homosexuality as a Subject of Anthropological Inquiry. *Anth. Quart.* 39: 73–82, 1966.

SYKES, A. J. M. Joking Relationships in an Industrial Setting. *Amer. Anth.* 68: 188–193, 1966.

part seven

Commercialized sex

We have, in this section, chosen to concentrate on what are perhaps the most widespread forms of commercialized sex: pornography and prostitution. These have in common more than merely being available for a price. They both provide outlets for sexual needs which some individuals find difficult to meet or for which they require supplementation; yet, there are interesting differences in their clienteles and manners of usage. In order for us to be able to further explore these topics it is necessary to begin with some definitions.

A prostitute is generally thought of as a person who provides sexual services for a price. This definition has led some to characterize certain marriages as "legalized prostitution" because of the absence of romantic involvement on the part of the women or more simply because of the exchange character of the marital relationship. We feel, however, that the term *prostitute* is better limited to those individuals who engage in sex with a variety of individuals more or less as a paid vocation. To be sure prostitutes ply their trade in a variety of ways: some work in brothels, others walk the street, and still others use the telephone to secure customers, but all of these variants are easily subsumed under our definition.

Pornography, which for many equals obscenity, is not easy to define. Even the Supreme Court has not come up with a workable definition of it, though they have tried. In the Roth decision of 1957 they defined sexual materials as "obscene" if they (1) dominantly appealed to a "prurient" sexual interest, (2) were offensive to "contemporary community standards," and (3) had no "redeeming social value." While at first glance these criteria might seem enforceable, it is extraordinarily difficult to do so. Community standards vary, they are not the same in New York City as they are in Des Moines, much less in Pine Bluff. Furthermore, where one man sees "redeeming social value" another man sees only smut, as is shown by the pages of testimony read into court records by literary experts at various obscenity trials, for example, the *Fanny Hill* case.

Perhaps the easiest way out of this dilemma is to forego the question of obscenity, which is obviously highly subjective, and simply resort to the classical definition of pornography as "books to be read with one hand," or in deference to art and movies, "to be seen with one hand." If we view pornography as material of a sexual character which is used as an adjunct to masturbation, we escape many of the pitfalls associated with other definitions. Obviously, some will look with horror at a definition that lumps together *Lady Chatterley's Lover* with *Nympho Coed,* but since they both may provide grist for masturbatory fantasies the definition has validity. One final word on definitions before we move on. We recognize that pornography need not be used exclusively as masturbatory material; it can and has been used for sexual instruction (Japanese pillow books) as well as a stimulant for other sexual activity, i.e., a means of arousal.

We noted earlier that pornography and prostitution are similar in certain respects. Ned Polsky in his essay "On the Sociology of Pornography," has explored, drawing upon the work of Kingsley Davis, an important point of congruence between them.[1] Using the above definition he claims that pornography like prostitution might be thought of as a safety valve which allows the draining off of "anti-social" sexual impulses. Were these impulses allowed expression in other arenas they might be destructive of prevailing institutions (e.g., monogamous marriage) or potentially dangerous to the safety of individuals (e.g., rape). The individual who uses pornography as a masturbatory stimulant need not be tempted to have an affair with the neighbor's spouse or assault the neighbor's child. While this interpretation of the functions of pornography has some face validity, it is, like all functional explanations, difficult to test. There are those who have seen a relationship between the liberalization of pornography laws and a subsequent reduction of sex crimes, but the relevant evidence is far from convincing.

Patterns of consumption for pornography and prostitution show some interesting and provocative variations. In the excerpt from *The Report of the Commission on Obscenity and Pornography* included in this section, it is observed that the typical patron of "adult" bookstores is a white, middle-class, married male. These are not surprising findings. The Kinsey study reports that better educated males were more responsive to erotic stories than those from lower educational levels.[2] Buying and using books, pornographic or otherwise, requires not merely a certain level of literacy, but also a general orientation which allows the reader to share in the experiences of a book's characters. This class pattern does not hold for other forms of erotica. Stag films, for example, are still *largely* consumed by upper-lower-class and lower-middle-class members of voluntary groups such as lodges and volunteer fire companies. Such class differences are not hard and fast. We find members of virtually all classes making use of pornography in all its varied forms; but, nevertheless, these findings do suggest how socio-cultural factors may affect one's taste for a particular type of erotic material.

Continuing along this line of analysis we must comment on sexual differences in response to pornography. Pornography has long been believed to be something produced by males for males. Therefore, it is important to explore not

230

merely the differential exposure of men and women to pornography but their differential response as well. According to the Commission report, cited above, more men see pornography than women, but since this is essentially a product of opportunity structures, the more significant question becomes what differences if any characterize their respective responses once they are exposed to such material. The Kinsey group found considerably fewer women than men (32 per cent compared with 77 per cent) reported being aroused by "portrayals of sexual action," e.g., drawings, photos, etc.[3] These findings have long been taken as evidence that women were less responsive to pornography than men. Recent experimental studies both in this country and in Europe have come up with somewhat different findings. For example, a research group at the University of Hamburg in Germany has reported that while slightly fewer females than males report being aroused by pictures and movies with sexual themes, they do not differ in their body (e.g., sensation in genitals) or behavioral (increase in sexual activity in the twenty-four hours following exposure) responses.[4] While this and similar studies have used far from representative samples (in almost all cases the subjects have been undergraduates), they do suggest that the kinds of changes in sexual attitude discussed throughout this book are making themselves felt in a variety of areas. Younger and more liberated females are probably much more responsive to a variety of sexual stimuli than are their mothers.

Turning to prostitution we see even more marked class and sex variations in patterns of consumption. There is virtually no male heterosexual prostitution, though a considerable, some claim growing, amount of homosexual prostitution among males currently exists. The former is probably a reflection of the fact that males have been granted sexual privileges both in and outside of marriage that until recently have been denied females. Furthermore, as we indicated in the section on female sexuality, women have been taught that they have to be romantically involved with a man to want to have sex with him.

Kinsey and his associates found that 74 per cent of the men in their sample who had not completed high school had had experience with prostitutes, while the same was true for only 28 per cent of the college men; or, if we look at it in terms of occupation, the figures for unskilled and semi-skilled workers were almost eight times higher than those for professionals and similarly high ranking males.[5] What this meant in terms of the general male population was that about two thirds of U.S. males had one or more contacts with prostitutes; however, less than 20 per cent had such contacts on a regular basis. In their recent book, *The Lively Commerce,* Winick and Kinsie remark that:

Probably roughly the same proportion of men visit prostitutes today as thirty years ago [when the Kinsey research was done], but the number of contacts per man has dropped somewhat. One reason for the decline is the decrease in the number of brothels.[6]

However, they also claim that the number of younger men (under thirty) both married and unmarried visiting prostitutes has declined — in earlier decades such men made up a significant part of the prostitute's clientele. Winick and Kinsie present no hard data to support their claims, but the latter seem plausible in light of the changing patterns of premarital and marital sex we have discussed earlier in this book. More and more women are reporting premarital sexual experience, and significantly an increasing amount of this is occurring in the dating situation, in contrast to a decade ago when the common setting was the engagement period. We have also seen a growing acceptance of varied forms of marital sexuality. In the past, a man might visit a prostitute because he felt reluctant or ashamed to ask his wife to engage in oral-genital sex; this is now less frequently the case. As the current generation of younger people mature there is reason to believe that we will see a further reduction in the amount of prostitution; the seeds for it apparently have been sown.

While prostitution appears to be declining, pornography is booming. Growth figures are not available, but there is reason to believe that the pornography industry is flourishing as never before. We see evidence of this not only in the multimillion dollar sales reported by the Commission on Obscenity and Pornography, but also in the surge of "sexually liberated tabloids" such as *Screw* and *Ball* (*Screw* began as a modest publishing venture in 1968 and now sells over 130,000 copies on a weekly basis despite its having at least ten competitors) and the proliferation of 16MM movie houses that show only "skin" films.

This apparent expansion of the pornography industry seems somewhat paradoxical in face of what is happening to prostitution, especially since we have claimed that the two serve similar needs. The resolution of this paradox is to be found in the age composition of the consumers of pornography. We noted earlier that most patrons of bookstores specializing in erotica are middle-aged, the same holds for movie theaters specializing in sex films (the proverbial bald-headed row); young people are not very much in evidence in such establishments. As the reader will recall, these patterns resemble those Winick and Kinsie claim currently characterize prostitution, the difference being that pornography is now widely available while prostitutes are, they maintain, harder and harder to find. It will not be surprising if as the current generation of younger people mature we see a decline in the pornography industry. For one thing, explicitly sexual material is becoming increasingly available in the legitimate media such as national magazines and Hollywood movies, and therefore is to some extent becoming de-eroticized. Of greater importance are, as we continue to emphasize, changing patterns of sexual behavior — like the man said, why pay for what you can get for free?

Notes

1. Polsky, Ned, "On the Sociology of Pornography," in Ned Polsky (ed.) *Hustlers, Beats and Others;* Chicago: Aldine, 1967, pp. 186–202.
2. Kinsey, Alfred C., Wardell Pomeroy, Clyde E. Martin, and Paul W. Gebhard, *Sexual Behavior in the Human Female,* Philadelphia: W. B. Saunders Co., p. 670.
3. Ibid.
4. Schmidt, Gunter and Volkmar Sigusch, "Sex Differences in Response to Psycho-Sexual Stimulation by Films and Slides," *Journal of Sex Research,* November, 1970, pp. 268–283.
5. Kinsey, Alfred C., Wardell Pomeroy and Clyde E. Martin, *Sexual Behavior in the Human Male,* Philadelphia: W. B. Saunders Co., 1948, p. 601.
6. Winick, Charles and Paul M. Kinsie, *The Lively Commerce,* Chicago: Quadrangle Books, 1970, pp. 185–186.

15

Apprenticeships in Prostitution

James H. Bryan

While theoretical conceptions of deviant behavior range from role strain to psychoanalytic theory, orientations to the study of the prostitute have shown considerable homogeneity. Twentieth century theorizing concerning this occupational group has employed, almost exclusively, a Freudian psychiatric model. The prostitute has thus been variously described as masochistic, of infantile mentality, unable to form mature interpersonal relationships, regressed, emotionally dangerous to males and as normal as the average women.[1] The call girl, the specific focus of this paper, has been accused of being anxious, possessing a confused self-image, excessively dependent, demonstrating gender-role confusion, aggressive, lacking internal controls, and masochistic.[2]

The exclusive use of psychoanalytic models in attempting to predict behavior, and the consequent neglect of situational and cognitive processes, has been steadily lessening in the field of psychology. Their inadequacy as

Reprinted from *Social Problems*, Vol. 12, No. 3, pp. 287–297, Winter, 1965, by permission of The Society for the Study of Social Problems and the author.

This data was collected when the author was at the Neuropsychiatric Institute, UCLA Center for the Health Sciences. I wish to acknowledge the considerable aid of Mrs. Elizabeth Gordon, Miss Carol Kupers, and Mr. Saul Sherter in the preparation and the analysis of this data. I am greatly indebted to Dr. Evelyn Hooker for both her intellectual and moral support, and to Vivian London for her excellent editorial advice. I particularly wish to express my great gratitude to my wife, Virginia, for her tolerance, encouragement, and understanding.

models for understanding deviancy has been specifically explicated by Becker, and implied by London.[3] The new look in the conceptualization and study of deviant behavior has focused on the interpersonal processes which help define the deviant role, the surroundings in which the role is learned, and limits upon the enactment of the role. As Hooker has indicated regarding the study of homosexuals, one must not only consider the personality structure of the participants, but also the structure of their community and the pathways and routes into the learning and enactment of the behavior.[4] Such "training periods" have been alluded to by Maurer in his study of the con man, and by Sutherland in his report on professional thieves. More recently, Lindesmith and Becker have conceptualized the development of drug use as a series of learning sequences necessary for the development of steady use.[5]

This paper provides some detailed, albeit preliminary, information concerning induction and training in a particular type of deviant career: prostitution, at the call girl level. It describes the order of events, and their surrounding structure, which future call girls experience in entering their occupation.

The respondents in this study were 33 prostitutes, all currently or previously working in the Los Angeles area. They ranged in age from 18 to 32, most being in their mid-twenties. None of the interviewees were obtained through official law enforcement agencies, but seven were found within the context of a neuropsychiatric hospital. The remaining respondents were gathered primarily through individual referrals from previous participants in the study. There were no obvious differences between the "psychiatric sample" and the other interviewees on the data to be reported.

All subjects in the sample were call girls. That is, they typically obtained their clients by individual referrals, primarily by telephone, and enacted the sexual contract in their own or their clients' place of residence or employment. They did not initiate contact with their customers in bars, streets, or houses of prostitution, although they might meet their customers at any number of locations by pre-arrangement. The minimum fee charged per sexual encounter was $20.00. As an adjunct to the call girl interviews, three pimps and two "call boys" were interviewed as well.[6]

Approximately two thirds of the sample were what are sometimes known as "outlaw broads"; that is, they were not under the supervision of a pimp when interviewed. There is evidence that the majority of pimps who were aware of the study prohibited the girls under their direction from participating in it. It should be noted that many members of the sample belonged to one or another clique; their individually expressed opinions may not be independent.

The interviews strongly suggest that there are marked idiosyncrasies from one geographical area to another in such practices as fee-splitting, involvement with peripheral occupations (e.g., cabbies), and so forth. For example, there appears to be little direct involvement of peripheral occupations with call girl activities in the Los Angeles area, while it has been estimated that up to 10% of the population of Las Vegas is directly involved in activities of prostitutes.[7] What may be typical for a call girl in the Los Angeles area is not necessarily typical for a girl in New York, Chicago, Las Vegas, or Miami.

Since the professional literature (e.g., Greenwald; Pomeroy) concerning this occupation and its participants is so limited in quantity, and is not concerned with training per se, the present data may have some utility for the social sciences.[8]

All but two interviews were tape recorded. All respondents had prior knowledge that the interview would be tape recorded. The interviewing was, for the most part, done at the girls' place of work and/or residence. Occasional interviews were conducted in the investigator's office, and one in a public park. Interviews were semi-structured and employed open-ended questions. One part of the interview concerned the apprenticeship period or "turning out" process.

The Entrance

> I had been thinking about it [becoming a call girl] before a lot. . . . Thinking about wanting to do it, but I had no connections. Had I not had a connection, I probably wouldn't have started working. . . . I thought about starting out. . . . Once I tried it [without a contact]. . . . I met this guy at a bar and I tried to make him pay me, but the thing is, you can't do it that way because they are romantically interested in you, and they don't think that it is on that kind of basis. You can't all of a sudden come up and want money for it, you have to be known beforehand. . . . I think that is what holds a lot of girls back who might work. I think I might have started a year sooner had I had a connection. You seem to make one contact or another . . . if it's another girl or a pimp or just someone who will set you up and get you a client. . . . You can't just, say, get an apartment and get a phone in and everything and say "Well, I'm gonna start business," because you gotta get clients from somewhere. There has to be a contact.

Immediately prior to entrance into the occupation, all but one girl had personal contact with someone professionally involved in call girl activities (pimps or other call girls). The one exception had contact with a customer of call girls. While various occupational groups (e.g., photographers) seem to be peripherally involved, often unwittingly, with the call girl, there was no report of individuals involved in such occupations being contacts for

236

new recruits. The novice's initial contact is someone at the level at which she will eventually enter the occupation: not a street-walker, but a call girl; not a pimp who manages girls out of a house of prostitution, but a pimp who manages call girls.

Approximately half of the girls reported that their initial contact for entrance into the profession was another "working girl." The nature of these relationships is quite variable. In some cases, the girls have been long standing friends. Other initial contacts involved sexual realtionships between a Lesbian and the novice. Most, however, had known each other less than a year, and did not appear to have a very close relationship, either in the sense of time spent together or of biographical information exchanged. The relationship may begin with the aspiring call girl soliciting the contact. That is, if a professional is known to others as a call girl, she will be sought out and approached by females who are strangers:[9]

> I haven't ever gone out and looked for one. All of these have fell right into my hands. . . . They turned themselfs out. . . . They come to me for help.

Whatever their relationship, whenever the professional agrees to aid the beginner, she also, it appears, implicitly assumes responsibility for training her. This is evidenced by the fact that only one such female contact referred the aspirant to another girl for any type of help. Data are not available as to the reason for this unusual referral.

If the original contact was not another call girl but a pimp, a much different relationship is developed and the career follows a somewhat different course. The relationship between pimp and girl is typically one of lovers, not friends:

> . . . because I love him very much. Obviously, I'm doing this mostly for him. . . . I'd do anything for him. I'm not just saying I will, I am. . . . [After discussing his affair with another woman] I just decided that I knew what he was when I decided to do this for him and I decided I had two choices — either accept it or not, and I accepted it, and I have no excuse.

Occasionally, however, a strictly business relationship will be formed:

> Right now I am buying properties, and as soon as I can afford it, I am buying stocks. . . . It is strictly a business deal. This man and I are friends, our relationship ends there. He handles all the money, he is making all the investments and I trust him. We have a legal document drawn up which states that half the investments are mine, half of them his, so I am protected.

Whether the relationship is love or business, the pimp solicits the new girl.[10] It is usually agreed that the male will have an important managerial role in the course of the girl's career, and that both will enjoy the gains from the girl's activities for an indefinite period:

> Actually a pimp has to have complete control or else its like trouble with him. Because if a pimp doesn't, if she is not madly in love with him or something in some way, a pimp won't keep a girl.

Once the girl agrees to function as a call girl, the male, like his female counterpart, undertakes the training of the girl, or refers the girl to another call girl for training. Either course seems equally probable. Referrals, when employed, are typically to friends and, in some cases, wives or ex-wives.

Although the data are limited, it appears that the pimp retains his dominance over the trainee even when the latter is being trained by a call girl. The girl trainer remains deferential to the pimp's wishes regarding the novice.

Apprenticeship

Once a contact is acquired and the decision to become a call girl made, the recruit moves to the next stage in the career sequence; the apprenticeship period. The structure of the apprenticeship will be described, followed by a description of the content most frequently communicated during this period.

The apprenticeship is typically served under the direction of another call girl, but may occasionally be supervised by a pimp. Twenty-four girls in the sample initially worked under the supervision of other girls. The classroom is, like the future place of work, an apartment. The apprentice typically serves in the trainer's apartment, either temporarily residing with the trainer or commuting there almost daily. The novice rarely serves her apprenticeship in such places as a house of prostitution, motel, or on the street. It is also infrequent that the girl is transported out of her own city to serve an apprenticeship. Although the data are not extensive, the number of girls being trained simultaneously by a particular trainer has rarely been reported to be greater than three. Girls sometimes report spending up to eight months in training, but the average stay seems to be two or three months. The trainer controls all referrals and appointments, novices seemingly not having much control over the type of sexual contract made or the circumstances surrounding the enactment of the contract.

The structure of training under the direction of a pimp seems similar, though information is more limited. The girls are trained in an apartment in the city they intend to work and for a short period of time. There is some evidence that the pimp and the novice often do not share the same apartment as might the novice and the girl trainer. There appear to be two reasons for the separation of pimp and girl. First, it is not uncommonly thought that cues which suggest the presence of other men displease the girl's customers:

> Well, I would never let them know that I had a lover, which is something that you never ever let a john know, because this makes them very reticent to give you money, because they think you are going to go and spend it with your lover, which is what usually happens.

(Interestingly, the work of Winick suggests that such prejudices may not actually be held by many customers.)[11] Secondly, the legal repercussions are much greater, of course, for the pimp who lives with his girl than for two girls rooming together. As one pimp of 19 years experience puts it:

> It is because of the law. There is a law that is called the illegal cohabitation that they rarely use unless the man becomes big in stature. If he is a big man in the hustling world, the law then employs any means at their command. . . .

Because of the convenience in separation of housing, it is quite likely that the pimp is less directly involved with the day-to-day training of the girls than the call girl trainer.

The content of the training period seems to consist of two broad, interrelated dimensions one philosophical, the other interpersonal. The former refers to the imparting of a value structure, the latter to "do's" and "don'ts" of relating to customers and, secondarily, to other "working girls" and pimps. The latter teaching is perhaps best described by the concept of a short range perspective. That is, most of the "do's" and "don'ts" pertain to ideas and actions that the call girl uses in problematic situations.[12] Not all girls absorb these teachings, and those who do incorporate them in varying degrees.

Insofar as a value structure is transmitted it is that of maximizing gains while minimizing effort, even if this requires transgressions of either a legal or moral nature. Frequently, it is postulated that people, particularly men, are corrupt or easily corruptible, that all social relationships are but a reflection of a "con," and that prostitution is simply a more honest or at least no more dishonest act than the everday behavior of "squares." Furthermore, more, not only are "johns" basically exploitative, but they are easily exploited; hence they are, in some respects, stupid. As explained by a pimp:

> . . . [in the hustling world] the trick or the john is known as a fool . . . this is not the truth. . . . He [the younger pimp] would teach his woman that a trick was a fool.

Since the male is corrupt, or honest only because he lacks the opportunity to be corrupt, then it is only appropriate that he be exploited as he exploits.

> Girls first start making their "scores" — say one guy keeps them for a while or maybe she gets, you know, three or four grand out of him, say a car or a coat. These are your scores. . . .

The general assumption that man is corrupt is empirically confirmed when the married male betrays his wife, when the moralist, secular or religious, betrays his publicly stated values, or when the "john" "stiffs" (cheats) the girl. An example of the latter is described by a girl as she reflects upon her disillusionment during her training period.

> It is pretty rough when you are starting out. You get stiffed a lot of times. . . . Oh sure. They'll take advantage of you anytime they can. And I'm a trusting soul, I really am. I'll believe anybody till they prove different. I've made a lot of mistakes that way. You get to the point, well, Christ, what the heck can I believe in people, they tell me one thing and here's what they do to me.

Values such as fairness with other working girls, or fidelity to a pimp, may occasionally be taught. To quote a pimp:

> So when you ask me if I teach a kind of basic philosophy, I would say that you could say that. Because you try to teach them in an amoral way that there is a right and wrong way as pertains to this game . . . and then you teach them that when working with other girls to try to treat the other girl fairly because a woman's worst enemy in the street [used in both a literal and figurative sense] is the other woman and only by treating the other women decently can she expect to get along. . . . Therefore the basic philosophy I guess would consist of a form of honesty, a form of sincerity and complete fidelity to her man [pimp].

It should be noted, however, that behavior based on enlightened self-interest with concomitant exploitation is not limited to customer relationships. Interviewees frequently mentioned a pervasive feeling of distrust between trainer and trainee, and such incidents as thefts or betrayal of confidences are occasionally reported and chronically guarded against.

Even though there may be considerable pressure upon the girl to accept this value structure, many of them (perhaps the majority of the sample) reject it.

> People have told me that I wasn't turned out, but turned loose instead. . . . Someone who is turned out is turned out to believe in a certain code of behavior, and this involves having a pimp, for one thing. It also involves never experiencing anything but hatred or revulsion for "tricks" for another thing. It involves always getting the money in front [before the sexual act] and a million little things that are very strictly adhered to by those in

240

the "in group," which I am not. . . . Never being nice or pleasant to a trick unless you are doing it for the money, getting more money. [How did you learn that?] It was explained to me over a period of about six months. I learned that you were doing it to make money for yourself so that you could have nice things and security. . . . [Who would teach you this?] [The trainer] would teach me this.[13]

It seems reasonable to assume that the value structure serves, in general, to create in-group solidarity and to alienate the girl from "square" society, and that this structure serves the political advantage of the trainer and the economic gains of the trainee more than it allays the personal anxieties of either. In fact, failure to adopt these values at the outset does not appear to be correlated with much personal distress.[14] As one girl describes her education experiences:

Some moral code. We're taught, as a culture . . . it's there and after awhile you live, breathe, and eat it. Now, what makes you go completely against everything that's inside you, everything that you have been taught, and the whole society, to do things like this?

Good empirical evidence, however, concerning the functions and effectiveness of this value structure with regard to subjective comfort is lacking.

A series of deductions derived from the premises indicated above serve to provide, in part, the "rules" of interpersonal contact with the customer. Each customer is to be seen as a "mark," and "pitches" are to be made.

[Did you have a standard pitch?] It's sort of amusing. I used to listen to my girl friend [trainer]. She was the greatest at this telephone type of situation. She would call up and cry and say that people had come to her door. . . . She'd cry and she'd complain and she' dsay "I have a bad check at the liquor store, and they sent the police over," and really . . . a girl has a story she tells the man. . . . Anything, you know, so he'll help her out. Either it's the rent or she needs a car, or doctor's bills, or any number of things.

Any unnecessary interaction with the customer is typically frowned upon, and the trainee will receive exhortations to be quick about her business. One girl in her fourth week of work explains:

[What are some of the other don'ts that you have learned about?] Don't take so much time. . . . The idea is to get rid of them as quickly as possible.

Other content taught concerns specific information about specific customers.

241

> . . . she would go around the bar and say, now look at that man over there, he's this way and that way, and this is what he would like and these are what his problems are. . . .
>
> . . . she would teach me what the men wanted and how much to get, what to say when I got there . . . just a line to hand them.

Training may also include proprieties concerning consuming alcohol and drugs, when and how to obtain the fee, how to converse with the customers and, occasionally, physical and sexual hygiene. As a girl trainer explains:

> First of all, impress cleanliness. Because, on the whole, the majority of girls, I would say, I don't believe there are any cleaner women walking the streets, because they've got to be aware of any type of body odor. . . . You teach them to French [fellatio] and how to talk to men.
>
> [Do they [pimps] teach you during the turning out period how to make a telephone call?] Oh, usually, yes. They don't teach you, they just tell you how to do it and you do it with your good common sense, but if you have trouble, they tell you more about it.

Interestingly, the specific act of telephoning a client is often distressing to the novice and is of importance in her training. Unfortunately for the girl, it is an act she must perform with regularity as she does considerable soliciting.[15] One suspects that such behavior is embarrassing for her because it is an unaccustomed role for her to play — she has so recently come from a culture where young women do *not* telephone men for dates. Inappropriate sex-role behavior seems to produce greater personal distress than does appropriate sex-role behavior even when it is morally reprehensible.

> Well, it is rather difficult to get on the telephone, when you've never worked before, and talk to a man about a subject like that, and it is very new to you.

What is omitted from the training should be noted as well. There seems to be little instruction concerning sexual techniques as such, even though the previous sexual experience of the trainee may have been quite limited. What instruction there is typically revolves around the practice of fellatio. There seems to be some encouragement not to experience sexual orgasms with the client, though this may be quite variable with the trainer.

> . . . and sometimes, I don't know if it's a set rule or maybe it's an unspoken rule, you don't enjoy your dates.
>
> Yes, he did [teach attitudes]. He taught me to be cold. . . .

It should be stressed that, if the girls originally accepted such instructions and values, many of them, at least at the time of interviewing, verbalized a rejection of these values and reported behavior which departed considerably

242

from the interpersonal rules stipulated as "correct" by their trainers. Some experience orgasms with the customer, some show considerable affect toward "johns," others remain drunk or "high" throughout the contact.[16] While there seems to be general agreement as to what the rules of interpersonal conduct are, there appears to be considerable variation in the adoption of such rules.

A variety of methods are employed to communicate the content described above. The trainer may arrange to eavesdrop on the interactions of girl and client and then discuss the interaction with her. One trainer, for example, listened through a closed door to the interaction of a new girl with a customer, then immediately after he left, discussed, in a rather heated way, methods by which his exit may have been facilitated. A pimp relates:

> The best way to do this [teaching conversation] is, in the beginning, when the phone rings, for instance . . . is to listen to what she says and then check and see how big a trick he is and then correct her from there.
> . . . with everyone of them [trainees] I would make it a point to see two guys to see how they [the girls] operate.

In one case a girl reported that her pimp left a written list of rules pertaining to relating to "johns." Direct teaching, however, seems to be uncommon. The bulk of whatever learning takes place seems to take place through observation.

> It's hard to tell you, because we learn through observation. But I watched her and listened to what her bit was on the telephone.

To summarize, the structure of the apprenticeship period seems quite standard. The novice receives her training either from a pimp or from another more experienced call girl, more often the latter. She serves her initial two to eight months of work under the trainer's supervision and often serves this period in the trainer's apartment. The trainer assumes responsibility for arranging contacts and negotiating the type and place of the sexual encounter.

The content of the training pertains both to a general philosophical stance and to some specifics (usually not sexual) of interpersonal behavior with customers and colleagues. The philosophy is one of exploiting the exploiters (customers) by whatever means necessary and defining the colleagues of the call girl as being intelligent, self-interested and, in certain important respects, basically honest individuals. The interpersonal techniques addressed during the learning period consist primarily of "pitches," telephone conversations, personal and occasionally sexual hygiene, prohibitions against alcohol and dope while with a "john," how and when to obtain the fee, and specifics concerning the sexual habits of particular customers.

Specific sexual techniques are very rarely taught. The current sample included a considerable number of girls who, although capable of articulating this value structure, were not particularly inclined to adopt it.

Contacts and Contracts

While the imparting of ideologies and proprieties to the prospective call girl is emphasized during the apprenticeship period, it appears that the primary function of the apprenticeship, at least for the trainee, is building a clientele. Since this latter function limits the degree of occupational socialization, the process of developing the clientele and the arrangements made between trainer and trainee will be discussed.

Lists ("books") with the names and telephone numbers of customers are available for purchase from other call girls or pimps, but such books are often considered unreliable. While it is also true that an occasional pimp will refer customers to girls, this does not appear to be a frequent practice. The most frequent method of obtaining such names seems to be through contacts developed during the apprenticeship. The trainer refers customers to the apprentice and oversees the latter in terms of her responsibility and adequacy in dealing with the customer. For referring the customer, the trainer receives forty to fifty per cent of the total price agreed upon in the contract negotiated by the trainer and customer.[17] The trainer and trainees further agree, most often explicitly, on the apprentice's "right" to obtain and to use, on further occasions, information necessary for arranging another sexual contract with the "john" without the obligation of further "kick-back" to the trainer. That is, if she can obtain the name and telephone number of the customer, she can negotiate another contract without fee-splitting. During this period, then, the girl is not only introduced to other working colleagues (pimps and girls alike) but also develops a clientele.

There are two obvious advantages for a call girl in assuming the trainer role. First, since there seems to be an abundant demand for new girls, and since certain service requirements demand more than one girl, even the well established call girl chronically confronts the necessity for making referrals. It is then reasonable to assume that the extra profit derived from the fee-splitting activities, together with the added conveniences of having a girl "on call," allows the trainer to profit considerably from this arrangement. Secondly, contacts with customers are reputedly extremely difficult to maintain if services are not rendered on demand. Thus, the adoption of the trainer role enables the girl to maintain contacts with "fickle" customers under circumstances where she may wish a respite from the sexual encounter without terminating the contacts necessary for re-entry into the call girl role. It is also possible that the financial gains may conceivably be much greater for most trainers than for most call girls, but this is a moot point.

244

A final aspect of the apprenticeship period that should be noted is the novice's income. It is possible for the novice, under the supervision of a competent and efficient trainer, to earn a great deal of money, or at least to get a favorable glimpse of the great financial possibilities of the occupation and, in effect, be heavily rewarded for her decision to enter it. Even though the novice may be inexperienced in both the sexual and interpersonal techniques of prostitution, her novelty on the market gives her an immediate advantage over her more experienced competitors. It seems quite likely that the new girl, irrespective of her particular physical or mental qualities, has considerable drawing power because she provides new sexual experience to the customer. Early success and financial reward may well provide considerable incentive to continue in the occupation.

A final word is needed regarding the position of the pimp vis-à-vis the call girl during the apprenticeship period. While some pimps assume the responsibility for training the girl personally, as indicated above, as many send the novice to another girl. The most apparent reason for such referral is that it facilitates the development of the "book." Purposes of training appear to be secondary for two reasons: (1) The pimp often lacks direct contact with the customers, so he personally cannot aid directly in the development of the girl's clientele; (2) When the pimp withdraws his girl from the training context, it is rarely because she has obtained adequate knowledge of the profession. This is not to say that all pimps are totally unconcerned with the type of knowledge being imparted to the girl. Rather, the primary concern of the pimp is the girl's developing a clientele, not learning the techniques of sex or conversation.

The apprenticeship period usually ends abruptly, not smoothly. Its termination may be but a reflection of interpersonal difficulties between trainer and trainee, novice and pimp, or between two novices. Occasionally termination of training is brought about through the novice's discovery and subsequent theft of the trainer's "book." Quite frequently, the termination is due to the novice's developing a sufficient trade or other business opportunities. The point is, however, that no respondent has reported that the final disruption of the apprenticeship was the result of the completion of adequate training. While disruptions of this relationship may be due to personal or impersonal events, termination is not directly due to the development of sufficient skills.

Discussion and Summary

On the basis of interviews with 33 call girls in the Los Angeles area, information was obtained about entrance into the call girl occupation and the initial training period or apprenticeship therein.

The novice call girl is acclimated to her new job primarily by being thoroughly immersed in the call girl subculture, where she learns the trade through imitation as much as through explicit tutoring. The outstanding concern at this stage is the development of a sizable and lucrative clientele. The specific skills and values which are acquired during this period are rather simple and quickly learned.

In spite of the girl's protests and their extensive folklore, the art of prostitution, at least at this level, seems to be technically a low-level skill. That is, it seems to be an occupation which requires little formal knowledge or practice for its successful pursuit and appears best categorized as an unskilled job. Evidence for this point comes from two separate sources. First, there seems to be little technical training during this period, and the training seems of little importance to the career progress. Length or type of training does not appear correlated with success (i.e., money earned, lack of subjective distress, minimum fee per "trick," etc.). Secondly, the termination of the apprenticeship period is often brought about for reasons unrelated to training. It seems that the need for an apprenticeship period is created more by the secrecy surrounding the rendering or the utilization of the call girl service than by the complexity of the role. In fact, it is reasonable to assume that the complexity of the job confronting a street-walker may be considerably greater than that confronting a call girl. The tasks of avoiding the police, sampling among strangers for potential customers, and arrangements for the completion of the sexual contract not only require different skills on the part of the street-walker, but are performances requiring a higher degree of professional "know-how" than is generally required of the call girl.[18]

As a pimp who manages both call girls and "high class" street-walkers explains:

> The girl that goes out into the street is the sharper of the two, because she is capable of handling herself in the street, getting around the law, picking out the trick that is not absolutely psycho . . . and capable of getting along in the street. . . . The street-walker, as you term her, is really a prima donna of the prostitutes . . . her field is unlimited, she goes to all of the top places so she meets the top people. . . .

The fact that the enactment of the call girl role requires little training, and the introduction of the girl to clients and colleagues alike is rather rapid, gives little time or incentive for adequate occupational socialization. It is perhaps for this reason rather than, for example, reasons related to personality factors, that occupational instability is great and cultural homogeneity small.

In closing, while it appears that there is a rather well defined apprenticeship period in the career of the call girl, it seems that it is the secrecy rather

246

than the complexity of the occupation which generates such a period. While there is good evidence that initial contacts, primarily with other "working girls," are necessary for entrance into this career, there seems no reason, at this point, to assume that the primary intent of the participants is anything but the development of an adequate clientele.

Notes

[1] H. Benjamin "Prostitution Reassessed," *International Journal of Sexology*, 26 (1951), pp. 154-160; H. Benjamin & A. Ellis, "An Objective Examination of Prostitution," *International Journal of Sexology*, 29 (1955), pp. 100-105; E. Glover, "The Abnormality of Prostitution," In A. M. Krich, editor, *Women*, New York: Dell Publishing Company, Inc., 1953; M. H. Hollander, "Prostitution, The Body, and Human Relatedness." *International Journal of Psychoanalysis*, XLII (1961), pp. 404-413; M. Karpf, "Effects of Prostitution on Marital Sex Adjustment," *International Journal of Sexology*, 29 (1953), pp. 149-154; J. F. Oliven, *Sexual Hygiene and Pathology*, Philadelphia: J. B. Lippencott Co., 1955; W. J. Robinson, *The Oldest Profession in the World*, New York: Eugenics Publishing Co., 1929.

[2] H. Greenwald, *The Call Girl*, New York: Ballentine Books, 1960.

[3] H. S. Becker, *Outsiders: Studies in the Sociology of Deviance*, New York: Free Press of Glencoe, 1963. Also see *The Other Side*, H. S. Becker, editor, New York: Free Press of Glencoe, 1964. P. London, *The Modes and Morals of Psychotherapy*, New York: Holt, Rinehart and Winston, Inc. 1964. For recent trends in personality theory, see N. Sanford, "Personality: Its Place in Psychology" and D. R. Miller, "The Study of Social Relationships: Situation, Identify, and Social Interaction." Both papers are presented in S. Koch, editor *Psychology: A Study of a Science*, Vol. 5, New York: McGraw-Hill Book Co., Inc., 1963.

[4] Evelyn Hooker, "The Homosexual Community." *Proceedings of the XIV International Congress of Applied Psychology*, 1961, pp. 40-59. See also A. Reiss, "The Social Integration of Queers and Peers," *Social Problems*, 9 (1961), pp. 102-120.

[5] D. W. Maurer, *The Big Con*, New York: Signet Books, 1940. H. S. Becker, *Outsiders, op. cit.* E. H. Sutherland, *The Professional Thief*, Chicago: University of Chicago Press, 1937. A. R. Lindesmith, *Opiate Addiction*, Evanston: Principia Press, 1955.

[6] This definition departs somewhat from that offered by Clinard. He defines the call girl as one dependent upon an organization for recruiting patrons and one who typically works in lower-class hotels. The present sample is best described by Clinard's category high-class independent professional prostitute. M. D. Clinard, *Sociology of Deviant Behavior*, New York: Rinehart & Co., Inc., 1957.

[7] E. Reid and O. Demaris, *The Green Felt Jungle*, New York: Pocket Books, Inc., 1963.

[8] H. Greenwald, *op. cit.* W. Pomeroy, *Some Aspects of Prostitution*, unpublished paper.

[9] A point also made in the autobiographical account of a retired call girl. Virginia McManus, *Not For Love*, New York: Dell Publishing Co., Inc., 1960, p. 160.

[10] Two of the pimps denied that this was very often so and maintained that the girls will solicit them. The degree to which they are solicited seems to depend upon the nature and extent of their reputations. It is difficult to judge the accuracy of these reports as there appears to be a strong taboo against admitting to such solicitation.

[11] C. Winick, "Prostitutes' Clients' Perception of the Prostitute and Themselves," *International Journal of Social Psychiatry*, 8 (1961-62), pp. 289-297.

[12] H. S. Becker, Blanche Geer, and E. C. Hughes, A. L. Strauss, *Boys in White*, Chicago: University of Chicago Press, 1961.

[13] The statements made by prostitutes to previous investigators and mental helpers may have been parroting this particular value structure and perhaps have misled previous investigators into making the assumption that "all whores hate men." While space prohibits a complete presentation of the data, neither our questionnaire nor interview data suggest that this is a predominant attitude among call girls.

[14] There is, from the present study, little support for the hypothesis of Reckless concerning the association of experience trauma and guilt with abruptness of entry into the occupation. W. C. Reckless, *The Crime Problem*, New York: Appleton-Century-Crofts, Inc., 1950.

[15] The topic of solicitation will be dealt with in a forthcoming paper.

[16] In the unpublished paper referred to above, Pomeroy has indicated that, of 31 call girls interviewed, only 23% reported never experiencing orgasms with customers.

[17] The fee-splitting arrangement is quite common at all levels of career activity. For example, cooperative activity between two girls is often required for a particular type of sexual contract. In these cases, the girl who has contracted with the customer will contact a colleague, usually a friend, and will obtain 40%-50% of the latter's earnings. There is suggestive evidence that fee-splitting activities vary according to geographical areas and that Los Angeles is unique for both its fee-splitting patterns and the rigidity of its fee-splitting structure.

[18] Needless to say, however, all of the sample of call girls who were asked for status hierarchies of prostitution felt that the street-walker had both less status and a less complex job. It *may* well be that the verbal exchange required of the call girl requires greater knowledge than that required of a street-walker, but the non-verbal skills required of the street-walker may be considerably greater than those of the call girl.

16

The Professional Prostitute

Travis Hirschi

Prostitution is an occupation. It should be fruitful, therefore, to compare it with, and contrast it to, other occupations. In every occupation a period of time is required to learn the trade: certain skills must be acquired if one is to be successful. One's occupation puts one in contact with certain groups and classes while it restricts contact with yet others. Each occupation develops an ideology by which it justifies its existence, and each bestows upon its members a certain degree of prestige. Some occupations require direct and personal contact with a customer or client. These are the service occupations, of which prostitution is one.[1]

Prostitution is usually defined as the emotionally indifferent selling of sexual favors on a promiscuous basis.[2] It is possible, therefore, to place prostitution within a still narrower occupational category:

> A *personal-service occupation* may be defined, ideally, as one whose practitioner performs a specialized personal service for a set of individuals where the service requires him to engage in direct personal communication with each of them and where he is not otherwise bound to the person he serves.[3]

It has been pointed out that there are elements of prostitution in many sex relationships in our culture.[4] This insight leads to comparisons between marriage and prostitution and, in so doing, tends to over-emphasize the de-

Reprinted from the *Berkeley Journal of Sociology*, Vol. VII, No. 1, pp. 33–9, by permission of the publisher and author.

gree to which prostitution differs from other occupations. Following the same line of reasoning, it can be seen that most men are, at one time or another, engaged in activities analogous to those of the physician, the cabdriver, the teacher, etc. Therefore, to avoid any confusion on this point, in this paper I will be concerned only with full-time, *professional* prostitutes. The housewife who occasionally engages in *pure* prostitution (as defined above) on week-ends is not, according to my usage, a prostitute. This does not, of course, exclude the call girl, although she may speak of others as prostitutes while reserving some other appellation for herself.[5]

Learning the Trade

"From a purely economic point of view," says Kingsley Davis, "prostitution comes perilously near the situation of getting something for nothing."[6] Davis is not alone in his judgment. Others have argued that the prostitute is "too lazy to work," that she needs little skill or training, that all it takes to become a prostitute is the decision to accept the social stigma that attaches to the profession.[7] It is doubtful whether any prostitute would agree. In order to survive, she must be able to 1) find customers, 2) "sell" them, 3) provide a suitable place in which to transact business, 4) please the customer, 5) collect her money, 6) protect herself from disease, pregnancy, and physical injury, 7) avoid the police. An examination of these problems and the skills that must be acquired if they are to be overcome may enable us to give at least a partial answer to Davis's "hard" question: "The hard question is not why so many women become prostitutes, but why so few of them do."[8]

One of the easiest ways to find customers, it would seem, would be to go to work in a brothel. The problem, however, is not so simple. Polly Adler reports that she had "to turn away thirty or forty girls for every one she was able to accommodate."[9] Reitman maintains that at the height of the Depression as high as 75% of the prostitutes in Chicago were unemployed.[10] But finding a job in a brothel is only half the problem. The other half is keeping it.

> Julia, the madame, liked me so well that I stayed two weeks instead of one. That was a record, as *she never keeps anyone more than one week.*[11]

Nor does simply "going into the streets" automatically put one in business. Rolph reports that women in London sometimes go for hours without finding a customer; that it is sometimes necessary to solicit as many as twenty men before a sale is made.[12] The prostitute must find where customers are most likely to be; she must solicit in areas appropriate to her dress, beauty, and demeanor.[13] Of course, if one has friends already in the trade, such lessons come easier, as is true in any occupation. And, if one has a business agent, he may be able to take care of these problems himself. Also, as we shall see later, the problem is sometimes simplified by the phenomenon known to the business world as the "regular customer." In periods of economic prosperity and short supply, this problem may be a minor one, requiring little skill. But in ordinary times it remains a chronic problem.

After locating a potential customer, the prostitute's next task is to make the sale. The oldest technique, of course, is to make exorbitant claims about the quality of the service. This technique, to be used effectively, presupposes knowledge of what the customer is likely to have in mind.[14] Many girls report losing customers early in their careers simply because they didn't know what was being asked of them. Initiative and skill are important characteristics of the successful salesman. If he is working on a straight commission basis, he must make every effort to sell his product if he is to survive. The prostitute faces the same contingency:

> The ability of a girl to make money does not depend upon beauty, although that may be an asset. It depends entirely upon her ability to flatter and please men. . . . The result is that in the same house there will often be a beautiful woman *who does not make expenses* and a remarkably plain one who is 'coining money.'[15] [italics mine]

The businessman rents office space, the prostitute an apartment or a hotel room.[16] Moving, draperies, carpets, telephone transfers, etc., are all expensive. The successful prostitute learns to carry on her business in such a manner that costly moves are kept at a minimum. This is one of the dilemmas of the business. Many potential customers have no place of their own, but if the prostitute uses her room the management is likely either to increase the rent or to ask her to leave. When special equipment is needed to perform the service (whips, canes, costumes, etc.) a permanent place for business is even more essential.[17] Although hotels and apartments may be found, the problems and costs involved easily exceed those of most professions. A common solution is to maintain two apartments: one for living and sleeping, the other for business.[18] Nor should it be supposed that overhead expenses are the only costs involved in moving. A prostitute usually depends on the regular customer for a large portion of her business. Although she usually has some means of letting her old customers know where she is, her new location may be inconvenient for many of them.

If she is to have regular customers, the prostitute must provide the service they demand. As usual, the satisfied customer is the best advertisement. The mere selling of the body, according to many professionals, does not assure a steady business. Although other reasons have been advanced as explana-

251

tions of the prostitute's "very rapid and gross provocations to sexual consummation,"[19] the economic advantages of this approach are fairly obvious. The simulation of passion 1) assures a satisfied customer and 2) decreases the time required to complete the sex act.[20] There are other skills which must be learned if the customer is to be satisfied:

> Kid, a notch house is a place of business and the customer must be satisfied. Nowadays few men want it straight. They want it half and half . . . if you're going to hustle in any kind of a joint you've got [sic] to learn to be French, and maybe Greek.[21]

Almost all professionals mention the times they were not paid by the customer and how they have solved this problem by demanding payment in advance. The following could well have been written by a hotel desk-clerk telling about his first few days on the job:

> Twice in one week I let men go without paying me . . . discipline required that I pay for the time consumed . . . the very next day I offended one of the best customers of the house by asking him for money in advance.[22]

Disease, pregnancy, and physical assault make prostitution a hazardous occupation. Disease means time off the job and is a threat to regular customers.[23] Pregnancy also means lost time and heavy expenses. The consequences of physical injury are obvious. There is evidence that as the professional learns her trade, the incidence of venereal disease and pregnancy decreases.[24] She learns what to use, where to get it, and why it is necessary. In addition, she learns to detect and refuse diseased customers. To protect herself from the violent customer, the prostitute often employs a maid or works only within hearing range of her pimp or friends. When she must work alone, she may refuse customers whose actions arouse her suspicions and, in some cases, she may carry a knife.

Finally, the prostitute must learn to avoid or come to terms with the police. This is no simple matter, especially when plain-clothesmen are utilized.

> We used to play the Hustler's Game. A girl made believe she was working the street or she could be in a bar if she wanted. Another girl was supposed to be a bull. She pulled all the tricks bulls pull. The girl who was doing the hustling had to figure ways to spot the bulls and say nay. What a hot game. I learned plenty: like what you got to do before you begin to talk price with a trick is feel all over his body to make sure he's got no gun on. Another thing's to make sure his hands are rough if he claims to be a worker.[25]

Codes are often used over the telephone to reduce the chances of arrest as a result of evidence gathered from wire-tapping. Bribery or some other

252

working agreement with the police appears to be a common pattern, although it appears that the "rotation system" makes even a well-bribed policeman unable to refrain from an occasional arrest.[26] Little is known, of course, about prostitutes who successfully avoid arrest.

Advertising the Service

We have seen that the prostitute must learn the techniques of attracting customers. Like the doctor, conventional means of advertisement are closed to her and she is forced to rely on the "good-will" of her client. Unlike the doctor, however, the prostitute is not protected by a taboo on "shopping-around," nor can she assure her client that she is an expert and that he doesn't know or need to know anything about the quality of the service. Other comparative disadvantages include the fact that she is often forced to change her place of business, to deny that she is a prostitute, and to protect herself from exploiters, the police, and others at the same time she is trying to attract the attention of customers. Historically, the prostitute had (?) one definite advantage over the physician: she could dress, walk, act, and make herself up like a prostitute. Whether she still uses this mode of advertisement is a question confused by conflicting claims. As long ago as 1935 social scientists were saying that "in the great modern cities there is no basis for singling out by abode or dress even the avowedly professional prostitute."[27] More recently (1951) Lemert says that "the external differentiae of the prostitute have vanished."[28] However, Rolph (1955) reports that:

> The prostitute often assumes not only a uniform but also a mask, the over-emphasized lips, etc., being familiar to everyone, *though they are not often apparent in the daytime on the same women.*[29]

The uniform includes platform-soled shoes and brightly colored clothing.[30] The argument could be resolved, of course, by simply admitting a British-American difference in the behavior of prostitutes. However, the popular image of the prostitute's behavior and uniform persists. If it is true, the advantages of occupational symbolism could well account for the distinctive dress and demeanor of the professional. If, on the other hand, the popular image of the prostitute is false, if, in fact, she is no longer socially visible, then there are two possible explanations: 1) Most women dress and make themselves up much as did prostitutes early in the century or, 2) legal restrictions have forced the professional deliberately to reduce her visibility.[31]

References can be found to girls who advertise as models,[32] psychologists,[33] and as night-club performers.[34] There is reason to believe that other techniques are used, but the evidence on this point is skimpy.[35]

As is the case in any business, the seller must adjust his hours to the convenience of the customer. Thus the prostitute usually works at night. Generally, she sets aside certain hours for business and will not accept customers at other hours.[36] In large cities such as London, New York, and Chicago, there is, apparently, a large noon-time and early evening trade. The businessman taking an extended lunch hour and the commuter on his way home to the suburbs provide the prostitute with an other than late evening clientele.[37] The prostitute's habit of sleeping late, often accounted for as evidence of laziness, is an inevitable result of working until late at night. The majority of prostitutes seem to spend their off-duty hours shopping and attending movies. Their habits probably do not differ considerably from those of other members of their social class as far as entertainment and recreation are concerned. There is some disagreement as to whether they take a three to seven day monthly vacation because of menstruation.[38] Although there is considerable variation from area to area and from class to class, it should not be supposed that prostitutes wander aimlessly in search of customers. They usually have a particular street-corner or area to which they return night after night. The same regularity is also to be found in the behavior of those who frequent bars. This is a large subject and space will not permit us to explore it further here. Suffice it to say that the prostitute's occupation largely determines the pattern and form of her interactions with others.

A. *The Customer:* Kinsey reports that as the male gets older an increasing proportion of his extra-marital intercourse involves prostitutes and that there is an inverse relation between social class and contacts with them. His figures indicate that 69% of the white male population has had or will have some contact with prostitutes.[39] One writer lists 15 separate categories which tend to frequent prostitutes. These range from the sexually curious adolescent to the middle-aged man, from the unmarried to the dissatisfied husband, from those with low socioeconomic status to the wealthy playboy.[40] Neither the absolute numbers nor the rates of contact with prostitutes are of special concern here. For that matter, these figures are often little more than guesses. Although there is little doubt that the call girl, for example, could not survive without a demand for her services among those with means, and that other types of prostitutes may have a majority of their contacts with members of the lower classes, the important thing, as far as the prostitute's perception of the situation is concerned, is that she is often able to say, "I've seen them all."[41]

Much of the interaction between the prostitute and her customer has been covered earlier. Perhaps the most commonly mentioned feature of this interaction is the regularity with which the customer asks the girl to tell the story of her "fall into sin." This story may be, and often is, a rather clever fabrication, an "atrocity tale."[42] At other times, the girl's response is the equivalent of the proverbial "just lucky, I guess." The customer, for his part, often attempts to justify his presence to the prostitute. This too, in many instances, takes the form of a hard-luck story.[43]

B. *Fellow Workers:* The literature on the pimp often notes that he serves as one of the few relatively stable friends of the prostitute. Adler maintains that the girl's "relationship with the pimp constitutes the only important human tie"[44] she has. From this it is often inferred that the prostitute has few long-lasting stable relationships with her fellow workers. There are several additional reasons for the belief that the prostitute is essentially isolated from her fellow workers. Maurer explains the absence of a professional argot among prostitutes as a consequence (at least partially) of the fact that they tend to view each other as rivals.[45] Lemert makes much the same point when he says: "Solidarity is precluded by the keen competition, the social and cultural heterogeneity of the girls, and their rapid turnover."[46] However, there is evidence that this aspect of prostitution has been highly overemphasized. Even in the most competitive and mobile occupations, friendships and cooperation are the rule rather than the exception. And, in fact, cooperation among prostitutes is not uncommon at all.

Call girls who have more customers than they can handle will refer them to a friend. The friend, in turn, either returns the favor or a fee-splitting arrangement is worked out.[47] Girls working in houses assist each other with unruly customers; when a girl is sick or in jail her friends will often attempt to preserve as much of her practice as possible. The girls frequently share apartments either for business or for living and sleeping.

Like others who share the same profession, prostitutes spend much of their time talking about events on the job.

> At breakfast the discussion was always about their bedfellows of the night before, given with the most minute detail, particularly of abhorrent perversions, and comparisons of the bed manners of men who had at different times been with the different girls.[48]

Another apparently well liked topic of conversation is the girl who has "made good." Prostitutes all seem to know wives of prominent politicians or businessmen who were once "on the game." Likewise, movie stars may be known as ex-customers or co-workers.[49] There is to be found in these discussions of ex-prostitutes a mixture of contempt, envy, and pride.

> This man, to whom she was afterward married, rose to a high position in the affairs of the nation, and she, his wife, became famous for her political acumen and her social graces. Society placed no scarlet brand upon her nor upon her kind . . .[50]

255

Not only do prostitutes enjoy talking about those who have left the profession to return to respectable society, they also seem to treasure the stories of those who descended from respectability to join their ranks.[51]

It is a mistake, then to assume that prostitutes are so individuated that friendship groups and even clubs of a sort do not form. The girls have an occupation and its many problems in common; they share a common status, working hours, friends, and area. It is not surprising, then, that they speak of "we." They may not have a peculiar jargon, but they have a peculiar fund of experiences and, as Rolph's informant indicates, old words take on new meanings within the sisterhood of a common occupation.

> The trouble is that if you're in London and you meet your *old friends* they'll make fun of you for working — 'Softie, for working,' they'll say — then you might go back again.[52]

C. *The Pimp, the Madam, or Both:* The pimp occupies perhaps the most despised role known to conventional society. He not only takes almost all of the earnings of the prostitute, he also seduces young girls into the business and gives them dope to keep them there, or, at least, so the story goes, as told by many prostitutes,[53] police officials,[54] and madams.[55] The problems involved in a description of the pimp-prostitute relationship are, as a result, fantastic. The question usually asked, "why a pimp?", is usually answered in terms of the loneliness of the prostitute. Reitman contends, on the other hand, that the pimp is a functional necessity: the prostitute simply couldn't get along without him. "He is the woman's protector against the police, her employment agent, her guard and bouncer, her impresario, and her man."[56] I have argued earlier that prostitution is a difficult occupation and that certain skills must be acquired if it is to be followed successfully. Certainly the pimp can be, and often is, helpful in this respect. But this explanation of the prostitute's pimp should not be over-worked. The similarity of the pimp-prostitute relationship to the husband-wife relationship, with the *economic roles reversed,* is too obvious to overlook. I have no explanation for marriage but it is, to evade the question, traditional, just as is the prostitute-pimp relationship.[57]

Interestingly enough, a large proportion of the pimps in the United States and Great Britain are Negroes. (Estimates in some areas run as high as 90 percent.[58]) Many explanations of this phenomenon have been offered. Lemert suggests that white prostitutes "prefer Negro to white pimps for the reason that they can more easily dominate the relationship."[59] But this, too, ignores a heavily documented empirical proposition. Status equals tend to inter-marry. Socially, a man living with a woman he knows is a prostitute, if he allows her to contribute to their mutual expenses and helps her find work, etc., is a pimp. It is not a case of the man "creating" the prostitute, nor is it a case of the woman "selecting" a pimp: her occupation makes

256

them both what they are. There is little reason to wonder why people of the same social level, circulating in the same *milieu*, tend to associate with each other.[60]

The pimp frequently "gambles the prostitute's money away;" he also frequently abuses her physically. If he gambles, he probably gambled before he met the prostitute. Again, it is not a case of the pimp being a gambler On the contrary, gamblers and prostitutes often come in contact with each other. If they decide to form some sort of semi-permanent association, then the gambler becomes a pimp. Much of the physical abuse of the prostitute by the pimp can be accounted for as the lower class equivalent of the middle class family argument. Still more of it could be the prostitute's "excuse" for turning the pimp in to the police when she wishes to rid herself of him.[61]

Any discussion of the pimp would be incomplete without some reference to the story which appears again and again in discussions of the prostitute-pimp relationship. This story, usually told by the prostitute, goes somewhat as follows: "My man tells me that he is putting our money in the bank so that in a year or two we will be able to quit the game and buy a business of our own." This story is often quoted as evidence of the pimp's mendacity and the prostitute's gullibility. In a culture which assumes that the man will "make the living," however, this story can be seen as a rather obvious ideological justification supporting a deviation from this cultural assumption.

The prostitute's relationship with the madam does not pose serious problems as does her relationship with the pimp. The madam is, simply, the prostitute's employer. She hires and fires, makes rules, punishes those who break them, and generally supervises the activities of girls on the job. She often keeps lists of customers and girls who may be available if extra help is needed. She may find it necessary to employ accessory personnel such as maids, cooks, bouncers, and spotters. Her contacts with madams in other cities enable her to assist girls in finding new positions.[62] Her problems include those involved in meeting the sometimes rapidly changing tastes of her customers and of working out some sort of stable arrangement with city officials and the police. Although the prostitute usually sees or works for a madam during the course of her career, and although she may, on occasion, associate with her during off-duty hours, there is little doubt that she is less important as an associate than either the pimp or the fellow prostitute.

D. *Family, Friends, other "Squares"*: Just as one's choice of an occupation determines the type of people one will meet both on and off the job, so this choice influences the pattern and form of interactions with all members of the larger community.

Members of "respectable society" can be divided, as far as the prostitute is concerned, into five categories: 1) the customer; 2) the potential exploiter; 3) the suppressor; 4) the casual acquaintance; 5) the relative or "old" friend. It is to the prostitute's advantage to conceal her occupational identity from all of these persons except the customer.[63] The necessity of revealing her identity to the potential customer, of course, complicates the problem of concealing her occupational identity from others. The suppressor and the exploiter can discover her identity simply by posing as a potential customer. In fact, some exploiters (bell-hops, desk-clerks, etc.) exploit knowledge of the prostitute's identity by becoming simply non-paying customers.[64] Mere awareness of her identity on the part of almost any member of respectable society exposes the prostitute to the possibility of black-mail, extortion, and ridicule.

Although the problem of concealing her identity from family and old friends may be somewhat magnified by the tendency to imagine the prostitute as being reared in an equivalent to the unbroken, middle-class family, the fact remains that few are "orphans" and few would care to have their relatives know their occupation. If Lemert's conjecture that prostitutes are largely "rural immigrants to urban areas, or perhaps even more . . . migrants from small towns"[65] is correct, then the relative stability of the rural family would seem to increase the probability that the prostitute has relatives who are close enough to her to desire frequent information about her activities.

Reitman's pimp's budget contains an item, "annual trip to the girl's folks, $60.00."[66] Undoubtedly, on these occasions, the pimp poses as a boyfriend or husband.[67] If this is the case, then the prostitute may well have to account later for the break-up of her marriage or the loss of her boyfriend. But this is probably easier than explaining how she lives without a job (or lying about the job she doesn't have), why she moves so often, and so on. There are still other complications resulting from the sources of the prostitute's income:

> I knew that my family would not only refuse my aid, but that they would discard me if they should find out my mode of living. . . . It was not the fear of their repudiating me *which made my life a burden in the effort to keep my secret.* It was the grief it would bring them which blanched my face with fear every time I thought of the possibility of their discovering my manner of life. . . . *It was not possible for me to send them much money, for I had no way of accounting for the possession of it.*[68] [italics mine]

The prostitute's fear of the police is often as much a fear of the publicity or jail sentence which would reveal her occupation to friends and family as it is a fear of punishment. If the prostitute is jailed and her occupation revealed to her family, she is almost certain to get letters much like the following:

> *I have never . . . been so ashamed* in all my life. . . . We hope that you will admit that you've made a mess of your life . . . we

258

are so tired of having to lie about what you're doing and cover up and of never having anything good to tell . . .

. . . if you come home to see your mother I will simply take a trip until you've gone.[69] [italics in original]

Another fairly common response, when exposure occurs, is for the family to send a representative or come themselves in an effort to get the prostitute to quit her job. Although the girl working in a house is relatively safe, the street-walker (and the call-girl) is faced with the possibility of meeting old friends or relatives while plying her trade. Several accounts of such encounters are available.[70]

While the problem of protecting her identity from friends and relatives is an occasional problem, the prostitute must interact almost daily with members of respectable society whose knowledge of her occupation would cost her. The landlord, the taxi-driver, the grocer, the launderer, and the neighbor must be, as far as possible, kept ignorant of her "true" identity. Exploitation and abuse are the price of failure in this effort. The dilemma in this situation often is a result of a need for advertisement. On the one hand, the cab-driver, the desk-clerk, or the bell-hop may be of assistance. On the other, he may demand more than his services are worth.[71] It is hard to explain to the curious what kind of a job one has that lasts from eight in the evening until four in the morning. If such a job can be discovered, it may still fail to account for or square with the prostitute's style of life.[72] Even if the prostitue decides to find another occupation, she is still faced with the problem. If she marries someone other than a customer, she faces the possibility of "exposure." Courtship with a man unaware of her occupation is exceedingly complicated.[73]

We have already discussed the problems involved in keeping one's identity from the policeman. Although the prostitute may learn to spot a potential customer, it is not always she who initiates interaction. As a matter of fact, Rolph says that "comparatively few men become customers as a result of a prostitute's suggestions."[74] The prostitute who is asked something like "Are you a naughty girl?" must decide rather hurriedly whether to say "no" and lose a potential customer or to say "yes" and thereby admit her occupation to a policeman.[75] There are other dilemmas. In some areas of London a loitering woman is assumed to be a prostitute.[76] To solicit in areas known to be frequented by other professionals is only good business. But the police also are aware of this fact and the risk of apprehension increases.

I have considered, very briefly, some of the things the prostitute must do, some of the people she meets, and some of the problems she faces in carrying on her profession. In the sections which follow, I will analyze two further aspects of this job using rather conventional categories for the study of a group of workers: job satisfaction and occupational ideology.

Job Satisfaction

There are several indices of job satisfaction. It is usual to ask the worker, to observe his behavior on the job, and to determine how long he keeps it.

The popular conception is that prostitution soon "destroys" a woman mentally and physically. It is true that prostitution seldom occupies more than a small fraction of a woman's adult years, although it is probably not as temporary as the following quotation suggests.

> Even regular prostitution is not and has never been so fixed a status as we should suppose; it is rather a transitory stage from which the girl seeks to emerge by marriage or otherwise. . . . 'it is usually abandoned during the first year.'[77]

Few prostitutes are found beyond age 35 and the peak age of entry appears to be around 20. The average length of a career as a prostitute would then be somewhat less than seven years with 15 years an unusually long career.[78] Adler, with a somewhat different frame of reference, says the prostitute "has ten money-making years at the outside."[79] Gosling, on the other hand, argues that a prostitute "who took reasonable care of herself" could remain in the higher income brackets for 25 years.[80] A glance at the case-histories reported in several different volumes reveals that prostitutes with more than 15 years "on the game" are not uncommon. And some of these women did not enter prostitution until their late twenties or early thirties. Although the old notion that "fallen women die in a few years" is, of course, no longer accepted, the notion that women will leave prostitution at the earliest opportunity is still found in interpretations of "length of service" figures. It remains true, however, that there is no basis for concluding from such data that the prostitute is extraordinarily unhappy with her occupational role. As beauty declines, so does earning power and other occupations are able to compete more favorably with prostitution. Since it can be assumed that many prostitutes eventually marry and leave the profession, it is also reasonable to assume that those who marry do not necessarily do so simply to escape prostitution any more than does the female clerk. For that matter, it is likely that figures on prostitution do not differ considerably from those of other occupations populated largely by women of marriageable ages.

Inferences of much the same order have often been drawn from the prostitute's use of drugs and alcohol. Lemert argues that the users of drugs are often only secondarily prostitutes. They enter prostitution because they need money to buy drugs. Likewise, he maintains, the alcoholic woman is apt to meet conditions under which prostitution is somewhat unavoidable.[81] Adler claims she refused prostitutes who were on drugs, unless they agreed to "take the cure."[82] Also, it is likely that the prostitute cannot operate successfully for long if she uses alcohol to excess. She is often in a position in which she must drink with the customer, however, and she probably meets dope pushers as frequently as do the members of any other occupational category.[83] Thus there is little reason, other than the popular superstition, to believe that her use of drugs reflects her hatred of her profession.

The following statements by prostitutes are not, it is true, a representative sample of their comments on this subject. Nevertheless, the writings of prostitutes often reflect considerable satisfaction or, at least, acceptance of their choice of an occupation.

> I was there nine weeks, and met many men. I stayed with them and grew prosperous. Since there was no other way for me to make a living, why not make the most of this? I was good looking, and men liked my company. So I had money for clothes, money to pay my hotel bill, plenty of food and drink. I had no regrets . . . I now committed my sins with open eyes.[84]

A call girl, who taught school prior to entering prostitution, sums up her feelings as follows:

> I'm not really complaining. I hate to live this way . . . but I feel the same way about typing letters for other people or filing or thinking their thoughts or doing their housework. . . . and I think this is a fairly useful thing to do and it pays well and I don't have to do it eight hours a day.[85]

Rolph presents a cogent argument to the effect that the prostitute goes through a period of personal disorganization *before* entering prostitution. There is probably an analogous period preceding entrance to any profession. The fact that most "case histories" of prostitutes focus on this period can, therefore, account for much of the belief that the prostitute herself is disorganized. The facts, however, are a different matter.

> Once a girl has become a professional prostitute one perceives the phenomenon of stabilization in her personality and behavior . . . . she has acquired a profession where she is needed, and needed by men, where she has regular hours and colleagues, and most important of all, where she finds herself in the company of people who are like herself in personality and outlook.[86]

While there is little doubt that the excerpt which follows is an overstatement of the prostitute's general feelings about her job, and comes near the "daughter of joy" position that society imputes to the prostitute (along with the belief that she is extremely demoralized), there seems little reason to doubt the sincerity of the statement:

> Life became fuller and more beautiful than I had ever thought it could be. . . . I awakened to find myself the most sought-after girl in town, and I rejoiced in my popularity. . . . I was happy.[87]

261

There is little question that an impressive array of quotations could be gathered to document the position that the prostitute is miserable, unhappy, depressed, and lonely. For that matter, contradictory evidence on this point could be gathered from the members of any profession. I have over-painted one side of the picture of prostitution; the other side will take care of itself.

Occupational Ideology

Every occupational group has a peculiar set of beliefs, rationalizations, or what have you, that serve to justify the existence of the profession both to those within and to those without. Thus the social scientist prefaces his texts with the comment that knowledge is good for its own sake or that it is necessary if social reform programs are to be effective. The physician, motivated by altruism, heals the sick. The garbage collector consoles himself with the statement that his work is not only honest, it is also necessary. One thing all such occupational ideologies have in common is that they are based on value premises shared by most, if not all, of the members of the larger society. The occupation of prostitution is no exception.

Almost all occupational ideologies have a "functionalist" orientation: "we contribute to society," "we perform a necessary social service." This is a major element of the ideology of prostitution.

> The prostitute's 'value' to the community is constantly being established by the reassertions of her apparent indispensability. Flossie told me [with pride] about the boxer, who, being in training for a fight, had asked only to be allowed to walk around the park with her . . .[88]

The prostitute realizes, of course, that she satisfies a rather imperious sexual need. Box-Car Bertha, after her first day of work, notes: "At the end of the day I had [sic] forty tricks, forty sex-hungry men that I had satisfied."[89] But she is apt to think of her social service as more than one of simply satisfying sexual needs.

> I think that the release of talking about an unhappy home situation may well have *saved many a marriage*, and *possibly even lives*, when nerves have been strained to a breaking point. It is well known that it is easier to unburden serious trouble onto a total stranger . . . Easier still to tell a girl whose time you have bought, whom nothing will surprise, and who is in no position to despise you . . .[90]

In addition to satisfying "normal" sex needs of "normal" people and listening to sad tales, the prostitute takes care of those who are unable to find other sexual outlets.

262

We get 'em all. The kids who are studying to be doctors and lawyers and things, and men whose wives hate the thought of sex. And men whose wives are sick or have left them. What are such men going to do? *Pick on married women . . . or run around after underage girls?* They're better off with us. That's what we're for.[91]

. . . I could endure a surprising amount of humiliation for the *handicapped person . . . .* most of the girls felt morally obliged to see the handicapped Johns and be unusually kind to them.[92]

Not only does the prostitute maintain that she performs a useful, necessary, and humanitarian service, she also believes that she is, in many respects, morally superior to many members of respectable society. She recognizes the element of prostitution implicit in many female-male relationships. "And how about the society girls who marry older men they don't love — who just happen to have money? I'll say they're different from us."[93] Greenwald, although he lists his excerpts under the heading "defenses," quotes the following as typical of the prostitute's attitude toward respectable women: "Let the poor bum figure up how many times a year she lets him have her, divide it by what he gives her, and she'd see if she's not the higher-priced whore."[94]

Even when the element of prostitution is missing, the behavior of the respectable woman may be morally inferior to that of the honest prostitute: "I was no 'gold digger,' who begged favors from a man *without giving something in return. . . .* I had pride."[95]

But above all else, according to the ideology of prostitution, the prostitute is not, as is the member of respectable society, a hypocrite.

We come into continual contact with upright, respected citizens whose voices are loudly raised against us in public, and yet who visit us in private . . . If they are afraid at all . . . their fear is not that they are sinning against the laws of God or of decency, or even so much that they may pass on to their wives and families whatever disease we may be suffering from, and never that they are adding to the demand whose supply they have so virtuously condemned, but rather that they will somehow be discovered consorting with us and lose thereby the respect of their fellows.[96]

Conclusion

I have tried to look at prostitution as an occupation. This occupation is one of the most despised in the Western world. As one result, non-scientific literature on the subject is marked by its lack of objectivity and its preoccupation with the question, "how could a girl stoop to selling her body for gain?" For that matter, sociological writing often reflects an inability to look upon this subject with a disinterested eye:

> Prostitution is a basic threat to family life. It degrades the sexual function of marriage in a special sense, for it undermines the capacity of men to confine their sex experience within the limits of marriage.[97]

Another result of prostitution's status as a despised occupation is that many approaches to the subject are potentially fruitful for sociology. The social reaction to the profession, for example, offers an excellent opportunity to the student seeking a "sociological explanation of moral attitudes."[98] Or, this same reaction may be treated as an independent variable and prostitution itself analyzed "as a dynamic response to the mythology, societal definitions, and manipulations in the name of reform that compose the societal reaction."[99]

While interest in prostitution as deviance may have resulted in neglect of prostitution as occupation, the difficulties involved in studying the subject certainly do not justify this neglect. In fact, viewing prostitution as an occupation may enable the student to cut through the elaborate mythology surrounding it and, in so doing, learn something about both prostitution and the service occupations in general.

Notes

1. This characteristic of the service occupations is discussed in Becker, Howard S., "The Professional Dance Musician and His Audience," *The American Journal of Sociology*, Vol. 58, September, 1951, p. 136.
2. Geoffrey May, "Prostitution," *Encyclopaedia of the Social Sciences*, Vol. 12, (New York: The MacMillan Company, 1935), p. 553.
3. Erving Goffman, *Asylums*, (Garden City, New York: Doubleday & Company, 1961), p. 324.
4. Kingsley Davis, "The Sociology of Prostitution," *American Sociological Review*, Vol. 2, 1937, pp. 744–755.
5. Harold Greenwald, *The Call Girl*, (New York: Ballantine Books, 1958), p. 25.
6. Davis, *op. cit.*, p. 750.
7. David W. Maurer, "Prostitutes and Criminal Argots," *American Journal of Sociology*, Vol. 24, 1939, p. 548. Edwin M. Lemert, *Social Pathology*, (New York: McGraw-Hill Book Company, 1951), p. 272.
8. Davis, *op. cit.*, p. 750. In a recently revised and expanded version of this paper, Davis replaces "hard" with "interesting." He goes on to say: "The answer of course is that the harlot's return is not primarily a reward for labor, skill, capital, or land (rent). It is primarily a reward for loss of social standing." Kingsley Davis, "Prostitution," in Robert K. Merton and Robert A. Nisbet (editors), *Contemporary Social Problems*, (New York: Harcourt, Brace & World, 1961), p. 277.
9. Polly Adler, *A House is not a Home*. (New York: Popular Library, 1955), p. 82.

10. Ben L. Reitman, *The Second Oldest Profession,* (New York: The Vanguard Press, 1931), p. 89.
11. O. W., *No Bed of Roses: The Diary of a Lost Soul,* (New York: Sheridan House, 1930), p. 175. I am reluctant to defend my occasional use of references as old as this one. Therefore, I call the reader's attention to the intermixing of materials written at different times and simply suggest that this practice is not wholly attributable to the scarcity of data on prostitution.
12. C. H. Rolph, (ed.), *Women of the Streets,* (London: Secker & Warburg, 1955), p. 82.
13. Anonymous, *Streetwalker,* (New York: Dell Publishing Co., 1961), pp. 31–32.
14. John M. Murtagh, and Sara Harris, *Cast the First Stone,* (New York: Pocket Books, Inc., 1958), p. 4–5.
15. Anonymous, *Madeleine — An Autobiography,* (New York: Pyramid Books, 1961), p. 64. (Copyright 1919).
16. There are, of course, many other places of resort, e.g., parks, alleys, and taxi-cabs. See Rolph, *op. cit.,* pp. 58–59.
17. Susan Kale, *The Fire Escape,* (Garden City, New York: Doubleday & Company, Inc., 1960), pp. 234–237.
18. *Streetwalker,* p. 17.
19. Lemert, *op. cit.,* p. 270. See also p. 245.
20. *Streetwalker,* p. 30.
21. Ben L. Reitman, *Sister of the Road: The Autobiography of Box-Car Bertha,* (New York: The Macaulay Company, 1937), p. 178.
22. *Madeleine,* p. 43.
23. *Streetwalker,* p. 95.
24. Rolph, *Women of the Streets,* p. 93.
25. Murtagh, *Cast the First Stone,* p. 27.
26. Rolph reports that "Bribery of police by prostitutes, either in cash or in kind, is uncommon" in London. *Women of the Streets,* p. 43. This, if our information is accurate, cannot be said for the United States.
27. May, *Encyclopaedia of the Social Sciences,* (1935), p. 559. Reckless made the same point even earlier. "The activities of modern women . . . have erased the outward distinction between the painted sport and the paler protected lady." Walter C. Reckless, *Vice in Chicago* (Chicago: University of Chicago Press, 1933), pp. 58 and 159.
28. Lemert, *Social Pathology,* p. 254.
29. Rolph, *Women of the Streets,* pp. 76–77.
30. *Streetwalker,* p. 31.
31. Lemert, *Social Pathology,* p. 254.
32. John Gosling and Douglas Warner, *City of Vice,* (New York: Hillman Books, 1961), p. 50.
33. Kale, *The Fire Escape,* p. 198.
34. Jess Stearn, *Sisters of the Night,* (New York: Popular Library, 1957), p. 59.
35. The need for some form of advertisement is illustrated by the following: "The Lord Chief Justice of England has ruled that it's legal for call girls to advertise in shop windows . . . [The following ad had appeared in a shop window] 'Model Susan 40–28–40. Full personal service. Hours 10 a. m. to 10 p. m.' Such advertisements have blossomed in store windows in seedier areas of London since Parliament, in 1958, decreed stiffer penalties for soliciting on the streets." *San Francisco Chronicle,* February, 1962.
36. Rolph, *Women of The Streets,* p. 65.
37. Gosling, *op. cit.,* p. 65.

38. Reitman, *The Second Oldest Profession*, p. 22. Rolph, *Women of the Streets*, p. 97.
39. Alfred C. Kinsey *et al.*, *Sexual Behavior in the Human Male*, (Philadelphia: W. B. Saunders Company, 1948), pp. 597–600.
40. Lemert, *Social Pathology*, pp. 244–245.
41. Gosling, *City of Vice*, p. 76.
42. *Madeleine*, p. 44. A discussion of the "sad tale" among mental patients and other deviants, including prostitutes, is found in Goffman, *Asylums*, pp. 150–155.
43. *Streetwalker*, p. 158.
44. Adler, *A House is not a Home*, p. 108.
45. Maurer, "Prostitutes and Criminal Argots," p. 547.
46. Lemert, *Social Pathology*, p. 248.
47. Greenwald, *The Call Girl*, p. 24.
48. *Madeleine*, p. 66.
49. Virginia McManus, *Not For Love*, (New York: G. P. Putnam's Sons, 1960), p. 161.
50. *Madeleine*, p. 97.
51. Adler, *A House is not a Home*, pp. 92–93.
52. Rolph, *Women of the Streets*, p. 136.
53. Murtagh, *Cast the First Stone*, p. 49.
54. Harold R. Danforth and James D. Horan, *Big City Crimes*, (New York: Permabook, 1957). pp. 104–140.
55. Adler, *A House is not a Home*, pp. 102 ff. In contrast: "But the one girl I never met in all these years and in all these countries that I visited was the pure girl who had been trapped and violated and sold into slavery, and held a prisoner unable to effect her escape — the so-called 'white slave' " *Madeleine*, p. 114.
56. Reitman, *The Second Oldest Profession*, p. 14.
57. *Ibid.*, pp. 37–38. An excellent discussion of this question is found in Havelock Ellis, *Studies in the Psychology of Sex*, Vol. 6, (Philadelphia: F. A. Davis Company, 1918), p. 271.
58. Murtagh, *Cast the First Stone*, p. 124.
59. Lemert, *Social Pathology*, p. 275.
60. Rolph, *Women of the Streets*, p. 119.
61. *Ibid.*
62. O. W., *No Bed of Roses*, p. 159–160.
63. The orientation of this section is drawn from class lectures by Erving Goffman on deviance and concealment of stigma.
64. O. W., *No Bed of Roses*, p. 122.
65. Lemert, *Social Pathology*, p. 241.
66. Reitman, *The Second Oldest Profession*, p. 92.
67. The pimp *is*, of course, a boy-friend or husband.
68. *Madeleine*, pp. 84–85.
69. McManus, *Not for Love*, pp. 204 and 256.
70. *Streetwalker*, pp. 194–197.
71. Also, he may miss the point and inadvertently expose her. While working in a hotel, the writer had occasion to observe the following: A young bell-hop, new to the job, told the desk-clerk, "I can't understand it, but it sure is great! The lady in 212 gives me a dollar every time she goes up or down on the elevator." The "lady," of course, was asked to leave.
72. McManus, *Not For Love*, p. 143.
73. O. W., *No Bed of Roses*, esp. p. 157.
74. Rolph, *Women of the Streets*, p. 56.
75. At least in many American cities.

266

76. Rolph, *ibid.*
77. W. I. Thomas, *The Unadjusted Girl,* (Boston: Little, Brown, and Company, 1928), p. 120. Thomas is quoting Ellis, *op. cit.,* p. 261. Ellis, in turn, is quoting works written in the middle of the last century.
78. Lemert, *Social Pathology,* pp. 270–271.
79. Adler, *A House is not a Home,* p. 128.
80. Gosling, *City of Vice,* p. 74.
81. Lemert, *Social Pathology,* p. 277.
82. Adler, *A House is not a Home,* p. 102.
83. Comparison with another occupation whose practitioners are exposed to drugs is revealing: "The incidence of opiate addiction among physicians has been estimated by the U. S. Commissioner of Narcotics as being about one addict among every 100 physicians, in contrast to a rate of one in 3,000 in the general population." Charles Winnick, "Physician Narcotic Addicts," *Social Problems,* Vol. 9, Fall, 1961, p. 174.
84. O. W., *No Bed of Roses,* p. 102.
85. McManus, *Not For Love,* p. 155.
86. Rolph, *Women of the Streets,* pp. 108–109.
87. *Madeleine,* p. 95.
88. Rolph, *Women of the Streets,* p. 88.
89. Reitman, *Sister of the Road,* p. 178.
90. *Streetwalker,* p. 21.
91. Gosling, *City of Vice,* p. 82.
92. McManus, *Not For Love,* p. 174.
93. Stearn, *Sisters of the Night,* p. 28.
94. Greenwald, *The Call Girl,* p. 132.
95. O. W., *No Bed of Roses,* p. 134.
96. *Streetwalker,* p. 156.
97. Mabel A. Elliott and Francis E. Merrill, *Social Disorganization,* (New York: Harper & Brothers, 1950), p. 162.
98. Davis, "Prostitution," in Merton & Nisbet, eds., *Contemporary Social Problems,* p. 262.
99. Lemert, *Social Pathology,* p. 237.

17

Pornography: Patterns of Exposure and Patrons

Commission on Obscenity and Pornography

Section F. Patterns of Exposure to Erotic Material

The following pages contain an attempt to spell out in some detail patterns of experience with sexually explicit materials among adults and young people.

Not many scientific investigations have collected data on experience with erotic materials. Those few studies that have been reported asked a variety of questions that are often not strictly comparable. Nevertheless, there is a growing body of knowledge regarding this experience, and a consistent picture is beginning to emerge.

Adults

Abelson and his associates (1970) carried out a large national survey to provide information regarding the nature of the experience that adults in the United States have had with erotic materials. This survey involved face to face interviews with a sample of 2,486 adults, age 21 and older, who were selected into the sample by a technique that provided an approxi-

From *The Report of the Commission on Obscenity and Pornography*, September, 1970.

mately equal probability for each adult in the United States to be included. The results of this survey should accurately reflect the experience of adults in the United States. The survey asked questions about both seeing and reading depictions of the following types: emphasizing the sex organs of a man or woman; mouth-sex organ contact between a man and woman; a man and woman having sexual intercourse; sexual activities between people of the same sex; and sex activities which include whips, belts or spankings. Eighty-four percent of the men and 69% of the women in the representative national sample reported having been exposed to at least one of these kinds of depictions.

Athanasiou (1970) analyzed the responses of over 20,000 readers of the magazine, Psychology Today, to a questionnaire on sex attitudes and practices that was contained in the July 1970 issue of the magazine. The respondents were obviously not representative of the general population: 77% were less than 35 years old and 89% had some college experience. In response to the question, "Have you voluntarily obtained or seen erotic or pornographic books, movies, magazines, etc.?", 92% of the males and 72% of the females said, "Yes."

The same question was asked of over 450 members of professional and community service groups in metropolitan Detroit (Wallace & Wehmer, 1970). About 63% were men and 37% women. Eighty percent of these people indicated that they had voluntarily obtained erotic materials.

Goldstein and his associates (1970) conducted intensive clinical interviews regarding experience with a variety of sexual materials with a sample of normal males in metropolitan Los Angeles. These subjects were predominantly lower-middle class in the age range of 20–40 years. The sample included 53 whites and 39 blacks. At least 85% of the whites and 76% of the blacks reported having been exposed to photographic depictions of sexual intercourse and at least 92% of the whites and 90% of the blacks had seen photos of fully nude females.

Massey (1970), in a questionnaire study of several hundred predominantly middle-class men and women members of social, professional, service, and church groups in Denver, found that 83% had seen at sometime in their life depictions of people engaged in a sex act, and a similar percentage had seen depictions of people with all private sex organs fully exposed.

These several studies of selected samples are quite consistent in their results and provide estimates of exposure very similar to that provided by the national survey reported by Abelson and his associates (1970). Approximately 85% of men and 70% of women report specific instances of having been exposed to explicit sexual materials depicting at a minimum nudity with genitals exposed.

The proportion of people in the United States who have been exposed to erotic materials is very similar to the proportion of adults in Copenhagen, Denmark, who report having seen pornographic books and magazines. Kutschinsky (1970) surveyed a representative sample of 398 men and women regarding their attitudes toward sex crimes and toward pornography. The responses to a series of questions regarding exposure to pornography indicated that 87% of men and 73% of women had consumed at least one book and a similar percentage had consumed at least one pornographic magazine (Kutschinsky, 1970).

Fewer adults report recent experience with erotic materials than report ever having been exposed. The national survey (Abelson, et al., 1970) reveals that whereas 84% of males report having been exposed at some time in the past to at least one of the ten depictions that were included in the study, only 40% report having experience with visual depictions of intercourse during the past two years. The comparable figures for women are 69% and 26%. Goldstein and his associates (1970) report a similar phenomenon among normal male adults. Whereas at least 85% of the white males report having been exposed to photos of heterosexual intercourse at sometime in their life, only 71% report exposure to such photos in the past year; the corresponding figures for blacks are 76% and 54%.

Three studies reveal no consistent differences between textual and visual media as being the more likely medium of exposure (Abelson, et al., 1970; Goldstein, et al., 1970; Massey, 1970). The more common medium changes from group to group and from depiction to depiction and does not form a coherent pattern.

Experience does vary, however, according to the content of the material. The national survey indicates that depictions of sex organs and heterosexual intercourse are most common, homosexual activities and oral sex are in between, and sadomasochistic materials are the least common (Abelson, et al., 1970). The data of Goldstein and his associates (1970) on normal adult males are in general agreement with the national survey, but they found more differentiation between full nudity and intercourse, and between homosexual and oral sex content. The rank ordering of likelihood of having been seen was: fully nude women, heterosexual intercourse, oral sex, homosexual, and sadomasochistic. Thus, portrayals of sex that conform to general cultural norms are more likely to be seen, and portrayals of sexual activity that deviate from these norms are less likely to be seen. Portrayals of combinations of sex and violence are relatively rare in the experience of normal adults in our society. Massey (1970) found that reported exposure decreased as material became more explicit within the range from partial nudity to sexual activity with full exposure of sex organs.

Experience with sexual materials also varies according to the characteristics of the viewer. Our chief source of information on this topic is the national survey referred to above (Abelson, et al., 1970). We have already seen that men are more likely to be exposed to erotic materials than are

270

women, and this gender difference holds in Copenhagen, Denmark, as well as in the United States. Younger adults are more likely to have experience with sexual materials than are older adults, and this holds for both men and women. People with some college attendance are more likely to have experience with erotic materials than people with only high school attendance who are, in turn, more likely to have been exposed to erotica than people who attended school eight years or less. These educational differences hold for both men and women. Males living in relatively large metropolitan areas are likely to have more experience with sexual materials than males living in small metropolitan areas of nonmetropolitan areas, but this does not hold for females. There are differences in amount of exposure among different geographical areas of the country for males but not for females. The most exposure for males occurs in the Northeast section and the least in the North Central section. People who read general books, magazines, and newspapers more and who see general movies more also see more erotic stimuli. People who are socially and politically active are exposed to more erotic materials. Both of these latter two findings hold for both men and women. People who attend religious services more often are somewhat less likely to be exposed to erotica.

Several of these differences in exposure to erotica were also found by Wallace and Wehmer (1970) in their more circumscribed study. They report that college students were most likely among their subjects to have voluntarily obtained or seen erotic or pornographic stimuli, followed by members of professional groups, community service groups, and church groups in that order.

Prosecuting attorneys from large urban areas are more likely to report that the volume of traffic and patterns of distribution are a matter of serious concern in their community than are prosecuting attorneys from smaller communities (Wilson, Horowitz, and Friedman, 1970).

These differences in experience with sexual materials may be summarized by the following profiles. Persons who have the greater amount of experience with erotic materials tend to be male, younger, better educated, urban, to consume more mass communication media, to be more socially active, more politically active, and less active in religious affairs. Those who have less experience with erotic materials tend to be female, older, less educated, to live in small circles or rural areas, to be less exposed to general communication media, less socially active, less politically active, and more active in religious affairs. Similar profiles are reported for Sweden by Zetterberg (1970).

Although most males in our society have been exposed to erotic stimuli at sometime in their lives, a small proportion have had relatively extensive experience with erotica. Eighty percent of the male adults in the national sample reported having ever seen in a visual medium at least one of the

271

five kinds of depictions asked about, but only 49% reported having seen three or more of these types of stimuli. Yet, approximately a third (34%) report having seen four or five of these different types. Only 17% of the females have seen three or more of these different kinds of stimuli.

The national survey data on more recent experience with erotica also demonstrates that extensive experience with sexual materials is not the usual case. Whereas 61% of the men report having been exposed to at least one of the above depictions in either visual or textual form during the past two years, only 26% have been exposed to five or more of the ten possible depictions. The figures for women are 50% and 11%.

The national survey also asked how many different times an individual had seen a given visual depiction during the past two years. Fourteen percent of the men and 5% of the women report having seen the given depiction more than five times in the two-year interval (Abelson, et al., 1970). These figures are low estimates because the depiction queried varied from individual to individual in such a way as to more often ask about the types of depictions that are least often seen.

Goldstein and his colleagues (1970) also report data on frequency of recent exposure. Thirty-two percent of the normal white males report seeing photos of heterosexual intercourse more than ten times during the past year, 27% report seeing photos of oral-genital activity that frequently, and only 14% report seeing sadomasochistic materials that frequently. The figures for the black sample are 36%, and 19%, and 9%. The frequency of exposure to textual and movie stimuli is less than that for still photographic depictions. It should be noted that the people in this sample were relatively young and lived in a large urban community and would, therefore, be expected to have had greater exposure than average for males.

Thus, somewhere around one-fifth or one-quarter of the male population in the United States has somewhat regular experience with sexual materials as explicit as intercourse.

There are no exactly comparable figures for frequency of exposure for countries other than the United States. Kutschinsky (1970) found that 18% of the representative adult male sample from Copenhagen, Denmark, report having consumed 50 or more pornographic magazines in their lifetime, and 39% reported having seen a pornographic magazine within the past month at the time of the interview.

Americans have their first exposure to erotic materials at a relatively young age. Three-quarters (74%) of the national sample (Abelson, et al., 1970) of male adults report having seen sexual materials at least as explicit as nudity with genitals before they were 21 years old, over half (54%) before age 18, and nearly one-third (30%) before age 15. Women report a later age of first exposure: about one-half (51%) before 21, one-third (33%) before 18, and one-sixth (17%) before 15. This early age of exposure will be explored further when we look at the experience of adolescents.

272

Few people report that they buy erotic materials. Only 5% of the men who have seen nonmovie visual depictions in the past two years report having bought the most recent depiction that they have seen; an additional 8% report having seen it at a newsstand or bookstore; but 53% report having been shown the depiction or given it by someone else. A larger proportion of men report having bought the most recent textual depiction they have read, 26%; only 4% read it at a bookstore or newsstand; 64% report having obtained it from someone else at no cost. The figures for women are roughly comparable (Abelson, et al., 1970). These figures may be low estimates because the depiction asked about varied in explicitness from person to person and the more explicit materials are less often purchased.

Massey (1970) asked his subjects if they had ever seen and if they had ever purchased sexual materials of several degrees of explicitness. Fifty-nine percent of those who had ever seen depictions of private sex organs but no sex activity had also bought such materials; 47% of those who had ever seen depictions of sexual activity but no sex organs exposed had bought; 35% of those who had ever seen depictions of sex play with sex organs exposed but not in contact had bought; and only 26% of those who had seen depictions of sex acts with full exposure of sex organs had also bought these materials at some time. These figures are perhaps higher than one would obtain in general since the subjects of the study were relatively well educated, young middle aged, urban and socially active. The figures are also not comparable to the ones reported in the national survey since Massey's figures reporting having *ever* bought, and the national survey figures report having bought the most recent exposure.

Several generalizations may be derived from these data. First, most exposure to erotica occurs outside the commercial context. Two, erotica is a durable material for which there are several consumers for each purchase. Three, although the proportion of the population purchasing erotic materials is relatively small, the absolute number of purchasers may constitute a sizable market.

The responses to the national survey (Abelson, et al., 1970) indicate that approximately 3% of the most recent exposures to erotic material occurred as a result of unsolicited mail.

Within the general adult public, exposure to erotica is a social or quasi-social activity. The principal source of both visual and textual erotica is a friend or acquaintance. Most people go to see skinflicks or "stag" movies with someone else, although a sizable minority of men (14%) go alone. The sexes differ in terms of with whom they attend erotic movies: men most often go in the company of other men, while women most often go in the company of men or a mixed group of both sexes (Abelson, et al., 1970).

The informal distribution of erotica among friends is an asymmetrical communication network. Many more people have had sexual materials shown or given to them than have shown or given these materials to others.

A relatively few people seem to be the central points of the communication network and initially obtain sexual materials and then share them with several others. Only 31% of men and 18% of women report knowing of a shop which specializes in sexual materials. Sharing is predominantly with a friend of the same sex or with a spouse (Abelson, et al., 1970).

Minors

Although much concern has been expressed regarding young people's potential exposure to explicit sexual materials, there have been until recently almost no formal reports of information about how often this occurs. Two adults may in a conversation about pornography recall certain experiences that occurred in their own childhood, but the sharing of these recollections seldom occurs. Kinsey included questions about age of exposure to erotic materials in his interviews, but these data have never been formally reported.

The national survey funded by the Commission and reported by Abelson and his associates (1970) did ask adults to try to recall the age at which they had first been exposed to explicit sexual materials. We mentioned earlier that of this representative sample of American adult males roughly three-quarters reported having been exposed before age 21, one-half before age 18, and one-third before age 15; and that females report being exposed about two years later than males. These figures may report later exposure than actually occurred, however, because it may be difficult for older people to make differentiations of a few years when recalling teenage experience. For example, although 19% of all male adults report first exposure at 12 years of age or younger, 34% of men age 21–29 report first exposure at age 12 or younger. This difference in reporting may reflect errors in recall among the older respondents or it may reflect actual changes in experience in more recent decades. In either case, we may expect higher rates of earlier exposure to be reported by today's youth.

Goldstein and his associates (1970) asked their subjects (normal, lower middle class, young and middle-aged males) to report on their exposure in adolescence. More than 90% of both whites and blacks reported exposure to photos of fully nude women and about 70% of both groups reported having seen these depictions more than ten times during adolescence. Eighty percent of the whites and 75% of the blacks reported seeing photos of heterosexual intercourse in adolescence, with approximately half of both groups reporting more than ten different exposures to these depictions. Over half of both groups reported seeing photos of homosexual activity, 75% of the whites and 58% of the blacks had seen photos of mouth-genital activity, and 43% of the whites and 30% of the blacks had seen photos of sadomasochistic activity in adolescence.

Both of these studies suggest that there has been considerable exposure to explicit sexual materials by adolescents in the past.

A recent national survey of sex educators and counselors (Wilson and Jacobs, 1970) asked the respondents to estimate the age at which roughly half of boys had been exposed to explicit sexual materials. A similar question was asked about girls. There was virtual consensus (91%) that half of the boys had been exposed to explicit sexual materials by the time they were 16 years old. About two-thirds (64%) of the sex educators and counselors felt that half of the boys are exposed to these materials by the time they are 14 years old. Generally, these experts estimated that girls were one to two years later than boys in their exposure to erotica.

White (1970) asked a total of 300 college students, male and female, from five different universities in New York, Providence, and Boston, at what age they were first exposed to pornography in any form. (Pornography was not defined, but each respondent had been asked to define the term earlier. Their responses indicate that they were thinking of explicit portrayals of genitals and sexual activity.) Nearly three-quarters (71%) said they had been exposed by age 13 and 97% had been exposed by age 17. Only 12% reported that they had never voluntarily exposed themselves to pornography, and 20% reported that they often voluntarily exposed themselves to pornography.

Roach and Kreisberg (1970) asked similar questions in a self-administered questionnaire to a total of 625 students of both sexes from eight colleges in Westchester County, New York. Nearly half of the males (49%) reported having been exposed to pornography before age 13 and 50% of the females had been exposed by age 15. Seven percent of the males and 12% of the females reported never having been exposed voluntarily to pornography, while 32% and 15%, respectively, reported voluntary exposure often.

Berger and his associates (1970a) report on a survey of a national random sample of college students conducted in 1967. The survey asked if the person had seen pornographic photographs depicting sexual activity, pornographic or stag movies depicting sexual intercourse, or pornographic writing. Ninety-eight percent of the males and 82% of the females reported exposure to at least one of these. There was no relationship between having been exposed and year in college, and the authors concluded that first exposure is primarily a precollege phenomenon. Thirty-nine percent of the males and 10% of the females reported frequent exposure to at least one of these types of pornography.

The reports of the college students indicate a greater degree of exposure to explicit sexual materials during adolescence than do the retrospective reports of older adults. This difference may be due to differential recall of the teenage experience, different experiences across generations, different experiences across social class groupings, or all three. Fortunately, we are

275

not limited to inferences based on retrospective reporting for information about contemporary experience of minors with erotic materials. Several recent investigations have directly questioned minors themselves about their experiences in this realm.

The national survey conducted for the Commission also included a sample of 769 adolescents age 15–20 who were living at home; the sample leaves out household members age 15–20 who were away at school, in the armed services, etc. The adolescent sample was asked many of the same questions that were asked the adults, including whether they had seen the various kinds of depictions of explicit sexual material in both pictorial and textual form and the circumstances of a recent exposure experience.

Ninety-one percent of the males and 88% of the females in this national sample age 15–20 reported having seen at least one of the ten depictions queried. Forty-nine percent of the males and 45% of the females reported having seen five or more of the depictions. Thirty-two percent of the males and 29% of the females report that they have seen a given visual depiction more than five times during the past two years. This is probably a low frequency estimate because different depictions were asked about for different respondents, and some of the depictions are likely to have lower frequencies of exposure than others. Minors report considerably more exposure to erotica than do adults in general. However, the experience of the minors with sexual materials is similar to that of adults who are nearest them in age, the 21–29 year olds (Abelson, et al., 1970).

Other studies of more circumscribed groups of minors are consistent with these findings.

Fersch (1970) asked several mixed male and female groups, including public high school students, private high school students, street corner gangs, and college students, about their exposure to books with stories of sadism, masochism, orgies, or wild parties in them, to "girlie" picture magazines, and to "more-censored" pictures and magazines. The subjects ranged from 14 to 22 years old, cut across several socio-economic status classifications, and represented a variety of religious groups. Ninety-seven percent reported that they had read books with sexual stories, 95% had looked at "girlie" picture magazines, and 80% had seen "more-censored" magazines. Half of these minors reported seeing "currently-censored" materials at age 13 or younger and two thirds at age 14 or younger.

Berger, Gagnon and Simin (1970b) used a self-administered questionnaire to gather information from 473 working-class, white, predominantly Catholic, adolescents age 13–18. Ninety-five percent of the males and 65% of the females had seen pictures of nudes with genitals exposed; 53% of the males and 16% of the females reported having seen such pictures more than ten times. Seventy-seven percent of the males and 35% of the females had seen pictures of sexual intercourse; 32% of males and 4% of females had seen such pictures more than ten times. Sixty percent of the males and 38% of the females had seen movies of sexual intercourse; 27% of the males and 9% of the females had seen such movies five or more times. Seventy-nine percent of the males and 78% of the females had been exposed to books describing sexual activities in slang terms; 20% of the males and 10% of the females had read more than ten such books.

Elias (1970) administered a questionnaire to over 300 11th and 12th grade students in a public school in a working-class suburb of Chicago. The respondents were nearly all white and Christian with slightly over half belonging to the Catholic Church. Ninety-four percent of the males and 66% of the females reported that they had seen photographs of nude females showing genitalia. Eighty-one percent of the males and 43% of the females report having seen photographs of nude males and females engaging in sex behavior. Ninety-five percent of males and 72% of females report having been exposed to printed material describing sexual intercourse. Among the males 40% report seeing photographs of nude females "often," 16% report seeing pictures of intercourse often, and 24% report seeing textual descriptions of intercourse often.

Propper (1970) studied inmates in a youth reformatory in a Northeastern city. The subjects were mostly ages 17–20 (97%), and predominantly from minority ethnic groups (67% black and 21% Puerto Rican). Eighty-five percent reported having seen visual depictions of sex organs, 82% had seen depictions of mouth-sex organ contact, 84% had seen pictures of heterosexual intercourse, 62% had seen homosexual pictures, and 46% had seen visual depictions of sex activities involving whips, belts, and spankings. With regard to frequency, the following percentages had been exposed more than ten times to visual depictions of sex organs, oral sex, intercourse, homosexual activities, and sadomasochistic activity, respectively: 49%, 36%, 44%, 23%, and 13%.

These various studies are quite consistent among themselves in finding that there is considerable exposure to explicit sexual materials on the part of minors. We may conservatively estimate from all these figures that 80% of boys and 70% of girls have seen visual depictions or read textual descriptions of sexual intercourse by the time they reach age 18. Substantial proportions of adolescents have had more than an isolated exposure or two, although the rates of exposure do not indicate an obsession with erotic materials. A great deal of exposure to explicit sexual materials occurs in the preadolescent and early adolescent years. More than half of the boys would appear to have some exposure to explicit sexual materials by age 15. Exposure on the part of girls lags behind that of boys by a year or two. Exposure to genitals and to heterosexual intercourse occurs earlier and more often. Exposure to oral-genital and homosexual materials occurs later and less frequently. Experience with depictions of sadomasochistic materials is much rarer, although it does occur.

Sex educators and counselors are overwhelmingly of the opinion that the principal source of sexual materials on the part of adolescents is from friends about the same age (Wilson & Jacobs, 1970). Eighty-seven percent mention this source. Twenty percent mention a newsstand or bookstore, 15% mention an older relative or find it at home, while 3% mention the mails, buying from an adult, and from an older person who is trying to seduce the adolescent.

The data from the national survey (Abelson, et al., 1970) are not adequate for a definitive statement on this topic, but they do seem to confirm, in general, the sex educators' opinions. About 5% of the adolescents who reported being exposed to a visual sexual depiction in the past two years said that they had bought it at a bookstore or newsstand, and another 5% said that they had seen it at a bookstore or newsstand. The mails, both solicited and unsolicited, are reported as negligible sources of exposure to erotica; and no one reported underground newspapers as a source. The most common source of exposure to sexual materials is a friend and this exposure appears to be a part of the normal social activity centered around house and school.

These findings of the national survey are consistent with the findings of the other more intensive studies carried out with more circumscribed groups.

Berger, Gagnon and Simon (1970b) found that friends were reported to be the most common source of exposure to pictures of sexual intercourse by 70% of the male adolescents and 59% of the female adolescents; other members of family were named by 5% of the males and 11% of the females; stores were named by 6% of the males and none of the females; and mails (about half solicited and half unsolicited) were named by 4% of both males and females. Similar kinds of findings were obtained regarding nudes with genitals exposed and books describing sexual activity in slang terms, except that stores were a more common source for the latter. Exposure to erotic materials appears to be primarily defined as a social activity rather than a sexual activity. Only 11% of these adolescents reported that the usual setting for viewing pictures of sexual intercourse was to be alone, and only 6% indicated that the usual setting was with the other sex. Forty-eight percent usually viewed these pictures with friends of the same sex only and 35% in a mixed sex group. There were sex differences in these reports, with females being more likely to view in mixed company and less likely to view only with their sex. Similar results were found for males regarding viewing movies of sexual intercourse, but females were more likely to view these movies with the opposite sex. Reading books describing sexual activity is more of a solitary activity than viewing pictures with about half the adolescents reporting that the usual setting for reading was to be alone. Still, a social setting with either friends of the same sex only or with mixed company is reported about 12 times more often than reading in the company of the other sex only.

Elias (1970) reports on the basis of interviews with over a hundred high school students that friends approximately the same age are the predominant sources of erotic material, although 45% have found erotic materials hidden at home.

In Propper's (1970) sample only 7% indicate that they bought a picture of sexual intercourse while 72% indicate that they either borrowed it, were given it or saw it some place. Mail is mentioned by 7% as a source of such pictures and stores are mentioned by 4%, while friends are mentioned as a source by over half.

Fersch (1970) reports that his subjects ranked friends, then stores, then adults, and finally mails as a source of "censored" materials, with friends named as source by approximately 60%.

These data suggest very strongly that exposure to explicit sexual materials in adolescence is widespread and occurs primarily in a group of peers of the same sex or a group involving several members of each sex, at school or at home or in the neighborhood. There are some suggestions in the data (Berger, et al., 1970a; Propper, 1970) that young people who are less active socially are less likely to be acquainted with sexual materials. Young people rarely purchase explicit sexual materials; most of their exposure comes in a social situation where materials are freely passed around among friends.

Section G. Patrons of Adult Bookstores and Movies

The "consumer of pornography" has been a vague and shadowy concept in American folk myth, not well defined but nevertheless obviously an undesirable type. Yet, in spite of the debate regarding the legal control of obscenity that has been growing the past 15 years, not one empirical study had been reported of the characteristics of people who bought erotic materials when the Commission came on the scene. The Commission has funded a few pilot studies of the patrons of adult bookstores and movie theaters, and these together begin to sketch in a more definite image of the "consumer of pornography."

Adult Bookstore Patrons

Massey (1970) observed 2,477 people who entered two bookstores carrying sex-oriented materials in Denver, Colorado. The observations were made over a six-day period in August 1969. One of the stores carried exclu-

279

sively sex-oriented materials, while the other was a segregated section of a larger bookstore-newsstand. The sex-oriented sections were clearly marked "for adults only." Trained observers attempted to classify each patron in terms of sex, age, ethnic group membership, type of dress and the presence or not of a wedding band.

The patrons were almost exclusively male. Almost three-quarters (74%) were estimated to be in the age range of 26–55, while 22% were 21–25, and 4% were over 55; less than 1% were possibly under 21. Eighty-nine percent of the patrons were white, 4% black, and 5% Spanish-American. Over half the sample were casually dressed, 26% wore suits and ties, 13% were blue-collar workers; the remainder were soldiers, students, tourists, hippies and clergymen. One-third of the patrons whose left hands were observable had on wedding bands. Jewelers estimate that roughly half of married males wear wedding bands, so well over half of these patrons were probably married.

Massey also inserted postcards in the purchases of 500 customers asking for demographic information. Only 52 of these postcards were returned, but the results were very similar to the observations. The purchaser who returned the postcard was male, age 26–35, had some education beyond high school, was married, a resident of the city, had an annual income of $10,000–$15,000, and had a professional or white collar occupation.

Massey reports that approximately one-third of the patrons in the 26–55 age group made purchases, but only about one-quarter of the younger and older groups purchased anything.

Massey attempted to interview some of the patrons, but soon gave up. The customers were quite skittish and generally silent while in the store; they appeared poised for flight. If someone spoke to them, they tended to respond in a monosyllable and move away. Customers did not interact with each other and interacted with cashier-clerks as little as possible.

Finkelstein (1970a) reports the results of a total of 14 hours of observation of 10 adult bookstores in Boston. The observations were made on three week days between 10:00 a.m. and 3:30 p.m. in May 1970. A total of 493 people were observed entering the stores, all but one of whom were male. Sixty-one percent were estimated to be 40 years of age or older and 39% to be in their 20's and 30's. Only one or two cases that might have been under 21 were observed. Fifty-one percent were dressed in jacket and tie, 38% were neat and casually dressed, 7% had on work clothes, and less than 1% had on a military uniform. Only 3% were disheveled in appearance. Ninety-five percent were white with the remaining equally divided between black and oriental. Ninety-five percent of the patrons entered the stores alone; younger shoppers were more likely to enter the stores in the company of others. Slightly more than one-third of the shoppers (36%) made purchases, and this figure was essentially the same across age groups and dress groups.

Booksellers' descriptions of their customer populations were quite consistent with the objective observations. Most of the stores claimed a steady clientele who buy materials regularly, as well as transients who rarely come in more than once, but no estimates of the proportions of these two types could be made.

Nawy (1970) observed 950 customers in 11 adult bookstores in San Francisco. Only three percent of these were females and they were mostly accompanied by a male escort. About 8 out of 10 of the customers were over 25 years old and less than 1% were possibly under 18. The ethnic composition of the customers approximated the ethnic composition of San Francisco as given in the United States Census; predominantly white with a small proportion of blacks and orientals. Middle-class customers, as indicated by dress style, predominated. It is estimated, based on the number of wedding bands observed, that most customers were married. Nine out of ten shopped alone. Approximately one customer in every five made a purchase.

Winick (1970a) reports observations of 1800 patrons of bookstores, 300 in each of six cities: Mid-town Manhattan, Los Angeles, Chicago, Detroit, Atlanta, and Kansas City. Ninety-nine percent of the patrons were male. Approximately 80% were white, 15% black, and smaller percentages were Spanish-American and oriental. The variations across cities in ethnic composition of customers seemed to reflect the differing ethnic composition of the cities. A little over one-third (36%) were in the age range 19–27, 39% were 28–40, and 24% were 41–60. Borderline youth cases were extremely rarely observed (far less than 1%) and few elderly men entered the stores. The age distribution was roughly the same across the cities. Twenty-six percent of the patrons wore business clothes, 41% casual, and 33% work clothes; few military uniforms were observed. There were considerable variations from city to city regarding costume: Atlanta, New York, and Kansas City had lower proportions of business attire and higher proportions of work clothes; Chicago and Los Angeles had higher proportions of business attire. The observers estimated the social class of the patrons as 44% lower class, 47% middle class, and 8% upper middle class. The downtown Manhattan figures inflated the lower class proportions considerably. Almost all (96%) shopped alone.

The profile of the patron of adult bookstores that emerges from these observations in different parts of the United States is: white, middle aged, middle class, married, male, dressed in business suit or neat casual attire, shopping alone.

Kutschinsky (1970) made systematic observations in about half of the pornography shops in Copenhagen in the winter of 1970. His characterization of the people in these shops was middle aged, middle class, white males. This characterization is very similar to that of the American adult bookstore patron. At least one-fourth of the patrons of the Danish shops were estimated to be from another country on the basis of their language or accent. Approximately one out of four people who entered the shops made purchases. Although selling pornography to 16–19 year olds is legal in Denmark, no persons under age 20 were observed in the shops.

Adult Movie Theater Patrons

Winick (1970a) observed 5,000 customers of adult movie theaters in nine different communities that provided a considerable spread of size, geographic, cultural, ethnic, and socioeconomic characteristics. The observations in eight of these locations were relatively consistent, but one was quite different from the others. We will describe the results of the observations on the eight and then discuss the ninth location.

Seventeen percent of the attendees were estimated to be in the age category 19–27, 32% in the 28–40 category, 41% in the 41–60 age group, and 10% were estimated to be over 60 years old. These figures did not vary significantly from city to city. Eighty percent were white, 14% black, 5% Spanish-American and 2% oriental. These figures did vary from city to city, but the variation appears to reflect the ethnic makeup of the community. Ninety-eight percent of the patrons were male; more females were observed in suburban locations than in downtown locations. All the females were with a male escort or in a mixed-gender group. Ninety percent of the men attended alone. Attending alone was even more characteristic for the downtown theaters; roughly 15% of the patrons of neighborhood theaters attended in groups of two or more males. Twenty-nine percent of the patrons were estimated to be lower class, 55% middle class, and 16% upper middle class. These proportions differed widely from situation to situation reflecting the character of the area in which the theater was located. For example, 62% of the patrons of New York neighborhood theaters were lower class, 69% of those in Kansas City were middle class, and 48% of patrons of New York suburban adult theaters were upper middle class. Forty-one percent wore suits and ties, 50% wore neat casual clothes, and 10% wore work clothes. This also varied by community. Downtown and suburban theaters had more suits and ties and neighborhood theaters had more work clothes; Los Angeles had more casually dressed patrons. Approximately 15% of the customers scrutinized the outside display and a similar proportion exhibited a conflicted demeanor in entering the theater. Very few juveniles were observed looking at the displays outside the theater.

The one theater whose patrons did not fit this general description was a theater in a relatively small city that contained several colleges. The patrons of this theater were more likely to be younger, white, and casually dressed; there was also more attendance of male-female couples.

Winick (1970b) also conducted interviews with 100 patrons of an adult

282

movie theater which provided validation for the classifications based on external observation. He classified each of the patrons in terms of age, ethnicity, and social class on the basis of external observations before the interview and then again after the interview on the basis of the interview data. The two sets of classifications correspond very closely; the main difference was reclassification of a few cases from upper middle class to middle class. These data confirm the possibility of making such judgments accurately from external observation, and heightened our confidence in the descriptions provided by such observations.

A small pilot study of theater patrons in Denver (Massey, 1970) produced observations that fit well within the range of the observations reported by Winick (1970a).

Nawy (1970) observed a total of 2,791 customers at three adult theaters in San Francisco. Ninety-seven percent of these customers were male. Eleven percent were age 18–25, 28% were age 26–35, 32% were age 36–45, 20% were age 46–55, and 9% were over age 55. Very few customers appeared to possibly be under 18 years old. Seventy percent of the patrons were white, 5% were black, 14% were Chinese, and 8% were Japanese. Blacks are underrepresented and Chinese overrepresented in comparison to their population in the city. Thirty-nine percent wore suit and tie, 49% wore neat casual clothes, 6% were dressed in sloppy casual clothes, 4% were in "hip" costumes, and 2% in blue collar work clothes. Thirty-one percent wore a wedding band, 58% did not, and 11% could not be observed; this provides an estimate that about 60% are married based on the assumption that half of married men wear wedding bands. Eighty-five percent of the customers entered the theater alone, 6% were with the opposite sex, and 8% were in a group of the same sex. Twenty-three percent of the patrons appeared to be regular customers.

Nawy (1970) also collected questionnaire data from 251 of these adult movie theater patrons. The demographic data on this questionnaire sample is very similar to the description of the total sample of patrons based on external observation. Thirteen percent were under age 26, 78% were age 26–55, and 9% were over 55 years old. Fifty-eight percent of the questionnaire sample were married. Fifty-two percent of this sample were college graduates. Forty-three percent report professional, managerial, or semiprofessional occupations, and another 24% report other white collar occupations; 11% did not report on occupation. Forty-one percent of these patrons reported annual incomes over $15,000 and 26% reported incomes between $9,000 and $15,000 a year; 12% did not report their income. Thus, the external observations are validated and amplified by the self reports.

Patrons of adult movie theaters may be characterized on the basis of these observations to be predominantly white, middle class, middle aged, married, males, who attend alone. This contrasts very much with the characteristics of patrons of general movie theaters who tend to be young heterosexual couples (Yankelovich, 1968).

Nawy (1970) reports that his observations revealed that over half of the adult movie theater business is conducted during the 9:00 a.m. to 5:00 p.m. working day. This may be less true for neighborhood and suburban theaters than for downtown theaters. This business pattern contrasts sharply with that of the general motion picture theaters which often do not open until 6:00 p.m.

Nawy (1970) and Winick (1970a) both noted that black and Spanish-American customers tend to be younger than the white customers in both bookstores and movie houses.

Arcade Patrons

Two pilot studies of adult film arcade patrons have been made (Massey, 1970; Nawy, 1970). Both of these indicate that females are not allowed in these arcades.

Massey (1970) observed 236 persons entering an adult film arcade in a single day's complete coverage. He concludes that, "the general type and characteristics of consumers observed in the bookstores continued to be seen in the arcade."

Nawy (1970) observed a total of 367 patrons in all six of the known adult film arcades in San Francisco. The characteristics of these customers were similar to those of the patrons of the bookstores and the movie houses: white, middle aged, middle class, married males. Chinese were less often found in the arcades than in the movies. During business week lunch hours and around 5:00 p.m., three out of four patrons of the arcade were dressed in suit and tie.

Interview and Questionnaire Studies of Consumers of Erotic Materials

Several investigators (Goldstein, et al., 1970; Massey, 1970; Nawy, 1970; Winick, 1970b) have attempted to study patrons of adult bookstores and adult movie theaters. All have reported a great deal of difficulty in securing the cooperation of members of these potential subject populations. Customers in adult bookstores appear more reluctant to participate in a study than patrons of adult movie houses. The response rates in the successful studies were all less than 50%. This low response rate may introduce an undetermined bias into the results because those who agree to filling out the questionnaire or to the interview may be different in some other way from those who do not agree to participate. The distribution of demographic data on the people who participated in the more intensive studies is very similar to that found for the larger samples of observed customers, however; this would suggest that the other data may be fairly representative, too. The fact that data from three independent investigations are consistent with each other lends additional support to the possibility that the findings are representative.

Winick (1970b) conducted informal "discussion interviews" with 100 patrons of adult movie theaters. These interview subjects were selected so as to have a distribution on a variety of externally observable demographic characteristics similar to the distribution of these characteristics among a large sample of adult movie patrons (Winick, 1970a). Fifteen percent of the sample reported attending such movies once a week or more; 37% attended less than once a week but more often than once every two months; 23% reported attending occasionally; 18% did not see such movies on a systematic basis; and no information was obtained from 7%. Regular customers of adult movies usually have been attending such films for several years and have well developed consumer patterns. Many of the theater patrons also referred in the interviews to other types of erotic materials, with the suggestion that they are familiar with several forms of erotica.

The most common response to the movies made in the interviews was a critical and comparative evaluation of adult movies from the viewpoint of the connoisseur. Sixty-five percent of the patrons commented along these lines; these people tended to be older and fairly frequent movie goers. Fifty-six percent of these viewers identified aspects of information as significant elements in adult films. Fantasy reactions to the movies, usually sexual and often humorous, were commented upon by 56% of the interviewees. Thirty-nine percent of the subjects mentioned the social context of viewing the film. The majority of these expressed positive sentiments regarding the sharing of an experience with others even though the sharing was very impersonal — indeed the impersonal aspect appeared to be essential. The minority of negative and ambivalent aspects of the social context specifically referred to the need to remain alone and separate from the others. Approximately one-quarter (27%) referred to the sexual stimulus value of the movies. The kind of content which acts as a stimulus to these people is the literally and explicitly sexual, with novel or forbidden fruit providing a further increment.

Nawy (1970) administered questionnaires to two samples of patrons of adult movie theaters, using two different methods. In one case, questionnaires were left at an accessible place in the theater to be filled out and returned; of 800 questionnaires, 190 or 24% were returned. In another case every third person leaving the theater was approached and requested to complete the questionnaire; 44% of those approached complied with the request, and this resulted in 61 completed questionnaires. The distribution of demographic variables was very similar and the two samples were combined for analysis. The distribution on demographic variables for this combined sample was not statistically significantly different from the total sample of over 3,000 patrons observed.

Nawy (1970) found that the patrons of adult movies generally lead active and varied sex lives. Ninety-three percent have a regular partner; most have intercourse twice a week or more often; and most report having had intercourse with more than one person during the past year. Most of these viewers of adult movies say that their sex partners are aware of their interest in sex films. Fifty-four percent report that sex is more enjoyable since they have been viewing sex films and less than one percent report that attendance at such films has had a negative effect on their sexual relations. Seventy-nine percent report that the films have motivated them to introduce new variety into their sex lives. This variety was within fairly circumscribed limits, however, for these people were overwhelming heterosexual; only one of the respondents indicated an interest in experimenting with sadomasochism, and none indicated a desire to engage in bestiality or pedophilia.

Thirty-six percent of these patrons report attending adult movies once a week or oftener. They do not feel guilty about such attendance. Their reported reasons for attending these movies are: for entertainment only, 45%; to get new ideas, 36%; viewing is satisfying in itself, 35%; to pass time, 24%. Seventy-one percent of the movie patrons have purchased material at adult bookstores. Forty percent of these people report having spent more than $100 in the past year on erotic materials.

These customers of adult movie theaters manifest a good deal of upward socioeconomic mobility. Consistent with this upward mobility is that they report larger percentages delaying first intercourse experience until after high school years than does a national sample of men generally (Kinsey, 1948) or a national sample of college students (Berger, et al., 1970a).

Goldstein and his colleagues (1970) interviewed 52 volunteer customers of adult bookstores and adult movie theaters using standardized clinical interviews of approximately two and one-half hours length that inquired intensively into history of experience with erotic materials, attitudes toward sex, and sexual history. The responses from this sample are compared with responses from 53 control subjects to the same interview. The two groups are fairly similar in terms of a variety of demographic variations except that the consumers of erotic materials are better educated and have higher level current occupations.

The buyers of erotic material tend to report more parental permissiveness when they were growing up regarding nudity around the home and exposure to erotic materials than do the controls, but there were no differences in the amount of either erotica around the house or conversation about sex. The two groups report essentially the same source of sex information, but

286

the buyers of erotica tend to have been less likely to have had a sex education course in school.

The buyers are more likely to have had their first sexual intercourse after age 18 than are the controls, and they report less experience with erotica during adolescence.

As adults, the buyers of erotica report frequencies of intercourse fairly similar to that of the controls and a similar degree of enjoyment of intercourse. They are more permissive toward a variety of sexual practices, feeling that every individual should be free to decide for himself what to do in the sexual realm. In practice they also are more likely to have extramarital sexual experience and more often to achieve orgasm through nonintercourse means. The buyers of erotica differ from the controls most in the amount of experience that they have had with pictorial and textual erotic materials; they do not differ, however, in exposure to live erotic shows.

Most patrons of adult bookstores and movie houses appear to have had less sexually related experiences in adolescence than the average male, but to be more sexually oriented as an adult. This high degree of sexual orientation in adulthood encompasses, in addition to pictorial and textual erotica, a variety of partners and a variety of activities within a consensual framework. Activities most frowned upon by our society, such as sadomasochism, pedophilia, bestiality and nonconsensual sex, are also outside the scope of their interest.

Notes

1. Reference should be made to the Report of the Positive Approaches Panel of the Commission which conducted an in-depth analysis of the movie rating system.

2. No individual reports were disclosed, of course; only aggregate statistics were furnished by the Census Bureau.

3. Of course, 16mm can refer merely to the size of film used, not to the content of the film. All of the films discussed previously are exhibited in 35mm, although a few may originally have been filmed in 16mm and "blown up" for presentation in theaters. In the industry, however, the term "16mm films" has come to denote the type of sexually oriented films described in this section, primarily because such films are almost always exhibited in 16mm (sometimes in 8mm, but never in 35mm).

4. Sixteen millimeter films are not included in this estimate.

5. At one time, many arcades were not operated in conjunction with retail book and magazine sales, but in 1970 most arcades are part of "adult bookstores."

6. Based on a response of 220 of the 550 members of the Council for Periodical Distributors Association, who were asked by the Commission to provide such data because they were familiar with the areas they serve, although they do not handle secondary materials.

7. For a more complete discussion of the legal aspects of mail-order advertising, see the Report of the Legal Panel.

8. The Postal Inspection Service was extremely cooperative throughout the survey. Indeed, all divisions of the Post Office were extremely helpful.

9. Disclosures of individual or corporate tax returns are prohibited; the Internal Revenue Service supplied only industry-wide sales and income statistics.

10. Some judges have employed the term "hard-core pornography" as a synonym for "material which can be legally suppressed." In this Report, the term is used as a synonym for "under-the-counter" or covertly sold materials. This is, in effect, the definition of hard-core applied in the marketplace. It can be argued that because of the confusion about the meaning of the term, which stems primarily from an undefined legal concept, it would be well to avoid the use of the term altogether.

References

Abelson, H., Cohen, R., Heaton, E., and Suder, C. Public attitudes toward and experience with erotic materials. *Technical reports of the Commission on Obscenity and Pornography,* Vol. 6. Washington, D. C.: U. S. Government Printing Office, 1970.

Annual report of the postmaster general, 1969. Washington, D. C.: U. S. Government Printing Office, 1970.

Athanasiou, R., Shaver, P., and Tavris, C. Sex, *Psychology Today,* July, 1970, pp. 39–52.

Berger, A., Gagnon, J., and Simon, W. Pornography: High school and college years, *Technical reports of the Commission on Obscenity and Pornography,* Vol. 9. Washington, D.C.: U. S. Government Printing Office. 1970, (a).

Berger, A., Gagnon, J., and Simon, W. Urban working-class adolescents and sexually explicit media. *Technical reports of the Commission on Obscenity and Pornography,* Vol. 9. Washington, D. C.: U. S. Government Printing Office, 1970. (b)

Bestsellers, January, 1969–July, 1970.

Department of Commerce, Bureau of the Census, *1967 census of business.* (Preliminary Report) Washington, D. C.: U. S. Government Printing Office, 1970. (a)

Department of Commerce, Business and Defense Services Administration. *U. S. Industrial Outlook, 1970.* Washington, D. C.: U. S. Government Printing Office, 1970. (b)

Elias, J. Exposure to erotic materials in adolescence. Unpublished manuscript, Commission files, 1970.

Fersch, E. The relationship between students' experience with restricted-access erotic materials and their behaviors and attitudes. Unpublished manuscript, Commission files, 1970.

Finkelstein, M. M. Traffic in sex-oriented materials, Part I: Adult bookstores in Boston, Massachusetts. *Technical Reports of the Commission on Obscenity and Pornography,* Vol. 4. Washington, D. C.: U. S. Government Printing Office, 1970. (a)

Finkelstein, M. M. Traffic in sex-oriented materials, Part II: Criminality and organized crime. *Technical reports of the Commission on Obscenity and Pornography,* Vol. 2. Washington, D. C.: U. S. Government Printing Office, 1970. (b)

Goldstein, M. J., and Kant, H. Exposure to pornography and sexual behavior in deviant and normal groups. *Technical reports of the Commission on Obscenity and Pornography,* Vol. 7. Washington, D. C.: U. S. Government Printing Office, 1970.

International motion picture almanac, 1969. New York: Quigley Publications, 1969.

Knight, A., and Alpert, H. The history of sex in the cinema, Part XVI: The nudies. Playboy, June, 1967, p. 124 ff.

288

Kutschinsky, B. Pornography in Denmark: Studies on producers, sellers, and users. *Technical reports of the Commission on Obscenity and Pornography*, Vol. 4. Washington, D. C.: U. S. Government Printing Office, 1970.

Laven, F. D. APDA survey of secondary publishers. Unpublished manuscript, Commission files, 1970.

Lynch, T., and O'Brien, C. A report to the California legislature on obscenity: The law and the nature of the business. Unpublished manuscript, Commission files, 1967.

Magazine industry newsletter. December 9, 1969.

Massey, M. E. A market analysis of sex-oriented materials in Denver, Colorado, August, 1969 — A pilot study. *Technical reports of the Commission on Obscenity and Pornography*, Vol. 4. Washington, D. C.: U .S. Government Printing Office, 1970.

Nawy, H. The San Francisco erotic marketplace. *Technical reports of the Commission on Obscenity and Pornography*, Vol. 4. Washington, D. C.: U. S. Government Printing Office, 1970.

Paperback books in print. New York: R. R. Bowker, 1970.

President's Commission on Postal Organization. *Towards postal excellence.* Washington, D. C.: U. S. Government Printing Office, 1968.

Propper, M. Exposure to sexually oriented materials among young male prison offenders. *Technical reports of the Commission on Obscenity and Pornography*, Vol. 9. Washington, D. C.: U. S. Government Printing Office, 1970.

Publisher's weekly. May 25, 1970. (a)

Publisher's weekly. June 29, 1970. (a)

Randall, R. S. *Censorship of the movies.* Madison: University of Wisconsin Press, 1968.

Randall, R. S. Classification by the motion picture industry. *Technical reports of the Commission on Obscenity and Pornography*, Vol. 10. Washington, D. C.: U. S. Government Printing Office, 1970. (a)

Randall, R. S. Gross receipts for MPAA — rated and unrated films. Unpublished manuscript, Commission files, 1970. (b)

Roach, W. J., and Kreisberg, L. Westchester college students' views on pornography. *Technical reports of the Commission on Obscenity and Pornography*, Vol. 1. Washington, D. C.: U. S. Government Printing Office, 1970.

Sampson, J. J. Commercial traffic in sexually oriented materials in the United States, 1969–70. *Technical reports of the Commission on Obscenity and Pornography*, Vol. 3. Washington, D. C.: U. S. Government Printing Office, 1970.

Smith, A., and Locke, B. Response of police and prosecutors to problems in arrests and prosecutions for obscenity and pornography. *Technical reports of the Commission on Obscenity and Pornography*, Vol. 2. Washington, D. C.: U. S. Government Printing Office, 1970.

Sonnenschein, D. Pornography: A false issue. *Psychiatric opinion.* February, 1969.

Sonnenschein, D., Ross, M., Bauman, R., Swartz, L., and Maclachlan, M. A study of mass media erotica: The romance or confession magazine. *Technical reports of the Commission on Obscenity and Pornography*, Vol. 9. Washington, D. C.: U. S. Government Printing Office, 1970.

Valenti, J. Testimony before the Commission on Obscenity and Pornography, May 12, 1970. *Technical reports of the Commission on Obscenity and Pornography*, Vol. 11. Washington, D. C.: U. S. Government Printing Office, 1970.

Variety, January 7, 1970. (a)

Variety, June 17, 1970. (b)

Wallace, D., and Wehmer, G. Contemporary standards of visual erotica. *Technical reports of the Commission on Obscenity and Pornography*, Vol. 9. Washington, D. C.: U. S. Government Printing Office, 1970.

White, D. M. College students' experience with erotica. *Technical reports of the Commission on Obscenity and Pornography*, Vol. 1. Washington, D. C.: U. S. Government Printing Office, 1970.

Wilson, W. C., Horowitz, B., and Friedman, J. The gravity of the pornography situation and the problems of control: A survey of prosecuting attorneys. *Technical reports of the Commission on Obscenity and Pornography*, Vol. 2. Washington, D. C.: U. S. Government Printing Office, 1970.

Wilson, W. C., and Jacobs, S. Sex educators' opinions regarding adolescents' experience with erotica: A national survey. *Technical reports of the Commission on Obscenity and Pornography*, Vol. 10. Washington, D. C.: U. S. Government Printing Office, 1970.

Winick, C. A. A study of consumers of explicitly sexual materials: Some functions served by adult movies. *Technical reports of the Commission on Obscenity and Pornography*, Vol. 4. Washington, D. C.: U. S. Government Printing Office, 1970. (a)

Winick, C. Some observations of patrons of adult theaters and bookstores. *Technical reports of the Commission on Obscenity and Pornography*, Vol. 4. Washington, D. C.: U. S. Government Printing Office, 1970.

Yankelovich, Inc. Public survey of movie-goers — 1967. In *A year in review*, New York: Motion Picture Association of America, 1968, pp. 11–12.

Zetterberg, H. L. The consumers of pornography where it is easily available: The Swedish experience. *Technical reports of the Commission on Obscenity and Pornography*, Vol. 9. Washington, D. C.: U. S. Government Printing Office, 1970.